The Data Warehouse ETL Toolkit

The Data Warehouse ETL Toolkit

Practical Techniques for Extracting, Cleaning, Conforming, and Delivering Data

Ralph Kimball
Joe Caserta

Wiley Publishing, Inc.

Published by
Wiley Publishing, Inc.
10475 Crosspoint Boulevard
Indianapolis, IN 46256
www.wiley.com

Published simultaneously in Canada

ISBN: 0-764-56757-8

C9780764567575_151123

For general information on our other products and services please contact our Customer Care Department within the United States at (800) 762-2974, outside the United States at (317) 572-3993 or fax (317) 572-4002.

Wiley also publishes its books in a variety of electronic formats. Some content that appears in print may not be available in electronic books.

Library of Congress Cataloging-in-Publication Data

Kimball, Ralph.
    The data warehouse ETL toolkit : practical techniques for extracting, cleaning, conforming, and delivering data / Ralph Kimball, Joe Caserta.
        p.   cm.
    Includes index.
    ISBN 0-7645-6757-8 (paper/website)
    1. Data warehousing.   2. Database design.   I. Caserta, Joe, 1965-   II. Title.

QA76.9.D37K53   2004
005.74—dc22   2004016909

Printed and bound by CPI Group (UK) Ltd, Croydon, CR0 4YY

Credits

Vice President and Executive Group Publisher:
Richard Swadley

Vice President and Publisher:
Joseph B. Wikert

Executive Editorial Director:
Mary Bednarek

Executive Editor:
Robert Elliot

Editorial Manager:
Kathryn A. Malm

Development Editor:
Adaobi Obi Tulton

Production Editor:
Pamela Hanley

Media Development Specialist:
Travis Silvers

Text Design & Composition:
TechBooks Composition Services

Contents

Acknowledgments

First of all we want to thank the many thousands of readers of the Toolkit series of data warehousing books. We appreciate your wonderful support and encouragement to write a book about data warehouse ETL. We continue to learn from you, the owners and builders of data warehouses.

Both of us are especially indebted to Jim Stagnitto for encouraging Joe to start this book and giving him the confidence to go through with the project. Jim was a virtual third author with major creative contributions to the chapters on data quality and real-time ETL.

Special thanks are also due to Jeff Coster and Kim M. Knyal for significant contributions to the discussions of pre- and post-load processing and project managing the ETL process, respectively.

We had an extraordinary team of reviewers who crawled over the first version of the manuscript and made many helpful suggestions. It is always daunting to make significant changes to a manuscript that is "done" but this kind of deep review has been a tradition with the Toolkit series of books and was successful again this time. In alphabetic order, the reviewers included: Wouleta Ayele, Bob Becker, Jan-Willem Beldman, Ivan Chong, Maurice Frank, Mark Hodson, Paul Hoffman, Qi Jin, David Lyle, Michael Martin, Joy Mundy, Rostislav Portnoy, Malathi Vellanki, Padmini Ramanujan, Margy Ross, Jack Serra-Lima, and Warren Thornthwaite.

We owe special thanks to our spouses Robin Caserta and Julie Kimball for their support throughout this project and our children Tori Caserta, Brian Kimball, Sara (Kimball) Smith, and grandchild(!) Abigail Smith who were very patient with the authors who always seemed to be working.

Finally, the team at Wiley Computer books has once again been a real asset in getting this book finished. Thank you Bob Elliott, Kevin Kent, and Adaobi Obi Tulton.

About the Authors

Ralph Kimball, Ph.D., founder of the Kimball Group, has been a leading visionary in the data warehouse industry since 1982 and is one of today's most well-known speakers, consultants, teachers, and writers. His books include *The Data Warehouse Toolkit* (Wiley, 1996), *The Data Warehouse Lifecycle Toolkit* (Wiley, 1998), *The Data Webhouse Toolkit* (Wiley, 2000), and *The Data Warehouse Toolkit, Second Edition* (Wiley, 2002). He also has written for *Intelligent Enterprise* magazine since 1995, receiving the Readers' Choice Award since 1999.

Ralph earned his doctorate in electrical engineering at Stanford University with a specialty in man-machine systems design. He was a research scientist, systems development manager, and product marketing manager at Xerox PARC and Xerox Systems' Development Division from 1972 to 1982. For his work on the Xerox Star Workstation, the first commercial product with windows, icons, and a mouse, he received the Alexander C. Williams award from the IEEE Human Factors Society for systems design. From 1982 to 1986 Ralph was Vice President of Applications at Metaphor Computer Systems, the first data warehouse company. At Metaphor, Ralph invented the "capsule" facility, which was the first commercial implementation of the graphical data flow interface now in widespread use in all ETL tools. From 1986 to 1992 Ralph was founder and CEO of Red Brick Systems, a provider of ultra-fast relational database technology dedicated to decision support. In 1992 Ralph founded Ralph Kimball Associates, which became known as the Kimball Group in 2004. The Kimball Group is a team of highly experienced data warehouse design professionals known for their excellence in consulting, teaching, speaking, and writing.

Joe Caserta is the founder and Principal of Caserta Concepts, LLC. He is an influential data warehousing veteran whose expertise is shaped by years of industry experience and practical application of major data warehousing tools and databases. Joe is educated in Database Application Development and Design, Columbia University, New York.

Introduction

The Extract-Transform-Load (ETL) system is the foundation of the data warehouse. A properly designed ETL system extracts data from the source systems, enforces data quality and consistency standards, conforms data so that separate sources can be used together, and finally delivers data in a presentation-ready format so that application developers can build applications and end users can make decisions. This book is organized around these four steps.

The ETL system makes or breaks the data warehouse. Although building the ETL system is a *back room* activity that is not very visible to end users, it easily consumes 70 percent of the resources needed for implementation and maintenance of a typical data warehouse.

The ETL system adds significant value to data. It is far more than plumbing for getting data out of source systems and into the data warehouse. Specifically, the ETL system:

- Removes mistakes and corrects missing data
- Provides documented measures of confidence in data
- Captures the flow of transactional data for safekeeping
- Adjusts data from multiple sources to be used together
- Structures data to be usable by end-user tools

ETL is both a simple and a complicated subject. Almost everyone understands the basic mission of the ETL system: to get data out of the source and load it into the data warehouse. And most observers are increasingly appreciating the need to clean and transform data along the way. So much for the simple view. It is a fact of life that the next step in the design of the ETL system breaks into a thousand little subcases, depending on your own weird data sources, business rules, existing software, and unusual destination-reporting applications. The challenge for all of us is to tolerate the thousand little subcases but to keep perspective on the simple overall mission of the ETL system. Please judge this book by how well we meet this challenge!

The Data Warehouse ETL Toolkit is a practical guide for building successful ETL systems. This book is not a survey of all possible approaches! Rather, we build on a set of consistent techniques for delivery of dimensional data. Dimensional modeling has proven to be the most predictable and cost effective approach to building data warehouses. At the same time, because the dimensional structures are the same across many data warehouses, we can count on reusing code modules and specific development logic.

This book is a roadmap for planning, designing, building, and running the back room of a data warehouse. We expand the traditional ETL steps of extract, transform, and load into the more actionable steps of extract, clean, conform, and deliver, although we resist the temptation to change ETL into ECCD!

In this book, you'll learn to:

- Plan and design your ETL system
- Choose the appropriate architecture from the many possible choices
- Manage the implementation
- Manage the day-to-day operations
- Build the development/test/production suite of ETL processes
- Understand the tradeoffs of various back-room data structures, including flat files, normalized schemas, XML schemas, and star join (dimensional) schemas
- Analyze and extract source data
- Build a comprehensive data-cleaning subsystem
- Structure data into dimensional schemas for the most effective delivery to end users, business-intelligence tools, data-mining tools, OLAP cubes, and analytic applications
- Deliver data effectively both to highly centralized and profoundly distributed data warehouses using the same techniques
- Tune the overall ETL process for optimum performance

The preceding points are many of the big issues in an ETL system. But as much as we can, we provide lower-level technical detail for:

- Implementing the key enforcement steps of a data-cleaning system for column properties, structures, valid values, and complex business rules

- Conforming heterogeneous data from multiple sources into standardized dimension tables and fact tables

- Building replicatable ETL modules for handling the natural time variance in dimensions, for example, the three types of slowly changing dimensions (SCDs)

- Building replicatable ETL modules for multivalued dimensions and hierarchical dimensions, which both require associative bridge tables

- Processing extremely large-volume fact data loads

- Optimizing ETL processes to fit into highly constrained load windows

- Converting batch and file-oriented ETL systems into continuously streaming real-time ETL systems

For illustrative purposes, Oracle is chosen as a common dominator when specific SQL code is revealed. However, similar code that presents the same results can typically be written for DB2, Microsoft SQL Server, or any popular relational database system.

And perhaps as a side effect of all of these specific recommendations, we hope to share our enthusiasm for developing, deploying, and managing data warehouse ETL systems.

Overview of the Book: Two Simultaneous Threads

Building an ETL system is unusually challenging because it is so heavily constrained by unavoidable realities. The ETL team must live with the business requirements, the formats and deficiencies of the source data, the existing legacy systems, the skill sets of available staff, and the ever-changing (and legitimate) needs of end users. If these factors aren't enough, the budget is limited, the processing-time windows are too narrow, and important parts of the business come grinding to a halt if the ETL system doesn't deliver data to the data warehouse!

Two simultaneous threads must be kept in mind when building an ETL system: the Planning & Design thread and the Data Flow thread. At the highest level, they are pretty simple. Both of them progress in an orderly fashion from left to right in the diagrams. Their interaction makes life very

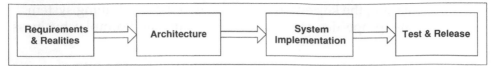

Figure Intro-1 The Planning and Design Thread.

interesting. In Figure Intro-1 we show the four steps of the Planning & Design thread, and in Figure Intro-2 we show the four steps of the Data Flow thread.

To help you visualize where we are in these two threads, in each chapter we call out process checks. The following example would be used when we are discussing the requirements for data cleaning:

PROCESS CHECK Planning & Design:

Requirements/Realities → Architecture → Implementation → Test/Release

Data Flow: Extract → *Clean* → Conform → Deliver

The Planning & Design Thread

The first step in the Planning & Design thread is accounting for all the *requirements and realities*. These include:

- Business needs
- Data profiling and other data-source realities
- Compliance requirements
- Security requirements
- Data integration
- Data latency
- Archiving and lineage

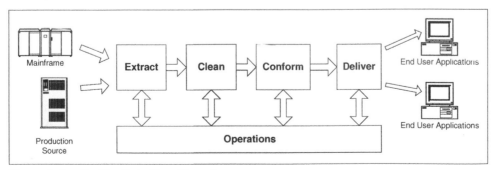

Figure Intro-2 The Data Flow Thread.

- End user delivery interfaces
- Available development skills
- Available management skills
- Legacy licenses

We expand these individually in the Chapter 1, but we have to point out at this early stage how much each of these bullets affects the nature of your ETL system. For this step, as well as all the steps in both major threads, we point out the places in this book when we are talking specifically about the given step.

The second step in this thread is the *architecture* step. Here is where we must make big decisions about the way we are going to build our ETL system. These decisions include:

- Hand-coded versus ETL vendor tool
- Batch versus streaming data flow
- Horizontal versus vertical task dependency
- Scheduler automation
- Exception handling
- Quality handling
- Recovery and restart
- Metadata
- Security

The third step in the Planning & Design thread is *system implementation*. Let's hope you have spent some quality time on the previous two steps before charging into the implementation! This step includes:

- Hardware
- Software
- Coding practices
- Documentation practices
- Specific quality checks

The final step sounds like administration, but the design of the test and release procedures is as important as the more tangible designs of the preceding two steps. Test and release includes the design of the:

- Development systems
- Test systems

- Production systems
- Handoff procedures
- Update propagation approach
- System snapshoting and rollback procedures
- Performance tuning

The Data Flow Thread

The Data Flow thread is probably more recognizable to most readers because it is a simple generalization of the old E-T-L extract-transform-load scenario. As you scan these lists, begin to imagine how the Planning & Design thread affects each of the following bullets. The *extract* step includes:

- Reading source-data models
- Connecting to and accessing data
- Scheduling the source system, intercepting notifications and daemons
- Capturing changed data
- Staging the extracted data to disk

The *clean* step involves:

- Enforcing column properties
- Enforcing structure
- Enforcing data and value rules
- Enforcing complex business rules
- Building a metadata foundation to describe data quality
- Staging the cleaned data to disk

This step is followed closely by the *conform* step, which includes:

- Conforming business labels (in dimensions)
- Conforming business metrics and performance indicators (in fact tables)
- Deduplicating
- Householding
- Internationalizing
- Staging the conformed data to disk

Finally, we arrive at the payoff step where we *deliver* our wonderful data to the end-user application. We spend most of Chapters 5 and 6 on delivery techniques because, as we describe in Chapter 1, you still have to serve the food after you cook it! Data delivery from the ETL system includes:

- Loading flat and snowflaked dimensions
- Generating time dimensions
- Loading degenerate dimensions
- Loading subdimensions
- Loading types 1, 2, and 3 slowly changing dimensions
- Conforming dimensions and conforming facts
- Handling late-arriving dimensions and late-arriving facts
- Loading multi-valued dimensions
- Loading ragged hierarchy dimensions
- Loading text facts in dimensions
- Running the surrogate key pipeline for fact tables
- Loading three fundamental fact table grains
- Loading and updating aggregations
- Staging the delivered data to disk

In studying this last list, you may say, "But most of that list is modeling, not ETL. These issues belong in the front room." We respectfully disagree. In our interviews with more than 20 data warehouse teams, more than half said that the design of the ETL system took place at the same time as the design of the target tables. These folks agreed that there were two distinct roles: data warehouse architect and ETL system designer. But these two roles often were filled by the same person! So this explains why this book carries the data all the way from the original sources into each of the dimensional database configurations.

The basic four-step data flow is overseen by the *operations* step, which extends from the beginning of the extract step to the end of the delivery step. Operations includes:

- Scheduling
- Job execution
- Exception handling
- Recovery and restart
- Quality checking

- Release
- Support

Understanding how to think about these two fundamental threads (Planning & Design and Data Flow) is the real goal of this book.

How the Book Is Organized

To develop the two threads, we have divided the book into four parts:

    I. Requirements, Realities and Architecture

    II. Data Flow

    III. Implementation and Operations

    IV. Real Time Streaming ETL Systems

This book starts with the requirements, realities, and architecture steps of the planning & design thread because we must establish a logical foundation for the design of any kind of ETL system. The middle part of the book then traces the entire data flow thread from the extract step through to the deliver step. Then in the third part we return to implementation and operations issues. In the last part, we open the curtain on the exciting new area of real time streaming ETL systems.

Part I: Requirements, Realities, and Architecture

Part I sets the stage for the rest of the book. Even though most of us are eager to get started on moving data into the data warehouse, we have to step back to get some perspective.

Chapter 1: Surrounding the Requirements

The ETL portion of the data warehouse is a classically overconstrained design challenge. In this chapter we put some substance on the list of requirements that we want you to consider up front before you commit to an approach. We also introduce the main architectural decisions you must take a stand on (whether you realize it or not).

This chapter is the right place to define, as precisely as we can, the major vocabulary of data warehousing, at least as far as this book is concerned. These terms include:

- Data warehouse
- Data mart

- ODS (operational data store)
- EDW (enterprise data warehouse)
- Staging area
- Presentation area

We describe the mission of the data warehouse as well as the mission of the ETL team responsible for building the *back room* foundation of the data warehouse. We briefly introduce the basic four stages of Data Flow: extracting, cleaning, conforming, and delivering. And finally we state as clearly as possible why we think dimensional data models are the keys to success for every data warehouse.

Chapter 2: ETL Data Structures

Every ETL system must stage data in various permanent and semipermanent forms. When we say *staging*, we mean writing data to the disk, and for this reason the ETL system is sometimes referred to as the staging area. You might have noticed that we recommend at least some form of staging after each of the major ETL steps (extract, clean, conform, and deliver). We discuss the reasons for various forms of staging in this chapter.

We then provide a systematic description of the important data structures needed in typical ETL systems: flat files, XML data sets, independent DBMS working tables, normalized entity/relationship (E/R) schemas, and dimensional data models. For completeness, we mention some special tables including legally significant audit tracking tables used to prove the provenance of important data sets, as well as mapping tables used to keep track of surrogate keys. We conclude with a survey of metadata typically surrounding these types of tables, as well as naming standards. The metadata section in this chapter is just an introduction, as metadata is an important topic that we return to many times in this book.

Part II: Data Flow

The second part of the book presents the actual steps required to effectively extract, clean, conform, and deliver data from various source systems into an ideal dimensional data warehouse. We start with instructions on selecting the system-of-record and recommend strategies for analyzing source systems. This part includes a major chapter on building the cleaning and conforming stages of the ETL system. The last two chapters then take the cleaned and conformed data and repurpose it into the required dimensional structures for delivery to the end-user environments.

Chapter 3: Extracting

This chapter begins by explaining what is required to design a logical data mapping after data analysis is complete. We urge you to create a logical data map and to show how it should be laid out to prevent ambiguity in the mission-critical specification. The logical data map provides ETL developers with the functional specifications they need to build the physical ETL process.

A major responsibility of the data warehouse is to provide data from various legacy applications throughout the enterprise data in a single cohesive repository. This chapter offers specific technical guidance for integrating the heterogeneous data sources found throughout the enterprise, including mainframes, relational databases, XML sources, flat files, Web logs, and enterprise resource planning (ERP) systems. We discuss the obstacles encountered when integrating these data sources and offer suggestions on how to overcome them. We introduce the notion of conforming data across multiple potentially incompatible data sources, a topic developed fully in the next chapter.

Chapter 4: Cleaning and Conforming

After data has been extracted, we subject it to cleaning and conforming. *Cleaning* means identifying and fixing the errors and omissions in the data. *Conforming* means resolving the labeling conflicts between potentially incompatible data sources so that they can be used together in an enterprise data warehouse.

This chapter makes an unusually serious attempt to propose specific techniques and measurements that you should implement as you build the cleaning and conforming stages of your ETL system. The chapter focuses on data-cleaning objectives, techniques, metadata, and measurements.

In particular, the techniques section surveys the key approaches to data profiling and data cleaning, and the measurements section gives examples of how to implement data-quality checks that trigger alerts, as well as how to provide guidance to the data-quality steward regarding the overall health of the data.

Chapter 5: Delivering Dimension Tables

This chapter and Chapter 6 are the payoff chapters in this book. We believe that the whole point of the data warehouse is to deliver data in a simple, actionable format for the benefit of end users and their analytic applications. Dimension tables are the context of a business' measurements. They are also the entry points to the data because they are the targets for almost all data warehouse constraints, and they provide the meaningful labels on every row of output.

The ETL process that loads dimensions is challenging because it must absorb the complexities of the source systems and transform the data into simple, selectable dimension attributes. This chapter explains step-by-step how to load data warehouse dimension tables, including the most advanced ETL techniques. The chapter clearly illustrates how to:

- Assign surrogate keys
- Load Type 1, 2 and 3 slowly changing dimensions
- Populate bridge tables for multivalued and complex hierarchical dimensions
- Flatten hierarchies and selectively snowflake dimensions

We discuss the advanced administration and maintenance issues required to incrementally load dimensions, track the changes in dimensions using CRC codes, and contend with late-arriving data.

Chapter 6: Delivering Fact Tables

Fact tables hold the measurements of the business. In most data warehouses, fact tables are overwhelmingly larger than dimension tables, but at the same time they are simpler. In this chapter we explain the basic structure of all fact tables, including foreign keys, degenerate dimension keys, and the numeric facts themselves. We describe the role of the fact-table provider, the information steward responsible for the delivery of the fact tables to end-user environments.

Every fact table should be loaded with a surrogate key pipeline, which maps the natural keys of the incoming fact records to the correct contemporary surrogate keys needed to join to the dimension tables.

We describe the three fundamental grains of fact tables, which are sufficient to support all data warehouse applications.

We discuss some unusual fact table varieties, including factless fact tables and fact tables whose sole purpose is to register the existence of complex events, such as automobile accidents.

Finally, we discuss the basic architecture of aggregations, which are physically stored summaries that, much like indexes, serve solely to improve performance.

Part III: Implementation and Operations

The third part of the book assumes the reader has analyzed his or her requirements, heeded the realities of his or her data and available resources, and visualized the flow of data from extraction to delivery. Keeping all this in mind, Part 3 describes in some detail the main approaches to system implementation and to organizing the operations of the ETL system. We discuss the role of metadata in the ETL system and finally the various responsibilities of the ETL team members.

Chapter 7: Development

Chapter 7 develops the techniques that you'll need to develop the initial data load for your data warehouse, such as recreating history for slowly changing dimensions and integrating historic offline data with current on-line transactions, as well as historic fact loading.

The chapter also provides estimation techniques to calculate the time it should take to complete the initial load, exposes vulnerabilities to long-running ETL processes, and suggests methods to minimize your risk.

Automating the ETL process is an obvious requirement of the data ware-house project, but how is it done? The order and dependencies between table loads is crucial to successfully load the data warehouse. This chapter reviews the fundamental functionality of ETL scheduling and offers cri-teria and options for executing the ETL schedule. Once the fundamentals are covered, topics such as enforcing referential integrity with the ETL and maintaining operational metadata are examined.

Chapter 8: Operations

We begin this chapter by showing the approaches to scheduling the various ETL system jobs, responding to alerts and exceptions, and finally running the jobs to completion with all dependencies satisfied.

We walk through the steps to migrate the ETL system to the production environment. Since the production environment of the ETL system must be supported like any other mission-critical application, we describe how to set up levels of support for the ETL system that must be utilized upon failure of a scheduled process.

We identify key performance indicators for rating ETL performance and explore how to monitor and capture the statistics. Once the ETL key per-formance indicators are collected, you are armed with the information you need to address the components within the ETL system to look for oppor-tunities to modify and increase the throughput as much as possible.

Chapter 9: Metadata

The ETL environment often assumes the responsibility of storing and man-aging the metadata for the entire data warehouse. After all, there is no better place than the ETL system for storing and managing metadata because the environment must know most aspects of the data to function properly. Chapter 9 defines the three types of metadata—business, technical, and process—and presents the elements within each type as they apply to the ETL system. The chapter offers techniques for producing, publishing, and utilizing the various types of metadata and also discusses the opportunity for improvement in this area of the data warehouse. We finish the chapter by discussing metadata standards and best practices and provide recommended naming standards for the ETL.

Chapter 10: Responsibilities

The technical aspects of the ETL process are only a portion of the ETL lifecycle. Chapter 10 is dedicated to the managerial aspects of the lifecycle required for a successful implementation. The chapter describes the duties and responsibilities of the ETL team and then goes on to outline a detailed project plan that can be implemented in any data warehouse environment. Once the basics of managing the ETL system are conveyed, the chapter dives into more-detailed project management activities such as project staffing, scope management, and team development. This somewhat nontechnical chapter provides the greatest benefit to ETL and data warehouse project managers. It describes the roles and skills that are needed for an effective team; and offers a comprehensive ETL project plan that can be repeated for each phase of the data warehouse. The chapter also includes forms that managers need to lead their teams through the ETL lifecycle. Even if you are not a manager, this chapter is required reading to adequately understand how your role works with the other members of the ETL team.

Part IV: Real Time Streaming ETL Systems

Since real-time ETL is a relatively young technology, we are more likely to come up against unique requirements and solutions that have not yet been perfected. In this chapter, we share our experiences to provide insight on the latest challenges in real-time data warehousing and offer recommendations on overcoming them. The crux of real-time ETL is covered in this chapter, and the details of actual implementations are described.

Chapter 11: Real-Time ETL

In this chapter, we begin by defining the real-time requirement. Next, we review the different architecture options available today and appraise each. We end the chapter with a decision matrix to help you decide which real-time architecture is right for your specific data warehouse environment.

Chapter 12: Conclusion

The final chapter summarizes the unique contributions made in this book and provides a glimpse into the future for ETL and data warehousing as a whole.

Who Should Read this Book

Anyone who is involved or intends to be involved in a data-warehouse initiative should read this book. Developers, architects, and managers will benefit from this book because it contains detailed techniques for delivering a dimensionally oriented data warehouse and provides a project management perspective for all the back room activities.

Chapters 1, 2, and 10 offer a functional view of the ETL that can easily be read by anyone on the data warehouse team but is intended for business sponsors and project managers. As you progress through these chapters, expect their technical level to increase, eventually getting to the point where it transforms into a developers handbook. This book is a definitive guide for advice on the tasks required to load the dimensional data warehouse.

Summary

The goal of this book is to make the process of building an ETL system understandable with specific checkpoints along the way. This book shows the often under-appreciated value the ETL system brings to data warehouse data. We hope you enjoy the book and find it valuable in your workplace. We intentionally remain vendor-neutral throughout the book so you can apply the techniques within to the technology to your liking. If this book accomplishes nothing else, we hope it encourages you to get thinking and start breaking new ground to challenge the vendors to extend their product offerings to incorporate the features that the ETL team requires to bring the ETL (and the data warehouse) to full maturity.

Requirements, Realities, and Architecture

Surrounding the Requirements

Ideally, you must start the design of your ETL system with one of the toughest challenges: surrounding the requirements. By this we mean gathering in one place all the known requirements, realities, and constraints affecting the ETL system. We'll refer to this list as the *requirements*, for brevity.

The requirements are mostly things you must live with and adapt your system to. Within the framework of your requirements, you will have many places where you can make your own decisions, exercise your judgment, and leverage your creativity, but the requirements are just what they are named. They are required. The first section of this chapter is intended to remind you of the relevant categories of requirements and give you a sense of how important the requirements will be as you develop your ETL system.

Following the requirements, we identify a number of architectural decisions you need to make at the beginning of your ETL project. These decisions are major commitments because they drive everything you do as you move forward with your implementation. The architecture affects your hardware, software, coding practices, personnel, and operations.

The last section describes the mission of the data warehouse. We also carefully define the main architectural components of the data warehouse, including the back room, the staging area, the operational data store (ODS), and the presentation area. We give a careful and precise definition of data marts and the enterprise data warehouse (EDW). Please read this chapter very carefully. The definitions and boundaries we describe here drive the whole logic of this book. If you understand our assumptions, you will see why our approach is more disciplined and more structured than any other data warehouse design methodology. We conclude the chapter with a succinct statement of the mission of the ETL team.

PROCESS CHECK
Planning & Design: *Requirements/Realities* → Architecture →
Implementation → Test/Release
   Data Flow: Haven't started tracing the data flow yet.

Requirements

In this book's introduction, we list the major categories of requirements we think important. Although every one of the requirements can be a show-stopper, business needs have to be more fundamental and important.

Business Needs

Business needs are the information requirements of the end users of the data warehouse. We use the term *business needs* somewhat narrowly here to mean the information content that end users need to make informed business decisions. Other requirements listed in a moment broaden the definition of business needs, but this requirement is meant to identify the extended set of information sources that the ETL team must introduce into the data warehouse.

Taking, for the moment, the view that business needs directly drive the choice of data sources, it is obvious that understanding and constantly examining business needs is a core activity of the ETL team.

In the *Data Warehouse Lifecycle Toolkit*, we describe the process for interviewing end users and gathering business requirements. The result of this process is a set of expectations that users have about what data will do for them. In many cases, the original interviews with end users and the original investigations of possible sources do not fully reveal the complexities and limitations of data. The ETL team often makes significant discoveries that affect whether the end user's business needs can be addressed as originally hoped for. And, of course, the ETL team often discovers additional capabilities in the data sources that expand end users' decision-making capabilities. The lesson here is that even during the most technical back-room development steps of building the ETL system, a dialog amongst the ETL team, the data warehouse architects, and the end users should be maintained. In a larger sense, business needs and the content of data sources are both moving targets that constantly need to be re-examined and discussed.

Compliance Requirements

In recent years, especially with the passage of the Sarbanes-Oxley Act of 2002, organizations have been forced to seriously tighten up what they report and provide proof that the reported numbers are accurate, complete, and have not been tampered with. Of course, data warehouses in regulated businesses like telecommunications have complied with regulatory reporting requirements for many years. But certainly the whole tenor of financial reporting has become much more serious for everyone.

Several of the financial-reporting issues will be outside the scope of the data warehouse, but many others will land squarely on the data warehouse. Typical due diligence requirements for the data warehouse include:

- Archived copies of data sources and subsequent stagings of data
- Proof of the complete transaction flow that changed any data
- Fully documented algorithms for allocations and adjustments
- Proof of security of the data copies over time, both on-line and off-line

Data Profiling

As Jack Olson explains so clearly in his book *Data Quality: The Accuracy Dimension*, data profiling is a necessary precursor to designing any kind of system to use that data. As he puts it: "[Data profiling] employs analytic methods for looking at data for the purpose of developing a thorough understanding of the content, structure, and quality of the data. A good data profiling [system] can process very large amounts of data, and with the skills of the analyst, uncover all sorts of issues that need to be addressed."

This perspective is especially relevant to the ETL team who may be handed a data source whose content has not really been vetted. For example, Jack points out that a data source that perfectly suits the needs of the production system, such as an order-taking system, may be a disaster for the data warehouse, because the ancillary fields the data warehouse hoped to use were not central to the success of the order-taking process and were revealed to be unreliable and too incomplete for data warehouse analysis.

Data profiling is a systematic examination of the quality, scope, and context of a data source to allow an ETL system to be built. At one extreme, a very clean data source that has been well maintained before it arrives at the data warehouse requires minimal transformation and human intervention to load directly into final dimension tables and fact tables. But a dirty data source may require:

- Elimination of some input fields completely
- Flagging of missing data and generation of special surrogate keys
- Best-guess automatic replacement of corrupted values
- Human intervention at the record level
- Development of a full-blown normalized representation of the data

And at the furthest extreme, if data profiling reveals that the source data is deeply flawed and cannot support the business' objectives, the data-warehouse effort should be cancelled! The profiling step not only gives the ETL team guidance as to how much data cleaning machinery to invoke but protects the ETL team from missing major milestones in the project because of the unexpected diversion to build a system to deal with dirty data. Do the data profiling up front! Use the data-profiling results to prepare the business sponsors for the realistic development schedules, the limitations in the source data, and the need to invest in better data-capture practices in the source systems. We dig into specific data- profiling and data-quality algorithms in Chapter 4.

Security Requirements

The general level of security awareness has improved significantly in the last few years across all IT areas, but security remains an afterthought and an unwelcome additional burden to most data warehouse teams. The basic rhythms of the data warehouse are at odds with the security mentality. The data warehouse seeks to publish data widely to decision makers, whereas the security interests assume that data should be restricted to those with a need to know.

Throughout the Toolkit series of books we have recommended a role-based approach to security where the ability to access the results from a data warehouse is controlled at the final applications delivery point. This means that security for end users is not controlled with grants and revokes to individual users at the physical table level but is controlled through roles defined and enforced on an LDAP-based network resource called a directory server. It is then incumbent on the end users' applications to sort out what the authenticated role of a requesting end user is and whether that role permits the end user to view the particular screen being requested. This view of security is spelled out in detail in *Data Warehouse Lifecycle Toolkit*.

The good news about the role-based enforcement of security is that the ETL team should not be directly concerned with designing or managing end user security. However, the ETL team needs to work in a special environment, since they have full read/write access to the physical tables of the data warehouse. The ETL team's workstations should be on a separate subnet behind a packet-filtering gateway. If the ETL team's workstations are on the regular company intranet, any malicious individual on that intranet can quietly install a packet sniffer that will reveal the administrative passwords to all the databases. A large percentage, if not the majority, of malicious attacks on IT infrastructure comes from individuals who have legitimate physical access to company facilities.

Additionally, security must be extended to physical backups. If a tape or disk pack can easily be removed from the backup vault, security has been compromised as effectively as if the on-line passwords were compromised.

Data Integration

Data integration is a huge topic for IT because ultimately IT aims to make all systems work together seamlessly. The *360 degree view of the business* is the business name for data integration. In many cases, serious data integration must take place among the primary transaction systems of the organization before any of that data arrives at the data warehouse. But rarely is that data integration complete, unless the organization has settled on a single enterprise resource planning (ERP) system, and even then it is likely that other important transaction-processing systems exist outside the main ERP system.

In this book, data integration takes the form of conforming dimensions and conforming facts. Conforming dimensions means establishing common dimensional attributes (often textual labels and standard units of measurement) across separate databases so that *drill across* reports can be generated using these attributes. This process is described in detail in Chapters 5 and 6.

Conforming facts means agreeing on common business metrics such as key performance indicators (KPIs) across separate databases so that these numbers can be compared mathematically by calculating differences and ratios.

In the ETL system, data integration is a separate step identified in our data flow thread as the *conform* step. Physically, this step involves enforcing common names of conformed dimension attributes and facts, as well as enforcing common domain contents and common units of measurement.

Data Latency

The data latency requirement describes how quickly the data must be delivered to end users. Data latency obviously has a huge effect on the architecture and the system implementation. Up to a point, most of the traditional batch-oriented data flows described in this book can be sped up by more clever processing algorithms, parallel processing, and more potent hardware. But at some point, if the data latency requirement is sufficiently urgent, the architecture of the ETL system must convert from batch oriented to streaming oriented. This switch is not a gradual or evolutionary change; it is a major paradigm shift in which almost every step of the data-delivery pipeline must be reimplemented. We describe such streaming-oriented real time systems in Chapter 11.

Archiving and Lineage

We hint at these requirements in the preceding compliance and security sections. But even without the legal requirements for saving data, every data warehouse needs various copies of old data, either for comparisons with new data to generate change capture records or for reprocessing.

In this book, we recommend staging the data at each point where a major transformation has occurred. In our basic data flow thread, these staging points occur after all four steps: extract, clean, conform, and deliver. So, when does staging (writing data to disk) turn into archiving (keeping data indefinitely on permanent media)?

Our simple answer is conservative. All staged data should be archived unless a conscious decision is made that specific data sets will never be recovered. It is almost always less of a headache to read data back in from permanent media than it is to reprocess data through the ETL system at a later time. And, of course, it may be impossible to reprocess data according to the old processing algorithms if enough time has passed.

And, while you are at it, each staged/archived data set should have accompanying metadata describing the origins and processing steps that produced the data. Again, the tracking of this lineage is explicitly required by certain compliance requirements but should be part of every archiving situation.

End User Delivery Interfaces

The final step for the ETL system is the handoff to end user applications. We take a strong and disciplined position on this handoff. We believe the ETL team, working closely with the modeling team, must take responsibility for the content and the structure of data, making the end user applications simple and fast. This attitude is much more than a vague motherhood statement. We believe it is irresponsible to hand data off to the end user application in such a way as to increase the complexity of the application, slow down the final query or report creation, or make data seem unnecessarily complex to end users. The most elementary and serious error is to hand across a full-blown normalized physical model and to walk away from the job. This is why Chapters 5 and 6 go to such length to build dimensional physical structures that comprise the actual final handoff.

In general, the ETL team and the data modelers need to work closely with the end user application developers to determine the exact requirements for the final data handoff. Each end user tool has certain sensitivities that should be avoided, and certain features that can be exploited, if the physical data is in the right format. The same considerations apply to data prepared for OLAP cubes, which we describe in Chapter 6.

Available Skills

Some of the big design decisions when building an ETL system must be made on the basis of who builds and manages the system. You shouldn't build a system that depends on critical C++ processing modules if those programming skills are not in house, and you cannot reasonably acquire and keep those skills. You may be much more confident in building your ETL system around a major vendor's ETL tool if you already have those skills in house and you know how to manage such a project.

In the next section, we look in depth at the big decision of whether to hand code your ETL system or use a vendor's package. Our point here is that technical issues and license costs aside, you should not go off in a direction that your employees and managers find unfamiliar without seriously considering the implications of doing so.

Legacy Licenses

Finally, in many cases, major design decisions will be made for you implicitly by senior management's insistence that you use existing legacy licenses. In many cases, this requirement is one you can live with and for which the advantages in your environment are pretty clear to everyone. But in a few cases, the use of a legacy system for your ETL development is a mistake. This is a difficult position to be in, and if you feel strongly enough about it, you may need to bet your job. If you must approach senior management and challenge the use of an existing legacy system, be well prepared in making your case, and be man enough (or woman enough) to accept the final decision or possibly seek employment elsewhere.

Architecture

The choice of architecture is a fundamental and early decision in the design of the ETL system. The choice of architecture affects everything, and a change in architecture almost always means implementing the entire system over again from the very start. The key to applying an architectural decision effectively is to apply it consistently. You should read each of the following subsections with the aim of first making a specific architectural choice and then applying it everywhere in your ETL system. Again, while each one of the categories in this section can be a showstopper, the most important early architectural choice is whether to build the ETL system around a vendor's ETL tool or to hand code the system yourself. Almost every detail of the design of your ETL system will depend on this choice.

PROCESS CHECK
Planning & Design: Requirements/Realities → *Architecture* →
Implementation → Test/Release
Data Flow: Haven't started tracing the data flow yet.

ETL Tool versus Hand Coding (Buy a Tool Suite or Roll Your Own?)

The answer is, "It depends." In an excellent Intelligent Enterprise magazine article (May 31, 2003, edited by Ralph Kimball), Gary Nissen sums up the tradeoffs. We have augmented and extended some of Gary's points.

Tool-Based ETL Advantages

- A quote from an ETL tool vendor: "The goal of a valuable tool is not to make trivial problems mundane, but to make impossible problems possible."
- Simpler, faster, cheaper development. The tool cost will make up for itself in projects large enough or sophisticated enough.
- Technical people with broad business skills who are otherwise not professional programmers can use ETL tools effectively.
- Many ETL tools have integrated metadata repositories that can synchronize metadata from source systems, target databases, and other BI tools.
- Most ETL tools automatically generate metadata at every step of the process and enforce a consistent metadata-driven methodology that all developers must follow.
- Most ETL tools have a comprehensive built-in scheduler aiding in documentation, ease of creation, and management change. The ETL tool should handle all of the complex dependency and error handling that might be required if things go wrong.
- The metadata repository of most ETL tools can automatically produce data lineage (looking backward) and data dependency analysis (looking forward).
- ETL tools have connectors prebuilt for most source and target systems. At a more technical level, ETL tools should be able to handle all sorts of complex data type conversions.
- ETL tools typically offer in-line encryption and compression capabilities.
- Most ETL tools deliver good performance even for very large data sets. Consider a tool if your ETL data volume is very large or if it will be in a couple of years.

- An ETL tool can often manage complex load-balancing scenarios across servers, avoiding server deadlock.

- Most ETL tools will perform an automatic change-impact analysis for downstream processes and applications that are affected by a proposed schema change.

- An ETL-tool approach can be augmented with selected processing modules hand coded in an underlying programming language. For example, a custom CRC (cyclic redundancy checksum) algorithm could be introduced into an ETL vendor's data flow if the vendor-supplied module did not have the right statistical performance. Or a custom seasonalization algorithm could be programmed as part of a data-quality step to determine if an observed value is reasonable.

Hand-Coded ETL Advantages

- Automated unit testing tools are available in a hand-coded system but not with a tool-based approach. For example, the JUnit library (www.junit.org) is a highly regarded and well-supported tool for unit testing Java programs. There are similar packages for other languages. You can also use a scripting language, such as Tcl or Python, to set up test data, run an ETL process, and verify the results. Automating the testing process through one of these methods will significantly improve the productivity of your QA staff and the quality of your deliverables.

- Object-oriented programming techniques help you make all your transformations consistent for error reporting, validation, and metadata updates.

- You can more directly manage metadata in hand-coded systems, although at the same time you must create all your own metadata interfaces.

- A brief requirements analysis of an ETL system quickly points you toward file-based processing, not database-stored procedures. File-based processes are more direct. They're simply coded, easily tested, and well understood.

- Existing legacy routines should probably be left as-is.

- In-house programmers may be available.

- A tool-based approach will limit you to the tool vendor's abilities and their unique scripting language. But you can develop a hand-coded system in a common and well-known language. (In fairness, all the ETL tools allow *escapes* to standard programming languages in isolated modules.)

■ Hand-coded ETL provides unlimited flexibility, if that is indeed what you need. You can literally do anything you want. In many instances, a unique approach or a different language can provide a big advantage.

We would add one more advantage to the ETL Tool suite list: It is likely that the ETL tool suite will be more self-documenting and maintainable over a period of years, especially if you have a typical IT staff *churn*. The counter argument to this is that if your ETL development staff has a strong software-development tradition and good management, documentation and maintenance will not be as big a problem.

Using Proven Technology

When it comes to building a data warehouse, many initial costs are involved. You have to buy dedicated servers: at least one database server, a business intelligence server, and typically a dedicated ETL server. You need database licenses, and you have to pay for the ability of your users to access your business intelligence tool. You have to pay consultants and various other costs of starting up a new project. All of these costs are mandatory if you want to build a data warehouse. However, one cost is often not recognized as mandatory and is often avoided in an effort to reduce costs of the project—the cost of acquiring a dedicated ETL tool. It is possible to implement a data warehouse without a dedicated tool, and this book does not assume you will or won't buy one. However, it is advised that you do realize in the long run that purchasing an ETL tool actually reduces the cost of building and maintaining your data warehouse. Some additional benefits of using proven ETL technology are as follows:

■ **Define once, apply many.** Share and reuse business rules and structured routines, keeping your data consistent throughout the data warehouse.

■ **Impact analysis.** Determine which tables, columns, and processes are affected by proposed changes.

■ **Metadata repository.** Easily create, maintain, and publish data lineage; inherit business definitions from a data-modeling tool, and present capture metadata in your BI tool.

■ **Incremental aggregation.** Dynamically update summary tables by applying only new and changed data without the need to rebuild aggregates with each load process.

■ **Managed batch loading.** Reduce shell scripts and enable conditional loading, load statistics, automated e-mail notification, and so on.

- **Simpler connectivity** to a wide variety of complex sources such as SAP and mainframes.
- **Parallel pipe-lined multithreaded operation**.
- **Vendor experience,** including success with dimensional models and a proven track record of supporting data warehouses.

More important than taking advantage of advanced functionality is that investing in a proven ETL tool can help you avoid reinventing the wheel. These tools are designed for one purpose: to do exactly what you are trying to do—load a data warehouse. Most have evolved into stable, robust ETL engines that have embedded capabilities to extract data from various heterogeneous sources, handle complex data transformations, and load a dimensional data warehouse.

> Don't add new and untested products to your ETL configuration. The dashboard-of-the-month approach, which has a certain charm in the end user environment, is too reckless in the back room. Be conservative and wait for ETL technologies to mature. Work with vendors who have significant track record and who are likely to support your products five years down the road.

Batch versus Streaming Data Flow

The standard architecture for an ETL system is based on periodic batch extracts from the source data, which then flows through the system, resulting in a batch update of the final end user tables. This book is mostly organized around this architecture. But as we describe in Chapter 11, when the real-time nature of the data-warehouse load becomes sufficiently urgent, the batch approach breaks down. The alternative is a streaming data flow in which the data at a record level continuously flows from the source system to users' databases and screens.

Changing from a batch to a streaming data flow changes everything. Although we must still support the fundamental data flow steps of extract, clean, conform, and deliver, each of these steps must be modified for record-at-a-time processing. And especially with the fastest streaming flows, many of the usual assumptions about the arrival of data and even referential integrity have to be revisited. For instance, the basic numeric measures of a sales transaction with a new customer can arrive before the description of the customer arrives. Even after the customer is identified, an enhanced/cleaned/deduplicated version of the customer record may be introduced hours or even days after the original event. All of this requires logic and database updating that is probably avoided with batch-oriented data flow.

At the beginning of this section, we advise applying each architectural decision uniformly across the entire data warehouse. Obviously, in the case of choosing a batch or streaming approach, the choice should be made on an application-by-application basis. In Chapter 11, we discuss the points of commonality between the two approaches and show where the results of the batch approach can be used in the streaming context.

Horizontal versus Vertical Task Dependency

A horizontally organized task flow allows each final database load to run to completion independently. Thus, if you have both orders and shipments, these two database loads run independently, and either or both can be released on time or be late. This usually means that the steps of extract, clean, conform, and deliver are not synchronized between these two job flows.

A vertically oriented task flow synchronizes two or more separate job flows so that, above all, the final database loads occur simultaneously. Usually, the earlier steps are synchronized as well, especially if conformed dimensions like customer or vendor are used by more than one system. Either all the job streams reach the conform step and the delivery step or none of them do.

Scheduler Automation

A related architectural decision is how deeply to control your overall ETL system with automated scheduler technology. At one extreme, all jobs are kicked off by a human typing at a command line or starting an icon. At the other extreme, a master scheduler tool manages all the jobs, understands whether jobs have run successfully, waits for various system statuses to be satisfied, and handles communication with human supervisors such as emergency alerts and job flow status reporting.

Exception Handling

Exception handling should not be a random series of little ad-hoc alerts and comments placed in files but rather should be a system-wide, uniform mechanism for reporting all instances of exceptions thrown by ETL processes into a single database, with the name of the process, the time of the exception, its initially diagnosed severity, the action subsequently taken, and the ultimate resolution status of the exception. Thus, every job needs to be architected to write these exception-reporting records into the database.

Quality Handling

Similarly, you should decide on a common response to quality issues that arise while processing the data. In addition to triggering an exception-reporting record, all quality problems need to generate an *audit record* attached to the final dimension or fact data. Corrupted or suspected data needs to be handled with a small number of uniform responses, such as filling in missing text data with a question mark or supplying least biased estimators of numeric values that exist but were corrupted before delivery to the data warehouse. These topics are further developed in Chapter 4.

Recovery and Restart

From the start, you need to build your ETL system around the ability to recover from abnormal ending of a job and restart. ETL jobs need to be re-entrant, otherwise impervious to incorrect multiple updating. For instance, a job that subtracts a particular brand sales result from an overall product category should not be allowed to run twice. This kind of thinking needs to underlie every ETL job because sooner or later these jobs will either terminate abnormally or be mistakenly run more than once. Somewhere, somehow, you must keep this from happening.

Metadata

Metadata from DBMS system tables and from schema design tools is easy to capture but probably composes 25 percent of the metadata you need to understand and control your system. Another 25 percent of the metadata is generated by the cleaning step. But the biggest metadata challenge for the ETL team is where and how to store process-flow information. An important but unglamorous advantage of ETL tool suites is that they maintain this process-flow metadata automatically. If you are hand coding your ETL system, you need to implement your own central repository of process flow metadata. See Chapter 9.

Security

Earlier in this chapter, we describe our recommended architecture for role-based security for end users. Security in the ETL environment is less granular than in the end user environment; nevertheless, a systematic approach to security demands that physical and administrative safeguards surround every on-line table and every backup tape in the ETL environment. The most sensitive and important data sets need to be instrumented with operating system printed reports listing every access and every command performed by all administrators against these data sets. The print log should be produced on a dedicated impact printer locked in a room that cannot be opened by any of the normal IT staff. Archived data sets should be stored with checksums to demonstrate that they have not been altered in any way.

The Back Room – Preparing the Data

PROCESS CHECK

**Planning & Design: Requirements → *Architecture* → Implementation → Release
Data Flow: Extract → Clean → Conform → Deliver.**

The back room and the front room of the data warehouse are physically, logically, and administratively separate. In other words, in most cases the back room and front room are on different machines, depend on different data structures, and are managed by different IT personnel.

Figure 1.1 shows the two distinct components of a typical data warehouse.

Preparing the data, often called *data management*, involves acquiring data and transforming it into information, ultimately delivering that information to the query-friendly front room. *No query services are provided in the back room*. Read that sentence again! Our approach to data warehousing assumes that data access is prohibited in the back room, and therefore the front room is dedicated to just this one purpose.

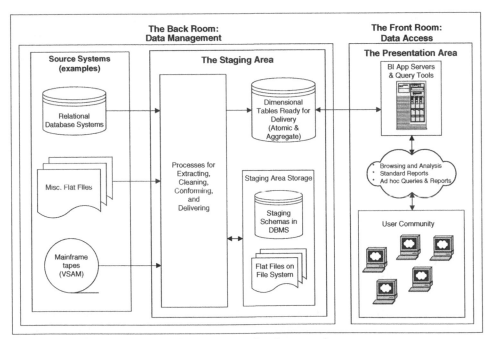

Figure 1.1   The back room and front room of a data warehouse.

Think of a restaurant. Imagine that patrons of the restaurant are end users and the food is data. When food is offered to patrons in the dining room, it is served and situated exactly as they expect: clean, organized, and presented in a way that each piece can be easily identified and consumed.

Meanwhile, before the food enters the dining room, it is prepared in the kitchen under the supervision of an experienced chef. In the kitchen the food is selected, cleaned, sliced, cooked, and prepared for presentation. The kitchen is a working area, off limits to the patrons of the restaurant. In the best restaurants, the kitchen is completely hidden from its customers— exposure to the kitchen, where their food is still a work-in-progress, spoils the customer's ultimate dining experience. If a customer requests information about the preparation of food, the chef must come out from the kitchen to meet the customer in the dining room—a safe, clean environment where the customer is comfortable—to explain the food preparation process.

The staging area is the kitchen of the data warehouse. It is a place accessible only to experienced data integration professionals. It is a back-room facility, completely off limits to end users, where the data is placed after it is extracted from the source systems, cleansed, manipulated, and prepared to be loaded to the presentation layer of the data warehouse. Any metadata generated by the ETL process that is useful to end users must come out of the back room and be offered in the presentation area of the data warehouse.

Prohibiting data access in the back room kitchen relieves the ETL team from:

- Providing detailed security at a row, column, or applications level
- Building query performance-enhancing indexes and aggregations
- Providing continuous up-time under service-level agreements
- Guaranteeing that all data sets are consistent with each other

We need to do all these things, but in the front room, not the back room. In fact, the issue of data access is really the crucial distinction between the back room and the front room. If you make a few exceptions and allow end user clients to access the back room structures directly, you have, in our opinion, fatally compromised the data warehouse.

Returning to the kitchen, we often use the word *staging* to describe discrete steps in the back room. Staging almost always implies a temporary or permanent physical snapshot of data. There are four staging steps found in almost every data warehouse, as shown in Figure 1.2, which is the same four-step data flow thread we introduce in the this book's introduction, but with the staging step explicitly shown. Throughout this book, we assume that every ETL system supporting the data warehouse is structured with these four steps and that data is staged (written to the disk) in parallel with

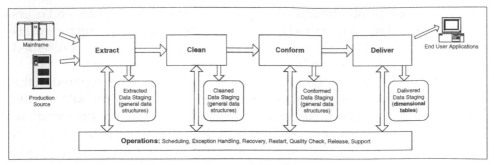

Figure 1.2   The Four Staging Steps of a Data Warehouse.

the data being transferred to the next stage. The central chapters of this book are organized around these steps. The four steps are:

1. **Extracting**. The raw data coming from the source systems is usually written directly to disk with some minimal restructuring but before significant content transformation takes place. Data from structured source systems (such as IMS databases, or XML data sets) often is written to flat files or relational tables in this step. This allows the original extract to be as simple and as fast as possible and allows greater flexibility to restart the extract if there is an interruption. Initially captured data can then be read multiple times as necessary to support the succeeding steps. In some cases, initially captured data is discarded after the cleaning step is completed, and in other cases data is kept as a long-term archival backup. The initially captured data may also be saved for at least one capture cycle so that the differences between successive extracts can be computed.

   💡 **We save the serious content transformations for the cleaning and conforming steps, but the best place to resolve certain legacy data format issues is in the extract step. These format issues include resolving repeating groups, REDEFINEs, and overloaded columns and performing low-level data conversions, including converting bit encoding to character, EBCDIC to ASCII, and packed decimal to integer. We discuss these steps in detail in Chapter 3.**

2. **Cleaning.** In most cases, the level of data quality acceptable for the source systems is different from the quality required by the data warehouse. Data quality processing may involve many discrete steps, including checking for valid values (is the zip code present and is it in the range of valid values?), ensuring consistency across values (are the zip code and the city consistent?), removing duplicates (does the same customer appear twice with slightly different attributes?), and checking whether complex business rules and procedures have been enforced (does the Platinum customer have the associated extended

credit status?). Data-cleaning transformations may even involve human intervention and the exercise of judgment. The results of the data-cleaning step are often saved semipermanently because the transformations required are difficult and irreversible. It is an interesting question in any environment whether the cleaned data can be fed back to the sources systems to improve their data and reduce the need to process the same data problems over and over with each extract. Even if the cleaned data cannot be physically fed back to the source systems, the data exceptions should be reported to build a case for improvements in the source system. These data issues are also important for the final business intelligence (BI) user community.

3. **Conforming.** Data conformation is required whenever two or more data sources are merged in the data warehouse. Separate data sources cannot be queried together unless some or all of the textual labels in these sources have been made identical and unless similar numeric measures have been mathematically rationalized so that differences and ratios between these measures make sense. Data conformation is a significant step that is more than simple data cleaning. Data conformation requires an enterprise-wide agreement to use standardized domains and measures. We discuss this step extensively in the book when we talk about conformed dimensions and conformed facts in Chapters 5 and 6.

4. **Delivering.** The whole point of the back room is to make the data ready for querying. The final and crucial back-room step is physically structuring the data into a set of simple, symmetric schemas known as dimensional models, or equivalently, star schemas. These schemas significantly reduce query times and simplify application development. Dimensional schemas are required by many query tools, and these schemas are a necessary basis for constructing OLAP cubes. We take the strong view in this book that dimensionally modeled tables should be the target of every data warehouse back room. In Chapter 5 we carefully describe the structures of dimensional tables, and we give a fairly complete justification for building the data warehouse around these structures. For a more comprehensive treatment of dimensional modeling, please refer to the other Toolkit books, especially the *Data Warehouse Toolkit*, Second Edition (Wiley, 2002).

💡 **Figure 1.2 makes it look like you must do all the extracting, cleaning, conforming and delivering serially with well-defined boundaries between each pair of steps. In practice, there will multiple simultaneous flows of data in the ETL system, and frequently some of the cleaning steps are embedded in the logic that performs extraction.**

 **The ODS has been absorbed by the data warehouse.**

Ten years ago, the operational data store (ODS) was a separate system that sat between the source transactional systems and the data warehouse. It was a *hot extract* that was made available to end users to answer a narrow range of urgent operational questions, such as "was the order shipped?" or "was the payment made?" The ODS was particularly valuable when the ETL processes of the main data warehouse delayed the availability of the data or aggregated the data so that these narrow questions could not be asked.

In most cases, no attempt was made to transform a particular ODS's content to work with other systems. The ODS was a hot query extract from a single source.

The ODS also served as a source of data for the data warehouse itself because the ODS was an extraction from the transactional systems. In some cases, the ODS served only this function and was not used for querying. This is why the ODS has always had two personalities: one for querying and one for being a source for the data warehouse.

The ODS as a separate system outside the data warehouse is no longer necessary. Modern data warehouses now routinely extract data on a daily basis, and some of the new real-time techniques allow the data warehouse to always be completely current. Data warehouses in general have become far more operationally oriented than in the past. The footprints of the conventional data warehouse and the ODS now overlap so completely that it is not fruitful to make a distinction between the two kinds of systems.

Finally, both the early ODSs and modern data warehouses frequently include an interface that allows end users to modify production data directly.

The Front Room – Data Access

Accessing data in the presentation area of the data warehouse is a client, or follow-on, project that must be closely coordinated with the building and managing of the ETL system. The whole purpose of the ETL system is to feed the presentation layer of dimensionally modeled tables that are directly accessed by query tools, report writers, dashboards, and OLAP cubes. The data in the front room is what end users actually see.

Data marts are an important component of the front room. A data mart is a set of dimensional tables supporting a business process. Some authors refer to business processes as subject areas. *Subject area* is a fuzzy phrase with multiple meanings. For example, we've heard people refer to subject areas as *products, customers, and orders*. But we believe there is a big difference between product and customer entities and true measurement-intensive processes such as orders. In our view, data marts are always measurement-intensive subject areas (like orders), and they are surrounded by descriptive entities like products and customers.

Although this book is not about using data marts, we need to make some strong statements about them.

1. **Data marts are based on the source of data, not on a department's view of data.** In other words, there is only one orders data mart in a product-oriented company. All the end user query tools and applications in various departments access this data mart to have a single, consistently labeled version of orders.

2. **Data marts contain all atomic detail needed to support drilling down to the lowest level.** The view that data marts consist only of aggregated data is one of the most fundamental mistakes a data warehouse designer can make. Aggregated data in the absence of the lowest-level atomic data *presupposes the business question* and makes drilling down impossible. We will see that a data mart should consist of a continuous pyramid of identically structured dimensional tables, always beginning with the atomic data as the foundation.

3. **Data marts can be centrally controlled or decentralized.** In other words, an enterprise data warehouse can be physically centralized on a single machine and the deployment of data marts can wait until a certain level of integration takes place in the ETL staging areas, or the data marts can be developed separately and asynchronously while at the same time participating in the enterprise's conformed dimensions and facts. We believe that the extreme of a fully centralized and fully prebuilt data warehouse is an ideal that is interesting to talk about but is not realistic. A much more realistic scenario is the incrementally developed and partially decentralized data warehouse environment. After all, organizations are constantly changing, acquiring new data sources, and needing new perspectives. So in a real environment, we must focus on incremental and adaptable strategies for building data warehouses, rather than on idealistic visions of controlling all information before a data warehouse is implemented.

There are many tasks and responsibilities in the front room that are outside the scope of this book. Just so there is no confusion, we do *not* talk in this book about:

- Indexing dimensional tables in the presentation area for query performance
- Choosing front-end tools, including query tools, report writers, and dashboards
- Writing SQL to solve end user queries

- Data-mining techniques
- Forecasting, behavior scoring, and calculating allocations
- Security on the tables and applications accessible by end users
- Metadata supporting end user tools
- End user training and documentation

This book is about the ETL systems for getting data out of its original source system and delivering it to the front room.

The Mission of the Data Warehouse

The mission of the data warehouse is to publish the organization's data assets to most effectively support decision making. The key word in this mission statement is *publish*. Just as the success of a conventional publication like a magazine begins and ends with its readers, the success of a data warehouse begins and ends with its end users. Since the data warehouse is a decision support system, our main criterion of success is whether the data warehouse effectively contributes to the most important decision-making processes in the organization. Although the costs of hardware, software, labor, consulting services, and maintenance have to be managed carefully, the hidden costs of failing to support the important decisions of an organization are potentially much larger. The tangible costs of a data warehouse, managed by IT, are tactical, but the more important costs and benefits of decision support are strategic.

Transaction database applications have been penetrating the corporate world for over 30 years. Although we have entered data into dedicated transaction applications for decades, it has become apparent that getting the data out of these systems for analytic purposes is too difficult. Billions of dollars have been spent on database applications, and their data is kept prisoner within them. An immeasurable amount of time is spent trying to get data from transaction systems, but like navigating through a labyrinth, most of that time is spent hitting dead ends. The ETL system must play a major role in handing the data to the final end user applications in a usable form.

Building a comprehensive, reliable data warehouse is a significant task that revolves around a set of standard components. The most important and fundamental components of the data warehouse are the back room and the front room. This book is about the back room.

What the Data Warehouse Is

Data warehousing is the process of taking data from legacy and transaction database systems and transforming it into organized information in a user-friendly format to encourage data analysis and support fact-based business decision making. The process that involves transforming data from its original format to a dimensional data store accounts for at least 70 percent of the time, effort, and expense of most data warehouse projects. After implementing many data warehouses, we've determined that a data warehouse should have the following definition:

> *A data warehouse is a system that extracts, cleans, conforms, and delivers source data into a dimensional data store and then supports and implements querying and analysis for the purpose of decision making.*

We've come up with this definition to alleviate confusion about data-warehouse implementation costs. Historically, the most visible part of a data warehouse project is the data access portion—usually in the form of products—and some attention is brought to the dimensional model. But by spotlighting only those portions, a gaping hole is left out of the data warehouse lifecycle. When it comes time to make the data warehouse a reality, the data access tool can be in place, and the dimensional model can be created, but then it takes many months from that point until the data warehouse is actually usable because the ETL process still needs to be completed.

By bringing attention to building the back room data management component, data warehouse sponsors are better positioned to envision the real value of the data warehouse—to support decision making by the end users—and allot realistic budgets to building data warehouses.

 Unanticipated delays can make the data warehouse project appear to be a failure, but building the ETL process should not be an unanticipated delay. The data warehouse team usually knows that the ETL process consumes the majority of the time to build the data warehouse. The perception of delays can be avoided if the data warehouse sponsors are aware that the deployment of the data warehouse is dependent on the completion of the ETL process. The biggest risk to the timely completion of the ETL system comes from encountering unexpected data-quality problems. This risk can be mitigated with the data-profiling techniques discussed in Chapter 4.

What the Data Warehouse Is Not

What constitutes a data warehouse is often misunderstood. To this day, you can ask ten experts to define a data warehouse, and you are likely to get ten different responses. The biggest disparity usually falls in describing exactly what components are considered to be part of the data warehouse project. To clear up any misconceptions, anyone who is going to be part of a data warehouse team, especially on the ETL team, must know his or her boundaries.

The environment of a data warehouse includes several components, each with its own suite of designs, techniques, tools, and products. The most important thing to remember is that none of these things alone constitutes a data warehouse. The ETL system is a major component of the data warehouse, but many other components are required for a complete implementation. Throughout our experiences of implementing data warehouses, we've seen team members struggling with the same misconceptions over and over again. The top five things the data warehouse is mistaken to be are as follows:

1. **A product.** Contrary to many vendor claims, you cannot buy a data warehouse. A data warehouse includes system analysis, data manipulation and cleansing, data movement, and finally dimensional modeling and data access. No single product can achieve all of the tasks involved in building a data warehouse.

2. **A language.** One cannot learn to *code* a data warehouse in the way you learn to implement XML, SQL, VB, or any other programming language. The data warehouse is composed of several components, each likely to require one or more programming or data-specification languages.

3. **A project.** A properly deployed data warehouse consists of many projects (and phases of projects). Any attempt to deploy a data warehouse as a single project will almost certainly fail. Successful data warehouses plan at the enterprise level yet deploy manageable dimensional data marts. Each data mart is typically considered a separate project with its own timeline and budget. A crucial factor is that each data mart contains conformed dimensions and standardized facts so that each integrates into a single cohesive unit—the enterprise data warehouse. The enterprise data warehouse evolves and grows as each data mart project is completed. A better way to think of a data warehouse is as a **process**, not as a project.

4. **A data model.** A data model alone does not make a data warehouse. Recall that the data warehouse is a comprehensive process that, by definition, must include the ETL process. After all, without data, even the best-designed data model is useless.

5. **A copy of your transaction system.** A common mistake is to believe copying your operational system into a separate reporting system creates a data warehouse. Just as the data model alone does not create a data warehouse, neither does executing the data movement process without restructuring the data store.

Industry Terms Not Used Consistently

In this section, we call out industry terms that are given different meanings by different writers. There is probably no realistic hope of getting the industry to settle on uniform definitions of these terms, but at least we can take a clear stand on how we use the terms in this book.

Data Mart

Other authors frequently define a data mart as an *aggregated set of data pre-built to answer specific business questions for a given department*. Of course, this definition contains its own criticism! In this book and in our writings for the last decade, we have consistently defined a data mart as a process-oriented subset of the overall organization's data based on a foundation of atomic data, and that depends only on the physics of the data-measurement events, not on the anticipated user's questions. Note the differences among data mart definitions:

CORRECT DEFINITION	MISGUIDED DEFINITION
Process Based	Department Based
Atomic Data Foundation	Aggregated Data Only
Data Measurement Based	User Question Based

Our data marts (call them *dimensional data marts*) look the same to all observers and would be implemented identically by anyone with access to the underlying measurement events. Furthermore, since dimensional data marts are always based on the most atomic data, these data marts are impervious to changes in application focus; by definition, they contain all the detail that is possible from the original sources. Data marts constructed according to the misguided definitions will be unable to handle changing business requirements because the details have been presummarized.

Enterprise Data Warehouse (EDW)

EDW is sometimes used as the name the name for a specific design approach (as contrasted with the uncapitalized *enterprise data warehouse*, which refers generically to the data warehouse assets of a large organization). Many people also refer to the EDW as the *CIF*, or *Corporate Information Factory*. The EDW approach differs materially from the Data Warehouse Bus Architecture approach described in our Toolkit books. EDW embodies a number of related themes that need to be contrasted individually with the DW Bus approach. It may be helpful to separate logical issues from physical issues for a moment.

Logically, both approaches advocate a consistent set of definitions that rationalize the different data sources scattered around the organization. In the case of the DW Bus, the consistent set of definitions takes the form of conformed dimensions and conformed facts. With the EDW approach, the consistency seems much more amorphous. You must take it on faith that if you have a single, highly normalized ER model of all the enterprise's information, you then know how to administer hundreds or thousands of tables consistently. But, overlooking this lack of precision, one might argue that the two approaches are in agreement up to this point. Both approaches strive to apply a unifying coherence to all the distributed data sources.

Even if we have a tenuous agreement that both approaches have the same goal of creating a consistent representation of an organization's data, as soon as you move into physical design and deployment issues, the differences between the EDW and the DW Bus become really glaring.

Conformed dimensions and conformed facts take on specific forms in the DW Bus architecture. Conformed dimensions have common fields, and the respective domains of the values in these fields are the same. That guarantees that you can perform separate queries on remote fact tables connected to these dimensions and you will be able to merge the columns into a final result. This is, of course, drill across. We have written extensively on the steps required to administer conformed dimensions and conformed facts in a distributed data warehouse environment. We have never seen a comparable set of specific guidelines for the EDW approach. We find that interesting because even in a physically centralized EDW, you have to store data in physically distinct table spaces, and that necessitates going through the same logic as the replication of conformed dimensions. But we have never seen systematic procedures described by EDW advocates for doing this. Which tables do you synchronously replicate between table spaces and when? The DW Bus procedures describe this in great detail.

The denormalized nature of the dimensions in the DW Bus design allows us to administer the natural time variance of a dimension in a predictable way (SCD types 1, 2, and 3). Again, in the highly normalized EDW world, we have not seen a comparable description of how to build and administer the equivalent of slowly changing dimensions. But it would seem to require copious use of time stamps on all the entities, together with a lot more key administration than the dimensional approach requires. By the way, the surrogate key approach we have described for administering SCDs actually has nothing to do with dimensional modeling. In an EDW, the root table of a normalized, snowflaked *dimension* would have to undergo exactly the same key administration (using either a surrogate key or a natural key plus a date) with the same number of repeated records if it tracked the same slowly changing time variance as the DW Bus version.

The denormalized nature of dimensions in the DW Bus design allows a systematic approach to defining aggregates, the single most powerful and cost effective way to increase the performance of a large data warehouse. The science of dimensional aggregation techniques is intimately linked to the use of conformed dimensions. The *shrunken* dimensions of an aggregate fact table are perfectly conformed subsets of the base dimensions in the DW Bus architecture. The EDW approach, again, has no systematic and documented approach for handling aggregates in the normalized environment or giving guidance to query tools and report writers for how to use aggregates. This issue interacts with *drilling down*, described in a moment.

Most important, a key assumption built into most EDW architectures is that the centralized data warehouse *releases* data marts. These data marts are often described as *built to answer a business question*, as described in the previous subsection on data-mart definitions. A final, unworkable assumption of the EDW is that if the user wants to ask a precise question involving atomic data, he or she must leave the aggregated dimensional data mart and descend into the 3NF atomic data located in the back room. EVERY-THING is wrong with this view in our opinion. All of the leverage we developed in the DW Bus is defeated by this two level architecture: drilling down through conformed dimensions to atomic data; uniform encoding of slowly changing dimensions; the use of performance-enhancing aggregates; and the sanctity of keeping the back room data-staging area off limits to query services.

Resolving Architectural Conflict: The Hybrid Bus Approach

Is it possible to reconcile the two architectural approaches? We think so. Throughout this book, we support the judicious use of normalized data structures for data cleaning. A really dirty data source benefits from the discipline of enforcing the many-to-1 relationships brought to the surface by the process of normalization. THEN we urge the ETL team to convert any such normalized structures into simple dimensional structures for the conforming and final handoff steps. This includes the atomic base layer of data. At this point, an IT organization that has already invested in normalized physical structures can leverage that investment. We can call this the *Hybrid Bus Approach*.

How the Data Warehouse Is Changing

As we write this book, the data warehouse is undergoing a significant change, perhaps the most significant change since the beginning of data warehousing. Everything we have said in this chapter about the data warehouse supporting decision making remains true, but the focus of new development in the data warehouse is in many cases drastically more *operational* and *real time*. Although the basic front room and back room components of the data warehouse are still very necessary for these real-time applications, the traditional batch-file-oriented ETL processing is giving way to streaming ETL processing, and the traditional user-driven query and reporting tools are giving way to data-driven and event-driven dashboards. We describe these new developments and how they extend the central concepts of the data warehouse in Chapter 11.

The Mission of the ETL Team

We are finally in a position to succinctly describe the mission of the ETL team, using the vocabulary of this chapter. *The mission of the ETL team at the highest level is to build the back room of the data warehouse.* More specifically, the ETL system must:

- Deliver data most effectively to end user tools
- Add value to data in the cleaning and conforming steps
- Protect and document the lineage of data

We will see that in almost every data warehouse the back room must support four keys steps:

- Extracting data from the original sources
- Quality assuring and cleaning data
- Conforming the labels and measures in the data to achieve consistency across the original sources
- Delivering data in a physical format that can be used by query tools, report writers, and dashboards.

This book deals with each of these steps in great detail.

ETL Data Structures

The back room area of the data warehouse has frequently been called the staging area. Staging in this context means *writing to disk* and, at a minimum, we recommend staging data at the four major checkpoints of the ETL data flow. The ETL team will need a number of different data structures to meet all the legitimate staging needs, and thus the purpose of this chapter is to describe all the types of data structures you are likely to need.

This chapter does not describe all the source data types you must extract from. We leave that to Chapter 3!

PROCESS CHECK Planning & Design:
Requirements/Realities → *Architecture* → *Implementation* → Test/Release

Data Flow: Extract → Clean → Conform → Deliver

We also try to step back from the details of the data structures to recommend general design principles for the staging area, including planning and design standards and an introduction to the metadata needed to support staging. Metadata is a big topic, and we gather a number of more specific metadata designs in Chapter 4 in the cleaning and conforming steps. Also, we tie all the metadata topics together toward the end of the book in Chapter 9.

To Stage or Not to Stage

The decision to store data in a physical staging area versus processing it in memory is ultimately the choice of the ETL architect. The ability to develop efficient ETL processes is partly dependent on being able to determine the right balance between physical input and output (I/O) and in-memory processing.

The challenge of achieving this delicate balance between writing data to staging tables and keeping it in memory during the ETL process is a task that must be reckoned with in order to create optimal processes. The issue with determining whether to stage your data or not depends on two conflicting objectives:

- Getting the data from the originating source to the ultimate target as fast as possible
- Having the ability to recover from failure without restarting from the beginning of the process

The decision to stage data varies depending on your environment and business requirements. If you plan to do all of your ETL data processing in memory, keep in mind that every data warehouse, regardless of its architecture or environment, includes a staging area in some form or another. Consider the following reasons for staging data before it is loaded into the data warehouse:

- **Recoverability.** In most enterprise environments, it's a good practice to stage the data as soon as it has been extracted from the source system and then again immediately after each of the major transformation steps, assuming that for a particular table the transformation steps are significant. These *staging tables* (in a database or file system) serve as recovery points. By implementing these tables, the process won't have to intrude on the source system again if the transformations fail. Also, the process won't have to transform the data again if the load process fails. When staging data purely for recovery purposes, the data should be stored in a sequential file on the file system rather than in a database. Staging for recoverability is especially important when extracting from operational systems that overwrite their own data.

- **Backup.** Quite often, massive volume prevents the data warehouse from being reliably backed up at the database level. We've witnessed catastrophes that might have been avoided if only the load files were saved, compressed, and archived. If your staging tables are on the file system, they can easily be compressed into a very small footprint and saved on your network. Then if you ever need to reload the data warehouse, you can simply uncompress the load files and reload them.

- **Auditing.** Many times the data lineage between the source and target is lost in the ETL code. When it comes time to audit the ETL process, having staged data makes auditing between different portions of the ETL processes much more straightforward because auditors (or programmers) can simply compare the original input file with the logical transformation rules against the output file. This staged data is especially useful when the source system overwrites its history. When questions about the integrity of the information in the data warehouse surface days or even weeks after an event has occurred, revealing the staged extract data from the period of time in question can restore the trustworthiness of the data warehouse.

Once you've decided to stage at least some of the data, you must settle on the appropriate architecture of your staging area. As is the case with any other database, if the data-staging area is not planned carefully, it will fail. Designing the data-staging area properly is more important than designing the usual applications because of the sheer volume the data-staging area accumulates (sometimes larger than the data warehouse itself). The next section discusses staging-area design considerations and options.

Designing the Staging Area

The staging area stores data on its way to the final presentation area of the data warehouse. Sometimes, data in the staging area is preserved to support functionality that requires history, while other times data is deleted with each process. When history is maintained in the staging area, it is often re-ferred to as a *persistent staging area*. When data is deleted with each load, the area is considered transient. It's perfectly valid for the data-staging area to be a hybrid, composed of a mixture of persistent and transient staging tables.

> Make sure you give serious thought to the various roles that staging can play in your overall data warehouse operations. There is more to staging than just building temp files to support the execution of the next job. A given staging file can also be used for restarting the job flow if a serious problem develops downstream, and the staging file can be a form of audit or proof that the data had specific content when it was processed.

Regardless of the persistence of the data in the staging area, you must adhere to some basic rules when the staging area is designed and deployed. The following rules all have the same underlying premise: If you are not on the ETL team, keep out! You must establish and practice the following rules for your data warehouse project to be successful:

- **The data-staging area must be owned by the ETL team.** The data-staging area, and all of the data within it, is off limits to anyone other than the ETL team. The data-staging area is not designed for presentation. There are no indexes or aggregations to support querying in the staging area. There are no service-level agreements for data access or consistency in the staging area. All of these data access requirements are handled in the presentation area.

- **Users are not allowed in the staging area for any reason.** Data in the staging area must be considered a *construction site area*. Allowing unauthorized personnel into the area can cause injuries. Curious users allowed in the area often misuse the data and reduce the perceived integrity of the data warehouse.

- **Reports cannot access data from the staging area.** The data-staging area is a work site. Tables are added, dropped, or modified by the ETL team without notifying the user community. This concept does not mean that the area is a free-for-all with tables being added, dropped, and modified by programmers at will. However, it does mean that the area is intended to be a workbench, not a display case. The area is a controlled environment, meaning that modifications to tables in the production-staging area must go through the same lifecycle of tables in the data warehouse presentation layer. However, unlike changes to production data warehouse tables, data-staging tables can be changed without notifying users, *breaking* reports that might be using the altered table. Accordingly, do not allow any reports to point to the staging area even when such pointing is *temporary*.

- **Only ETL processes can write to and read from the staging area.** Every data warehouse requires data sets that don't have a conventional outside source, such as a table of data-quality status types. When the data warehouse requires data that does not exist in any existing external database environment, nevertheless it must come into the data-staging area like other data. Keep in mind that the data-staging area is not a transaction environment and that you should not allow data to be manually entered into it. If manual tables must be maintained, an application should be developed outside of the data-staging area, and the resulting data should be provided to the ETL team and incorporated into the staging area via an ETL process.

The ETL group owns the data-staging area. That means that the ETL architect designs the tables within it and decides whether a table belongs in the database or, based on the requirements of its respective ETL processes, is best suited for the file system. When the staging area is initially set up, the ETL architect must supply the database administrator (DBA) team and OS administrators with an overall data storage measure of the staging area so they can estimate the space allocations and parameter settings for the staging database, file systems, and directory structures. Figure 2.1 shows a sample staging area volumetric worksheet, focusing on the final delivery

Table Name	Update Strategy	Load Frequency	ETL Job(s)	Initial Rowcount	Avg Row Length	Grows with	Expected Monthly Rows	Expected Monthly Bytes	Initial Table Size Bytes	Table Size 6 mo. (MB)
S_ACCOUNT	Truncate / Reload	Daily	SAccount	39,933	27	New accounts	9,983	269,548	1,078,191	2.57
S_ASSETS	Insert / Delete	Daily	SAssets	771,500	78	New assets	192,875	15,044,250	60,177,000	143.47
S_BUDGET	Truncate / Reload	Monthly	SBudget	39,932	104	Refreshed monthly	9,983	1,038,232	4,152,928	9.90
S_COMPONENT	Truncate / Reload	On demand	SComponent	21	31	Components added to Inventory	5	163	651	0.00
S_CUSTOMER	Truncate / Reload	Daily	SCustomer	38,103	142	New customers added daily	9,526	1,352,657	5,410,626	12.90
S_CUSTOMER_HISTORY	Truncate / Reload	Daily	SCustomerHistory	2,307,707	162	Refresh with each bulk load	576,927	93,462,134	373,848,534	891.32
S_CUSTOMER_TYPE	Truncate / Reload	On demand	SCustomerType	5	21	New customer types	1	26	105	0.00
S_DEFECT	Truncate / Reload	On demand	SDefect	84	27	New defect names	21	567	2,268	0.01
S_DEFECTS	Insert Only	Daily	SDefects	8,181,132	132	Transaction defects	2,045,283	269,977,356	1,079,909,424	2,574.70
S_DEPARTMENT	Truncate / Reload	On demand	SDepartment	45	36	Departments established	11	405	1,620	0.00
S_FACILITY	Truncate / Reload	Daily	SFacility	45,260	32	New or changed facilities worldwide	11,315	362,080	1,448,320	3.45
S_HISTORY_FAIL_REASON	Insert / Delete	On demand	SHistoryFailReason	6	27	New failure codes	2	41	162	0.00
S_OFFICE	Truncate / Reload	Daily	SOffice	14	56	New offices opened	4	196	784	0.00
S_PACKAGE_MATL	Truncate / Reload	Daily	SPackageMatl	54	18	New packaged material categories	14	243	972	0.00
S_PRODUCT	Truncate / Reload	Daily	SProduct	174,641	73	New products	43,660	3,187,198	12,748,793	30.40
S_PROVIDER	Truncate / Reload	On demand	SProvider	63	45	Service providers	16	709	2,835	0.01
S_REGION	Truncate / Reload	Daily	SRegion	333	37	New or changed global regions	83	3,080	12,321	0.03
S_RESPONSES	Insert Only	Daily	SResponses	5,199,095	105	Response transaction	1,299,774	136,476,244	545,904,975	1,301.54
S_SURVEY	Truncate / Reload	Daily	SSurvey	45,891	83	Survey conducted	11,473	952,238	3,808,953	9.08

Figure 2.1 Staging tables volumetric worksheet.

tables at the end of the ETL data flow. A full volumetric tracking system would have similar worksheets for copies of source data and the staging files that followed the cleaning and conforming steps.

The volumetric worksheet lists each table in the staging area with the following information:

- **Table Name.** The name of the table or file in the staging area. There is one row in the worksheet for each staging table.

- **Update Strategy.** This field indicates how the table is maintained. If it is a persistent staging table, it will have data appended, updated, and perhaps deleted. Transient staging tables are truncated and reloaded with each process.

- **Load Frequency.** Reveals how often the table is loaded or changed by the ETL process. Quite often, it is daily. It can be weekly, monthly, or any interval of time. In a real-time environment, tables in the staging area can be updated continuously.

- **ETL Job(s).** Staging tables are populated or updated via ETL jobs. The ETL job is the job or program that affects the staging table or file. When many jobs affect a single staging table, list all of the jobs in this section of the worksheet.

- **Initial Row Count.** The ETL team must estimate how many rows each table in the staging area initially contains. The initial row count is usually based on the rows in the source and/or target tables.

- **Average Row Length.** For size-estimation purposes, you must supply the DBA with the average row length in each staging table. In an Oracle environment, we create the table in a development environment, run statistics, and gather this information from the ALL_TABLES table. For instance, in Oracle, the DBMS_STATS package can be used to populate the appropriate statistics columns.

- **Grows With.** Even though tables are updated on a scheduled interval, they don't necessarily grow each time they are touched. The Grows With field is based on business rules. You must define when each table in the staging area grows. For example, a status table grows each time a new status is added. Even though the table is touched daily to look for changes, the addition of new statuses is quite rare.

- **Expected Monthly Rows.** This estimate is based on history and business rules. Anticipated growth is required for the DBA to allocate appropriate space to the table. The monthly row count is a building block to calculate how many bytes the table grows each month.

- **Expected Monthly Bytes.** Expected Monthly Bytes is a calculation of Average Row Length times Expected Monthly Rows.

- **Initial Table Size.** The initial table size is usually represented in bytes or megabytes. It is a calculation of Average Row Length times Initial Row Count.

- **Table Size 6 Months.** An estimation of table sizes after six months of activity helps the DBA team to estimate how the staging database or file system grows. This measurement is usually represented in megabytes. It is a calculation of (Average Row Length times Initial Row Count) + (Average Row Length times Expected Monthly Rows times 6) / 1,048,576).

So far, the details discussed in this section are mostly applicable to tables within a database management system (DBMS). The staging area normally consists of both DBMS tables and flat text files on the file system. Flat files are especially important when using a dedicated ETL tool. Most of the tools utilize an area in the file system for placing data down to optimize its workflow. In many cases, you need to stage your data outside of a DBMS in flat files for fast sequential processing. You can also use the volumetric worksheet for file-system planning. A general practice is to set the files down in a development area and record the space they occupy to provide the statistics to the appropriate personnel for official space allocation.

The next sections of this chapter provide information to help you select the appropriate architecture for your staging tables.

> The ETL architect needs to arrange for the allocation and configuration of data files that reside on the file system as part of the data-staging area to support the ETL process. ETL vendors whose tools use the file system should recommend appropriate space allocation and file-system configuration settings for optimal performance and scalability. For nonvendor data files explicitly created by the ETL process, use the standard volumetric worksheet.

Data Structures in the ETL System

In this section, we describe the important types of data structures you are likely to need in your ETL system.

Flat Files

In many cases, you won't need to stage your data within the confines of a DBMS. If you are not using a dedicated ETL tool and are doing all of the ETL tasks with SQL in your database, you need to create DBMS table structures to store all of your staging data. However, if you have an ETL tool or are utilizing shell scripts or scripting programs such as Perl, VBScript, or JavaScript, which can manipulate text files, you can store staging data right in your file system as simple text files.

When data is stored in columns and rows within a file on your file system to emulate a database table, it is referred to as a *flat* or *sequential file*. If your operating system is any flavor of UNIX or Windows, data in your flat files is in standardized character code known as American Standard Code for Information Interchange (ASCII). ASCII flat files can be processed and manipulated by ETL tools or scripting languages just as if they were database tables—and in certain cases much faster!

A DBMS requires overhead to maintain metadata about the data being processed, which in simple cases is not really needed in the data-staging environment. It has been the conventional wisdom that sorting, merging, deleting, replacing, and many other data-migration functions are much faster when they are performed outside the DBMS. Many utility programs are dedicated to text-file manipulation. Keep in mind when performing flat-file manipulations with scripting languages that you may have an obligation to separately advise your metadata tracking tables of the transformations you are making. If the metadata tracking (say, for compliance purposes) is as important as the transformations themselves, you should think instead about handling these operations through a dedicated ETL tool that can automatically supply the metadata context.

 Arguments in favor of relational tables.

It is always faster to WRITE to a flat file as long you are truncating or inserting. There is no real concept of UPDATING existing records of a flat file efficiently, which argues against using a flat file for a persistent staging table. Querying and other random access lookups are not supported well by operating system utilities or vendor tools. Finally, flat files cannot be indexed for fast lookups.

When you READ from a staging table in the ETL system, database storage is superior when filtering is anticipated and when joins between tables on the same system are performed. Although dedicated sort packages used to be the clear performance winners, relational databases have made significant progress recently in leveling the playing field. Being able to work in SQL and get automatic database parallelism for free is a very elegant approach.

The exact platform to store your data-staging tables depends on many variables, including corporate standards and practices. However, we've observed that it's most practical to use flat files over database tables for portions of the ETL process when the fundamental purpose of the process is one of the following:

■ **Staging source data for safekeeping and recovery.** When you extract data from its originating data source, you must quickly enter the system, select exactly what you need, and exit. If the ETL process fails after the data is extracted, you must be able to start without penetrating the source system again. The best approach to restart a failed process without constantly penetrating the source system is to dump the extracted data into a flat file for safe keeping. If the process fails at any point after the data has been placed in flat file, the process can easily restart by picking up the already extracted data from the flat file in the staging area. Further details on utilizing flat files to recover from ETL process failures are discussed in Chapter 8.

■ **Sorting data.** Sorting is a prerequisite to virtually every data integration task. Whether you are aggregating, validating, or doing look-ups, presorting data optimizes performance. Sorting data in the file system may be more efficient than selecting data from a database table with an ORDER BY clause. Since the nature of ETL is to integrate disparate data, merging data efficiently is a top priority that requires intensive sorting. A huge fraction of your ETL system's processor cycles will go to sorting. You should carefully simulate the biggest sorting tasks both in your DBMS and with a dedicated sort package, if that is possible, to decide whether to base your sorting on the DBMS or a dedicated package.

■ **Filtering.** Suppose you need to filter on an attribute that is not indexed on the source database. Instead of forcing the source system to create indexes that may hinder transaction processing, it might be faster to extract the whole data set into a flat file and grep (A UNIX command for filtering simple data files) only the rows that meet your requirements. Another benefit of having the ability to filter data without using a database is realized when data does not originate from a database but from data files. A common example of this is Web logs. While processing clickstream data, we use a grep statement with the -v switch to select all the rows that do not contain certain values such as .gif or .jpg so hits that are serving image files are excluded from the data warehouse. Filtering flat files is tremendously more efficient than inserting all data into a database table, indexing the table, and then applying a WHERE clause either to delete or select the data into another table.

■ **Replacing/substituting text strings.** The operating system can blaze through a text file, translating any string to any other string amazingly fast using the tr command. Doing substring searching and replacing data in a database can require nested scalar functions and update statements. This type of sequential file processing is much faster at the file-system level than it is with a database.

- **Aggregation.** Aggregation, discussed in Chapter 6, must be supported in two ways: in the regular ETL data flow before loading into a database and in the database itself when aggregating data that can only be requested with database filtering. Outside the database, it makes most sense to use a dedicated sort package. Inside the database, it almost always makes most sense to stay with the database sort capability, although occasionally it can pay to dump large volumes of data out of the database and use the sort package.

- **Referencing source data.** In normalized transaction systems, it is common to have a single reference table support many other tables. A generic Status table, for example, can support order statuses, shipping statuses, and payment statuses. Instead of querying the same table in the source system over and over, it's more efficient to extract the reference table and stage it in the staging area once. From there, you can look up data with your ETL tool. Most ETL tools can read a look-up table into memory and store it there for the life of the process. Accessing reference tables stored in memory is blazingly fast. Moreover, utilizing staged reference data keeps the queries that hit the source system simpler and more efficient because many of the table joins can be omitted.

XML Data Sets

At this point, XML data sets are not generally used for persistent staging in ETL systems. Rather, they are a very common format for both input to and output from the ETL system. It is likely that XML data sets will indeed become a persistent data-storage format in the ETL system and in the data warehouse queryable tables, but the hierarchical capabilities of XML will have to be integrated more deeply with relational databases before that will be common.

XML is a language for data communication. Superficially, XML takes the form of plain text documents containing both data and metadata but no formatting information. XML is expressed with much the same notation as HTML but departs from the architecture of an HTML document. HTML, by contrast, contains data and formatting information but no metadata.

Differences between XML and HTML are crucial to understanding how XML affects data warehousing. XML metadata consists of tags unambiguously identifying each item in an XML document. For instance, an invoice coded in XML contains sequences such as:

```
<Customer Name = "Bob" Address= "123 Main Street" City= "Philadelphia" />
```

Here *Customer* is an XML element whose definition has been established between the sending and receiving parties before the invoice is transmitted. The customer element has been defined to contain a number of XML attributes, including name, address, city, and possibly others.

XML has extensive capability for declaring hierarchical structures, such as complex forms with nested repeating subfields. These hierarchical structures do not directly map into standard two-dimensional relational tables with rows and columns. When the data warehouse receives an XML data set, there may be a complex extraction process to transfer the data permanently into a relational data warehouse. There has been some discussion of extending relational databases to provide native support for XML's hierarchical structures, but this would amount to a substantial extension of the syntax and semantics of SQL based relational databases, which as of this writing has not happened.

Setting aside the issues of complex hierarchical structures, XML is today an extremely effective medium for moving data between otherwise incompatible systems, since XML (and the XML Schemas that follow) provide enough information to do a full CREATE TABLE statement in a relational database and then populate this table with data with the right column types. XML defines a universal language for data sharing. That is its strength. The downside of XML for large-volume data transfer is the overhead of the XML document structure itself. If you are transmitting millions of similar and predictable records, you should seek a more efficient file structure than XML for data transfer.

DTDs, XML Schemas, and XSLT

In XML, the standard way for two parties to define a set of possible tags is by exchanging a special document known as a Document Type Definition (DTD). The DTD declaration for our customer example could be cast as:

```
<!ELEMENT Customer (Name, Address, City?, State?, Postalcode?)>
<!ELEMENT Name (#PCDATA)>
```

plus similar lines for Address, City, State, and Postalcode.

Here the question marks after City, State, and Postalcode indicate that these fields are optional. The #PCDATA declaration indicates that Name is an unformatted text string.

Notice that the DTD contains somewhat less information than an SQL CREATE TABLE statement. In particular, there is no field length.

DTDs have until now been the basis for setting up a *metadata understanding* between two parties exchanging XML. A number of industry groups have been defining standard DTDs for their subject areas. But as data warehousers, we don't get enough from DTDs to build a relational table. To rectify this problem, the W^{3}C standards organization has defined an industrial-strength successor to DTDs known as XML Schemas. XML Schemas contain much more database-oriented information about data types and how the XML elements relate to each other or, in other words, how tables can be joined.

When an XML Schema has been agreed upon and XML content has been received, the information content is rendered via another specification called Extensible Stylesheet Language Transformations (XSLT). Actually, XSLT is a general mechanism for translating one XML document into another XML document, but its most visible use is for turning XML into HTML for final on-screen presentation.

Relational Tables

Staging data can optionally be stored within the confines of a relational DBMS. Using database tables is most appropriate especially when you don't have a dedicated ETL tool. Using a database to store staging tables has several advantages:

- **Apparent metadata.** One of the main drawbacks of using flat files is that they lack apparent metadata. By storing data in a relational table, the DBMS maintains technical metadata automatically, and business metadata can easily be attached to the table within the DBMS. Information such as column names, data types and lengths, and cardinality is inherent to the database system. Table and column business descriptions are elements commonly added to DBMS data catalogs.

- **Relational abilities.** Enforcing data or referential integrity among entities is easy to accomplish in a relational environment. If you are receiving data from nonrelational systems, it might make sense to stage data in a normalized model before transforming into a dimensional model.

- **Open repository.** Once data is placed in a DBMS, the data can easily be accessed (assuming permission is granted) by any SQL-compliant tool. Access to the data is crucial during quality-assurance testing and auditing.

- **DBA support.** In many corporate environments, the DBA group is responsible only for data inside the DBMS. Data outside of the database, in the file system, is usually not looked after. Space allocation, backup and recovery, archiving, and security are tasks that the ETL team must coordinate when the staging data is not in a DBMS.

■ **SQL interface.** You will encounter many times when you need to write SQL to manipulate data and get it in just the right format. Most know that SQL is the standard language to *speak* to data—it is easy to write and is powerful. SQL is probably the most widely known programming language in the IT environment. Most database systems come packed with robust SQL functions that save numerous hours of manual coding. Oracle, for example, has overloaded functions such as to_char() that can take virtually any data type and convert it into a character string in a variety of formats. Besides enforcing referential integrity, having the ability to use native SQL is the primary reason to store staging data in a database environment.

Independent DBMS Working Tables

If you decide to store your staging data in a DBMS, you have several architecture options when you are modeling the data-staging schema. Designing tables in the staging area can be even more challenging than designing transaction or dimensional models. Remember, transaction databases are designed to get data in; dimensional designs get data out. Staging-area designs must do both. Therefore, it's not uncommon to see a mixture of data architectures in the staging area.

To justify the use of independent staging tables, we'll use one of our favorite aphorisms: Keep it simple. Independent tables get their name because they don't have dependencies on any other tables in the database. In the transactional environment, these tables are known as orphans because they don't have relationships with other tables in the schema. Because independent tables don't have relationships, they are prime candidates to store outside of a relational database.

Most of the time, the reason you create a staging table is to set the data down so you can again manipulate it using SQL or a scripting language. In many cases, especially smaller data warehouse projects, independent tables are all you need in the staging area.

Just because independent tables are not necessarily normalized, they must not be treated like dump files. Dump files are typically created arbitrarily without concern about disk space or query performance. Each field of an independent file or table must have a purpose and a logical definition. Superfluous columns are omitted from any independent table design. For database tables, a proper index plan must be established and implemented on all independent tables. Since all of the processes that hit each staging table are known because only ETL processes use these tables, there is less need for bitmapped indexes here than in the presentation area, which is dominated by end user tools and ad-hoc requests. You will find more for use for single column and compound column b-tree indexes in your ETL system.

Third Normal Form Entity/Relation Models

There are arguments that the data-staging area is perhaps the central repository of all the enterprise data that eventually gets loaded into the data warehouse. However, calling the data-staging area an enterprise-wide central repository is a misnomer that makes data architects believe that the area must be fully *normalized*. After all, what rightful data architect leaves any enterprise data vulnerable to the possibility of redundancy? To build on the analogy of the restaurant kitchen that we describe earlier in this chapter, imagine that certain foods—fish, for example—must be carefully selected, cleaned, portioned, filleted, and sautéed before they are finally served. Now suppose you also serve ice cream. You don't process ice cream the same way you process the fish before serving it—ice cream is essentially scooped and served. Forcing all data from every source system to go through the same normalization process—fitting it into a third normal form-data model—is like preparing ice cream as you would fish.

We rarely model the staging area in third normal form. We have had cases where data elements of a hierarchy have come from disparate data sources at different levels of granularity, including some external data from nonrelational sources. In those cases, it makes sense to model the data in a way that removes redundancy and enforces integrity before it is loaded it into the dimensional data model. But this ideally takes the form of focusing on isolated *problem dimensions* that need to be turned inside out to make sure that initially dirty data has been cleaned correctly. Remember that the main result of normalization is to enforce specific many-to-1 relationships. The typical annotations on an entity-relation diagram are not enforced or interpreted, except by humans examining the graphical depiction of the schema. Consider modeling decisions on a case-by-case basis, normalizing entities only as needed.

Don't assume that the data-staging area must be normalized. Remember two of the goals for designing your ETL processes we describe at the beginning of this chapter: Make them fast and make them recoverable. If you have stages in your process that are not physically manipulating data and do not enable speed or recoverability, they ought to be removed.

Nonrelational Data Sources

A common reason for creating a dedicated staging environment is to integrate nonrelational data. Your data-integration tasks seem much less challenging when all data is under one roof (DBMS). Integrating heterogeneous data sources is a challenge that ETL developers must constantly confront as the data warehouse expands its scope to include more and more subject areas.

In enterprise data warehouse projects, many of the data sources are from nonrelational data sources or relational data sources that are not necessarily related to each other. Nonrelational data sources can include COBOL copy books, VSAM files, flat files, spreadsheets, and so on.

Bringing all of the disparate data sources into a single DBMS is a common practice, but is it really necessary? The power of ETL tools in handling heterogeneous data minimizes the need to store all of the necessary data in a single database. Figure 2.2 illustrates how a platform-neutral ETL tool can integrate many heterogeneous data sources right from their native data stores, integrating the data on the fly to migrate it to the data warehouse. Notice that the ETL tool is linked to the physical staging database and external files and can optionally set the transient data down for interim manipulation if required.

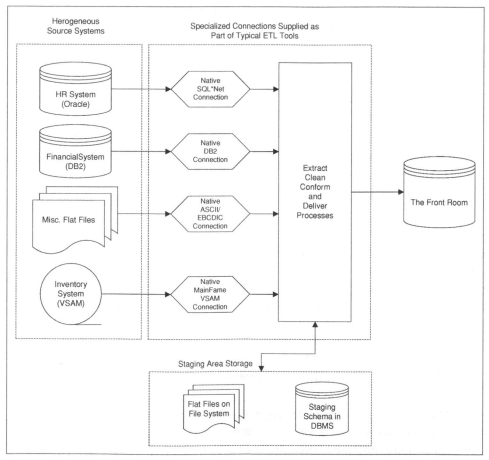

Figure 2.2 ETL tools natively integrate heterogeneous sources optionally using the data-staging area.

Integrating nonrelational data sources often requires some integrity checking. Data-integrity assurance is not free. It often requires real estate in the data-staging area and customized ETL processing to enforce business rules that would otherwise be enforced by the nature of a source system relational database. Relational means that tables have relationships—usually parent-to-child—enforced by the database. For instance, if an orders table has a status column, a status cannot be entered into that table without it preexisting in a separate status table. In this scenario, the status table is the *parent* of its associated *children* in the orders table. A parent record cannot be deleted unless all of its children are deleted as well; otherwise, the children become orphans. An orphan is any child record without a parent. Equivalently, we say that the primary key for an order cannot be deleted if there are foreign keys in the status table referring to that order. Orphans are a sign of referential integrity failure.

Nonrelational data sources do not enforce referential integrity. Nonrelational systems are essentially a collection of independent tables. Most often in legacy transaction systems, parent-child relationships are enforced only through the front-end application. Unfortunately, after years of operation, any data integrity that is not enforced within the database is inevitably put to risk by scripts or any other data manipulation performed outside the front-end application. It is practically guaranteed that nonrelational data sources include some data-quality issues.

As is not the case with transaction systems, it's a good practice to have integrity checks in the ETL process rather than in the database when designing your data staging area. The difference is due to the fact that transaction systems expect data to be entered correctly. Moreover, a human being who enters erroneous data can react to an error thrown by the database and reenter the data correctly. Conversely, the ETL process must know how to handle data anomalies in a more automatic way. The process cannot simply reject all data-integrity failures because there may be no one to reenter the data correctly in a timely manner. Instead, you need to establish business rules for different data-quality failure scenarios and implement them in the ETL process. When erroneous data is passed through the process, sometimes you want to transform the data on the fly; load the data as is; load the data with an associated code or description describing the impact or condition of the data; or if the data is unacceptable, reject the data completely and put it into a reject file for investigation.

> 💡 **Don't overuse the reject file! Reject files are notorious for being dumping grounds for data *we'll deal with later*. When records wind up in the reject file, unless they are processed before the next major load step is allowed to run to completion, the data warehouse and the production system are out of sync.**

Basic database referential integrity enforcement is not sufficient to enforce each of these scenarios. Hand-coded logic in the ETL process is almost always required to successfully integrate nonrelational data sources.

Dimensional Data Models: The Handoff from the Back Room to the Front Room

Dimensional data structures are the target of the ETL processes, and these tables sit at the boundary between the back room and the front room. In many cases, the dimensional tables will be the final physical-staging step before transferring the tables to the end user environments.

Dimensional data models are by far the most popular data structures for end user querying and analysis. They are simple to create, they are extremely stable in the presence of changing data environments, they are intuitively understandable by end users, and they are the fastest data structure for general relational database querying. Dimensional models are also the foundation for constructing all forms of OLAP cubes, since an OLAP cube is really just a high-performance dimensional model implemented on special-purpose software.

This section is a brief introduction to the main table types in a dimension model.

The other books in the Toolkit series discuss dimensional models in great detail and provide guidance and motivation for building them in many different business environments. We assume in this book that you have studied the motivations for dimensional models (or that you don't need motivation because you have been handed a specification for a particular dimensional design!). So in this section we introduce the basic physical structure of dimensional models without any of the usual business-content justification. In section 2 of this book we exhaustively illustrate all the known dimensional model variations and discuss the ETL system that feeds each of these structures.

Fact Tables

Dimensional models are built around measurement processes. A measurement is a real-world observation of a previously unknown value. Measurements are overwhelmingly numeric, and most measurements can be repeated over time, creating a time series.

A single measurement creates a single *fact table* record. Conversely, a single fact table record corresponds to a specific measurement event. Obviously, the observed measurement is stored in the fact table record. But we also store the *context* of the measurement in the same record. While we

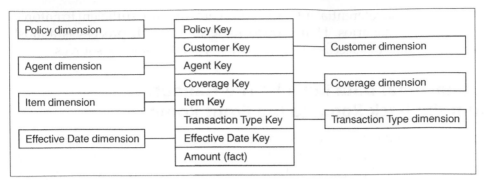

Figure 2.3 A dimensional model for an insurance policy transaction.

might be tempted to store this context in many verbose fields directly in the fact table record, we systematically normalize the contextual attributes out of the fact table by creating a number of *dimension* tables that can be viewed informally as *clumps of context*.

So, for example, if the measurement is the amount of an insurance premium booked by an insurance company on a particular policy, a particular customer, a particular agent, a particular coverage (such as collision damage), an insured item (perhaps an automobile), a specific transaction type (such as *establish premium*), on a certain effective date, typical dimensions attached to the fact record would be Policy, Customer, Agent, Coverage, Item, Transaction Type and Effective Date. See Figure 2.3, which illustrates this example.

The *grain* of a fact table is the definition of what constitutes a unique fact table record. In the dimensional-modeling world, the grain is always declared at the beginning of the design in business terms, not in database terms. The grain of our insurance example could be *insurance policy transaction*. Then, later in the design process, when the available dimensions are understood, the grain can be formally stated in terms of the key of the fact table. This key declaration will include some but usually not all of the foreign key references to the dimensions attached to the fact table. We assume that the key to our insurance fact table is Policy X Transaction Type X Time.

The structure and content of a dimensional model depend only on the physics of the measurement process itself.

Dimension Tables

The dimensional model does not anticipate or depend upon the intended query uses. It is a superbly flexible, symmetric framework suitable for all classes of queries. But there is still some room for designer discretion. Many of the dimensions for a particular fact table will be referenced directly in the original data source. But the data warehouse team can add dimensions that come from other sources, as long as they are *single valued* at the time of the measurement event. For instance, in our insurance example, a marketing-oriented promotion dimension might be added if that data were available. One of the great strengths of dimensional models is their ability to gracefully add dimensional context that is valid in the context of the measurement event.

Similarly, the best dimensions are *verbose* descriptions of the dimensional entities. So the Customer dimension in our example should have many descriptive fields. We call these descriptive fields dimensional *attributes*. Fortunately, all dimensional designs allow attributes to be added to dimensions incrementally over the life of the warehouse. The responsibility of the data warehouse architect is to identify these opportunities for additional attributes and to request that the ETL team add them to the physical schema.

Dimensional attributes are mostly textual or are numbers that take on discrete values. Dimension tables should always be built with a single primary key field that is a simple meaningless integer assigned by the ETL process. These keys are called *surrogate* keys. The many advantages of surrogate keys are described in the other Toolkit books. In this book, we describe how surrogate keys are created and administered in a number of important situations.

The primary surrogate keys in each dimension are paired with corresponding foreign keys in the fact table. When this primary-to-foreign key relationship is adhered to, we say that the tables obey *referential integrity*. Referential integrity is a constant requirement in all dimensional models. Failure to maintain referential integrity means that some fact table records are orphans that cannot be retrieved through constraints on the affected dimensions.

Atomic and Aggregate Fact Tables

You know that a dimensional data model is the best format for data to support user queries. You might at times need to utilize certain elements at an atomic level so the data can be presented at a higher level. However, you need to store the atomic-level facts to produce the precisely constrained requests required by the users. Often, business users don't want to analyze transaction-level facts because the cardinality of each dimension is so extensive that any atomic-level report would be pages long—making it humanly impossible to examine. However, you need to store the atomic-level facts to produce the periodic snapshot facts required by the users. When the time comes that the users request atomic-level data, you can simply migrate it from the staging area to the presentation layer.

It's good practice to partition fact tables stored in the staging area because its resulting aggregates will most likely be based on a specific period—perhaps monthly or quarterly. Creating partitions alleviates the database from scanning the entire table and enables it to go directly to the subsection that contains the data it needs for that period to create the aggregate. Partitioning also reduces the burden of pruning or archiving *old* data. Partitioned tables can simply drop the portion of a table that contains the old data.

Dimensionally designed tables in the staging area are in many cases required for populating on-line analytic processing (OLAP) cubes. Or you may implement a hybrid structure where you have the large atomic data layer in a dimensional RDBMS schema, with progressively more aggregated structures above the atomic layer in the form of OLAP cubes. Some of the OLAP systems can drill down through the OLAP cubes and access the lowest-level atomic data in a single application.

Surrogate Key Mapping Tables

Surrogate key mapping tables are designed to map natural keys from the disparate source systems to their master data warehouse surrogate key. Mapping tables are an efficient way to maintain surrogate keys in your data warehouse. These compact tables are designed for high-speed processing. Mapping tables contain only the most current value of a surrogate key—used to populate a dimension—and the natural key from the source system. Since the same dimension can have many sources, a mapping table contains a natural key column for each of its sources.

Mapping tables can be equally effective if they are stored in a database or on the file system. The advantage of using a database for mapping tables is that you can utilize the database sequence generator to create new surrogate keys. And also, when indexed properly, mapping tables in a database are very efficient during key value lookups.

Since key mapping tables serve no analytical value, they should never reside in the presentation layer of the data warehouse nor be exposed to end users.

CROSS-REFERENCE Details on how to utilize mapping tables to create surrogate keys for your dimensions are explained in Chapter 5, and utilizing them to populate fact tables is discussed in Chapter 6.

Planning and Design Standards

PROCESS CHECK Planning & Design:
Requirements/Realities → *Architecture* → Implementation → Test/Release

Data Flow: Extract → Clean → Conform → Deliver

The data-staging area must be managed and maintained as much, if not more, than any other database in your environment. Some staging areas are administered like a sandbox, where developers have a free for all—creating, dropping, and modifying tables at will. Naturally, because of the lack of control in these environments, troubleshooting and impact analysis take much longer than necessary, causing inflated costs to the project.

The data-staging area must be a controlled environment. Only the data architect should be able to design or modify a table in the staging area. All physical changes must be owned by the DBA responsible for the database. Also, if any developer needs a table, a strong chance exists that it can be used by another developer. As a rule of thumb: If you build a table, expect that it will be used by someone else for reasons other than you originally intended. People, especially developers, are very creative when it comes to reusing existing resources.

Impact Analysis

Impact analysis examines the metadata associated to an object (in this case a table or column) and determines what is affected by a change to its structure or content. Changing data-staging objects can *break* processes that are crucial to properly loading the data warehouse. Allowing ad-hoc changes to data-staging objects is detrimental to the success of your project.

Once a table is created in the staging area, you must perform impact analysis before any changes are made to it. Many ETL tool vendors provide impact analysis functionality, but this functionality is often overlooked during the ETL product proof-of-concept because it is a back-room function and not really important until the data warehouse is up and running and begins to evolve.

Impact analysis, an ETL function, is an onerous responsibility because changes to the source systems and the target data warehouse can be continuous and only the ETL process knows exactly which of these disparate elements are connected. Communication among the ETL project manager, source system DBA, and data warehouse modeling team is crucial to ensure that appropriate impact analysis is performed whenever changes to any of the systems to which the data warehouse is dependent occurs.

Metadata Capture

The topic of metadata is discussed in depth in Chapter 9, but it's necessary for you to understand what types of metadata you'll be responsible for while designing the data-staging area. Metadata has many different meanings depending on its context. Metadata, which describes or supports other data elements, is sprinkled throughout the components of the data warehouse. In the realm of the data warehouse, the data staging area is *not* the metadata repository. However, several metadata elements associated with the data-staging area are valuable to the data warehouse and must be presented to its end users.

Enable the presentation of metadata elements by designing the staging database with a data-modeling tool. Data-modeling tools store applicable metadata in their own repositories. Also, use an ETL tool that implicitly provides metadata about its processes and supports presentation of its transformations. Types of metadata derived by the staging area include the following:

- **Data Lineage.** Perhaps the most interesting of all data warehouse metadata, the data lineage, also known as the logical data mapping, illustrates transformations applied to a data element between its original data source and its ultimate target in the data warehouse.

- **Business Definitions.** Every table created in the data-staging area stems from a business definition. Business definitions can be captured in several different places including the data-modeling tool, the ETL tool, the database itself, or spreadsheets and Word documents. Use whatever standards are in place for capturing business definitions within the presentation layer of the data warehouse to maintain consistency.

- **Technical Definitions.** In the data-staging area specifically, technical definitions are likely to be more prevalent than business definitions. Remember: If it is not documented, it does not exist. Without proper documentation of the technical definitions of your staging tables, the tables might be recreated over and over, causing duplication of efforts and data explosion in the data-staging area. Technical definitions describe the physical attributes of data elements, including the structure, format, and location. Properly document technical metadata for all of your data-staging tables to minimize ambiguity and ensure reusability.

- **Process Metadata.** Processes that load data-staging tables must record their statistics along with the statistics of the data warehouse table loads. Although information regarding staging table loads need not be presented to end users, the ETL team must know exactly how many records were loaded into each staging table, with success and failure statistics for each process. A measure of data freshness is useful both for ETL administrators and end users.

All tables and files in the data-staging area must be designed by the ETL architect. Metadata must be well documented. Data-modeling tools offer metadata capture capabilities that would otherwise cause metadata documentation to be a laborious task. Use a data-modeling tool to capture appropriate metadata when designing staging tables, keeping in mind that the structure-oriented metadata from these tools is perhaps 25 percent of the total metadata picture. The next 25 percent of the metadata describes the results of data cleaning. To capture the additional process metadata, which is fully 50 percent of the metadata, make sure your ETL tool supplies the statistics required. At a minimum, the number of rows inserted, updated, deleted, and rejected should be available for each process. Also, the process start time, end time, and duration should be obtainable without any code enhancements.

Naming Conventions

The ETL team should not be in the business of developing naming standards for the data warehouse team. Nevertheless, data-staging tables must adhere to a standardized set of naming standards defined by the data warehouse architect. It's best practice to adopt the conventions in place in the rest of the data warehouse and apply those same rules to the staging area. On occasion, the data-staging area may contain tables or elements that are not in the data warehouse presentation layer and do not have established naming standards. Work with the data warehouse team and DBA group to embellish the existing naming standards to include special data-staging tables.

Many ETL tools and data-modeling tools insist on presenting long lists of table names alphabetically. You should pay careful attention to grouping your tables together in useful clumps by using their alphabetic sort!

Auditing Data Transformation Steps

The data transformations in a complex ETL system reflect intricate business rules. If you kept a formal audit trail of all data transformations used in your system, you would include at least the following list:

- Replacing natural keys with surrogate keys
- Combining and deduplicating entities
- Conforming commonly used attributes in dimensions
- Standardizing calculations, creating conformed key performance indicators (KPIs)
- Correcting and coercing data in the data cleaning routines

In volatile environments, the source system data is constantly changing; it's mandatory that the data warehouse have the ability to prove the data within it is accurate. But how is that accomplished when the source is constantly changing? The ETL process must maintain a snapshot of the *before* picture of the data before goes through the data-cleansing routines.

> 💡 **When data is significantly altered (cleansed) by the ETL process, an extract of the data before manipulation occurs must be retained for audit purposes. Furthermore, metadata for all data-cleansing logic must be available without sifting through code. The original source data, the data-cleansing metadata, and the final dimensional data must be displayed in a cohesive delivery mechanism to support questions arising from data-cleansing transformations.**

Snapshots of extract data are stored in the data-staging area and made available for audit purposes. A before and after glimpse of the data, along with the metadata describing the data-cleansing logic, depicts exactly how the data within the data warehouse is derived and promotes confidence in the quality of its data.

Summary

In this chapter, we have reviewed the primary data structures you need in your ETL system. We started by making the case for staging data in many places, for transient and permanent needs. You need to be especially diligent in supporting legal and financial compliance requirements. In these cases, you need not only to store data but to document the rules by which the data was created; if that isn't enough, you need to prove that the data hasn't been tampered with.

A mature ETL environment will be a mixture of flat files, independent relational tables, full-blown normalized models, and maybe some other kinds of structured files, especially XML documents. But in all cases, we urge you to remember that the whole point of the ETL system is the final result: data structures purposely built for ease of use by end user tools. And of course, we recommend that these purposely built tables take the form of dimensional models consisting of fact tables and dimension tables. Their close cousins, OLAP cubes, are usually created from dimensional schemas.

Finally, we touched on some best-practice issues, including adopting a set of consistent design standards, performing systematic impact analyses on your table designs, and changing those table designs as you move forward, and making sure that you capture metadata at each point in the ETL system. The big categories of metadata include table structure metadata (25 percent), data-cleaning results (25 percent), and process results (50 percent). Metadata is developed in depth in Chapter 4 and Chapter 9.

Now that we have all our working data structures organized, in Chapter 3 we dive into the source data structures we must read to populate the data warehouse.

Data Flow

Extracting

Once your data warehouse project is launched, you soon realize that the integration of all of the disparate systems across the enterprise is the real challenge to getting the data warehouse to a state where it is usable. Without data, the data warehouse is useless. The first step of integration is successfully extracting data from the primary source systems.

PROCESS CHECK Planning & Design:
Requirements/Realities → Architecture → Implementation → Test/Release

Data Flow: *Extract* → Clean → Conform → Deliver

While other chapters in this book focus on transforming and loading data into the data warehouse, the focal point of this chapter is how to interface to the required source systems for your project. Each data source has its distinct set of characteristics that need to be managed in order to effectively extract data for the ETL process.

As enterprises evolve, they acquire or inherit various computer systems to help the company run their businesses: point-of-sale, inventory management, production control, and general ledger systems—the list can go on and on. Even worse, not only are the systems separated and acquired at different times, but frequently they are logically and physically incompatible. The ETL process needs to effectively integrate systems that have different:

- Database management systems
- Operating systems
- Hardware
- Communications protocols

Before you begin building your extract systems, you need a logical data map that documents the relationship between original source fields and final destination fields in the tables you deliver to the front room. This document ties the very beginning of the ETL system to the very end. We show you how to build your logical data map in Part 1 of this chapter.

Part 2 of this chapter is a tour of the many flavors of source systems you are likely to encounter. We probe moderately deeply into each one to get you started choosing the right extraction approach.

At the end of this chapter, we introduce the subject of change data capture and deleted record capture. Fifteen years ago we thought that the data warehouse was immutable: a huge write-once library of data. With the benefit of lots of experience in the intervening years, we now know that data warehouses constantly need to be updated, corrected, and altered. The change data capture extraction techniques in this chapter are only the first step in this intricate dance. We need to revisit this subject in the data-cleaning chapter, the delivery chapters, and the operations chapter!

Let's dive into the logical data map.

Part 1: The Logical Data Map

The physical implementation can be a catastrophe if it is not carefully architected before it is implemented. Just as with any other form of construction, you must have a blueprint before you hit the first nail. Before you begin developing a single ETL process, make sure you have the appropriate documentation so the process complies logically and physically with your established ETL policies, procedures, and standards.

PROCESS CHECK Planning & Design:
Requirements/Realities → Architecture → *Implementation* → Test/Release

Data Flow: *Extract* → Clean → Conform → *Deliver*

The logical data map describes the relationship between the extreme starting points and the extreme ending points of your ETL system.

Designing Logical Before Physical

Diving right into physical data mapping wastes precious time and excludes documentation. This section describes how to develop the logical ETL process and use it to map out your physical ETL implementation. Ensure the following steps are achieved before you start any physical ETL development:

1. **Have a plan.** The ETL process must be figured out logically and documented. The logical data map is provided by the data warehouse architect and is the specification for the ETL team to create the physical ETL jobs. This document is sometimes referred to as the data lineage report. The logical data map is the foundation of the metadata that is eventually presented to quality-assurance testers and ultimately to end users to describe exactly what is done between the ultimate source system and the data warehouse.

2. **Identify data source candidates**. Starting with the highest-level business objectives, identify the likely candidate data sources you believe will support the decisions needed by the business community. Identify within these sources specific data elements you believe are central to the end user data. These data elements are then the inputs to the data profiling step.

3. **Analyze source systems with a data-profiling tool.** Data in the source systems must be scrutinized for data quality, completeness, and fitness for the purpose. Depending on your organization, data quality might or might not fall under the responsibility of the ETL team, but this data-profiling step must be done by someone with an eye for the needs of the decision makers who will use the data warehouse. Data in each and every source system must be analyzed. Any detected data anomaly must be documented, and best efforts must be made to apply appropriate business rules to rectify data before it is loaded into the data warehouse. You must hold open the possibility that the project STOPs with this step! If the data cannot support the business objectives, this is the time to find that out. More on data profiling in Chapter 4.

4. **Receive walk-though of data lineage and business rules.** Once the data sources have been qualified by the data-profiling step and the final target data model is understood, the data warehouse architect and business analyst must walk the ETL architect and developers through the data lineage and business rules for extracting, transforming, and loading the subject areas of the data warehouse, as best they understand these rules. Full understanding of the data lineage and business rules will not be achieved until the ETL team has encountered all the data realities, but this step aims to transfer as much knowledge as possible to the ETL team. The data-profiling step should have created two subcategories of ETL-specific business rules:

   4a. Required alterations to the data during the data-cleaning steps

   4b. Coercions to dimensional attributes and measured numerical facts to achieve standard conformance across separate data sources

5. **Receive walk-through of data warehouse data model.** The ETL team must completely understand the physical data model of the data warehouse. This understanding includes dimensional modeling concepts. Understanding the mappings on a table-by-table basis is not good enough. The development team must have a thorough understanding of how dimensions, facts, and other special tables in the dimensional model work together to implement successful ETL solutions. Remember that a principal goal of the ETL system is to deliver data in the most effective way to end user tools.

6. **Validate calculations and formulas.** Verify with end users any calculations specified in the data linage. This rule comes from the *measure twice, cut once* aphorism used in the construction business in New York City. Just as you don't want to be caught up on a skyscraper with the wrong-size material, you similarly don't want to be caught deploying the wrong measures in the data warehouse. It is helpful to make sure the calculations are correct before you spend time coding the wrong algorithms in your ETL process.

Inside the Logical Data Map

Before descending into the details of the various sources you will encounter, we need to explore the actual design of the logical data mapping document. The document contains the data definition for the data warehouse source systems throughout the enterprise, the target data warehouse data model, and the exact manipulation of the data required to transform it from its original format to that of its final destination.

Components of the Logical Data Map

The logical data map (see Figure 3.1) is usually presented in a table or spreadsheet format and includes the following specific components:

- **Target table name.** The physical name of the table as it appears in the data warehouse

- **Target column name.** The name of the column in the data warehouse table

- **Table type.** Indicates if the table is a fact, dimension, or subdimension (outrigger)

- **SCD (slowly changing dimension) type.** For dimensions, this component indicates a Type-1, -2, or -3 slowly changing dimension approach. This indicator can vary for each column in the dimension.

For example, within the customer dimension, the last name may require Type 2 behavior (retain history), while the first name may require Type 1 (overwrite). These SCD types are developed in detail in Chapter 5.

- **Source database.** The name of the instance of the database where the source data resides. This component is usually the connect string required to connect to the database. It can also be the name of a file as it appears in the file system. In this case, the path of the file would also be included.

- **Source table name.** The name of the table where the source data originates. There will be many cases where more than one table is required. In those cases, simply list all tables required to populate the relative table in the target data warehouse.

- **Source column name.** The column or columns necessary to populate the target. Simply list all of the columns required to load the target column. The associations of the source columns are documented in the transformation section.

- **Transformation.** The exact manipulation required of the source data so it corresponds to the expected format of the target. This component is usually notated in SQL or pseudo-code.

Columns in the logical data mapping document are sometimes combined. For example, the source database, table name, and column name could be combined into a single *source* column. The information within the concatenated column would be delimited with a period, for example, ORDERS.STATUS.STATUS_CODE. Regardless of the format, the content of the logical data mapping document has been proven to be the critical element required to efficiently plan ETL processes.

The individual components in the logical data mapping appear to be simple and straight-forward. However, when studied more closely, the document reveals many hidden requirements for the ETL team that might otherwise have been overlooked. The primary purpose of this document is to provide the ETL developer with a clear-cut blueprint of exactly what is expected from the ETL process. This table must depict, without question, the course of action involved in the transformation process.

Take a look at Figure 3.1.

Scrutinizing this figure, you may notice a few revelations that, if they were to go unnoticed, would cause a lot of time troubleshooting and debugging and ultimately delaying the project. For example, you might notice that the data types between the source and target for STATE get converted from 255 characters to 75 characters. Even though the data-scale reduction might be supported by the data-analysis documentation, should any future

	Target			SCD Type	Source				Transformation
Table Name	Column Name	Data Type	Table Type		Database Name	Table Name	Column Name	Data Type	
EMPLOYEE_DIM	EMPLOYEE_KEY	NUMBER	Dimension	1					Surrogate key.
EMPLOYEE_DIM	EMPLOYEE_ID	NUMBER	Dimension	1	HR_SYS	EMPLOYEES	EMPLOYEE_ID	NUMBER	Natural Key for employee in HR system
EMPLOYEE_DIM	BIRTH_COUNTRY_NAME	VARCHAR2(75)	Dimension	1	HR_SYS	COUNTRIES	NAME	VARCHAR2(75)	select c.name from employees e, states s, countries c where e.state_id = s.state_id and s.country_id = c.country
EMPLOYEE_DIM	BIRTH_STATE	VARCHAR2(75)	Dimension	1	HR_SYS	STATES	DESCRIPTION	VARCHAR2(255)	select s.description from employees e, states s where e.state_id = s.state_id
EMPLOYEE_DIM	DISPLAY_NAME	VARCHAR2(75)	Dimension	1	HR_SYS	EMPLOYEES	FIRST_NAME	VARCHAR2(75)	select initcap(salutation) ll' ll initcap(first_name) ll' ll initcap(last_name) from employee
EMPLOYEE_DIM	BIRTH_DATE	DATE	Dimension	1	HR_SYS	EMPLOYEES	DOB	DATE	trunc(DOB)
EMPLOYEE_DIM	SALUTATION	VARCHAR2(12)	Dimension	1	HR_SYS	EMPLOYEES	SALUTATION	VARCHAR2(12)	initcap(salutation)
EMPLOYEE_DIM	FIRST_NAME	VARCHAR2(30)	Dimension	1	HR_SYS	EMPLOYEES	FIRST_NAME	VARCHAR2(30)	initcap(first_name)
EMPLOYEE_DIM	LAST_NAME	VARCHAR2(30)	Dimension	1	HR_SYS	EMPLOYEES	LAST_NAME	VARCHAR2(30)	initcap(last_name)
EMPLOYEE_DIM	MARITAL_STATUS	VARCHAR2(12)	Dimension	2	HR_SYS	MARITAL_STATUS	DESCRIPTION	VARCHAR2(12)	select nvl(m.name,'Unknown') from employee e marital_status m where e.marital_status_id = m.marital_status_id
EMPLOYEE_DIM	DIVERSITY_CATEGORY	VARCHAR2(30)	Dimension	1	HR_SYS	EMPLOYEES	EEO_CLASS	VARCHAR2(30)	decode(eeo_class,null,'Not Stated', decode(eeo_class,'N', 'Not Stated',eeo_class))
EMPLOYEE_DIM	GENDER	VARCHAR2(12)	Dimension	1	HR_SYS	EMPLOYEES	SEX	VARCHAR2(12)	nvl(sex, Unknown)
EMPLOYEE_DIM	EMPLOYEE_STATUS	VARCHAR2(24)	Dimension	1	HR_SYS	EMPLOYEES	STATUS	VARCHAR2(24)	select es.name from employee e employee_status es where e.employee_status_id = m.employee_status_id
EMPLOYEE_DIM	POSITION_CODE	VARCHAR2(12)	Dimension	2	HR_SYS	POSITIONS	POSITION_CODE	VARCHAR2(12)	select p.code from employees e, positions p where p.position_id = e.position_id
EMPLOYEE_DIM	POSITION_CATEGORY	VARCHAR2(30)	Dimension	2	HR_SYS	POSITIONS	POSITION_CATEGORY	VARCHAR2(30)	select p.category from employees e, positions p where p.position_id = e.position_id
EMPLOYEE_DIM	HIRE_DATE	DATE	Dimension	1	HR_SYS	EMPLOYEES	DATE_HIRED	DATE	trunc(date_hired)
EMPLOYEE_DIM	DEPARTMENT_CODE	VARCHAR2(12)	Dimension	2	HR_SYS	DEPARTMENTS	CODE	VARCHAR2(12)	select d.code from employee p, employee_department pd, departments d where p.employee_ids=pd.employee_id and pd.department_id = d.department_id
EMPLOYEE_DIM	DEPARTMENT_NAME	VARCHAR2(75)	Dimension	2	HR_SYS	DEPARTMENTS	DESCRIPTION	VARCHAR2(75)	select d.description from employee p, employee_department pd, departments d where p.employee_ids=pd.employee_id and pd.department_id = d.department_id
EMPLOYEE_DIM	PART_TIME_FLAG	VARCHAR2(1)	Dimension	1	HR_SYS	EMPLOYEES	PERCENTAGE	VARCHAR2(1)	select decode(sign(percentage-100),-1,'Y','N') from employee
EMPLOYEE_CONTRACT_FACT	EFFECTIVE_DATE_KEY	NUMBER	Fact	N/A	DW_PROD, HR_SYS	DATE_DIM, EMPLOYEE_CONTRACT	DATE_KEY	NUMBER	where employee_contract.eff_date = dw_prod.date_dim.cal_date
EMPLOYEE_CONTRACT_FACT	END_DATE_KEY	NUMBER	Fact	N/A	DW_PROD, HR_SYS	DATE_DIM, EMPLOYEE_CONTRACT	DATE_KEY	NUMBER	where employee_contract.end_date = dw_prod.date_dim.cal_date
EMPLOYEE_CONTRACT_FACT	CURRENCY_KEY	NUMBER	Fact	N/A	DW_PROD, HR_SYS	CURRENCY_DIM, EMPLOYEE_CONTRACT	CURRENCY_KEY	NUMBER	where employee_contract.currency_code = dw_prod.currency_dim.currency_code
EMPLOYEE_CONTRACT_FACT	RATE_TYPE_KEY	NUMBER	Fact	N/A	DW_PROD, HR_SYS	RATE_TYPE_DIM, EMPLOYEE_CONTRACT	RATE_TYPE_KEY	NUMBER	where employee_contract.rate_type_id = dw_prod.rate_type_dim.rate_type_id
EMPLOYEE_CONTRACT_FACT	PROJECT_KEY	NUMBER	Fact	N/A	DW_PROD, HR_SYS	PROJECT_DIM, EMPLOYEE_CONTRACT	PROJECT_KEY	NUMBER	where employee_contrac.project_code = dw_prod.project_dim.project_code
EMPLOYEE_CONTRACT_FACT	EMPLOYEE_ROLE_KEY	NUMBER	Fact	N/A	DW_PROD, HR_SYS	EMPLOYEE_ROLE_DIM, EMPLOYEE_CONTRACT	EMPLOYEE_ROLE_KEY	NUMBER	where employee_contract.employee_role = employee_role_dim.contract_role_name
EMPLOYEE_CONTRACT_FACT	CONTRACT_TYPE_KEY	NUMBER	Fact	N/A	DW_PROD, HR_SYS	CONTRACT_TYPE_DIM, EMPLOYEE_CONTRACT	CONTRACT_TYPE_KEY, CONTRACT_TYPE_ID	NUMBER	where dw_prod.employee_contract.contract_type = contract_type_dim.contract_type_id
EMPLOYEE_CONTRACT_FACT	CONTRACT_NUMBER	NUMBER	Fact	N/A	DW_PROD, HR_SYS	EMPLOYEE_CONTRACT	CONTRACT_NUMBER	NUMBER	Degenerate Dimension
EMPLOYEE_CONTRACT_FACT	RATE_AMOUNT_LOCAL	NUMBER	Fact	N/A	DW_PROD, HR_SYS	EMPLOYEE_CONTRACT	AMOUNT	NUMBER	sum(amount)
EMPLOYEE_CONTRACT_FACT	RATE_AMOUNT_USD	NUMBER	Fact	N/A	DW_PROD, HR_SYS	EMPLOYEE_CONTRACT	AMOUNT	NUMBER	select ec.amount * avg(cc.conversion_rate) from employee_contract ec, currency_conversion cc where ec.currency = cc.from_currency and cc.effective_Date between ec.effective_date and ec.end_date group by ec.amount

Figure 3.1 The logical data map.

values with more than 75 characters be created, you would potentially lose the data. Moreover, some ETL tools would actually abort or fail the entire process with this kind of data overflow error. Notice the transformation notation for the STATE does not explicitly define this data conversion—the conversion is implied. By definition, no one explicitly accounts for *implied conversions*. Implied conversions are common and notorious for sneaking up and destroying your processes. To avoid calamity, the ETL team must assume responsibility for explicitly handling these types of implied data conversions.

> ETL tool suites typically keep track of these implied data conversions and can deliver reports that identify any such conversions.

The table type gives us our queue for the ordinal position of our data load processes—first dimensions, then facts.

Working with the table type, the SCD type is crucial while loading dimensions. As we explain earlier in this chapter, the structure of the table itself does not reveal what the slowly changing dimension strategy is. Misinterpreting the SCD strategies could cause weeks of development time gone to waste. Know exactly which columns have historic relevance and the strategy required for capturing the history before you begin the development of the load process. The value in this column may change over time. Usually during unit testing, when your selected users observe the data in the data warehouse for the first time, they see unexpected results. As hard as the data modeler may try, the SCD concepts are very hard to convey to users, and once they are exposed to the loaded dimension, they quite often want to *tweak* the SCD strategies. This request is common and should be handled through the data warehouse project manager and the change management process.

The transformation within the mapping is the *guts* of the process, the place where developers with strong technical abilities look first. But you must constrain yourself from being completely code focused and review the entire mapping before you drill into the transformation. The transformation can contain anything from the absolute solution to nothing at all. Most often, the transformation can be expressed in SQL. The SQL may or may not be the complete statement. Quite often, it is the segment of the code that cannot otherwise be implied from the other elements in the mapping, such as the SQL WHERE clause. In other cases, the transformation might be a method that is not SQL specific and is explained in plain English, like instructions to preload from a flat file or to base the load transformation on criteria outside of the database or to reject known data anomalies into a reject file. If the transformation is blank, this means the mapping is a straight load, from source-to-target, with no transformation required.

🔆 **Upon the completion of the logical data map, do a comprehensive walkthrough of the document with the ETL developer before any actual coding begins.**

Using Tools for the Logical Data Map

Some ETL and data-modeling tools directly capture logical data mapping information. There is a natural tendency to want to indicate the data mapping directly in these tools. Entering this information into a tool that enables us to share this metadata is a good practice. But, at the time of this writing, there is no standard for the appropriate data elements related to logical data mapping. The exact elements available in the various tools differ quite a bit. As the metadata standards in the data warehouse environment mature, a standard should be established for the elements defined in the logical data map. Established metadata standards will enable the tools to become more consistent and usable for this purpose. You should investigate the usability of your current toolset for storing the logical data map and take advantage of any features you have available. However, if your tools do not capture all of the elements you need, you will wind up having the logical data map in several locations, making maintenance a horrific chore. Be on the lookout for vast product improvements in this area.

Building the Logical Data Map

The success of data warehousing stems in large part from the fact that all data is in one logical place for users to perform cross-functional analysis. Behind the scenes, the ETL team integrates and transforms disparate, unorganized data seamlessly and presents it as if it has lived together since the beginning of time. A key criterion for the success of the data warehouse is the cleanliness and cohesiveness of the data within it. A unified data store requires a thorough insight of each of its source data systems. The importance of understanding the data in the data sources, and the systems of the sources themselves, is often overlooked and underestimated during the project-planning phase of the ETL. The complete logical data mapping cannot exist until the source systems have been identified and analyzed. The analysis of the source system is usually broken into two major phases:

- The data discovery phase
- The anomaly detection phase

Data Discovery Phase

Once you understand what the target needs to look like, you need to identify and examine the data sources. Some or all of the source systems may have been accumulated during the data-modeling sessions, but this cannot be taken for granted. Usually, only the major source systems are identified during the data-modeling sessions. It's important to note that the data modeler's main objective is to create a data model. Any logical data mapping derived from the data-modeling sessions is merely a byproduct—a starting point. Moreover, the data modeler spends most of his or her time with end users, so the source systems defined in the logical data mapping may not be the true originating or optimal source—the *system-of-record*. It is up to the ETL team to drill down further into the data requirements to determine each and every source system, table, and attribute required to load the data warehouse. Determining the proper source, or system-of-record, for each element is a challenge that must be reckoned with. Thorough analysis can alleviate weeks of delays caused by developing the ETL process using the wrong source.

Collecting and Documenting Source Systems

The source systems are usually established in various pieces of documentation, including interview notes, reports, and the data modeler's logical data mapping. More investigation is usually necessary by the ETL team. Work with the team's system and business analysts to track down appropriate source systems. In large organizations, you must ask the question "Who else uses this data?" and find the data source of each user group. Typical organizations have countless distinct systems. It is the ETL team's responsibility to keep track of the systems discovered and investigate their usefulness as a data warehouse source.

Keeping Track of the Source Systems

Once the source systems are identified, it makes sense to document these systems along with who is responsible for them. Figure 3.2 is a chart created for this purpose. This chart, the source system tracking report, has saved us many times from having to hunt down system administrators or business owners. If you are lucky, the data modeler will have started this list. Regardless of the originator, the maintenance of the list should be a collaborative effort between the ETL team and the data modeling team. If during your analysis systems are deemed inappropriate as a source system to the data warehouse, leave them on the list with the reason for their omission; they may be used in future phases.

Subject Area	Interface Name	Business Name	Priority	Department/Business Use	Business Owner	Technical Owner	DBMS	Platform	Daily User Count	DB Size (GB)	Transactions/Day	Comments
Human Resources	PeopleSoft	HR Information	1	Human Resource Mgmt	Daniel Bumis	Margaret Kartin	Oracle	AIX on RS/6000	850	3	8,000	Everything revolves around HR
Finance	Oracle Financials	Oracle Financials	2	General Accounting	Mabel Karr	Edmund Bykel	Oracle	AIX on S80	400	60	20,000	Driven sponsor ; Department likes slicing & dicing data
Materials Management	WMS	Warehouse Management System	3	Manufacturing Panning & Control	Annabel Giutu	Christina Hayim	Oracle	AIX on S80	350	200	5,000	Initiative to cut inventory of slow movers; Need analytical support.
Operations	BOMM	Bill of Materials Management	4	Production Planning	Lucy Kard	George Cimembis	Oracle	AIX on RS/6000	60	8	TBD	Need analysis of "kits", Want to build kits in-house
Marketing	IMCM	Internal/Marketing & Campaign Management	5	Marketing	Elizabeth Impzar	Brian Bridalurg	SQL Server	W2K on Compaq	50	350	Varies	Needs Data Mining Capabilities
Human Resources	Positions Website	Positions Website	5	Human Resource Mgmt	Florence Iyzar	Andrew Aoanthal	SQL Server	W2k on Compaq	50	1	10,000	Manager is new, eager for DW
Purchaing	PAS	Purchaing & Acquision System	6	Purchaing Department	Guy Croendil	Sybil Mai	SQL Server	NT on Compaq	75	4	1,500	
Customer Service	CSS	Customer Service System	7	Customer Care	Bernard Beais	Arthur Aticcio	Notes/Domino	NT on Compaq	275	6	1,500	Plans to move application to Oracle next year.
Operations	QCS	Quality Control System	8	Quality Control	Thomas Fryar	Elias Caye	SQL Server	NT on Compaq	450	12	500	Needs failure ratio analytics by product, by vendor, by year
Sales	SFA	Sales Force Automation	9	Sales	Anthony Aran	Emma Inalonm	DB2	AS/400	1200	10	2,500	Politically challenging; Interim reporting system in place

Figure 3.2 Source system tracking report.

The source system tracking report also serves as an outline for future phases of the data warehouse. If there are 20 source systems identified in the list, and phase 1 includes two or three systems, plan to be on the project for a long, long time.

- **Subject area.** Typically the name of the data mart that this system feeds

- **Interface name.** The name of the transaction application that the source system supports

- **Business name.** The name the system is commonly referred to by the business users.

- **Priority.** A ranking or ordinal position used to determine future phases. The priority is usually set after the data warehouse bus matrix has been completed.

- **Department/Business use.** The primary department using the database, for example, Accounting, Human Resources, and so on. If the application is used by many departments, indicate the business use, for example, Inventory Control, Client tracking, and so on.

- **Business owner.** The person or group to contact for issues or questions related to the use of the application or database. This person or group is typically the data steward for the subject area.

- **Technical Owner.** Typically the DBA or IT project manager responsible for maintaining the database

- **DBMS.** The source database management system name. In most cases, it will be a relational database such as Oracle, DB2, or Sybase. It can also be nonrelational data stores like Lotus Notes or VSAM.

- **Production server/OS.** When known, this column includes the physical name of the server where the database lives. It also includes the operating system. You need this column when designing OS level scripts for your ETL. For example, you cannot use UNIX shell scripts when the server is operating on NT.

- **# Daily users.** Gives you an idea of how many operational people in the organization the data is exposed to. This number is not the same as the potential end user data warehouse users.

- **DB size.** The DBA should be able to provide this information. Knowing the raw size of the source data can help you determine the ETL priorities and efforts. Generally speaking, the larger databases tend to be higher on the priority lists because performance is usually lacking when large tables or several joined tables are queried in the transaction system.

- **DB complexity.** The number of tables and view objects in the system

- **# Transactions per day.** Estimate that gives you an indication of the capacity requirements for the incremental load process

- **Comments.** Usually used for general observations found while researching the database. It may include notes about future version releases of the database or reasons why it is or isn't a system-of-record for certain entities.

Determining the System-of-Record

Like a lot of the terminology in the data warehouse world, the system-of-record has many definitions—the variations depend on who you ask. Our definition of the system-of-record is quite simple: It is the originating source of data. This definition of the system-of-record is important because in most enterprises data is stored redundantly across many different systems. Enterprises do this to make nonintegrated systems share data. It is very common that the same piece of data is copied, moved, manipulated, transformed, altered, cleansed, or made corrupt throughout the enterprise, resulting in varying versions of the *same* data. In nearly all cases, data at the end of the lineage will not resemble the originating source of data—the system-of-record. We were once on a project where the originally identified source data was four times removed from the system-of-record. In the process between systems 3 and 4, the data was transferred via an algorithm in an attempt to *clean* the data. The algorithm had an undetected bug, and it corrupted the data by inserting data from other fields into it. The bug was discovered by the ETL team during the data-discovery phase of the project.

 Dealing with Derived Data.

You may run into some confusion surrounding derived data. Should the ETL process accept calculated columns in the source system as the system-of-record, or are the base elements, the foundation of the derived data, desired? The answer to this depends partly on whether the calculated columns are addditive. Nonadditive measures cannot be combined in queries by end users, whereas additive measures can. So you may be forced to use the base elements and calculate the nonadditve measure yourself. But be thoughtful. Should you try to recreate the calculations in the ETL process, you will be responsible for keeping the calculations synchronized and for understanding the business rules that define these calculations. If the calculation logic changes in the source system, the ETL process will have to be modified and redeployed. It is necessary, therefore, to capture the calculation as metadata so users understand how it was derived.

Unless there is substantial evidence that the originating data is not reliable, we recommend you don't sway from our definition of system-of-record. Keep in mind that a goal of the data warehouse is to be able to share conformed dimensions across all subject areas. Should you chose not to use the system-of-record to load your data warehouse, conforming dimensions will be nearly impossible. Should you need to augment your dimensions with different versions of data for specific needs, those should be stored as additional attributes in your conformed dimension.

However, to each rule there is an exception. Identifying the database name or file name may not be as easy as you might think—especially if you are dealing with legacy systems. During a project, we once spent weeks tracking down the *orders* database. Everyone we spoke to referred to the database by a different name. We then discovered that each location had a local version of the database. Since the goal of the data warehouse was to report across the organization, we began documenting each location database name with the intent to migrate the data with the ETL process. During our research of the database names, a programmer finally came forward and said, "You can get the list of the databases you need by reading this replication program." To our surprise, there was already a process in place to replicate the local databases to a central repository. Rather than recreate the wheel, we chose to use this program to get the consolidated database name and loaded the data warehouse from the central repository. Even though the true originating source of data was in each location's database, using the central repository was the most efficient and reliable solution.

> 💡 The further downstream you go from the originating data source, the more you increase the risk of extracting corrupt data. Barring rare exceptions, maintain the practice of sourcing data only from the system-of-record.

Analyzing the Source System: Using Findings from Data Profiling

Once you've determined the system-of-record, your next step is to analyze the source systems to get a better understanding of their content. This understanding is normally accomplished by acquiring the entity relation (ER) diagrams for the systems you've selected to be the system-of-record, if they are based on relational technology. Should the ER diagrams not exist (and don't be surprised if there are none to be found) you may be able to create them. ER diagrams can be generated by *reverse engineering* the database. Reverse engineering is a technique where you develop an ER diagram by reading the existing database metadata. Data-profiling tools are available that make this quite easy. Just about all of the standard data-modeling tools provide this feature, as do some of the major ETL tools.

💡 *Reverse engineering* a system of record to get a proper ER model of the data is obviously useful. But it is not the same as *forward engineering* a complex ER model to build simple dimensional schemas. Data-modeling tools, in fact, fail miserably at this kind of forward engineering when you are trying to see the forest for the trees in a normalized environment with hundreds of tables.

Before diving into the ER diagram, look for a high-level description of the tables and fields in the database. If it exists, it may take the form of unstructured text descriptions, and it may be out of date, but it's far better to start with an overview than to try to discover the overview by looking at reams of mind-numbing detail. Also, don't forget to debrief the source-system guru who understands all the arcane logic and incremental changes that have occurred in the source system!

Having the ability to navigate an ER diagram is essential to performing data analysis. All members of the ETL team need to be able to read an ER diagram and instantly recognize entity relationships. Figure 3.3 illustrates a simple ER diagram.

In the numbered list that follows, we explain the significant characteristics that you want to discover during this phase, including unique identifiers, nullability, and data types. These are primary outputs of a data-profiling effort. But more important, we explain how to identify when tables are related to each other; and which columns have dependencies across tables. Specific characteristics in the ER diagram outlined in Figure 3.3 are:

1. **Unique identifiers and natural keys.** Unique identifiers depict the columns that uniquely represent a row in a table. This definition can be misleading, so we want to investigate it a bit further. From a referential integrity standpoint, a unique identifier is the primary key for a table. Most of the time, the primary key is artificial, and although it is unique from an ETL standpoint, it is not enough information to determine if the row is unique. In every properly designed transaction table, in addition to the primary key, there is at least one natural key. The natural key is what the business uses to uniquely describe the row. For example, a status table can have a status_id, status_code, and status_description. The status_id is clearly the primary key, but depending on the business rules, for purposes of the ETL, the status_code could be the unique identifier natural key. Special care must be taken when selecting the correct natural keys, especially when loading slowly changing dimensions.

2. **Data types.** Remember, as ETL analysts, you take nothing for granted. Column names do not infer data types. Just because a column is named Purchase_Order_Number, are we certain that only

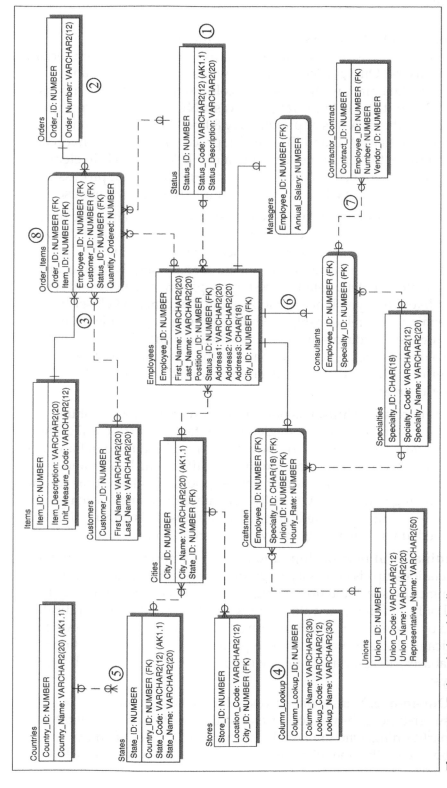

Figure 3.3 Entity relationship diagram.

numbers, not letters, are stored in the column? Additionally, if there are only numbers, are there leading zeros? Are these zeros important to end users? On a particular project, while building a human resource data mart, we had a source column named SCORE; it was a CHAR(2) data type. In the target, it was a NUMBER data type. As it turns out, the data was approximately 80-percent numbers and the rest were letters (A-D and F). The ETL process needed to convert any letter grades to their numerical equivalent. DATE and TIME elements are notorious for being stored as text. It is up to the ETL process to convert these dates while loading them into the data warehouse.

3. **Relationships between tables.** Understanding how tables are related is vital to ensuring accuracy in joins while retrieving data. If you are lucky, the ER diagram has lines connecting the related tables. Evaluation of table relationships includes analyzing the connecting lines. Unfortunately, data-processing people are not lucky and it is most likely that you'll need to look at the diagram a bit closer to determine table relationships. While loading a target table from heterogeneous sources, it is good practice to bring all of the sources into a data-modeling tool and map out the relationships. This integrated ER diagram lends itself to making the logical data map easier to create.

4. **Discrete relationships.** It is not uncommon for the design of the source system to include a single look-up table that stores all of the static reference data for all of the tables throughout the database. The look-up table contains a column that identifies which table and column the associated group of rows support. This takes time for the unknowing to discover. Carefully document the name of each group of rows and the associated tables and columns. This information will be needed while mapping many of the dimensions.

5. **Cardinality of relationships and columns.** Knowing the cardinality of relationships is necessary to predict the result of your queries. Using crow's feet notation, a single line means the cardinality is 1, and only 1 of the same value is allowed. A line and a circle indicate zero or 1 is allowed. The side with 3 lines in the form of a crow's foot indicates the same value can be repeated many times. In relational databases, all associated tables will be joined in one of the following ways:

   ▪ **One-to-one.** You see one-to-one relationships during super-type/sub-type scenarios and the practice of vertical table partitioning. One-to-one relationships can be identified by observing that the relationship is on the primary key of each table.

- **One-to-many.** This is the most commonly found relationship for foreign key references. It is easily identified by noting that a nonkey attribute in a table refers to the primary key of another table. We call this nonkey attribute a foreign key, and we insist that all the foreign keys are *good*, that is, they are instances of the primary key they point to.

- **Many-to-many.** This relationship usually involves three tables with two one-to-many relationships between them. More specifically, there are two tables with an *associative* table between them. The center or associative table has a compound primary key and two foreign keys, one to the primary key of one table and another to the primary key of the other table.

Frequently, source systems do not have foreign keys or referential integrity consistently defined in the database dictionary. These issues may also be discovered through simple column-name matching and more comprehensive data profiling.

Be sure you carefully study all data types in your sources, in your intermediate staging tables, and in the final tables to be delivered. It's quite common for the data modeling team to create data elements that don't exactly match their source. In some cases, you'll find data types are purposely mismatched. For example, some designers deliberately make all code fields allow alphanumeric characters, even if the current system uses only numbers and is a number data type. Also, be sure to evaluate the length of each field. In some cases, the target data warehouse can have smaller data lengths or numeric precision than the source database. Smaller data lengths in the target causes data truncation (lost data!). When you see disparities, check with the data modeling team to confirm their intentions. Either await database corrections or get business rules for conversion and truncation routines.

Data Content Analysis

Understanding the content of the data is crucial for determining the best approach for retrieval. Usually, it's not until you start working with the data that you come to realize the anomalies that exist within it. Common anomalies that you should be aware of include:

- **NULL values.** An unhandled NULL value can destroy any ETL process. NULL values pose the biggest risk when they are in foreign key columns. Joining two or more tables based on a column that contains NULL values will cause data loss! Remember, in a relational database NULL is not equal to NULL. That is why those joins fail. Check for NULL values in every foreign key in the source database. When NULL values are present, you must *outer* join the tables. An outer join returns all of the rows regardless of whether there is a matching value in the joined table. If the NULL data is not in a foreign key column but is in a column required by the business for the data warehouse, you must get a business rule on how the NULL data should be handled. We don't like to store NULL values in the data warehouse unless it is indeed an unknown measure. Whenever possible, create default values to replace NULL values while loading the data warehouse.

- **Dates in nondate fields.** Dates are very peculiar elements because they are the only logical elements that can come in various formats, literally containing different values and having the exact same meaning. Fortunately, most database systems support most of the various formats for display purposes but store them in a single standard format (for that specific database). But there are many situations where dates are stored in text fields, especially in legacy applications. The possible variations of date formats in nondate fields are boundless. Following is a sample of the possible variations of the same date that can be found when the date is stored in a text field:

13-JAN-02

January 13, 2002

01-13-2002

13/01/2002

01/13/2002 2:24 PM

01/13/2002 14:24:49

20020113

200201

012002

As you can imagine, it's possible to fill pages with variations of a single date. The problem is that when the source database system doesn't control or regulate the data entry of dates, you have to pay extra-close attention to ensure you are actually getting what you expect.

💡 **In spite of the most detailed analysis, we recommend using outer join logic when extracting from relational source systems, simply because referential integrity often cannot be trusted on remote systems.**

Collecting Business Rules in the ETL Process

You might think at this stage in the process that all of the business rules must have been collected. How could the data modelers create the data model without knowing all of the business rules, right? Wrong. The business rules required for the data modeling team are quite different from those required by the ETL team. For example, the data modeling definition of the status dimension might be something like:

Status Code—The status is a four-digit code that uniquely identifies the status of the product. The code has a short description, usually one word, and a long description, usually one sentence.

Conversely, the ETL definition of status might be expressed like this:

Status Code—The status is a four-digit code. However, there are legacy codes that were only three digits that are still being used in some cases. All three-digit codes must be converted to their four-digit equivalent code. The name of the code may have the word *OBSOLETE* embedded in the name. *OBSOLETE* needs to be removed from the name and these obsolete codes must have an obsolete flag set to 'Y'. The description should always be in sentence case, regardless of the case used when entered into the source system.

The business rules for the ETL process are much more technical than any other collection of business rules in the data warehouse project. Regardless of their technical appearance, these rules still stem from the business — the ETL team cannot be in the business of making up rules. It is up to the ETL architect to translate user requirements into usable ETL definitions and to articulate these technical definitions to the business people in a way they can understand. The ETL data definitions go through an evolution process. As you discover undocumented data anomalies, document and discuss them with the business—only they can dictate how the anomalies should be handled. Any transformations that come from these meetings have to be documented, properly approved, and signed off.

Integrating Heterogeneous Data Sources

The preceding sections of this chapter expose many of the common data systems that you might come across while sourcing your data warehouse. This section discusses the challenges you may face *integrating* the different data sources. But before you can integrate data, you need to know what *data integration* means. Integrating data means much more than simply collecting disparate data sources and storing that data in a single repository. To better understand what integration really means, consider a corporate merger. During corporate mergers, one or more companies are joined with other similar (or dissimilar) companies. When mergers occur, the business must decide which company is the surviving company and which gets consumed by the new parent. Sometimes, negotiations are made when the parent company recognizes value in certain practices and techniques of its subsidiaries and incorporates those practices in its modified organization. The result of a successful corporate merger is a cohesive organization that has a single business interest. This requires a heroic commitment to aligning terminology (dimension attributes) and aligning key performance indicators (facts in fact tables). If you think of integrating your data in the same fashion as a corporate merger, the result of your data warehouse is a single source of information organized to support the business interest.

But what about those half-finished mergers that allow their subsidiary companies to *do their own thing*? This situation causes a problem because the companies are not integrated—they are merely associated. When you build a data warehouse, integration can occur in several places. The most direct form of data integration is the implementation of conformed dimensions. In the data warehouse, conformed dimensions are the cohesive design that unifies disparate data systems scattered throughout the enterprise.

> **When a dimension is populated by several distinct systems, it is important to include the unique identifier from each of those systems in the target dimension in the data warehouse. Those identifiers should be viewable by end users to ensure peace of mind that the dimension reflects *their* data that they can tie back to in their transaction system.**

What happens when those idiosyncratic dimensions cannot completely conform? Unfortunately, this question is as much of a political issue as a technical one. Conformed dimensions and facts are crucial to the success of the data warehouse project. If the result of your project offers disparate dimensions that are not cohesive across business subject areas, you have not accomplished your goal. Chapter 5 discusses loading dimensions in painstaking detail, but we want to mention specific techniques for loading conformed dimensions in a disparate source system environment here.

1. **Identify the source systems.** During the data-profiling phase of the construction of the logical data mapping, the data warehouse team must work together to detect the various sources of your target dimensions and facts. The data warehouse architect should uncover most of the potential sources of each element in the data warehouse

and attempt to appoint a system-of-record to each element. The system-of-record is considered the *ultimate* source for the data being loaded.

2. **Understand the source systems (data profiling).** Once the source systems are identified, you must perform a thorough analysis of each system. This is also part of data profiling. Data analysis of the source systems uncovers unexpected data anomalies and data-quality issues. This phase declares the reliability of the source system for the elements under scrutiny. During this phase of the project, the assignment of the system-of-record can actually be reassigned if data-quality issues persist or if reliability of the data is problematic for any reason.

3. **Create record matching logic.** Once you understand all of the attributes of all of the entities of all of the systems under consideration (quite a tall order), your next objective is to design the matching algorithm to enable entities across the disparate systems to be joined. Sometimes, the matching algorithm is as simple as identifying the primary key of the various customer tables. But in many cases, disparate systems do not share primary keys. Therefore, you must join the tables based on *fuzzy* logic. Perhaps, there is a social security number that can be used to uniquely identify your customer or maybe you need to combine the last name, e-mail address, and telephone number. Our intention here is not to offer a matching solution but to get you thinking about how your customers can be linked. The various business areas must be involved with and approve of your final matching logic. Don't forget to make sure that this record-matching logic is consistent with the various legislated privacy rules, such as HIPAA in the health care arena.

4. **Establish survivorship rules.** Once your system-of-record has been identified and the matching logic has been approved, you can establish the *surviving record* when data collisions occur in your ETL process. This means that if you have a customer table in your accounts receivable, production control, and sales systems, the business must decide which system has overriding power when attributes overlap.

5. **Establish nonkey attribute business rules.** Remember, dimensions (and facts) are typically sourced from various tables and columns within a system. Moreover, many source systems can, and usually do, contain different attributes that ultimately feed into a target final dimension. For instance, a list of departments probably originated in your HR department; however, the accounting code for that

department probably comes from your financial system. Even though the HR system may be the system-of-record, certain attributes may be deemed more reliable from other systems. Assigning business rules for nonkey attributes is especially important when attributes exist in several systems but not in the system-of-record. In those cases, documentation and publication of the data lineage metadata is crucial to prevent doubt in the integrity of the data warehouse when users don't see what they expect to see.

6. **Load conformed dimension.** The final task of the data-integration process is to physically load the conformed dimension. This step is where you consider the slowly changing dimension (SCD) type and update late-arriving data as necessary. Consult Chapter 5 for details on loading your conformed dimensions.

The beauty of your data warehouse is that it has the ability to truly integrate data, yet also to enable users to see dimensions from their perspective. Conformed dimensions and facts are the backbone of the enterprise data warehouse.

Part 2: The Challenge of Extracting from Disparate Platforms

Each data source can be in a different DBMS and also a different platform. Databases and operating systems, especially legacy and proprietary ones, may require different procedure languages to communicate with their data. On enterprise-wide data warehouse projects, be prepared to have communication with source systems limited to specific languages. Even if there is no technical limitation, departments or subsystems can, and usually do, have a standard language that is *allowed* to interact with their data. Standards we've been asked to use include COBOL, FOCUS, EasyTrieve, PL/SQL, Transact-SQL, and RPG. When a specific language beyond the realm of your ETL toolset or experience becomes mandatory, request that the owner of the source system extract the data into a flat file format.

Connecting to Diverse Sources through ODBC

Open Database Connectivity (ODBC) was created to enable users to access databases from their Windows applications. The original intention for ODBC was to make applications *portable*, meaning that if an application's underlying database changed—say from DB2 to Oracle—the application layer did not need to be recoded and compiled to accommodate the change. Instead, you simply change the ODBC driver, which is transparent to the

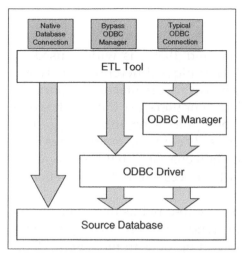

Figure 3.4 The topology of ODBC in the ETL process.

application. You can obtain ODBC drivers for practically every DBMS in existence on virtually any platform. You can also use ODBC to access flat files.

The drawback to ODBC's flexibility is that it comes at a performance cost. ODBC adds several layers of processing and passing of data to the data-manipulation process. For the ETL process to utilize data via ODBC, two layers are added between the ETL system and the underlying database. Figure 3.4 illustrates the layers involved in an ODBC environment.

- **ODBC manager.** The ODBC manager is a program that accepts SQL from the ETL application and routes it to the appropriate ODBC driver. It also maintains the connection between the application and the ODBC driver.

- **ODBC driver.** The ODBC driver is the real workhorse in the ODBC environment. The ODBC driver translates ODBC SQL to the native SQL of the underlying database.

As you might suspect, once you use ODBC you might lose much DBMS-specific functionality. Particular non-ANSI standard SQL commands are not accepted by the ODBC manager because it needs to maintain an *open* solution. ODBC, particularly Microsoft's OLE DB and .Net providers, have improved significantly in recent years, but for highest performance and native DBMS functionality you should look first to a native database driver. Just don't throw the baby out with the bath water. ODBC can provide a common format gateway to certain troublesome data sources that are otherwise not easily extracted.

Mainframe Sources

The mainframe computer, created in the mid 1960s, is widely used by most large enterprises around the world. The unique differentiator between mainframes and other computers is the hardware architecture. Nonmainframe, including minicomputers and microcomputers, use their central processing units (CPUs) for virtually all of their processing, including getting data to and from disk and other peripherals. By contrast, mainframes have a special architecture emphasizing peripheral channels that process all input/output, leaving the CPU dedicated to processing only data, such as calculating formulas and balances.

In many large companies, much of the day-to-day business data is processed and stored on mainframe systems (and certain minicomputer systems, such as the IBM AS/400) and integrating data from these systems into the data warehouse involves some unique challenges. There are several characteristics of mainframe systems that the ETL team must be familiar with and develop techniques to handle:

- COBOL copybooks
- EBCDIC character sets
- Numeric data
- Redefines fields
- Packed decimal fields
- Multiple OCCURS fields
- Multiple record types
- Variable record lengths

The rest of this section discusses these mainframe characteristics and offers techniques for managing them when they are encountered.

Working with COBOL Copybooks

COBOL remains the dominant programming language used on mainframe computers, and the file layout for data is described in COBOL copybooks. A copybook defines the field names and associated data types for a mainframe data file. As with other flat files you encounter in your ETL process, only two data types exist in mainframe flat files: text and numeric. However, numeric values are stored in a variety of ways that you need to understand to accurately process. Likewise, dates are stored simply as strings of numbers (or text) and typically require transformation to be stored in date columns in the data warehouse.

		Len	Positions	
01 EMP-RECORD.				
05 FIRST-NAME	PIC X(10).	10	1 –	10
05 MIDDLE-INITIAL	PIC X.	1	11 –	11
05 LAST-NAME	PIC X(15).	15	12 –	26
05 SSN	PIC X(9).	9	27 –	35
05 EMP-DOB.		8	36 –	43
10 DOB-YYYY	PIC 9(4).	4	36 –	39
10 DOB-MM	PIC 9(2).	2	40 –	41
10 DOB-DD	PIC 9(2).	2	42 –	43
05 EMP-ID	PIC X(9).	9	44 –	52
05 HIRE-DATE.		8	53 –	60
10 HIRE-YYYY	PIC 9(4).	4	53 –	56
10 HIRE-MM	PIC 9(2).	2	57 –	58
10 HIRE-DD	PIC 9(2).	2	59 –	60
05 TERM-DATE.		8	61 –	68
10 TERM-YYYY	PIC 9(4).	4	61 –	64
10 TERM-MM	PIC 9(2).	2	65 –	66
10 TERM-DD	PIC 9(2).	2	67 –	68
05 TERM-REASON_CODE	PIC X(2).	2	69 –	70

Figure 3.5 A simple copybook that describes an employee record.

Figure 3.5 illustrates a 70-byte, fixed length record that describes a simple employee record. Notice that the field names are preceded by level numbers. Nesting of level numbers is used to group related fields. COBOL programs can refer to field names at any defined level. For example, a program can refer to *HIRE-DATE* to capture the full date of hire or *HIRE-YYYY* if only the year portion is needed for processing.

Text and numeric data types are denoted using the PIC clauses. PIC X denotes text fields, while PIC 9 means the field is numeric. Field lengths are specified with numbers following the type. For example, the clause PIC 9(4) indicates a four-byte numeric field, whereas PIC X(15) indicates a 15-byte text field. PIC clauses can be coded alternatively by repeating the *X* or *9* data type indicator, such as *PIC 9999* for a four-byte numeric field.

The data file represented in Figure 3.5 can easily be transmitted via FTP and loaded into the data warehouse because all of the data is contained in *display* format. But before you try to transfer this file from the mainframe to the data warehouse platform, you need to take a short lesson on the difference between the familiar ASCII character set used on UNIX and Windows platforms and the EBCDIC character set used on the mainframe.

EBCDIC Character Set

Both the legacy mainframe systems and the UNIX- and Windows-based systems, where most data warehouses reside, are stored as *bits and bytes*. Each byte is made of eight bits, and each bit represents a binary (base-2) digit. The maximum number that can be represented by a byte made of binary bits is 255 (that is, 2^8-1). Thus, the number of unique characters (for example, A–Z, a–z, 0–9, punctuation, and special characters) that can be portrayed in a system made up of such bytes is 256 (including character 0).

Converting EBCDIC to ASCII

You might think that since both systems use bits and bytes, data from your mainframe system is readily usable on your UNIX or Windows system. But UNIX and Windows systems use the American Standard Code for Information Interchange (ASCII) character set, whereas mainframes use a different set, known as Extended Binary Coded Decimal Interchange Code (EBCDIC). EBCDIC uses more or less the same characters as ASCII but uses different 8-bit combinations to represent them.

For example, take the lowercase letter *a*. In ASCII, the letter *a* is character number 97 (01100001), but in EBCDIC, character number 97 is / (forward slash). In EBCDIC *a* is character 129 (10000001). In fact, none of the common characters are represented by the same character numbers in ASCII and EBCDIC. To use mainframe data on your UNIX or Windows system, you must first translate it from EBCDIC to ASCII.

Transferring Data between Platforms

Luckily, translating data from EBCDIC to ASCII is quite simple. In fact it's virtually automatic, assuming you use File Transfer Protocol (FTP) to transfer the data from the mainframe to your data warehouse platform. An FTP connection requires two nodes—a host and a client. When an FTP connection is made between systems, the FTP client identifies its operating system environment to the FTP host, and the host determines whether any translation is required when transferring data between the two systems. So when an FTP connection is made between a mainframe and a UNIX or Windows system, the FTP host translates mainframe data from EBCDIC to ASCII as it transfers the data. In addition, FTP adds the special line feed and carriage return characters used to designate the end of a line (or record) of data on UNIX and Windows. FTP also translates from ASCII to EBCDIC if the data movement is from UNIX or Windows to the mainframe.

If you receive mainframe data on magnetic tape cartridge or CD-ROM rather than via FTP, you need to explicitly translate the data from EBCDIC to ASCII on the data warehouse system. This translation can be performed using the UNIX dd command with the conv=ascii switch. For Windows, you can obtain a port of the dd—and many other useful UNIX commands—on the Internet. In addition, commercial products that handle character-translation duties are available. ETL tool suites all handle this conversion.

Most robust tools designed specifically for ETL can convert EBCDIC to ASCII on the fly.

> If your source data resides on a mainframe system, it is crucial that your ETL tool have the ability to implicitly convert EBCDIC data to ASCII. If at all possible, you want this to occur on the mainframe to avoid any corruption of low values and packed decimals. If data is received via tape or other media, the translation must occur by the ETL tool in the nonmainframe environment. At a minimum, the ETL tool must automatically execute FTP and process files *in stream*, passing the data directly from the mainframe through the ETL process to the target data warehouse.

As a final point, although mainframes and UNIX or Windows systems use different character sets, translating data from one system to another is a rather simple task—simple, that is, unless your mainframe data has some other traits that are typical of the mainframe world. The next few sections discuss specific characteristics that mainframe data may possess and recommend strategies for managing them during the ETL process.

Handling Mainframe Numeric Data

When you begin to work with quantitative data elements, such as dollar amounts, counts, and balances, you can see that there's more to these numbers than meets the eye. For one thing, you won't typically find decimal points in decimal data, because the decimal points are *implied*. For example, the value 25,000.01 is stored as 002500001. Worse, the value 2,500,001 is stored the same way. So how does the mainframe COBOL program know that 25,000.01 is meant rather than 2,500,001? It's in the PIC clause. The next section discusses the importance and power of the PIC clause in COBOL copybooks.

Using PICtures

You can see in Figure 3.6 that the PIC clause can give the same data value different meaning. To accurately process a numeric value that comes from a legacy mainframe system, you must first transform it to its display format before transmitting it to the data warehouse system; otherwise, your ETL tool has to handle interpreting these mainframe values on the UNIX or Windows platform. To resolve decimals in the numeric values, you might think that you can simply divide the numeric value by the power of ten equal to the number of implied decimal places. And if all numeric values were stored with only the decimal point implied, you'd be right. However, it's not quite that simple. You also have to consider signed numeric values.

PIC Clause	Value	DATA
PIC 9(9)	2,500,001	002500001
PIC 9(7)V99	25,000.01	002500001
PIC 9(6)V9(3)	2,500.001	002500001
PIC S9(W) DISPLAY SIGN LEADING SEPARATE	2,500.001	002500001
PIC S9(7)V99 DISPLAY SIGN LEADING SEPARATE	25,000.01	+002500001
PIC S9(7)V99 DISPLAY SIGN LEADING SEPARATE	(25,000.01)	-002500001
PIC S9(7)V99 DISPLAY SIGN TRAILING SEPARATE	25,000.01	002500001+
PIC S9(7)V99 DISPLAY SIGN TRAILING SEPARATE	(25,000.01)	002500001-
PIC S9(7)V99	25,000.01	00250000A
PIC S9(7)V99	(25,000.01)	00250000J

Figure 3.6 The PIC clause in a COBOL copybook indicates the decimal places of a numeric value.

In mainframe data, the signs may come before or after the numeric value. What's more, the sign may be embedded within the numeric value.

The most common format, *zoned numeric*, embeds the sign within the last numeric digit as shown in the last two rows of Figure 3.6. So, how does *A* in the last position connote both the digit *1* and the sign +, and likewise, how does *J* represent both *1* and -? The trick is that the last byte is treated as two separate half-bytes (each containing four bits) and each half-byte is interpreted separately—in hexadecimal, of course!

For positive numbers, the first half-byte is set to *C*, the hexadecimal value of 1100, and negative numbers are set to *D*, the hexadecimal value of 1101. The second half-byte is set to the hexadecimal value that corresponds to the desired numeric digit. When you combine the first half-byte—1100 for positive or 1101 for negative—to the second half-byte, you get resulting EBCDIC characters, as seen in Figure 3.7.

By now, you are probably scratching your head trying to figure out how to deal with numeric data from your mainframe system. Well, before you try to solve the problem, there's still one more twist that you are likely to encounter in most legacy mainframe systems.

BIN	HEX	EBCDIC
11000000	C0	unprintable
11000001	C1	A
11000010	C2	B
11000011	C3	C
11000100	C4	D
11000101	C5	E
11000110	C6	F
11000111	C7	G
11001000	C8	H
11001001	C9	I
11010000	D0	unprintable
11010001	D1	J
11010010	D2	K
11010011	D3	L
11010100	D4	M
11010101	D5	N
11010110	D6	O
11010111	D7	P
11011000	D8	Q
11011001	D9	R

Figure 3.7 Hexadecimal to EBCDIC.

Unpacking Packed Decimals

Though at present computer hard disk storage is relatively inexpensive, in the past disk storage was among the most expensive components of the computer system. To save disk space, software engineers devised creative formats to store numeric data using fewer bytes than the digits in the number. The most pervasive of these formats is COMP-3, also known as *packed numeric*.

In many mainframe systems, most if not all numeric data is stored in COMP-3 format. COMP-3 format is a simple space-saving technique that uses half-bytes—or *nibbles*—rather than full bytes to store numeric digits. Each numeric digit can be stored in binary format within the four bits of a nibble. The last nibble of a COMP-3 numeric field stores the sign (positive/negative) of the numeric value. Using half-bytes to store numeric digits saves nearly half the space used by the display format. But this simple space-saving technique throws a wrench into the EBCDIC to ASCII character-set translation.

As a result of this translation conundrum, mainframe data that contains numeric values stored using numeric storage formats such as Zoned Numeric or COMP-3 (not to mention COMP, COMP-1, and COMP-2) cannot simply be translated from EBCDIC to ASCII and then processed on the UNIX or Windows warehouse system.

One of the following techniques must be used to maintain the integrity of mainframe numeric data:

- Reformat data on the mainframe into its display format before transmitting it to the data warehouse system using a simple program written in COBOL, Assembler, or a fourth-generation language such as SAS, Easytrieve, or FOCUS. Once data is reformatted in this way, it can then be translated to ASCII via FTP as described earlier in this chapter.

- Transfer data to the warehouse system in its native EBCDIC format. This option is viable only if your ETL tools or process can process EBCDIC data. Several types of tools can perform this task.

  - Use robust ETL tools that can process native EBCDIC, including accurately handling numeric data store in any mainframe-type numeric formats.

  - Use a utility program that can reformat data into *display* format on the warehouse platform. If you receive EBCDIC data and are writing the ETL process without the aid of a specialized ETL tool, we strongly recommend purchasing a utility program that can perform the numeric format conversion and EBCDIC-to-ASCII translation duties. Some relatively inexpensive, commercially available programs handle this task quite well.

Working with Redefined Fields

Rather than wasting space—remember it used to be expensive—mainframe engineers devised REDEFINES, which allow mutually exclusive data elements to occupy the same physical space. Figure 3.8 contains an excerpt from a COBOL Copybook that helps illustrate the concept of REDEFINES in mainframe data files. The excerpt describes the data fields that represent an employee's wage information. Notice EMPLOYEE-TYPE, which is a one-byte code that indicates whether the employee is exempt or hourly. Also, notice that two separate series of fields carry the wage information for the employee. The field set used depends on whether the employee is exempt or hourly. Exempt employees' wages are represented in three fields (PAY-GRADE, SALARY, and PAY-PERIOD), which take up a total of eight

		Len	Positions		
05 EMPLOYEE-TYPE	PIC X.	1	71	–	71
88 EXEMPT VALUE 'E'.					
88 HOURLY VALUE 'H'.					
05 WAGES.		8	72	–	79
10 EXEMPT-WAGES.		8	72	–	79
15 PAY-GRADE	PIC X(2).	2	72	–	73
15 SALARY	PIC 9(6)V99 COMP3.	5	74	–	78
15 PAY-PERIOD	PIC X.	1	79	–	79
88 BI-WEEKLY	VALUE '1'.				
88 MONTHLY	VALUE '2'.				
10 NON-EXEMPT-WAGES		8	72	–	79
REDEFINES EXEMPT-WAGES.					
15 PAY-RATE	PIC 9(4)V99.	6	72	–	77
15 JOB-CLASS	PIC X(1).	1	78	–	78
15 FILLER	PIC X.	1	79	–	79

Figure 3.8 REDEFINES clause in a COBOL copybook.

bytes. Hourly employees use a different set of fields that take up seven bytes (PAY-RATE and JOB-CLASS).

Since an employee is exempt or hourly, never both, only one of the two field sets is ever used at a time. The exempt wage fields occupy positions 72 through 79 in the file, and the hourly wage fields occupy positions 72 though 78. Furthermore, notice that the fields for exempt and hourly wages use different data types even though they occupy the same positions. When reading the employee record, the program must determine how to interpret these positions based on the value of EMPLOYEE-TYPE in position 71.

The same positions can have more than one REDEFINES associated with them, so rather than just two possible uses, the same positions can have two, three, or more possible uses. REDEFINES introduce one further complication that renders mere EBCDIC-to-ASCII character-set translation insufficient.

💡 **When you encounter multiple REDEFINES in your sources, you should consider making each definition a separate pass of the extract logic over the source data if the subsequent processing is quite different (using Exempt versus Hourly as an example). This would allow you to build separate code lines for each extract rather than one complex job with numerous tests for the two conditions.**

Multiple OCCURS

Mainframe and COBOL precede relational databases and Edward Codd's normalization rules. Prior to utilizing relational theory to design databases, repeating groups were handled with mainframe COBOL programs that use an OCCURS clause to define data fields that repeat within a data file. For

		Len	Position		
05 PERFORMANCE-RATING-AREA	PIC X(100).	100	80	–	179
05 PERFORMANCE-RATINGS		100	80	–	179
REDEFINES PERFORMANCE-RATINGS-AREA.					
07 PERFORMANCE-RATING	OCCURS 5 TIMES.	20	80	–	99
15 PERF-RATING	PIC X(3).	3	80	–	82
15 REVIEWER-ID	PIC X(9).	9	83	–	91
15 REVIEW-DATE.		8	92	–	99
20 REVIEW-DATE-YYYY	PIC 9(4).	4	92	–	95
20 REVIEW-DATE-MM	PIC 9(2).	2	96	–	97
20 REVIEW-DATE-DD	PIC 9(2).	2	98	–	99

Figure 3.9   COBOL copybook with OCCURS clause to define repeating groups within a data record.

example, in Figure 3.9 you can see an area of an employee record that stores information about performance ratings. The record is designed to keep track of up to five performance ratings. But rather than creating the needed fields five times—remember, this precedes relational theory so there won't be a separate performance rating table with a foreign key that points back to the employee—they are named only once within a special OCCURS field. The OCCURS clause indicates the number of times the fields within it repeat. Essentially, the OCCURS clause defines an array contained within the file. Thus, in the employee record, data for the first performance rating occupies positions 80 to 99, the second rating from 100 to 119, the third from 120 to 139, the fourth from 140 to 159, and the fifth—and last—from 160 to 179.

In most cases, the ETL process needs to *normalize* any data contained in a OCCURS section of a mainframe file. Even though it is possible to manually program the ETL process to manage the repeating data, it is strongly recommended that you use a robust ETL tool that allows you to use the COBOL copybooks to define inputs or at least allows you to manually define input file arrays in some other way. If your tools do not support input arrays, you are stuck with the toil of writing code to deal with repeating groups within records sourced from your legacy mainframe systems.

> **Sometimes programmers use OCCURS to store different facts in an array, rather than storing the same fact N times. For example, suppose O-DATE occurs four times. The first date is CREATE, the second is SHIP, the third is ACKNOWLEDGE, and the fourth is PAYMENT. So in this case you don't normalize this OCCURS data but rather create discrete fields for each position in the array.**

To ensure data integrity, model data that results from a COBOL OC-CURS clause in a normalized fashion—a master table and child table—in the staging area of the data warehouse. It's good practice to stage this data in separate tables because the result of the process most likely loads data into a fact table and a dimension, two separate dimensions, or two separate fact tables. We find that in these situations it makes sense to set data down to *settle* before integrating it with the data warehouse.

Managing Multiple Mainframe Record Type Files

The concept of multiple record type files is touched upon in the section that discusses REDEFINES. The main difference between REDEFINES as discussed earlier and what we're introducing now is that instead of having just a small portion of a record contain multiple definitions, the entire record has multiple definitions. Multiple record types are often used to span a single logical record across two or more physical records. Figure 3.10 contains an extract of a COBOL copybook that illustrates the concept of redefining an entire record.

In Figure 3.10, the REDEFINES clause applies to the entire record. So now, instead of the file carrying only an employee's basic information, it also carries an employee's job history with the company as well. In this file, every employee has at least two records: one EMP-RECORD and one JOB-RECORD. When an employee transfers to a new job, a new JOB-RECORD is added to the file. So an employee's total job history is contained in two or more records on the file: one EMP-RECORD and one or more JOB-RECORD(s).

In this file, the physical order of the records is critically important because the JOB-RECORDs do not have any information to link them to their corresponding EMP-RECORDs. The JOB-RECORDs for an employee follow immediately after his or her EMP-RECORD. So to accurately process the job history of an employee, you must treat two or more physically adjacent records as one *logical* record.

The benefit of using multiple record types is—once again—to save space. The alternative, without using relational theory, is to have extremely wide, space-wasting records to carry all data in a single record. If, for example, you want to track job history for up to five prior positions, you have to add 255 bytes to each employee record (the base EMP-RECORD, plus five occurrences of JOB-RECORD fields (5×51 bytes). But the number of job history field segments is *situational*—it depends on how many jobs an employee has held.

By using multiple record types, the mainframe system can store job history records only as needed, so employees with only one job require only one JOB-RECORD (70 bytes including FILLER), saving 185 bytes on the file. Furthermore, you are no longer limited to a fixed number of jobs in file. An unlimited number of 70-byte JOB-RECORDs can be added for each employee.

			Len	Positions		
01 EMP-RECORD.			70	1	–	70
05 REC-TYPE		PIC X(1).	1	1	–	1
05 FIRST-NAME		PIC X(10).	10	2	–	11
05 MIDDLE-INITIAL		PIC X.	1	12	–	12
05 LAST-NAME		PIC X(15).	15	13	–	27
05 SSN		PIC X(9).	9	28	–	36
05 EMP-DOB.			8	37	–	44
10 DOB-YYYY		PIC 9(4).	4	37	–	40
10 DOB-MM		PIC 9(2).	2	41	–	42
10 DOB-DD		PIC 9(2).	2	43	–	44
05 EMP-ID		PIC X(8).	8	45	–	52
05 HIRE-DATE.			8	53	–	60
10 HIRE-YYYY		PIC 9(4).	4	53	–	56
10 HIRE-MM		PIC 9(2).	2	57	–	58
10 HIRE-DD		PIC 9(2).	2	59	–	60
05 TERM-DATE.			8	61	–	68
10 TERM-YYYY		PIC 9(4).	4	61	–	64
10 TERM-MM		PIC 9(2).	2	65	–	66
10 TERM-DD		PIC 9(2).	2	67	–	68
05 TERM-REASON_CODE		PIC X(2).	2	69	–	70
01 JOB-RECORD **REDEFINES** EMP-RECORD.			70	1	–	70
05 REC-TYPE		PIC X(1).	1	1	–	1
05 DIVISION		PIC X(8).	8	2	–	9
05 DEPT-ID		PIC X(3).	3	10	–	12
05 DEPT-NAME		PIC X(10).	10	13	–	22
05 JOB-ID		PIC X(3).	3	23	–	25
05 JOB-TITLE		PIC X(10).	10	26	–	35
05 START-DATE.			8	36	–	43
10 START-YYYY		PIC 9(4).	4	36	–	39
10 START-MM		PIC 9(2).	2	40	–	41
10 START-DD		PIC 9(2).	2	42	–	43
05 END-DATE.			8	44	–	51
10 END-YYYY		PIC 9(4).	4	44	–	47
10 END-MM		PIC 9(2).	2	48	–	49
10 END-DD		PIC 9(2).	2	50	–	51
05 FILLER		PIC X(19).	19	52	–	70

Figure 3.10 Recognizing multiple record types within the same file.

Our employee example has only two record types, but multiple REDE-FINES can be used to create any number of record types that can combine into a single logical record. If we expand the employee example, you might imagine a third record type to carry information about the employee's fringe benefits and a fourth type to carry information about the employee's family dependents.

The ETL process must manage multiple record types by retaining the values from the first physical record in a set—which is only the first part of the logical record—in memory variables so they can be joined to the rest of the data that follows in subsequent records.

Handling Mainframe Variable Record Lengths

In the previous section, we discuss how information related to a single entity is spanned across two or more records using multiple record types. A variable record length is another approach used in mainframe files to store situational information. Rather than storing the job history of an employee in separate JOB-RECORDs, each job is stored in an OCCURS job history segment. Furthermore, as illustrated in Figure 3.11, instead of the record having a fixed number of such segments, the number of segments varies between 0 and 20, based on the numeric value in the DEPENDING ON

		Len	LOGICAL Positions		
01 EMP-RECORD.		70	1	-	70
05 REC-TYPE	PIC X(1).	1	1	-	1
05 FIRST-NAME	PIC X(10).	10	2	-	11
05 MIDDLE-INITIAL	PIC X.	1	12	-	12
05 LAST-NAME	PIC X(15).	15	13	-	27
05 SSN	PIC X(9).	9	28	-	36
05 EMP-DOB.		8	37	-	44
10 DOB-YYYY	PIC 9(4).	4	37	-	40
10 DOB-MM	PIC 9(2).	2	41	-	42
10 DOB-DD	PIC 9(2).	2	43	-	44
05 EMP-ID	PIC X(8).	8	45	-	52
05 HIRE-DATE.		8	53	-	60
10 HIRE-YYYY	PIC 9(4).	4	53	-	56
10 HIRE-MM	PIC 9(2).	2	57	-	58
10 HIRE-DD	PIC 9(2).	2	59	-	60
05 TERM-DATE.		8	61	-	68
10 TERM-YYYY	PIC 9(4).	4	61	-	64
10 TERM-MM	PIC 9(2).	2	65	-	66
10 TERM-DD	PIC 9(2).	2	67	-	68
05 TERM-REASON_CODE	PIC X(2).	2	69	-	70
05 JOB-HISTORY-COUNT	PIC 9(2).	2	71	-	72
05 JOB-HISTORY OCCURS 20 TIMES		varies	73	-	varies
DEPENDING ON JOB-HISTORY-COUNT.					
05 DIVISION	PIC X(8).	8	73	-	80
05 DEPT-ID	PIC X(3).	3	81	-	83
05 DEPT-NAME	PIC X(10).	10	84	-	93
05 JOB-ID	PIC X(3).	3	94	-	96
05 JOB-TITLE	PIC X(10).	10	97	-	106
05 START-DATE.		8	107	-	106
10 START-YYYY	PIC 9(4).	4	107	-	110
10 START-MM	PIC 9(2).	2	111	-	112
10 START-DD	PIC 9(2).	2	113	-	114
05 END-DATE.		8	115	-	114
10 END-YYYY	PIC 9(4).	4	115	-	118
10 END-MM	PIC 9(2).	2	119	-	120
10 END-DD	PIC 9(2).	2	121	-	122

Figure 3.11 Variable record lengths in a COBOL copybook using the DEPENDING ON clause.

JOB-HISTORY-COUNT clause. Each additional employee job, up to a maximum of 20, adds 50 bytes to the length of the record.

Variable-length records that use DEPENDING ON clauses in the copybook make straightforward EBCDIC-to-ASCII character-set translation ineffective. The following is a list of ways to mitigate the risk of creating corrupt data from variable-length records during the ETL process.

- Convert all data to *display* format on the mainframe and convert to fixed-length records, adding space at the end of each record for all unused variable segment occurrences.

- Transfer the file in BINARY format to the data warehouse platform. This technique requires having tools that can interpret all of the nuances of mainframe data discussed throughout this chapter. Robust dedicated ETL tools handle most or all of these situations. If your data warehouse project does not include such a tool, third-party utility programs are available in various price ranges that can interpret and convert mainframe data on a UNIX or Windows platform.

- The last option is to develop your own code to handle all of the known nuances that can occur when dealing with legacy data. However, this option is not for the faint-hearted. The cost in time and effort to handle all of the possible data scenarios would most likely exceed the cost of either developing the reformat programs on the mainframe or purchasing one of the utilities to assist in handling the mainframe data.

Extracting from IMS, IDMS, Adabase, and Model 204

If you use any of these systems, you will need special extractors. For starters, there are ODBC gateways to each of these. It is beyond the scope of this book to discuss detailed extraction techniques for these legacy database systems, but we realize they may be important to some of you.

Flat Files

PROCESS CHECK Planning & Design:
Requirements/Realities → **Architecture** → *Implementation* → **Test/Release**

Data Flow: Extract → **Clean** → **Conform** → **Deliver**

Flat files are the mainstay of any data-staging application. In most data warehouse environments you cannot avoid flat files. Flat files are utilized by the ETL process for at least three reasons:

- **Delivery of source data.** When data is sourced by mainframes or external vendors, it is quite often FTP'd to the data-staging area in flat files. Data that comes from *personal* databases or spreadsheets is also usually delivered via flat files.

- **Working/staging tables.** Working tables are created by the ETL process for its own exclusive use. Most often, flat files are used because I/O straight reads and writes to the file system are much faster than inserting into and querying from a DBMS.

- **Preparation for bulk load.** If your ETL tool does not support *in-stream* bulk loading, or you want a load file for safekeeping or archiving, you need to create a flat file on the file system after all of the data transformations have occurred. Once a flat file is created, your bulk load processor can read the file and load it into your data warehouse.

Not all flat files are created equally. Flat files essentially come in two flavors:

- Fixed length
- Delimited

Processing Fixed Length Flat Files

At times, you cannot access the physical data required to populate the data warehouse from its originating system. In those cases, you need to have a flat file created for you by the programmers who support the source system. Quite often, those files will be fixed length—also known as *positional* flat files. One of us was once on a data warehouse project that required very complex calculations from the legacy source system. The names of the calculations were given to the data warehouse architect, but the sources and calculations were a mystery. After some time-consuming investigation and detective work, the fields were discovered on a report that was written in COBOL in 1977. Naturally, the programmers that designed the report were no longer with the company. Moreover, the source code was nowhere to be found. As it turned out, the calculations were not so much complex as they were nonexistent.

Unfortunately, telling business users that data could not be derived and would not be available in the data warehouse was not an option. The team's solution was to redirect the report containing the required data to output to a flat file and use the prederived data from the report as a data source. Because of the nature of the report—fixed columns—it was simply treated as a positional flat file and processed with the rest of the ETL processes.

Field Name	Length	Start	End	Type	Comments
Record Type	2	1	2	AlphaNumeric	Type of record can be either 'H' for header or 'D' for detail record.
SSN	9	3	11	Numeric	Employee's Social Security Number.
First Name	20	12	31	AlphaNumeric	First name of employee
Middle Initial	1	32	32	AlphaNumeric	Middle initial of employee
Last Name	20	33	52	AlphaNumeric	Last name of employee
Name Suffix	5	53	57	AlphaNumeric	Jr, Sr, III, etc.
Birth Date	8	58	65	Numeric	Employee's data of birth "YYYYMMDD".
Status Code	6	66	71	Numeric	Employee's Status ('A','R', 'T', etc).
Office Code	2	72	73	Numeric	The code of the employees branch office.
Department Code	2	74	75	Numeric	The code of the employees department within his/her office.
Position Code	2	76	77	Numeric	The code of the employees position in the organization.
Filler	1	78	78	AlphaNumeric	Filler space.
Add Date	8	79	86	Numeric	The date the record was add to the system.
Modified Date	8	87	94	Numeric	The date the record last modified.

Figure 3.12   Fixed length flat file layout.

Processing a fixed length flat file requires a file layout to illustrate the exact fields within the file, as illustrated in Figure 3.12. A fixed length file layout should include the file name, where the field begins; its length; and its data type (usually *text* or *number*). Sometimes, the end position is supplied. If it is not, you have to calculate the end position of each field based on its beginning position and length if it is required by your ETL tool.

In most ETL tools, you most likely have to manually input the file layout of the flat file once. After the layout is entered, the tool remembers the layout and expects that same layout each time it interacts with the actual flat file. If the file layout changes or the data shifts off of its assigned positions, the ETL process must be programmed to fail. Unfortunately, unlike XML, no implicit validation of the file layout occurs when you process fixed length flat files—an explicit preprocess test must be successful before the data is processed.

> When processing fixed length flat files, try to validate that the positions of the data in the file are accurate. A quick check to validate the positions is to test any date (or time) field to make sure it is a valid date. If the positions are shifted, the date field most likely contains alpha characters or illogical numbers. Other fields with very specific domains can be tested in the same way. XML offers more concrete validation abilities. If data validation or consistency is an issue, try to convince the data provider to deliver the data in XML format.

Positional flat files are often indicated on the file system by a .TXT extension. However, positional flat files can have virtually any file extension—or none at all—and be processed just the same.

Processing Delimited Flat Files

Flat files often come with a set of delimiters that separate the data fields within the file. Delimiters are used as an alternative to using positions to describe where fields begin and end. Delimited files can use any symbol or group of symbols to separate the fields in the flat file. The most common delimiter is the comma. Comma-delimited files can usually be identified by the .CSV extension on the file name. Obviously, however, other application-specific delimited flat files may simply have a .TXT extension or no extension.

Most ETL tools have a delimited file wizard that, once the developer indicates the actual delimiter characters, scans the flat file, or a sample of it, to detect the delimiters within the file and specify the file layout. Most often, the first row of delimited files contains its column names. The ETL tool should be intelligent enough to recognize the column names supplied in the first row to assign logical column names in the metadata layer and then ignore the row during all subsequent data processing.

Just as with positional flat files, no implicit validation on delimited files exists. They must have explicit validation tests written by the ETL team and embedded in the data-processing routines.

XML Sources

PROCESS CHECK Planning & Design:
Requirements/Realities → **Architecture** → *Implementation* → **Test/Release**

Data Flow: *Extract* → **Clean** → **Conform** → **Deliver**

Extensible Markup Language (XML) is slowly but surely becoming the standard for sharing data. Much excitement has been generated by this new paradigm that stores data in a *well-formed* document. After all of its hype, we thought by now virtually all data warehouse sources would involve XML. But so far, we've observed that methods for sharing internal data have not changed all that much. On the other hand, methods for sharing external data have radically evolved in the past year or so to become almost completely XML.

XML has emerged to become a universal language for exchanging data between enterprises. If your data warehouse includes data that comes from external sources—those from outside of your enterprise—odds are that those sources will be provided in XML.

To process XML, you must first understand how it works. XML has two important elements: its metadata and the data itself. XML metadata can be provided in various ways. The next section illustrates different forms of XML metadata and what each means to the ETL.

Character Sets

Character sets are groups of unique symbols used for displaying and printing computer output. The default character set for most relational database management systems is ISO8859-15 (Latin 9). The character set supersedes ISO8859-1 (Latin 1) by enabling the euro sign: € The Latin character sets are intended to be used in the Western world to support languages based on the English alphabet. However, since XML is primarily used as a language for the Internet, it must support languages and alphabets from all over the world, not just the Western world. Therefore, XML supports the UTF-8 character set. UTF-8 is a character set that preserves the basic ASCII encoding method and also supports Unicode (ISO10646), the Universal Character Set (UCS). UTF-8 supports most of the languages and alphabets from around the world.

Many problems can arise if the source XML document and the target data warehouse are not based on the same character set. Of course, this flawed synchronization is always a risk when you integrate disparate systems (not just XML data sets). But in most cases, the risk is minimal because with few exceptions database systems use the Latin character sets. Organizations that don't use Latin-based character sets, but Unicode to support specific alphabets or characters, should adopt an enterprise-wide standard character set to avoid integration difficulties. Whenever you have a requirement to integrate data, especially using XML, from external sources, you must be ready to deal with dissimilar character sets. The good thing is that in XML, you can at least tag the document with the appropriate metadata to indicate the character set being used. For instance, the tag `<?xml version="1.0" encoding="UTF-8" ?>` indicates that the XML document is encoded using the UTF-8 character set.

XML Meta Data

We hear quite often that XML is nothing more than a flat file that contains data. In our opinion, that could not be farther from the truth. The only thing that makes XML remotely similar to a flat file is that it is stored on the files system as opposed to in the database. And in fact, many database systems are adding the capability to read, create, and store XML natively, calling themselves XML *enabled*.

XML is an odd entity because it stores data but is considered a language. It's not an application; therefore, it is dependent on other applications to make it work. Yet it is not merely data because of its embedded tags. The tags in XML documents are what make XML so powerful. But the self-describing data comes at a cost. The tags, which contain its metadata, can consume 90 percent of the XML file size, leaving about ten percent of the XML file for actual data. If your current flat files were XML, they could potentially be ten times their original size—containing exactly the same amount of raw data.

We find it ironic that a primary objective of data warehousing is to keep data as lean as possible to process it as quickly as possible and that even though XML tags cause a deviation from that goal by adding a considerable amount of overhead to the data processes, many still insist on making it a standard for data exchange. Not only do the tags increase the size of the data files; they also add substantial complexity to them. Because of such inherent complexity, never plan on writing your own XML processing interface to parse XML documents. The structure of an XML document is quite involved, and the construction of an XML parser is a project in itself—not to be attempted by the data warehouse team. There are many XML parsers (or processors) on the market, and most ETL vendors now include them in their product offerings.

> **Do not try to parse XML files manually. XML documents need to be processed by an XML processor engine. Many of the major ETL tools now include XML processors in their suite. Make sure XML processing capabilities are in your ETL toolset proof-of-concept criteria.**

To process an XML document, you must first know the structure of the document. The structure of an XML document is usually provided in a separate file. The next few sections discuss each of the possible metadata files that might accompany your XML and provide the structure of the XML document.

DTD (Document Type Definition)

As someone who views XML as a *data* source as opposed to a programming language, we equate the DTD to the COBOL file layout. It is a file that describes the structure of data in the XML document or file. Definitions can be embedded within an XML document, but to enable validation, keep the metadata and the actual data files separate. The DTD can be quite complex, incorporating such allowable XML data structures as the following:

- **Base Data.** If an element must contain only data, it is tagged with the #PCDATA declaration.

- **Element structures.** The structure of an element in a DTD is specified by listing element names within an element. For example, `<!ELEMENT OrderLineItem (ProductID, QuantityOrdered, Price)>` indicates that an order line item is composed of the Product ID, the quantity ordered, and the price of the item at the time of the order.

- **Mixed Content.** When either data or elements are allowed, PCDATA is declared to indicate that the base data is allowed and element names are indicated to enable the nested elements.

- **Nillable.** That's not a typo! In XML, you indicate if a field can be NULL with the 'nill=' or 'nillable=' tags. In the DTD, you'll see a question mark (?) to indicate that a subelement is optional. For example, the code `<!ELEMENT Customer (FirstName, LastName, ZipCode?, Status)>` indicates that the first and last name and status are required but the zip code is optional.

- **Cardinality.** One-to-many is indicated by the plus sign (+). For example, `<!ELEMENT Customer (FirstName, LastName, ZipCode+, Status)>` means that the customer can have more than one zip code.

- **Allowed Values.** Similar to a check constraint, XML enforces allowed values by listing the acceptable values separated by vertical bars. For example, `<!ELEMENT State (Alabama|Louisiana| Mississippi )>` indicates that the state must contain *Alabama*, *Louisiana*, or *Mississippi*.

At the time of this writing, the XML paradigm is still evolving and changing. Today, the DTD is viewed by many as *dated* technology. Because XML is evolving into more data-centric roles, similar to relational databases, most likely the DTD will be replaced by XML Schemas as the standard metadata. The next section discusses XML Schemas and how they are different from the DTD.

XML Schema

The XML Schema is the successor of the DTD. XML Schemas are richer and more useful than the DTD because they were created to extend the DTD. An XML Schema allows an SQL CREATE TABLE statement to be defined directly. This is not possible with simple DTDs, because the detailed data types and field lengths are not specified in DTDs. Some features of the XML Schema include the following:

- Elements that appear in an XML document

- Attributes that appear in an XML document
- The number and order of child elements
- Data types of elements and attributes
- Default and fixed values for elements and attributes
- Extensible to future additions
- Support of namespaces

Namespaces

XML is growing in popularity because it forces disparate data sources to send *consistent and expected* data files. But the reality is that different systems always have slightly different meanings and usage for the same elements within an entity. For example, if you receive a customer file from both human resources and operations, they might have different definitions of a customer. One department may deal with organizations, while the other transacts with individuals. Even though both are customers, organizations and individuals have very different attributes. To alleviate this situation, an XML document can refer to a *namespace*. A namespace indicates where to get the definition of an element or attribute. The same entity can take on a different meaning based on its declared namespace. The same customer entity with the namespace tag `<Customer xmlns=http://www.website.com/xml/HRns>` can have different meaning than the same entity referring to `<Customer xmlns=http://www.website.com/xml/OPSns>`.

> 💡 Because XML is emerging as the data source for Web-based applications, you will most likely see that increasingly reflected in your data warehouse data sources. When you pick your ETL tool, make sure it can natively process XML and XML Schemas.

Web Log Sources

PROCESS CHECK Planning & Design:
Requirements/Realities → Architecture → *Implementation* → Test/Release

Data Flow: *Extract* → Clean → Conform → Deliver

Virtually every company in the world has a Web site. Beneath each Web site are logs—Web logs—that record every object either posted to or served from the Web server. Web logs are important because they reveal the user traffic on the Web site.

💡 **A Web log in this section is not a *weblog* or *blog* ! Our Web log is a control document automatically produced by every Web server. A blog is a kind of diary maintained and published by individuals, principally teenagers, for anyone to read.**

Understanding the behavior of users on your Web site is as valuable as following a customer around a store and recording his or her every move. Imagine how much more organized your store can be and how many opportunities you can have to sell more merchandise if you know every move your customers make while navigating your store. Web logs provide that information. The activity of parsing Web logs and storing the results in a data mart to analyze customer activity is known as clickstream data warehousing.

CROSS-REFERENCE An excellent source for more information on clickstream data warehousing is the book *Clickstream Data Warehousing* by Mark Sweiger, Mark R. Madsen, Jimmy Langston, and Howard Lombard (Wiley 2002).

From the data-modeling perspective, a clickstream data mart may be no more challenging than any other subject in the data warehouse. The ETL process, however, is significantly different from any other source you're likely to encounter. The difference is that the source to the clickstream is a text-based log that must be integrated with other source systems. Fortunately, the format of the text-based log is standardized. The standard is maintained by the World Wide Web Consortium (W^{3}C).

W3C Common and Extended Formats

Even though the format of Web logs is standardized, its format and the content can vary. The operating system (OS) of the Web server and the parameter settings that control the log contents affect exactly what is written to the logs. Regardless of the OS, Web logs have a common set of columns that usually include the following:

- **Date.** This field is in a common date format—usually dd/mm/yyyy. If the time zone is adjusted during the ETL process, you must concatenate the date and time and adjust them together; otherwise, you may be a day off. You can split them up again upon loading.
- **Time.** This is the time of the Web hit. The format is HH:MM:SS and is usually set to Greenwich Mean Time (GMT). However, the time zone can be changed. Be sure you know what time zone your Web servers

are set to. This usually involves conversion to the local time for the data mart.

- **c-ip.** This is the IP address of the user's Internet service provider (ISP). It is a standard IP address that can be used for domain name system (DNS) look-up to estimate where the user came from and *sessionizing*. Using the c-ip can be less than reliable because of known anomalies, such as AOL (the most popular ISP), which gives millions of users the same IP address and indicates that all of their users are from the same state in the United States, even though they might really be from all over the world.

- **Service Name.** This refers to the Internet service that was running on client computer, for example, w3svc1, w3svc2, w3svc3, and so on. This field identifies the site the log came from in environments that host many different Web sites or domains. This field is typically turned off for single-site environments.

- **s-ip.** This is the server IP address. It is standard IP address format. This is useful to identify individual Web servers in a Web farm environment. It also enables analysis of load balancing.

- **cs-method.** There are only two values possible in this field: POST or GET. Only GET records are usually stored in a Clickstream data mart.

- **cs-uri-stem.** This is the resource accessed (that is, the HTML or ASP page requested).

- **cs-uri-query.** This is the query the client passed. This field contains highly customizable, very valuable data. We call this and the cookie (discussed later in this list) the golden nuggets of the Web log. This field typically uses an ampersand (&) as a delimiter between label=value pairs, but any symbol is possible. More on parsing the cs-uri-query is discussed later in the "Name Value Pairs" section of this chapter.

- **sc-status.** This is the HTTP status, for example, 302 (redirect), 402 (error), and 200 (ok). A complete list of HTTP status codes can be found on the Web with a search for *HTTP status codes*. We recommend you preload the HTTP status dimension with all of the possible codes and their descriptions.

- **sc-bytes.** This is the number of bytes sent by the server. This is usually captured as a fact of the Hit.

- **cs(User-Agent).** This is the browser type and version used by the client. The user-agent, along with the date and time, can be used to determine unique visitors.

💡 You can refer to *The Data Webhouse Toolkit: Building the Web-Enabled Data Warehouse* by Ralph Kimball and Richard Merz (Wiley 2000) for more information on alternative methods on identifying unique users on your Web site.

- **cs(Cookie).** This is the content of the cookie sent or received, if any. This field is the other half, along with the cs-uri-query, of the gold found in the Web log. The cookie is highly customizable and very valuable. It can explicitly identify the user and many other characteristics about the user's session.
- **cs(Referrer).** This is the URL describing the site that directed the user to the current site.

The following fields are available in the W^3C extended format, but it is not an all-inclusive list. For an exhaustive list of the fields available in your environment, refer to your Web server documentation or the W^3C Web site (www.w3c.org).

- **Server Name.** This is the name of the server on which the log was generated. This should be one-to-one with the s-ip, which is the IP address of the Web server.
- **cs-username.** This is the username and contains values only when the method is a POST.
- **Server Port.** This is the port number the client was connected to.
- **Bytes Received**. This is the number of bytes received by the user.
- **Time Taken**. This is the length of time the action took.
- **Protocol Version**. This is the protocol version used by the client, for example, HTTP 1.0, HTTP 1.1.

Name Value Pairs in Web Logs

Web logs consist of standard fields that are all distinct in content. For the most part, the content of the Web log can be extracted without too much transformation logic. This straightforwardness is especially true for the date, time, c-ip, service name, s-ip, cs-method, cs-uri-stem, sc-status, and sc-bytes. However, fields such as cs-uri-query and cs(Cookie) are not standard at all. In fact, it would be an extremely rare event to find two unrelated Web sites that have the same content in these fields. The cs-uri-query and cs(Cookie) contain customized name value pairs to capture specific attributes of a transaction that are important to the business.

The cs-uri-query typically contains detailed information about the transaction such as the product being served on the page. Consider the following cs-uri-query as an example:

```
/product/product.asp?p=27717&c=163&s=dress+shirt
```

Take a look at the query string and notice the following segments:

- **/product/**—The initial portion of the query string represents the directory that the executing program resides. The directory is always preceded and followed by a slash '/'. In this example, the product.asp program is in the product directory. If the program were in the *root* directory, a single slash would precede the program name.

- **product.asp**—This is the executing program file that generates the Web page. Common executing programs have the following extensions: .asp (active server pages) and .jsp (java server pages). The program file can be found immediately after directory.

- **?**—The question mark indicates that parameters were sent to the program file. In this example, there are three parameters: p, c, and s.

Before the question mark, the query string is pretty standard. After the question mark is where the custom parameters for the program are stored. A different set of parameters can be defined by the Web site developer for each program file. The parameters are captured in the Web log in name-value pairs. In this example, you can see three parameters, each separated by an ampersand (&).

- **p** indicates the product number
- **c** indicates the product category number
- **s** indicates the search string entered by the user to find the product

> The ampersand (&) is the most common delimiter for separating parameters in the Web log, but it is not guaranteed. Make sure you visually scan the logs during your analysis phase to ensure that the parameter delimiters are identified.

Notice in the s= parameter that the search string is written as *dress + shirt*. Actually, the user entered *dress shirt*. The + was automatically inserted by the Web browser because HTTP cannot handle spaces. Extra care must be taken when you are processing textual descriptions in the query string. The ETL process must substitute any + in textual descriptions with a <space> before they are used for look-ups or stored in the data warehouse.

The intent of this section is to expose you to Web logs to give you a head start on your clickstream data mart project. Again, if you are deep into a clickstream project or plan to be in the near future, you should invest in either of the two books referenced earlier in this section.

ERP System Sources

The existence of an ERP system has an immense effect on ETL system planning and design, as described in this section. This can range from treating the ERP system as a simple arms-length source of data, all the way to having the ERP system be the data warehouse and subsuming all the components, including the ERP system. We make recommendations in this section.

Data Flow: Extract → Clean → Conform (maybe) → Deliver

Enterprise resource planning (ERP) systems were created to solve one of the issues that data warehouses face today—integration of heterogeneous data. ERP systems are designed to be an integrated enterprise solution that enables every major entity of the enterprise, such as sales, accounting, human resources, inventory, and production control, to be on the same platform, database, and application framework.

As you can imagine, ERP systems are extremely complex and not easily implemented. They take months or years to customize so they contain the exact functionality to meet all of the requirements to run a particular business. As noble as the effort to be an all-inclusive solution is, it's very rare to see an entire enterprise use only an ERP system to run a company.

ERP systems are notoriously large, and because they are really a framework and not an application, their data models are comprehensive, often containing thousands of tables. Moreover, because of their flexibility, the data models that support ERP processing are incredibly difficult to navigate. The more popular ERP systems are SAP, PeopleSoft, Oracle, Baan, and J.D. Edwards.

Because of the sheer number of tables, attributes, and complexity of a typical ERP implementation, it is a mistake to attack these systems like any other transaction source system. Performing system and data analysis from scratch is cost and time prohibitive and leaves much room for error. If your data warehouse sources are from an existing ERP system, it is best to acquire someone with vast experience of the underlying database structure of your specific ERP system as well as the business objectives of the application.

To help you along, many of the major ETL vendors now offer ERP *adapters* to communicate with the popular ERP systems. If you are sourcing from an ERP system, take advantage of the available adapters. They can help you navigate the metadata in these systems and make sense of the application.

Special Considerations for SAP

Because of the marketplace dominance of SAP as an ERP system, we get asked about the role of SAP in the data warehouse. Here are our unvarnished recommendations.

You have probably heard the cliché that, from a decision-support standpoint, SAP ERP is like a black hole: Rivers of data flow in, but there is no way to get the information back out. Why?

A contemporary SAP ERP implementation is likely to have a data foundation that consists of tens of thousands of physical tables, exhibiting few DBMS-defined table relationships, with entity and attribute names rendered in abbreviated German! Thus, the SAP RDBMS, for all practical purposes, is incomprehensible and proprietary. SAP ERP comes with an extensive library of operational reports, but these typically fall short of fully addressing the decision-support needs of most business communities. This is not a design flaw. SAP's OLTP data architecture simply lacks support for fundamental business-reporting needs, such as historical retention of transactions and master data images, comprehensible and easily navigated data structures, and robust query performance characteristics.

Some early SAP adopters tried to free their operational data trapped inside the ERP labyrinth by creating ERP subject areas in their data warehouses, populated via hand-crafted ETL. Predictably, with few specialized tools to assist them in this heroic undertaking, many of these efforts achieved unremarkable degrees of success.

Recognizing this unmet and blossoming need, SAP created a decision-support extension to their ERP application called the Business Information Warehouse (SAP BW). Early generations of SAP BW were rather primitive and consisted mainly of SAP-specialized ETL feeding proprietary OLAP repositories, thus lacking many of the foundational architectural elements of the contemporary data warehouse. Newer releases of SAP BW have evolved considerably and now embrace many of the core tenets and structures of contemporary data warehousing: better support for non-SAP data sources and persistent mainstream data repositories (Staging Areas, ODS, Data Warehouse, Dimensional Data Marts, and OLAP cubes). Some of these repositories support open access by third-party reporting tools.

SAP BW value proposition, at face value, now offers a compelling price and timeframe *sales story* that is likely to attract the attention of CIOs. And so, the contemporary DW architect will likely be asked to define and defend a role for SAP BW within the corporation's overall data warehousing vision.

In the following table, we present pros, cons, and recommendations for several SAP BW role scenarios within an overall enterprise DW strategy. We humbly recognize that this is a rapidly evolving area, with many variables, in which few fully satisfactory solutions exist. BW and ETL tool capabilities will change, thereby modifying the decision balances that follow. But we hope nonetheless that our evaluation process will be useful to you and extensible to your unique situation and challenges.

BW as Enterprise DW	Utilize SAP BW as the foundational core of the enterprise data warehousing strategy.
	We cannot recommend using BW in this role. Making BW the centerpiece of an enterprise BI architecture seems, at present, to be architecturally indefensible. As of this writing, BW offers no unique capabilities for cleansing / integration of non-SAP data or for the delivery of non-SAP analytics. Also, packaged BI tends to offer reduced opportunity for competitive differentiation through analytic capabilities.
	Nonetheless, organizations that do not view BI as an area of strategic competitive differentiation and whose reporting requirements are SAP-centric and well addressed by SAP BW might consider using BW in this role.
BW on the Dimensional DW Bus	Utilize SAP BW as a set of satellite data marts that interoperate within a broader distributed dimensional data warehouse bus architecture.
	Although this may someday become an appropriate way to utilize BW, we find (as of this writing) that BW is not yet well suited to play the role of an ERP-centric data mart within a broader dimensional data warehouse bus architecture. As we write this book, SAP has announced a facility called Master Data Management that claims to handle cross-functional descriptions of products and customers. It is too early to tell if this offers unique capabilities for either creating enterprise-wide conformed dimensions or for incorporating externally conformed dimensions into its ETL processing stream and presenting its facts accordingly. Utilizing conformed dimensions and facts across subject areas is a core tenet of the dimensional data warehouse bus architecture.
	Nonetheless, IT organizations that already have dimensional data warehouses and *inherit* a BW may choose to take on the task of extending BW to utilize externally conformed dimensions, thereby allowing it to plug and play in the bus architecture. Be warned though: Maintenance of these extensions through SAP upgrades may not be a trivial undertaking.
ETL and Staging	Utilize SAP BW as a gateway and staging area for feeding ERP data to a downstream dimensional data warehouse.

This option appears at first to be quite compelling, because it purports to simplify and shorten the work effort to add ERP data into a dimensional data warehouse, while also providing, as a happy benefit, standard BW reporting capabilities for SAP-only reporting. But when comparing this option to the alternative of utilizing a specialized third-party ETL tool with good SAP connectivity (see "Forgo BW" as follows), it may no longer be the optimal solution. Using SAP as a data source through the ETL tool extracyors results in a single set of tables for the DW, typically offering greater control, flexibility, and metadata consistency.

We recommend this option for implementing your ETL system within SAP only to organizations with immature ETL teams under tight timeframes for ERP reporting, who find great value in the canned SAP BW reports. Others should look seriously at a mature ETL tool with good SAP connectors. See "Forgo BW" that follows.

Forgo BW	Utilize the SAP connectors offered by most good ETL tools to populate fully integrated ERP subject areas within a separate enterprise dimensional data warehouse bus architecture.

We're big believers in *buy versus build*, where appropriate. But based on BW's lack of a track record for either creating or publishing conformed dimensions or utilizing externally conformed dimensions, this is our recommended default BW architectural posture.

Part 3: Extracting Changed Data

PROCESS CHECK Planning & Design:
Requirements/Realities → **Architecture** → *Implementation* → **Test/Release**

Data Flow: *Extract* → **Clean** → **Conform** → **Deliver**

During the initial load, capturing changes to data content in the source data is unimportant because you are most likely extracting the entire data source or a potion of it from a predetermined point in time. But once that load is complete, the ability to capture data changes in the source system instantly becomes priority number one. If you wait until the initial load is complete to start planning for change data-capture techniques, you are headed for a heap of trouble. Capturing data changes is far from a trivial task. You must plan your strategy to capture incremental changes to the source data at the onset of your project.

The ETL team is responsible for capturing data-content changes during the incremental load. Desires and hopes are dictated by the users, and the realities of the feasibility of those hopes are revealed by the source system DBA team—if you're lucky. More often than not, a bit of research will be required to determine the best possible incremental load strategy for your specific situation. In this section, we offer several options and discuss the benefits and weaknesses of each. Naturally, you won't need all of these techniques for every situation. Choose the practice that best meets each ETL challenge throughout your project.

> 💡 Determining the appropriate strategy for identifying changed data in the source system may take some detective work. When analyzing source systems, never assume that what you see is what you get. In many cases, there will be unused or disabled audit columns or, even worse, columns used inconsistently. Be sure to allocate enough research time to investigate and determine the best approach to capture data-content changes for your incremental load process.

Detecting Changes

When managers talk about the maintenance of a data warehouse, most often they are talking about keeping the data current so it is a true reflection of the company's operational position. Capturing changes to the source system content is crucial to a successful data warehouse. The maintenance of the data content is dependent on the incremental load process. There are several ways to capture changes to the source data, and all are effective in their appropriate environments.

Using Audit Columns

In most cases, the source system contains audit columns. Audit columns are appended to the end of each table to store the date and time a record was added or modified. Audit columns are usually populated via database triggers fired off automatically as records are inserted or updated. Sometimes, for performance reasons, the columns are populated by the front-end application instead of database triggers. When these fields are loaded by any means other than database triggers, you must pay special attention to their integrity. You must analyze and test each of the columns to ensure that it is a reliable source to indicate changed data. If you find any NULL values, you must to find an alternative approach for detecting change.

The most common environment situation that prevents the ETL process from using audit columns is when the fields are populated by the front-end application and the DBA team allows *back-end* scripts to modify data. If this is the situation in your environment, you face a high risk that you will eventually miss changed data during your incremental loads. A preventative measure to minimize your risk is to stipulate that all back-end scripts be validated by a quality-assurance team that insists and tests that the audit fields are populated by the script before it is approved.

Once you are confident that audit columns are dependable, you need a strategy for utilizing them. There are various methods to implement the utilization of audit columns to capture changes to data. All of the methods have the same logical objective: to compare the last modified date and time of each record to the maximum date and time that existed during the previous load and take all those that are greater.

One approach we've found effective is to utilize the audit columns in the source system. Essentially, the process selects the maximum date and time from the create date and last modified date columns. Some last modified columns are updated upon insertion and with each change to the record. Others are left NULL upon insertion and updated only with changes after the record has already been inserted. When the last modified date is not populated, you must default it with an arbitrary *old* date in order to not lose new records. The following code can help resolve NULL modified dates:

```
select max(greatest(nvl(create_date,'01-JAN-0001'),
nvl(last_mod_date,'01-JAN-0001')))
```

In cases where the rows in the fact table are inserted but never updated, you can simply select records from the source system where the create date and time is greater than the maximum date and time of the previous load and ignore the last modified date column.

Since fact tables and dimension tables can be sourced from many different tables and systems, and since fact tables consist only of foreign keys and measures, you do not store the audit dates in the fact table directly. You need to create an ETL last-change table that captures each source table and the maximum date time found in the source system audit columns at the time of each extract. If your fact table requires audit statistics for its rows, consider implementing an audit dimension as described in Chapter 4.

Database Log Scraping or Sniffing

Log scraping effectively takes a snapshot of the database redo log at a scheduled point in time (usually midnight) and scours it for transactions that affect the tables you care about for your ETL load. Sniffing involves a polling of the redo log, capturing transactions on the fly. Scraping the log for transactions is probably the messiest of all techniques. It's not rare for transaction logs to blow-out, meaning they get full and prevent new transactions from occurring. When this happens in a production-transaction environment, the knee-jerk reaction for the DBA responsible is to empty the contents of the log so the business operations can resume. But when a log is emptied, all transactions within them are lost. If you've exhausted all other techniques and find log scraping is your last resort for finding new or changed records, persuade the DBA to create a special log to meet your specific needs. You presumably need transactions only for a few specific tables out of the hundreds in the source database. Those tables can populate your dedicated log via insert and update triggers.

If you want to pursue log sniffing, we recommend that you survey the available ETL tools in the market to find a proven solution rather than attempt to write the process from scratch. Many real-time ETL solution providers utilize log-sniffing techniques.

Timed Extracts

Select all of the rows where the date in the Create or Modified date fields equal SYSDATE-1, meaning you've got all of yesterday's records. Sounds perfect, right? Wrong. Loading records based purely on time is a common mistake made by most beginning ETL developers. This process is horribly unreliable.

Time-based data selection loads duplicate rows when it is restarted from midprocess failures. This means that manual intervention and data cleanup is required if the process fails for any reason. Meanwhile, if the nightly load process fails to run and misses a day, a risk exists that the missed data will never make it into the data warehouse. Unless your ETL process is extremely straightforward and the data volume is exceptionally small, avoid loading data based purely on time.

Process of Elimination

Process of elimination preserves exactly one copy of each previous extraction in the staging area for future use. During the next run, the process takes the entire source table(s) into the staging area and makes a comparison against the retained data from the last process. Only differences (deltas) are sent to the data warehouse. Albeit not the most efficient technique, the process of elimination is the most reliable of all incremental load techniques for capturing changed data. Because the process makes a row-by-row comparison, looking for changes, it's virtually impossible to miss any data. This technique also has the advantage that rows deleted from the source can be detected. These deleted rows are sometimes missed by other techniques.

This technique can be accomplished inside or out of a database management system. If you prefer using your DBMS, you must bulk load the data into the staging database for efficiency.

Initial and Incremental Loads

Create two tables: previous_load and current_load.

The initial process bulk loads into the current_load table. Since change detection is irrelevant during the initial load, the data continues on to be transformed and loaded into the ultimate target fact table.

When the process is complete, it drops the previous_load table, renames the current load table to previous load, and creates an empty current_load table. Since none of these tasks involve database logging, they are very fast!

The next time the load process is run, the current_load table is populated.

Select the current_load table MINUS the previous_load table. Transform and load the result set into the data warehouse.

Upon completion, drop the previous_load table and rename the current_load table to previous_load. Finally, create an empty current_load table.

Since MINUS is a notoriously slow technique when inside the database management system, you'll want to use the ETL tool or third-party application to perform the process-of-elimination routine.

Extraction Tips

Consider the following points as you approach the extract process:

- **Constrain on indexed columns.** Work with the DBA to ensure all of the columns in your WHERE clause are indexed in the source system; otherwise you will probably provoke a relation scan of the entire production database.

- **Retrieve the data you need.** The optimal query returns exactly what you need. You shouldn't retrieve an entire table and filter out unwanted data later in the ETL tool. One situation that might break this rule is if the transaction system DBA refuses to index columns needed to constrain the rows returned in your query. Another exception is when you are forced to download the entire source database to search for the deltas.

- **Use DISTINCT sparingly.** The DISTINCT clause is notoriously slow. Finding the balance between performing a DISTINCT during the extract query versus aggregating or grouping the results in your ETL tool is challenging and usually varies depending on the percentage of duplicates in the source. Because there are many other factors that can affect this decision, all we can recommend is to take care to test each strategy for the most efficient results.

- **Use SET operators sparingly.** UNION, MINUS, and INTERSECT are SET operators. These, like DISTINCT, are notoriously slow. It's understood that sometimes these operators cannot be avoided. A tip is to use UNION ALL instead of UNION. UNION performs the equivalent of a DISTINCT, slowing the process. The hitch is that UNION ALL returns duplicates, so handle with care.

- **Use HINT as necessary.** Most databases support the HINT keyword. You can use a HINT for all kinds of things, but most importantly to force your query to use a particular index. This capability is especially important when you are using an IN or OR operator, which usually opts for scanning a full table scan rather than using indexes, even when usable indexes exist.

- **Avoid NOT.** If at all possible, avoid non-equi constraints and joins. Whether you use the keyword NOT or the operators '< >', your database will most likely opt to scan a full table rather than utilize indexes.

- **Avoid functions in your where clause.** This is a difficult one to avoid, especially when constraining on dates and such. Experiment with different techniques before committing to use of a function in your WHERE clause. Try using comparison keywords instead of functions whenever possible. For example:

```
LIKE 'J%' instead of SUBSTR('LAST_NAME',1,1 ) = 'J'
EFF_DATE BETWEEN '01-JAN-2002' AND '31-JAN-2002' instead of
TO_CHAR(EFF_DATE, 'YYY-MON' ) = '2002-JAN'
```

The goal of the extract query is to get all of the relevant natural keys and measures. It can be as simple as selecting multiple columns from one table or as complex as actually creating nonexistent data and can range from joining a few tables to joining many tables across heterogeneous data sources. On a specific project, we had to create a periodic snapshot fact table that needed to present sales for every product in inventory even if there were no sales for the product during the specified period. We had to *generate* a product list, get all of the sales by product, and perform an outer join between the product list and the sales by product list, defaulting the nonselling product sales amounts with zero.

Detecting Deleted or Overwritten Fact Records at the Source

Measurement (fact) records deleted or overwritten from source systems can pose a very difficult challenge for the data warehouse if no notification of the deletion or overwrite occurs. Since it is usually infeasible to repeatedly re-extract old transaction records, looking for these omissions and alterations, the best we can offer are the following procedures:

- Negotiate with the source system owners, if possible, explicit notification of all deleted or overwritten measurement records.

- Periodically check historical totals of measurements from the source system to alert the ETL staff that something has changed. When a change is detected, drill down as far as possible to isolate the change.

When a deleted or modified measurement record is identified, the late-arriving data techniques of the previous section can be used. In cases of deleted or modified fact records, rather than just performing a deletion or update in the data warehouse, we prefer that a new record be inserted that implements the change in the fact by canceling or negating the originally posted value. In many applications, this will sum the reported fact to the correct quantity (if it is additive) as well as provide a kind of audit trail that the correction occurred. In these cases, it may also be convenient to carry an extra administrative time stamp that identifies when the database actions took place.

Summary

In this chapter, we have isolated the extract step of the ETL data flow. We recommended that you step back at the very start and make sure the proposed extracts are even worth it! You can make this go/no-go decision with a data-profiling tool that will tell you if data is of sufficient quality to meet your business objectives.

The next big step is preparing the logical data map that connects the original source data to the ultimate final data. Perhaps the most important part of the logical data map is the description of the transformation rules applied between these inputs and outputs. Since a certain amount of discovery and refinement will take place as you actually implement the ETL system, you should expect to go back and periodically update the logical data map. If it is well maintained, it will be perhaps the most valuable description of your ETL system. At some point, a new person will have to decipher what you did, and he or she should start with the logical data map.

The central focus of this chapter was a tour of the various source systems you are likely to encounter. We gave you more than a teaspoon of some of the extract complexities, but of course, nothing is as valuable as real experience.

The last part of the chapter described the challenge of extracting just the new data, the changed data, and even the deleted data. In subsequent chapters, we point out the special processing needed in these situations.

Cleaning and Conforming

Cleaning and conforming are the main steps where the ETL system adds value. The other steps of extracting and delivering are obviously necessary, but they only move and reformat data. Cleaning and conforming actually changes data and provides guidance whether data can be used for its intended purposes.

In this chapter, we urge you to build three deliverables: the data-profiling report, the error event fact table, and the audit dimension. You can build a powerful cleaning and conforming system around these three tangible deliverables.

The cleaning and conforming steps generate potent metadata. Looking backward toward the original sources, this metadata is a diagnosis of what's wrong in the source systems. Ultimately, dirty data can be fixed only by changing the way these source systems collect data. Did we say *business process re-engineering*?

Metadata generated in the cleaning and conforming steps accompanies real data all the way to the user's desktop. Or at least it should. The ETL team must make the cleaning and conforming metadata available, and that is where the audit dimension comes in.

Please stay with us in this chapter. It is enormously important. This chapter makes a serious effort to provide specific techniques and structure for an often amorphous topic. The chapter is long, and you should probably read it twice, but we think it will reward you with useful guidance for building the data cleaning and conforming steps of your ETL system.

If you are new to ETL system design, you may well ask "What should I focus on as a bare minimum?" Perhaps our best answer is: Start by performing the best data-profiling analysis you are capable of. You will then be much more usefully calibrated about the risks of proceeding with your potentially dirty or unreliable data. Armed with these understandings from the data-profiling step, you will have decomposed the problem and you will be more confident in designing a simple error event fact table and a simple audit dimension.

PROCESS CHECK Planning & Design:
Requirements/Realities → *Architecture* → *Implementation* → Test/Release

Data Flow: Extract → *Clean* → *Conform* → Deliver

This chapter is organized into four data-quality topics:

- Part 1: Design Objectives
- Part 2: Cleaning Deliverables
- Part 3: Screens and Their Measurements
- Part 4: Conforming Deliverables

This is a top-down explanation of data quality. In the objectives section, we urge you to be *thorough, fast, corrective* and *transparent*. The perspectives of the cleaning and conforming steps are less about the upside potential of the data and more about containment and control. In some ways, this is unfamiliar territory for the data warehouse team. In the deliverables section, we introduce the mainstay structures of the cleaning subsystem: the error event table and the audit dimension. We also urge you to study Appendix B of Jack Olson's book in order to design a systematic structure for the results of your up-front data-profiling pass.

Descending a level further, the screens section defines a set of checkpoints and filters that you set up in many places to measure data quality. With screens, we build a unified approach to capturing data-quality events and responding to these events with appropriate actions.

 Definition: data-quality screen.

Throughout this chapter, we refer to data-quality screens. We use the word *screen* both to mean report and filter. Thus, a data-quality screen is physically viewed by the ETL team as a status report on data quality, but it's also a kind of gate that doesn't let bad data through.

In the fourth part, we describe the big deliverables of the conforming step: the conformed dimensions and facts and how they are handed off. We also suggest some metadata approaches to keep track of the decisions the organization has made to standardize your dimensions and facts.

Finally, the measurements section is a kind of implementer's guide to specific data-quality issues. Much like the details of the different types of extraction issues we describe in Chapter 3, these data-quality measurements are a reasonable set for you to build upon.

This chapter draws liberally from the work of the leading data-quality authors Jack Olsen and Larry English. Their simple and most direct techniques for measuring data quality have been used in this chapter and placed within a kind of a template for building sensible data-quality ETL processes.

Defining Data Quality

Let's agree on some basic vocabulary, focused on *accuracy*. Accurate data means that the data is:

- **Correct.** The values and descriptions in data describe their associated objects truthfully and faithfully. For example, the name of the city in which one of the authors currently live is called New Hope. Therefore, accurate data about that home address needs to contain New Hope as the city name to be correct.

- **Unambiguous.** The values and descriptions in data can be taken to have only one meaning. For example, there are at least ten cities in the U.S. called New Hope, but there is only one city in Pennsylvania called New Hope. Therefore, accurate data about an address in this city needs to contain New Hope as the city name and Pennsylvania as the state name to be unambiguous.

- **Consistent.** The values and descriptions in data use one constant notational convention to convey their meaning. For example, the U.S. state Pennsylvania might be expressed in data as PA, Penn., or Pennsylvania. To be consistent, accurate data about current home addresses should utilize just one convention (such as the full name Pennsylvania) for state names and stick to it.

- **Complete.** There are two aspects of completeness.
    - The first is ensuring that the *individual* values and descriptions in data are defined (not null) for each instance, for example, by ensuring that all records that should have current addresses actually do.
    - The second aspect makes sure that the *aggregate* number of records is complete or makes sure that you didn't somehow lose records altogether somewhere in your information flow.

A related completeness issue surrounds the alternative meanings of missing values in data. A missing value represented as a null might mean that the true value is unknown or that it does not apply. Missing values may be represented as blanks, or strings of blanks, or as creative descriptions (Don't Know or Refused to Say).

Assumptions

The chapter makes a simplifying number of assumptions about the environment in which cleaning and conforming takes place. The first is that there are distinct points in the ETL job stream into which data-quality processing can be *injected*. Two such points are obvious from our model of the overall ETL data flow.

- The first processing milestone is when data has been *extracted*—which means that data has been extracted from some number of sources and placed into a physical or logical structure that is subject aligned. For example, customer information from various sources initially can be staged in a table, data file, or in-memory structure whose configuration is the same regardless of the data source. Such a structure could be used for incoming data from various data sources deposited and queued for ETL work. Little or no data cleansing or integration has yet been applied; data from one or several sources has simply been restructured and now sits waiting for further processing. This should not imply that data from multiple sources must be processed simultaneously, just that source-independent staging structures are utilized. The ETL data-quality techniques described still work even if source-specific staging structures and processing streams are used, but the metadata examples shown at the end of the chapter might need to be adjusted. We propose running lots of data-quality processes at this stage to get an accurate picture of the state of the organization's data quality while it is still *unvarnished* and to weed out hopelessly flawed data before it fouls up your data-cleansing and integration processes.

- The second milestone is when data has been *cleaned and conformed*—which means data has successfully passed through all of the data-preparation and integration components of the ETL stream and is ready for final packaging in the delivery step. We propose you run more data-quality processes at this stage, as a safety net for your data-cleansing and integration software. In essence, you want to run your newly manufactured information products through some quality-assurance checks before you turn them loose in the world.

For simplicity's sake, this chapter also assumes the use of batch ETL processing—rather than real-time or near real-time processing. We assume that batch processing aligns the techniques presented to the reality of most ETL environments and allows this chapter to direct its focus on data-quality issues and techniques rather than on the complexities of real-time ETL. We turn our attention to streaming ETL in Chapter 11.

Part 1: Design Objectives

PROCESS CHECK Planning & Design:
Requirements/Realities → Architecture → Implementation → Test/Release
Data Flow: Extract → *Clean* → Conform → Deliver

This part discusses the interrelated pressures that shape the objectives of data-quality initiatives and the sometimes conflicting priorities that the ETL team must aspire to balance. We propose some approaches to achieving this balance and in formulating a data-quality policy that meets the needs of important user constituencies.

Understand Your Key Constituencies

The data-quality subsystem must support the roles of data warehouse manager, the information steward, and the information-quality leader. Although these roles may be distributed in different ways across actual personnel, it's useful to characterize these roles.

Data Warehouse Manager

The data warehouse manager owns responsibility for the day-to-day decisions that need to be made in running the data warehouse, ensuring that it is an accurate reflection of the internal and external data sources and that data is processed according to the business rules and policies in place.

The cleaning and conforming subsystems should support the data warehouse manager and the surrounding business community by providing a history of the transformations applied to data as it is loaded into the warehouse, including a detailed audit of all exceptional conditions.

Information Steward

The information steward is accountable for defining the information strategy. This person formalizes the definition of analytic goals, selects appropriate data sources, sets information generation policies, organizes and publishes metadata, and documents limitations of appropriate use.

The cleaning and conforming subsystems should support the information steward by providing metrics on the operational data warehouse's day-to-day adherence to established business policy, issues with the source data that might be testing the boundaries of these policies, and data-quality issues that might call into question the appropriateness of the source data for certain applications.

Information-Quality Leader

The information-quality leader detects, corrects, and analyzes data-quality issues. This person works with the information steward to define policies for dealing with dirty data, setting publication quality thresholds, and balancing the completeness versus speed and corrective versus transparent tradeoffs described in the next section.

The data-quality subsystem should support the information-quality leader by providing data-quality measurements that describe the frequency and severity of all data-quality issues detected during the data warehouse ETL processes. This record should be a complete historical audit, allowing the information-quality leader to assess the success of data-quality improvement efforts over time.

Dimension Manager

The dimension manager creates and publishes one or more of the conformed dimensions used by the overall organization. There may be multiple dimension managers, each responsible for different dimensions. The dimension manager implements the agreements on common descriptive labels reached by various stakeholders in the overall data warehouse. The dimension manager creates and assigns surrogate keys and assigns version numbers to each release of a dimension to the target fact table environments. When a dimension is released to the data warehouse community, it is replicated simultaneously to all the destinations so that they may install the new version of the dimension simultaneously. The job of the dimension manager is centralized: A conformed dimension must have a single, consistent source. We provide more on the role of the dimension manager later in this chapter.

Fact Table Provider

The fact table provider is the local DBA who *owns* the single instance of a given fact table. The fact table provider is responsible for receiving dimensions from various dimension managers, converting local natural keys to the surrogate keys in the conformed dimensions, and making updated fact tables available to the user community. The fact table provider may have to make complex changes in existing fact tables if postdated (late) dimension records are received. Finally, the fact table provider is responsible for creating and administering aggregates, which are physically stored summary records used to accelerate performance of certain queries. We provide more on the role of the fact table provider later in this chapter.

Competing Factors

Four interrelated pressures or priorities shape the objectives of your data-quality system as depicted in Figure 4.1.

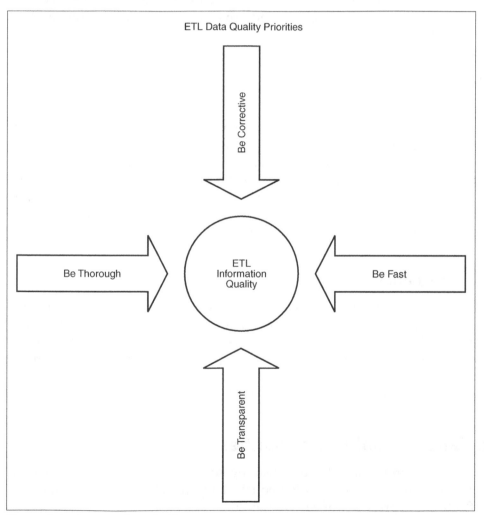

Figure 4.1 Data-quality priorities.

Be Thorough

The data-cleaning subsystem is under tremendous pressure to be thorough in its detection, correction, and documentation of the quality of the information it publishes to the business community. End users want to look to the data warehouse as a source of trusted information—a rock upon which to build their management metrics, strategies, and policies.

Be Fast

The whole ETL pipeline is under tremendous pressure to process ever-growing volumes of data in ever-shrinking windows of time. Some of the newest and most interesting customer touch points are very detailed and intimate—like Web clickstream—and drive huge data volumes into the data warehouse.

Be Corrective

Correcting data-quality problems at or as close to the source as possible is, of course, the only strategically defensible way to improve the information assets of the organization—and thereby reduce the high costs and lost opportunity of poor data quality. However, the reality is that many organizations have not yet established formal data-quality environments or information-quality leaders. In such cases, the data warehouse team might be the first to discover quality issues that have been festering for years. This team is expected to do all that can be done to fix these problems.

Be Transparent

The data warehouse must expose defects and draw attention to systems and business practices that hurt the data quality of the organization. These revelations ultimately drive business process re-engineering, where the source systems and data entry procedures are improved. Undertaking heroic measures to mask data-quality defects at the source might be one of those situations where the remedy can be worse than the disease.

Balancing Conflicting Priorities

Clearly, it is impossible for the cleaning subsystem to address in absolute terms all of these factors simultaneously. They must be properly balanced—reflecting the priorities of each situation.

Completeness versus Speed

The data-quality ETL cannot be optimized for both speed and completeness. Instead, we aspire to find an appropriate point on the exponential relationship curve (see Figure 4.2) that strikes the balance we seek.

A potentially revealing way to best strike this balance is by asking some tough questions about the latency and quality of the data in your to-be-built data warehouse, such as:

- At what point does data staleness set in?

  versus

- How important is getting the data verifiably correct?

If your data warehouse sponsors had to choose, for example, between a higher degree of confidence in data quality and a one-day delay in publication, which would they choose? A data warehouse that publishes daily might, for example, choose to trade one full day of latency for additional data-quality confidence, perhaps through expanded statistical variance testing or data standardization and matching or even selective manual review/auditing. If Monday's operational data were published on Wednesday

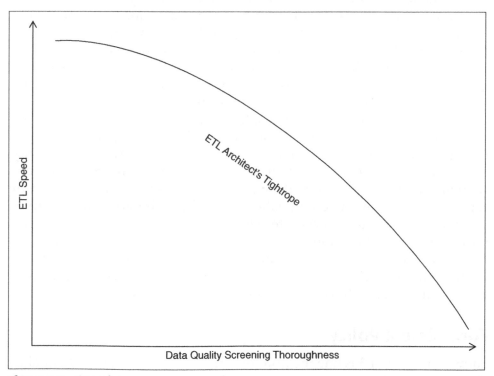

Figure 4.2   Completeness versus speed.

rather than Tuesday, would this be an acceptable trade-off? There are no easy answers to questions like these.

Corrective versus Transparent

The data-cleaning process is often expected to fix dirty data, yet at the same time provide an unvarnished view into the workings of the organization warts and all. Striking a proper balance here is essential: A transparency-at-all-costs system can yield a feeble business-intelligence system that dilutes potential for insight, and a too-corrective system hides/obscures operational deficiencies and slows organizational progress.

The solution is to establish a sensible policy boundary between the types of defects that are *corrected verses highlighted* by the cleaning and to produce an easy-to-use audit facility (the audit dimension) that dutifully documents the modifications, standardizations, and underlying rules and assumptions of the error- detection and data-reengineering components.

Data Quality Can Learn From Manufacturing Quality

The manufacturing quality revolution is now at least 30 years old. The seminal work on quality is W. Edwards Deming's total quality management (TQM) structure. His 14 points of managing TQM are worth reading while thinking about data quality, although outside the immediate scope of this book. But perhaps Deming's main point is that manufacturing quality requires a total commitment across every part of an organization: It is not a single inspector at the end of the assembly line!

Data quality can learn a great deal from manufacturing quality. One big step in this direction is the emergence of centralized data-quality groups in IT organizations. The data warehousing staff concerned with data quality must not operate independently from the data-quality group. The screens we define in this chapter should supplement other screens and assessment capabilities used by the data-quality team. These should feed a comprehensive database that incorporates results from all manner of data-quality measurements, not just the data warehouse. Most of the issues that come from ETL screens will result in demands to improve source systems, not in demands for more cleansing. All of the demands for improving data quality at the source need to be coordinated through the data-quality team.

Formulate a Policy

Shown in Figure 4.3 is one method for categorizing the set of data-quality challenges faced in data warehouse projects and isolating those that should be addressed by the ETL data-quality subsystems:

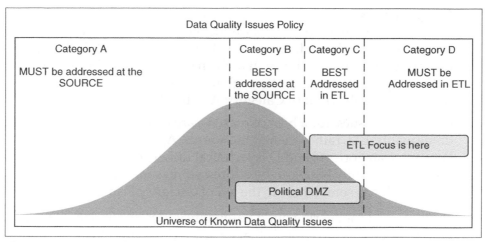

Figure 4.3   Data Quality Issues Policy.

- **Category A** issues, for whatever reason, simply must be addressed at the data source. Examples might include missing information about the subject of a customer complaint or bogus information entered into a field that subjectively captures customer receptivity to a sales call. There is simply no technological way to derive or recreate this information. It must be captured correctly at the source, or it is lost. When addressing Category A data-quality issues, the cleaning subsystems should recognize them as deficiencies at the source, remove any clearly bogus information from the primary reporting and analysis dimensions and facts, and clearly label the information as missing or bogus thereby drawing management focus directly on the source system defect. In most data warehouse projects, the majority of data-quality issues discovered fall into this category—data-quality issues that must be detected and clearly communicated to the end user community.

- **Category D** (we know we are skipping) data-quality issues can only be pragmatically resolved in the ETL system. Examples might include missing or incomplete information from independent third-party data suppliers that can be reliably corrected through integration or the correction of bad data from an inflexible operational source system. Category D issues tend to be relatively rare in most data warehouse projects. In dealing with Category D issues, the ETL system is granted license to undertake creative/heroic measures to correct the data defect, but it must ensure that its polices and actions are visible to users through descriptive and complete metadata.

- **Category B** issues should be addressed at the data source even if there might be creative ways of deducing or recreating the derelict information. The boundary between Categories A and B is therefore technical rather than political. If a given data issue can be addressed with acceptable confidence through technology, it clearly belongs somewhere to the right of Category A in this bell curve.

- **Category C** issues, for a host of reasons, are best addressed in the data-quality ETL rather than at the source. Again, the boundary between Categories C and D is technical rather than political. If a given data-quality issue can be addressed reasonably at the source, it clearly belongs somewhere to the left of Category D in this bell curve.

By dividing and conquering our data-quality issues, we find that the only really tough boundary to define is that between Categories B and C: issues that, from a technology standpoint, can be addressed either at the source or in the ETL system. This is the *Political DMZ (demilitarized zone)*.

Part 2: Cleaning Deliverables

A serious undertaking to improve data quality must be based on rigorous measurement. This should include keeping accurate records of the types of data-quality problems you look for, when you look, what you look at, and the results. Further, you need to be able to answer questions from the data warehouse manager, information steward, and information-quality leader about your processing and the data-quality insights discovered, such as:

- Is data quality getting better or worse?

- Which source systems generate the most/least data-quality issues?

- Are there interesting patterns or trends revealed in scrutinizing the data-quality issues over time?

- Is there any correlation observable between data-quality levels and the performance of the organization as a whole?

Perhaps the data warehouse manager also asks:

- Which of my data-quality screens consume the most/least time in my ETL window?

- Are there data-quality screens that can be retired because the types of issues that they uncover no longer appear in our data?

The data-cleaning subsystem follows the extract step in the overall ETL processing stream. The primary deliverables, discussed in the next three sections, are:

- Data-profiling results
- An error event table
- An audit dimension

Data Profiling Deliverable

Data cleaning must actually start before the first step of building the ETL system. We have strongly urged that you perform a comprehensive data-profiling analysis of your data sources during the up-front planning and design phase. Good data-profiling analysis takes the form of a specific metadata repository describing:

- Schema definitions
- Business objects
- Domains
- Data sources
- Table definitions
- Synonyms
- Data rules
- Value rules
- Issues that need to be addressed

Not only is data profiling a good quantitative assessment of your original data sources; this output should strongly influence the content of the two operations deliverables described as follows. Appendix B of Jack Olson's book, *Data Quality: The Accuracy Dimension*, has a comprehensive list of subcategories expanding the preceding list that should be created through data-profiling analysis to form the basis of the metadata repository.

Cleaning Deliverable #1: Error Event Table

The first major data-cleaning deliverable is a fact table called the error event table and a set of dimensions. This deliverable is structured as a dimensional data model, that is, as a dimensional *star schema*. (See Figure 4.4)

Each data-quality error or issue surfaced by the data-cleaning subsystem is captured as a row in the error event fact table. In other words, the grain of this fact table is each error instance of each data-quality check. Remember that a quality check is a screen. So, if you were to run ten separate screens against some set of data and each screen uncovered ten defective records, a total of 100 records would be written to the error event fact table.

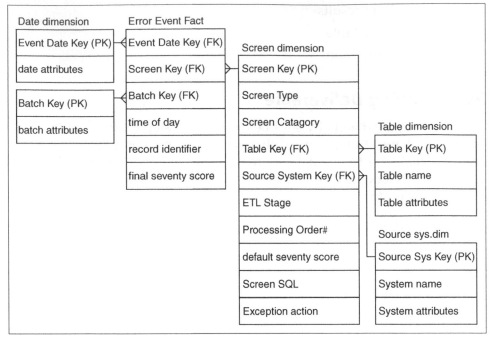

Figure 4.4   Error event table schema.

The event date is a standard dimension representing the calendar date. The time of day is represented in the fact table as the number of seconds since midnight, expressed as an integer.

The batch dimension contains a record for each invocation of the overall batch process—and typically contains interesting timestamps, and numbers of records processed.

The screen dimension table contains constant descriptive information about each data-quality check, or screen, applied. It is not a description of a specific run (that is what the fact table records) but rather is a description of what the screen does and where it is applied. One of its attributes, the default severity score, defines a severity value for each of the various types of errors it may encounter. These error-severity scores are used as the basis of the final severity score error event fact table. For example, the final severity score could be higher than the individual default scores if a large number had accumulated.

The attributes of the screen dimension are as follows:

- The **ETL Stage** describes the stage in the overall ETL process in which the data-quality screen is applied.
- The **Processing Order Number** is a primitive scheduling/ dependency device, informing the overall ETL master process of the order in which to run the screens. Data-quality screens with the same

processing-order number in the same ETL stage can be run in parallel.

- The **Default Severity Score** is used to define the error-severity score to be applied to each exception identified by the screen in advance of an overarching processing rule that could increase or decrease the final severity score as measured in the fact table.

- The **Exception Action** attribute tells the overall ETL process whether it should pass the record, reject the record, or stop the overall ETL process upon discovery of error of this type.

- The **Screen Type** and **Screen Category Name** are used to group data-quality screens related by theme, such as Completeness or Validation or Out-of-Bounds.

- And finally, the **SQL Statement** captures the actual snippet of SQL or procedural SQL used to execute the data-quality check. If applicable, this SQL should return the set of unique identifiers for the rows that violate the data-quality screen so that this can be used to insert new records into the error event fact table.

For reporting purposes, it is useful to associate each screen to the table or set of columns that it scrutinizes, so that the information-quality leader can run reports that identify areas of data-quality problems and track these over time. This is the purpose of the table foreign key in the screen dimension.

The source system dimension identifies the source of the defective data. Because data-quality screens are run against both staged data that belongs to a single data source and data that may have been distilled from several sources, error events can be associated with a special (dummy) *integrated* source system.

The unique identifier of the defective record that allows the error event to be traced directly to the offending record is represented in the fact table as a *degenerate dimension* consisting of the ROWID or other direct pointer to the record in question. Note that with this design there is an implied responsibility to maintain referential integrity between this identifier in the screen dimension table and the real record. If you delete the real record, the screen record will be left as an orphan. The screen category field is simply used to categorize the types of errors detected by the screen. Possible values might include: Incorrect, Ambiguous, Inconsistent, and Incomplete, allowing the analyst to aggregate error events into interesting classifications.

The error event fact table is the central table for capturing, analyzing, and controlling data quality in the ETL system. All error events from all ETL processes should be written to this table. The screen dimension, of course, is the main driver for this table. This schema is the basis of the master control panel for the ETL system.

Cleaning Deliverable #2: Audit Dimension

The error event fact table described in the previous section captures data-cleaning events at the grain of the individual record in any and all tables in the ETL system. Obviously, these events may not occur at the grain of an individual record in a final delivered table being sent across to the front room. To associate data-quality indicators with the final end user fact tables, we need to build a dimension that is single valued at the grain of these tables. We will call this the audit dimension. The audit dimension describes the complete data-quality context of a fact table record being handed to the front room.

The audit dimension is literally attached to each fact record in the data warehouse and captures important ETL-processing milestone timestamps and outcomes, significant errors and their frequency or occurrence for the that record, and an overall data-quality score. Audit dimension records are created as the final step of the processing for cleaned and conformed fact table records and must contain a description of the fixes and changes that have been applied to the record.

> **The audit dimension captures the specific data-quality context of an individual fact table record. This does not usually produce an enormous proliferation of audit dimension records, because the purpose of the audit dimension is to describe each type of data quality encountered. For instance, in the ideal case of a completely clean run of new data to be loaded into a fact table, only one audit record would be generated. Alternatively, if the run was clean except for a few input records that triggered out-of-bounds checks because of abnormally high values, two audit records would be generated: one for normal data records and one for out-of-bounds records. The vast majority of fact records would use the surrogate key for the normal audit record, and the few anomalous fact records would use the surrogate key for the out-of-bounds audit record.**

A representative audit dimension design is shown in Figure 4.5.

The data-quality attributes and overall score are calculated by examining all error event facts for the integrated record and its associated source system records. The audit dimension contains a number of attributes calculated from the error event fact table by summing the error scores of the fact record, the scores of the conformed dimension instances that it is associated with, and each of the source records from which the integrated dimensions and facts were created. If you classify each screen, the aggregated data-quality score for each of these classifications can be carried in the audit dimension as descriptive attributes, both in textual and numeric form. The textual forms are useful for labeling reports with qualitative descriptions of error conditions. The data-quality completeness, validation, and

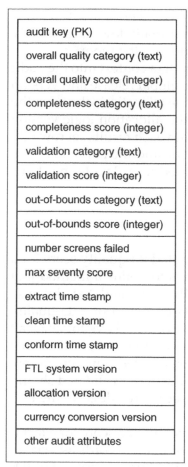

audit key (PK)
overall quality category (text)
overall quality score (integer)
completeness category (text)
completeness score (integer)
validation category (text)
validation score (integer)
out-of-bounds category (text)
out-of-bounds score (integer)
number screens failed
max seventy score
extract time stamp
clean time stamp
conform time stamp
FTL system version
allocation version
currency conversion version
other audit attributes

Figure 4.5 Audit dimension.

out-of-bounds, audit dimension attributes shown in Figure 4.4 are examples of this technique.

Similarly, you can count the total number of error events and the maximum severity score for any one event as interesting attributes to be carried into the audit dimension. Finally, the audit dimension is a perfect placeholder for all of the timestamps and ETL code lineage attributes that you have collected supporting the analysis and troubleshooting tasks of the data warehouse manager.

Perhaps the biggest payoff comes from exposing the audit dimension to the end user community. End user queries and reports can now be run in normal mode and instrumented mode. By simply dragging one of the audit dimension attributes into the query or report, the original results get exploded into the separate contributions made by records with various data-quality conditions. Thus, a reported sales total for a large number of stores could now be broken into three lines (stores with normal sales, stores with abnormally high sales, and stores with abnormally low sales) merely by dragging the out-of-bounds category attribute into the report.

Notice that we have sneaked some global metadata context into the audit dimension! At the bottom of the figure are some global release and version numbers. Thus, if you have changed your revenue allocation scheme in the middle of the reporting period, you can drag the allocation logic version number attribute into the report and it will expand each results set row into the parts that were computed with the old scheme and the parts that were computed with the new scheme. We have elevated metadata to the status of data.

Audit Dimension Fine Points

A broadly accepted method to calculate an overall data-quality score for a fact record has not yet matured. The challenge is to define a method that presents the level of data quality that has actually been validated, doing so in a form that survives anticipated adjustments to the set of data-quality screens performed over time. After all, you don't want to have to revisit all of your data-quality scores for all facts in the warehouse every time that the information-quality leader adjusts the screens. If very few screens are performed, for example, the level of data quality actually validated should be lower than if more comprehensive sets of screens are added to the ETL stream later.

One technique for calculating the validated overall data score for a fact is to sum the error-event severity scores for all error-event records associated to the fact. Of course, this assumes that a source-to-target mapping of IDs is produced as a byproduct of the ETL *matching* data integration function (described later in this chapter). This sum of observed event scores can be subtracted from a worst-case error score scenario to determine the overall validated data-quality score used in the audit dimension. Worst-case error scores represent the sum of the maximum error-severity scores for all screens performed against extracted, cleaned, and conformed data. Thus, if ten distinct screens are performed against a single fact record and nine dimension records—each capable of generating a worst-case, data-quality severity score of ten—the overall worst-cast score total is 100. Restated: If every screen found defects in every screen that it applied, the cumulative data-quality severity score would be 100. Knowing this, you might choose to give this *absolutely flawed* fact an overall score of zero and assign a fact that has zero error events an overall score of 100. This technique, therefore, provides a measure of the overall data quality against the set of screens actually applied. If the organization chooses to add more screens to the ETL process, validated data-quality scores have the potential to rise. This seems reasonable, since the organization is now validating its data to a higher level of quality.

The structure of the audit dimension can be made unique to each fact table. In other words, you may choose to build a family of audit-dimension designs rather than forcing al audit dimensions to contain the same information. This would allow individual diagnoses of the quality of separate facts to be represented in a single audit dimension record. The key here is to preserve the dimensional character of this table.

> 💡 **This section has discussed the design of an audit dimension that describes the data-quality diagnoses and actions pertaining to fact table records. As such, it is cleanly modeled as a dimension on each fact table. But is it possible to have an audit dimension for a dimension? Our answer is no; you don't need this. We prefer to embed the data-quality diagnoses and actions directly in the dimension table itself. Data-quality diagnoses of the overall reliability of the data should be included as additional fields in the dimension itself. Type 1 changes to a dimension (overwrites) can also be described in this way. Type 2 changes (alterations to atrributes at a particular point in time) already have extensive machinery available, including time stamps and reason codes, that can accomplish much of the purposes of a separate audit dimension. If a full audit trail of all changes to the data warehouse structures is needed for compliance reporting, you need to design special structures that record all these changes individually.**

Part 3: Screens and Their Measurements

We are now ready to do some detailed design. This section describes a set of fundamental checks and tests at the core of most data-cleaning engines. It describes what these functions do, how they do it, and how they build upon one another to deliver cleaned data to the dimensional data warehouse. We are greatly indebted to Jack Olsen for creating the organization and vocabulary of the following sections, as described in his book *Data Quality: The Accuracy Dimension*.

PROCESS CHECK Planning & Design:
Requirements/Realities → Architecture → *Implementation* → Test/Release

Data Flow: Extract → *Clean* → Conform → Deliver

Anomaly Detection Phase

A *data anomaly* is a piece of data that does not fit into the domain of the rest of the data it is stored with. Remember when as a child you would be given a picture and would be asked, "What is wrong with this picture?" You would point out the square tires on a bicycle or the upside-down stop sign. Data anomalies are the square tires in the database. Detecting these anomalies requires specific techniques and entails analytical scrutiny. In this section, we explain anomaly detection techniques that have been proven successful on our data warehouse projects.

What to Expect When You're Expecting

Exposure of unspecified data anomalies once the ETL process has been created is the leading cause of ETL deployment delays. Detecting data anomalies takes a great deal of time and analysis. By doing this analysis up front, you save time and reduce frustration. The alternative is to have your time consumed by rebuilding the same ETL jobs over and over again while attempting to correct failed mappings caused by undiscovered data anomalies.

💡 **Finding data anomalies may be perceived by some as data-quality issues outside the data warehouse, and they may well be, but unless your project is budgeted for a full-blown data-quality analysis subproject, chances are that detecting data anomalies will be the responsibility of the ETL team.**

Data Sampling

The simplest way to check for anomalies is to count the rows in a table while grouping on the column in question. This simple query, whose results are shown in Figure 4.6, reveals the distribution of values and displays potentially corrupt data.

```
select state, count(*)
  from order_detail
group by state
```

As you can see in Figure 4.6, data anomalies are instantly exposed. The outliers in the result set are data anomalies and should be presented to the business owner with a strong recommendation that they be cleaned up in the source system.

TECHNICAL NOTE Data-profiling tools are built to perform exactly this kind of data sampling.

Analyzing source data sounds easy, right? What happens when your source table has 100 million rows, with 250,000 distinct values? The best

State	Count(*)
Rhode Island	1
Missisippi	2
New Yourk	5
Connecticut	7
New Mexico	43,844
Vermont	64,547
Mississippi	78,198
Utah	128,956
Wyoming	137,630
Missouri	148,953
Rhode Island	182,067
Minnesota	195,197
North Dakota	203,286
Michigan	241,245
Washington	274,528
Pennsylvania	287,289
Montana	337,128
Louisiana	341,972
Virginia	346,691
West Virginia	359,848
Delaware	422,091
Iowa	456,302
Massachusetts	480,958
Tennessee	483,688
New York	494,332
Nevada	506,235
South Dakota	514,485
Indiana	553,267
Connecticut	562,436

Figure 4.6 Result of value distribution query.

approach to analyzing monster data sources is with *data samples*. We've used many different techniques for sampling data, ranging from simply selecting the first 1,000 rows to using the most elaborate algorithms, none of which are especially remarkable. We find that the following query, which simply counts the rows in the table and slices the table evenly into a specified number of segments, accurately samples the data regardless of the values in the table:

```
select a.*
from employee a,
(select rownum counter, a.*
 from employee a) B
where a.emp_id = b.emp_id and
mod(b.counter, trunc((select count(*)
 from employee)/1000,0)) = 0
```

To examine more or less data, simply alter the 1,000 to the number of rows you'd like returned in your sample.

Another approach involves adding a random number column to data, which can be sorted to select any desired fraction of the total table.

Once you have this sample data, you can perform your value-distribution analysis as usual. Selecting data by any other means, besides selecting all of it, can skew your tests results.

💡 **A common mistake we've noticed is selecting a specific range of dates to narrow a result set. Data corruption usually occurs by bugs in the application program or by untrained staff. Most anomalies we've come across happen temporarily; then either the application is corrected or the person is replaced, and the anomaly disappears. Selecting data within a date range can easily miss these anomalies.**

Types of Enforcement

It is useful to divide the various kinds of data-quality checks into four broad categories:

- Column property enforcement
- Structure enforcement
- Data enforcement
- Value enforcement

Column Property Enforcement

Column property enforcement ensures that incoming data contains expected values from the providing system's perspective. Useful column property enforcement checks include screens for:

- Null values in required columns
- Numeric values that fall outside of expected high and low ranges
- Columns whose lengths are unexpectedly short or long
- Columns that contain values outside of discrete valid value sets
- Adherence to a required pattern or member of a set of patterns
- Hits against a list of known wrong values where list of acceptable values is too long
- Spell-checker rejects

A number of specific screening techniques are discussed later in this chapter for performing precisely this set of validity checks and for capturing exceptions. Based on the findings of these screens, the ETL job stream can choose to:

1. Pass the record with no errors
2. Pass the record, flagging offending column values
3. Reject the record
4. Stop the ETL job stream

The general case is option two, passing records through the ETL stream and recording any validation errors encountered to the error event fact table to make these errors visible to the end user community and to avoid situations where data warehouse credibility is hurt by *Swiss cheese* data completeness. Data records that are so severely flawed that inclusion in the warehouse is either impossible or is damaging to warehouse credibility should be skipped completely, the error event duly noted, of course, in the error event fact table. And finally, data-validation errors that call into question the data integrity of the entire ETL batch should stop the batch process completely, so that the data warehouse manager can investigate further. The screen dimension contains an exception action column that associates one of these three possible actions to each screen.

Structure Enforcement

Whereas column property enforcement focuses on individual fields, structure enforcement focuses on the relationship of columns to each other. We enforce structure by making sure that tables have proper primary and foreign keys and obey referential integrity. We check explicit and implicit hierarchies and relationships among groups of fields that, for example, constitute a valid postal mailing address. Structure enforcement also checks hierarchical parent-child relationships to make sure that every child has a parent or is the supreme parent in a family.

Data and Value Rule Enforcement

Data and value rules range from simple business rules such as *if customer has preferred status, the overdraft limit is at least $1000* to more complex logical checks such as *a commercial customer cannot simultaneously be a limited partnership and a type C corporation*. Value rules are an extension of these reasonableness checks on data and can take the form of aggregate value business rules such as *the physicians in this clinic are reporting a statistically improbable number of sprained elbows requiring MRIs*. Value rules can also provide a probabilistic warning that the data may be incorrect. There indeed are boys named *Sue*, at least in Johnny Cash's song, but maybe such a record should be flagged for inspection. A priori if this record is incorrect, you don't know whether it is the name or the gender that should be corrected.

💡 **These kinds of findings are hard to include in the error event fact table because the violations involve multiple records. Individual incorrect records are impossible to identify. One is left with two choices: Either tag all such records (sprained elbow requiring MRI) as suspect, or establish a virtual aggregate table on which errors can be reported as a count of incidences.**

Measurements Driving Screen Design

PROCESS CHECK Planning & Design:
Requirements/Realities → Architecture → *Implementation* → Test/Release

Data Flow: Extract → *Clean* → Conform → Deliver

This section discusses what needs to go into the data-cleaning baseline for the data warehouse, including simple methods for detecting, capturing, and addressing common data-quality issues and procedures for providing the organization with improved visibility into data-lineage and data-quality improvements over time.

Overall Process Flow

A series of data-quality screens or *error checks* are queued for running—the rules for which are defined in metadata. Each screen is described in the screen dimension we build as part of the error event schema in the early part of this chapter. As each screen is run, each occurrence of errors encountered is recorded in an error event record. The metadata for each error check also describes the severity of the error event. The most severe data-quality errors are classified as fatal errors that will cause overall ETL processing to stop. An example of a condition that drives the creation of a fatal error event might be discovering that daily sales from several stores are completely missing or that an *impossible* invalid value for an important column has appeared for which there are no transformation rules.

When each of the data-quality checks has been run, the error event fact table is queried for fatal events encountered during the overall data-quality process. If none are found, normal ETL processing continues; otherwise, a *halt* condition is returned to the overall calling ETL process, which should then perform an orderly shutdown of the overall ETL process and proactively notify the data warehouse administrator and/or information-quality steward. This process is depicted in Figure 4.7.

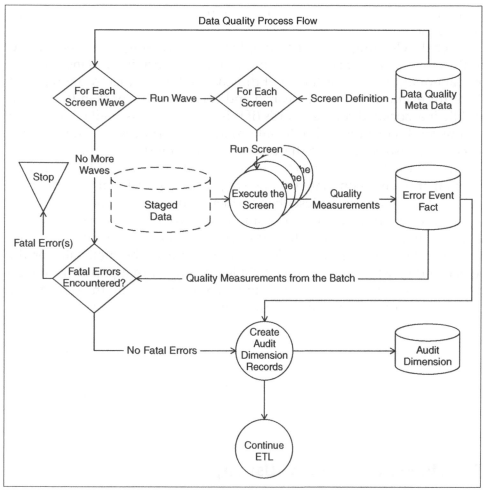

Figure 4.7   Overall process flow.

For highest performance, the goal of the data-cleaning subsystem processing stream is to invoke *waves* of screens that can be run in parallel. These screens identify data-quality issues and insert records into the error event fact table. To minimize database contention issues, you should avoid unneeded indexing or constraints on the error event fact table so that records can stream into this table from several screen processes simultaneously without causing problems. The calling process waits for each *wave* of screens to complete before invoking the next wave of screens—until there are no more screen waves left to run. As indicated earlier in this chapter, the processing-order number of the screen metadata table is used for scheduling screens. Screens with the same processing order can be run in parallel. Standard data warehouse job scheduling tools can also be utilized for more comprehensive scheduling of screens and management of their dependencies.

When the cleaning subsystem completes its processing of the cleaned and conformed records, it performs some additional work in deriving an overall data-quality score for the audit dimension. It does this by aggregating the error event facts for the cleaned and conformed records in the stream and their associated source records (if this relationship is available)—saved as a byproduct of the ETL integration/matching processes. Interestingly, screens can also be applied to the error event fact table itself, allowing special screens to be established that measure the number and types of data-quality errors that have accumulated at any stage of the overall data-cleaning job stream. This technique is described further in the next section.

The recommended method for running screens is to build a generic software module that can execute any screen, given a batch ID and a screen surrogate key as parameters. This module extracts the metadata for the screen and constructs a dynamic INSERT statement that populates the error event fact table for each offending record returned by the screen. The general form of the dynamic INSERT statement is as follows:

```
INSERT INTO data_quality_error_event_fact
        (etl_batch_surrogate_key, day and time of day surrogate keys,
        list of values from the Screen Meta Data record,
        offending_record_surrogate_key)
SELECT  offending_record_surrogate_keys provided by the Screen's SQL
Statement
```

The Show Must Go On—Usually

A guiding principle of the data-cleaning subsystem is to detect and record the existence of data-quality errors, not to skip records or to stop the ETL stream. Data-quality issues are an unfortunate fact of life in the data warehousing arena, and business managers are forced to make tough decisions every day in the face of incomplete and inaccurate data. This situation will not change overnight. Instead, you should aspire to provide the organization with tools to gauge the quality of the data they are utilizing and to measure their progress in improving data quality over time.

That said, the data-cleaning subsystem must also provide some mechanism for dealing with unexpected conditions, including data records that are simply too flawed to be permitted into the data warehouse or data records that indicate a systemic flaw so severe as to warrant a halt to the overall ETL process. For practical and political reasons, the thresholds for triggering these exceptional remedies must be balanced to allow the data warehouse to remain a viable and useful tool to the business, yet still provide enough assuredness of data quality to maintain system credibility within the end user community. This can be a tough balance to strike and is likely to be adjusted over time. So the ETL data-quality subsystem should support the ability to tune these thresholds and change the course of action to take when data-quality errors are encountered.

In some cases, exceptional actions might need to be taken if too many low-level error conditions are detected. For example, the existence of an invalid U.S. state code in a customer address record would typically cause an error event to be written to the data-quality subject area but would not stop the overall ETL process. If *all* of the records in the batch have invalid U.S. state codes, though, this probably indicates a severe problem in some upstream process—severe enough to call into question the overall integrity of all data in the ETL stream. It is recommended that cases like this be handled by creating additional data-quality screens run directly against the error event fact table, counting the number of data quality error event records captured in the overall data-cleaning batch and triggering exception processing.

> Take care with these special screens in their writing of their error findings back to the error event fact. They are reading from and writing to the same table—a recipe for database contention problems. Rather than writing error events for each offending record back to the fact, as do most other data-quality screens, they should instead aggregate error conditions of a specific type from a specific source table and write a single record error event fact if the aggregate exceeds the allowable threshold. This should sidestep most common contention issues.

Screens

Before screens can be run, you should have established an overall data-profiling baseline. This should include defining column specifications for nullity, numeric column ranges, character column length restrictions, and table counts. There is no substitute for performing in-depth research on data, on a source-by-source basis, for determining the characteristics of high-quality examples of data. This research should contain a review of the technical documentation of the data providers and a column-by-column review of the source data itself. For each data source to be loaded into the data warehouse, a data-profiling checklist should include:

- Providing a history of record counts by day for tables to be extracted
- Providing a history of totals of key business metrics by day
- Identifying required columns
- Identifying column sets that should be unique
- Identifying columns permitted (and not permitted) to be null

- Determining acceptable ranges of numeric fields
- Determining acceptable ranges of lengths for character columns
- Determining the set of explicitly valid values for all columns where this can be defined
- Identifying frequently appearing invalid values in columns that do not have explicit valid value sets

Without dedicated data-profiling tools, a limited subset of the data-profiling benefits can be obtained with hand-coded SQL, a team of subject matter experts, and time and effort. This make-versus-buy tradeoff mirrors the discussion of choosing an overall ETL tool we present at the beginning of this book. In other words, the vendor-supplied tools are continuously raising the bar, making it less and less practical to roll your own, unless your needs and aspirations are very modest. The findings from the data-profiling exercise should be maintained by the information-quality leader—who can then apply them directly to the data-quality screen metadata definitions that drive the ETL data-quality process.

Known Table Row Counts

In some cases, the information-quality leader absolutely knows, through business policy, the number of records to be expected of a given data type from a given data provider. An example of this might be a weekly inventory of parts from a warehouse, where the inventory of all active parts must be provided—even if zero. In other cases, the information-quality leader can infer a range of acceptable records to expect from a given data-provider-based history and build screens that detect record counts that are uncharacteristically high or low. The known table record count case can be handled by simple screen SQL, such as the following:

```
SELECT      COUNT(*)
FROM        work_in_queue_table
WHERE       source_system_name = 'Source System Name''
HAVING      COUNT(*) <> 'Known_Correct_Count'
```

Because this is a table-level screen, the cleaned or conformed record identifier of the error event fact should be stored as a NULL.

Column Nullity

The determination of which columns are required (versus allowed to be null) in data records is very important and typically varies by source system. For example, a point-of-sale operational system might be permitted to have missing customer address attributes, but a record from a shipping system might demand non-null values. The metadata structures proposed capture nullity rules on a source-by-source basis. In dimensional models, integrated records often have more restrictive nullity rules than source data, because nearly all dimensional attribute columns are required to be populated—even if with only *Unknown*, *Not Applicable*, or *Not Available* descriptive strings.

> 💡 **Systematically populating null text fields with an actual value removes the ambiguity of whether the field is missing or legitimately empty. This technique also simplifies many SQL lookups; unfortunately, relational databases treat the empty text field differently from the null text field. Even if a value is not supplied for the null text field, we recommend at least converting all null text fields to empty text fields.**

The proposed approach for testing nullity is to build a library of source-specific nullity SQL statements that return the unique identifiers of the offending rows, such as the following:

```
SELECT      unique_identifier_of_offending_records
FROM        work_in_queue_table
WHERE       source_system_name = 'Source System Name'
AND         column IS NULL
```

For screening errors from integrated records, you might adjust the SQL slightly to use your special *dummy* source system name, as follows:

```
SELECT      unique_identifier_of_offending_records
FROM        work_in_queue_table
WHERE       source_system_name = 'Integrated'
AND         column IS NULL
```

Rows are inserted into the error event fact for each offending record returned by this screen, and the unique identifiers of the offending rows are written into the fact table as degenerate dimensions.

Column Numeric and Date Ranges

Although many numeric and date columns in relational database tables tolerate a wide range of values, from a data-quality perspective, they may have ranges of validity that are far more restrictive. Is it believable that a single customer transaction is for one million units? Perhaps yes, if our business is a global B2B exchange, but no, if this is a consumer retail point-of-sale transaction. You want your data-cleaning subsystem to be able to detect and record instances of numeric columns that contain values that fall outside of what the information-quality leader defines as valid ranges. In some cases, these valid value ranges will be defined by the source system. In other cases, especially for numeric columns that participate in sensitive ETL calculations, these ranges might need to be set by the information steward. Here again, columns of integrated data may have valid numeric ranges different from those of any data source, so you need to validate these with separate screens. An example of a SQL SELECT statement to screen these potential errors follows:

```
SELECT      unique_identifier_of_offending_records
FROM        work_in_queue_table
WHERE       source_system_name = 'Source System Name'
AND         numeric_column IS NOT BETWEEN min AND max
```

💡 **Suppose we have a fact table that tracks daily sales in 600 stores, each of which has 30 departments. We therefore receive 18,000 sales numbers each day. This note describes a quick statistical check, based on calculating standard deviations, that allows us to judge each of the 18,000 incoming numbers for** *reasonableness.* **The technique also lets us quickly update the statistical base of numbers to get ready for tomorrow's data load.**

Remember that the standard deviation is the square root of the variance. The variance is the sum of the squares of the differences between each of the historical data points and the mean of the data points, divided by N-1, where N is the number of days of data. Unfortunately, this formulation requires us to look at the entire time history of sales, which, although possible, makes the computation unattractive in a fast-moving ETL environment. But if we have been keeping track of SUM_SALES and SUM_SQUARE_SALES, we can write the variance as (1/(N-1))*(SUM_SQUARE_SALES - (1/N)*SUM_SALES*SUM_SALES). Check the algebra!

So if we abbreviate our variance formula with VAR, our data-validity check looks like:

```
SELECT s.storename, p.departmentname, sum(f.sales)
FROM fact f, store s, product p, time t, accumulatingdept a
WHERE
   (first, joins between tables... )
f.storekey = s.storekey and f.productkey = p.productkey and
f.timekey = t.timekey and s.storename = a.storename and
p.departmentname = a.departmentname and
   (then, constrain the time to today to get the newly loaded data... )
t.full_date = #October 13, 2004# and
   (finally, invoke the standard deviation constraint... )
HAVING ABS(sum(f.sales) - (1/a.N)*a.SUM_SALES) > 3*SQRT(a.VAR)
```

We expand VAR as in the previous explanation and use the *a.* **prefix on N, SUM_SALES and SUM_SQUARE_SALES. We have assumed that departments are**

groupings of products and hence are available as a rollup in the product dimension.

Embellishments on this scheme could include running two queries: one for the sales MORE than three standard deviations above the mean and another for sales LESS than three standard deviations below the mean. Maybe there is a different explanation for these two situations. This would also get rid of the ABS function if your SQL doesn't like this in the HAVING clause. If you normally have significant daily fluctuations in sales (for example, Monday and Tuesday are very slow compared to Saturday), you could add a DAY_OF_WEEK to the accumulating department table and constrain to the appropriate day. In this way, you don't mix the normal daily fluctuations into our standard deviation test.

When you are done checking the input data with the preceding SELECT statement, you can update the existing SUM_SALES and SUM_SQUARE_SALES just by adding today's sales and today's square of the sales, respectively, to these numbers in the accumulating department table.

Column Length Restriction

Screening on the length of strings in textual columns is useful in both staged and integrated record errors. An example of this screen might check customer last names that you believe are too long or too short to be credible. Here is an example of a SQL SELECT that performs such a screening:

```
SELECT      unique_identifier_of_offending_records
FROM        work_in_queue_table
WHERE       source_system_name = 'Source System Name'
AND         LENGTH(numeric_column) IS NOT BETWEEN min AND max.
```

Column Explicit Valid Values

In cases where a given column has a set of known discrete valid values as defined by its source system, you can screen for exceptions by looking for occurrences of default *unknown* values in the processed columns. Alternatively, you can treat this as a staging screen by using the generic column validity reference table of valid values for columns from any data providers. Therefore, a representative SQL statement might be:

```
SELECT      unique_identifier_of_offending_records
FROM        work_in_queue_table Q
WHERE       source_system_name = 'Source System Name'
AND         column NOT EXISTS
(           SELECT anything
            FROM    column_validity_reference_table
            WHERE   column_name = "column_name"
```

```
          AND        source_system_name = 'Source System Name'
          AND        valid_column_value = Q.column_value
     )
```

Column Explicit Invalid Values

In cases where a given column is routinely populated with values known to be incorrect and for which there is no known set of discreet valid values, the information-quality leader might choose to explicitly screen for these invalid values. An example might be the periodic appearance of strings like UNKNOWN in a customer last name field—where the set of all potentially valid customer last names is undefined. The explicit invalid values screen should obviously not attempt to exhaustively filter out all possible invalid values—just pick off the frequent offenders. Other data-cleaning technologies, such as name and address standardization and matching, are far more appropriate for these tasks. For simplicity's sake, the example that follows hard-codes the offending strings into the screen's SQL statement.

```
SELECT      unique_identifier_of_offending_records
FROM        work_in_queue_table
WHERE       source_system_name = 'Source System Name'
AND         UPPER(column) IN ("UNKNOWN", "?", list of other
            frequent offenders... )
```

A slightly more elegant approach might compare the data values to a table full of frequent offenders, as in:

```
SELECT      unique_identifier_of_offending_records
FROM        work_in_queue_table Q
WHERE       source_system_name = 'Source System Name'
AND         EXISTS
( SELECT 'Got One' FROM Table_Of_Frequent_Offenders WHERE column_name =
Q.column_name)
```

If the set of valid values for a column is too large to be explicitly defined or is unknown, this type of screen has limited value, but in some useful cases the set of recently found violations can be used; data-entry people tend to repeat these violations over and over.

Checking Table Row Count Reasonability

This class of screens is quite powerful but a bit more complex to implement. It attempts to ensure that the number of rows received from a data source is reasonable—meaning that the row counts fall within a credible range based on previously validated record count histories. To test table row count reasonability, you can choose from a number of simple statistical tests such

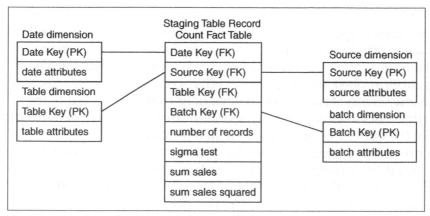

Figure 4.8 Table level reasonability metadata.

as calculating the number of standard deviations a value falls from the mean of previous similar values or opting for more advanced and professional value predictors such as the X.12 standard or even ARIMA (Autoregressive Integrated Moving Average) techniques. If you are interested in some of these powerful statistical tools, you'll need a few weeks of consulting with a good statistician. A good place to find such a statistician is in your marketing research department, if you have such a department.

The data-staging table record count table shown in Figure 4.8 captures the number of records processed from each data source each day for each table—one row per data source per day.

Figure 4.8 presents these tables in a dimensional structure. Some ETL tools create similar tables as a byproduct of their normal operation. Using the data-staging table record count table, the SQL for this screen might be handled in two passes, as follows:

```
SELECT      AVERAGE(Number_of_Records)-3 * STDDEV(Number_of_Records),
            AVERAGE(Number_of_Records) + 3 * STDDEV(Number_of_Records)
INTO        Min_Reasonable_Records,
            Max_Reasonable_Records
FROM        data_staging_table_record_count
WHERE       source_system_name = 'Source System Name"
;
SELECT      COUNT(*)
FROM        work_in_queue_table
WHERE       source_system_name = 'Source System Name"
HAVING      COUNT(*) NOT BETWEEN
            Min_Reasonable_Records AND Max_Reasonable_Records
;
```

Clever SQL gurus can implement the preceding screen as either multipass SQL (as shown), single pass SQL for each data source, or a single screen that validates table record count reasonability from all sources—depending on specific data-quality requirements and severity score flexibility needed. The information-quality leader might also choose to define multiple screens for the same table and source system, with a different number of standard deviation tolerances applied and different severity scores, for example, recording low severity errors at two standard deviations from mean, graduating to high severity errors at three standard deviations from mean and to outright stoppage of the entire ETL stream at four standard deviations.

The table row count screen can easily be extended to support reasonability testing of any additive metric in the data warehouse. For example, by adding a total sales metric to the table in Figure 4.8, screens can be written that identify situations when sales metrics are inexplicitly skewed:

```
SELECT      AVERAGE(Total_Sales_Dollars)-3
            * STDDEV(Total_Sales_Dollars),
            AVERAGE(Total_Sales_Dollars) + 3
            * STDDEV(Total_Sales_Dollars)
INTO        Min_Reasonable_Sales_Dollars,
            Max_Reasonable_Sales_Dollars
FROM        staging_table_record_count
WHERE       source_system_name = 'Source System Name"
;
SELECT      SUM(Total_Sales_Dollars)
FROM        work_in_queue_table
WHERE       source_system_name = 'Source System Name"
HAVING      SUM(Total_Sales_Dollars) NOT BETWEEN
            Min_Reasonable_Sales Dollars AND
            Max_Reasonable_Sales_Dollars
```

Checking Column Distribution Reasonability

The ability to detect when the distribution of data across a dimensional attribute has strayed from normalcy is another powerful screen. This screen enables you to detect and capture situations when a column with a discrete set of valid values is populated with a data distribution that is *skewed* abnormally. For example, the column being screened might be the product presented in a sales call fact from a sales force automation (SFA) system. Assume that history tells you that most sales calls are devoted to the presentation of product A (for which sales are highly compensated) and that very few present product B (which offers little reward to the sales force). You want to design a screen that will alert the information-quality leader if, say, you suddenly see too few sales calls for product A or too many sales calls for product B.

You build this screen by following an approach similar to the table row count reasonability technique described previously. Again, you are going to need a staging table to keep historical counts of the number of records seen for the valid values of a column over time, from which you can calculate means and standard deviations for your screen. Because there are often many possible values for a given column, and many columns with a discrete set of valid values, you will need to deviate from your metadata norms and propose staging tables that are specific to the table and sets of columns that are to be scrutinized by the screen. Of course, this increases the number of data-staging tables needed, but it affords the ETL architect much greater flexibility in physical implementation of these potentially large tables. In some cases, even this less-generalized data-staging approach generates a table that is too large to be used for high-performance ETL processing, so one can use the statistical technique described in a previous section for judging the mean and standard deviation of the data.

Note that the statistical approach described can also be used to support multicolumn screening—that is, testing for reasonability across several column combinations of valid values. Earlier in this chapter, we refer to this as value rule enforcement. An example of this might be scrutinizing daily sales by product and store, or daily sales by product, store, and day of the week, looking for results that are unreasonably skewed from historical norms.

Modifying the table in Figure 4.8 to add product as a dimension allows us capture daily sales-call counts by product. Using this table, the screen can compare the average sales-call totals by product code and source seen historically to those in the current ETL batch. Those products whose averages exceed the established threshold of standard deviations (as defined in the block of SQL in the screen definition) should have error event records written to the fact table.

Processing this type of screen using the technique described requires procedural programming on a level well supported by mainstream procedural SQL language extensions. This procedural SQL can be included in the screen SQL statement definition or handled outside of it. The important thing is for the ETL architect to be consistent in maintaining a screen metadata instance for all screens and in populating the error event fact for all error events surfaced by all screens.

Regardless of the implementation method chosen, the error event facts created by this screen are considered to be table-level screens, so the cleaned/conformed record identifier of the error event fact should be NULL.

General Data and Value Rule Reasonability

Data and value rules as defined earlier in the chapter are subject-matter specific, so we cannot give a list of specific checks for you to implement. But the form of the reasonableness queries clearly is similar to the simple data column and structure checks given in this section as examples.

Part 4: Conforming Deliverables

Integration of data means creating *conformed* dimension and fact instances built by combining the best information from several data sources into a more comprehensive view. To do this, incoming data somehow needs to be made structurally identical, filtered of invalid records, standardized in terms of its content, deduplicated, and then distilled into the new conformed image. In this section, we describe a three-step process for building conformed dimensions and facts:

- Standardizing
- Matching and deduplication
- Surviving

When we conform data, we may convert Gender Codes of (M, F), (M, W), and (Man, Woman) from three different data providers into a standard gender dimension attribute of (Male, Female). Similarly we can conform name and address information using specialized tools.

☀ **Conforming descriptive attributes across multiple data sources, multiple data marts, and multiple remote clients participating in a distributed data warehouse is one of the key development steps for the data warehouse architect and the ETL team. Much has been written on the technical, administrative, and organizational affects this of this subject in the other Toolkit books. The immediate concerns of the ETL team are capturing the full range of overlapping and conflicting inputs and supporting the needs of the dimension manager and the fact-table provider.**

Conformed Dimensions

Regardless of the hardware architecture, every data warehouse is distributed in a certain sense because separate kinds of measurements must always exist in separate fact tables. The same statement is true in an ER-modeled environment. So, for an end user application to combine data from separate fact tables, we must implement consistent interfaces to these fact tables so that data can be combined. We call these consistent interfaces *conformed dimensions* and *conformed facts*.

A conformed dimension means the same thing with every possible fact table to which it can be joined. Often, this means that a conformed dimension is identical for each fact table. A more precise definition of conformed dimensions is:

attribute from conformed dimension ↓	fact table 1	fact table 2	fact table 3	computed column
Product	Manufacturing Shipments	Warehouse Inventory	Retail Sales	Turns
Framis	2940	1887	761	21
Toggle	13338	9376	2448	14
Widget	7566	5748	2559	23

Procedure: 1) open separate connection to each source
2) assemble all three answer sets
3) merge answer sets on the conformed row headers (product).

Figure 4.9 Drilling across three fact tables.

Two dimensions are conformed if they share one or more attributes whose values are drawn from the same domains. A requesting application must use only these common attributes as the basis for constraints and groupings when using the conformed dimensions to drill across separate fact tables.

Figure 4.9 illustrates the drill-across process for three fact tables supporting a conformed product dimension.

Examples of dimensions frequently conformed include customer, product, location, deal (promotion), and calendar (time). A major responsibility of the central data warehouse design team is to establish, publish, maintain, and enforce conformed dimensions.

The establishment of a conformed dimension is a very significant step for an organization. We describe the organization decisions and the overall procedure for arriving at the definitions of conformed dimensions in *Data Warehouse Lifecycle Toolkit*. A conformed customer dimension is a master table of customers with a clean surrogate customer key and many well-maintained attributes describing each customer. It is likely that the conformed customer dimension is an amalgamation and a distillation of data from several legacy systems and possibly outside sources. The address fields in the customer dimension, for instance, should constitute the best mailable address known for each customer anywhere within the enterprise. It is often the responsibility of the central data warehouse team to create the conformed customer dimension and provide it as a resource to the rest of the enterprise, both for legacy use and for data warehouse use.

The conformed product dimension is the enterprise's agreed-upon master list of products, including all product rollups and all product attributes. A good product dimension, like a good customer dimension, should have at least 50 separate textual attributes.

The conformed calendar dimension will almost always be a table of individual days, spanning a decade or more. Each day will have many useful attributes drawn from the legal calendars of the various states and countries the enterprise deals with, as well as special fiscal calendar periods and marketing seasons relevant only to internal managers.

Conformed dimensions are enormously important to the data warehouse. Without strict adherence to conformed dimensions, the data warehouse cannot function as an integrated whole. If a dimension like customer or product is used in a nonconformed way, either the separate fact tables simply cannot be used together or, worse, attempts to use them together will produce wrong results. To state this more positively, conformed dimensions make possible a single dimension table to be used against multiple fact tables in the same database space, consistent user interfaces and consistent data content whenever the dimension is used, and a consistent interpretation of attributes and therefore rollups across different fact tables.

Designing the Conformed Dimensions

Identifying and designing the conformed dimensions should take a few weeks. Most conformed dimensions will naturally be defined at the most granular (atomic) level possible. The grain of the customer and product dimensions will naturally be the lowest level at which those entities are tracked in the source systems. The grain of the date dimension will usually be a day.

Taking the Pledge

If the central data warehouse team succeeds in defining and providing a set of master conformed dimensions for the enterprise, it is extremely important for the owners of separate fact tables to use these dimensions. The commitment to use the conformed dimensions is much more than a technical decision. It is a business-policy decision that is key to making the enterprise data warehouse function. The use of the conformed dimensions should be supported at the highest executive levels. This issue should be a sound bite for the enterprise CIO.

Permissible Variations of Conformed Dimensions

It is possible to create a subset of a conformed dimension table for certain fact tables if you know that the domain of the associated fact table contains only that subset. For example, the master product table can be restricted to just those products manufactured at a particular location if the data mart in question pertains only to that location. We can call this a simple data subset, since the reduced dimension table preserves all the attributes of the original dimension and exists at the original granularity.

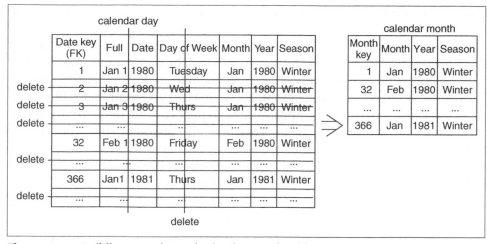

Figure 4.10 Building a conformed calendar month table.

A rollup data subset systematically removes both rows and columns from the original dimension table. For example, it is common to restrict the date dimension table from days down to months. In this case, we may keep only the record describing the first day of each month, but we must also remove all those attributes like Day-of-Week and Holiday-Flag that make sense only at a daily grain. See Figure 4.10.

Perhaps you are wondering how to create queries in an environment where the conformed dimensions can be subsetted? Which dimension table should be used where? Actually, it is much simpler than it sounds. Each dimension table is naturally paired with its companion fact table. Any application that drills across fact tables must inevitably use multipass SQL to query each data mart separately and in sequence. It is usually the case that a separate SQL query is generated for each column in a drill-across report. The beauty of using conformed dimensions is that the report will run to completion *only if* the dimension attributes used in the report are found in each dimension table. Since the dimensions are conformed, the business answers are guaranteed to be consistent. The numbers will also be comparable if we have established conformed fact definitions.

Conformed Facts

We have talked thus far about the central task of setting up conformed dimensions to tie our data marts together. This is 80 percent of the up-front architectural effort. The remaining 20 percent is establishing standard fact definitions.

Fortunately, identifying the standard fact definitions is done at the same time as the identification of the conformed dimensions. We need standard fact definitions when we use the same terminology across fact tables and when we build single reports that drill across fact tables as described in the previous section.

Establishing conformed dimensions is a collaborative process wherein the stakeholders for each fact table agree to use the conformed dimensions. During conforming meetings, stakeholders also need to identify similar facts present in each of the fact tables. For instance, several fact tables may report revenue. If end user applications expect to add or compare these revenue measures from separate fact tables, the business rules that define these revenue measures must be the same. Perhaps revenue is measured by one group at the end of the month, whereas another group measures revenue on a rolling billing period. Or perhaps one group measures total sales, but another group measures only the Generally Accepted Accounting Principles (GAAP) recognized portion of the sale.

Conformed facts can be directly compared and can participate in mathematical expressions such as sums or ratios. If the stakeholders of the fact tables can reach agreement, the data-preparation steps for some or all of the fact tables may involve transformations of the facts in order to meet the common definition.

The Fact Table Provider

Although this section is more of an operational discussion, we want to complete the picture of the conforming dance we have described in this part of the chapter. In the next section, we define the role of a dimension manager, a centralized authority who prepares and publishes conformed dimensions to the community. The *fact table provider* is the receiving client of the dimension manager. The fact table provider owns one or more fact tables and is responsible for how they are accessed by end users. If fact tables participate in any enterprise-wide drill across applications, by definition they must use conformed dimensions provided by the dimension manager, and they must carefully prepare the numeric facts that have been identified by the organization as conformed (standardized) facts.

The Dimension Manager: Publishing Conformed Dimensions to Affected Fact Tables

A conformed dimension is by necessity a centrally managed object. A master *dimension manager* needs to be appointed by the organization to administer and publish each conformed dimension.

When the dimension manager releases a new version of a dimension, it is incumbent on the fact table provider to update local copies of the dimension as soon as possible. Ideally, the published dimension contains a version number field in every record, and all drill-across applications are enforcing the equality of this version number as they combine separate answer sets in the final step of preparing reports. If the fact table provider is tardy in updating dimensions, the drill-across application should fail because the version numbers don't match. Although this sounds harsh, it is very important for this discipline to be enforced; different versions of the same dimension can lead to insidious, unobservable errors in the drill-across results.

Each conformed dimension should possess a Type 1 version number field in every record (see the discussion of Type 1, 2, and 3 slowly changing dimensions in the Chapter 5 if this is unfamiliar vocabulary). This version number field is overwritten in every record whenever the dimension manager releases the dimension to the separate fact tables. Any drill-across query that combines data from two or more fact tables using two or more separate copies of a dimension must make sure that the version numbers of the dimensions match exactly. This requires the dimension manager to replicate any revised dimensions to all client fact tables simultaneously. In an environment supporting drill-across queries between fact tables, failure to enforce the equality of dimension versions is a very serious error, because applications may well run to completion, but sums and groupings can be insidiously wrong, with no real way to detect inconsistencies in the final reports.

In a single tablespace in a single DBMS on a single machine, managing conformed dimensions is somewhat simpler because there needs to be only one copy of a dimension. This single copy is joined at query time to all the fact tables resident in the tablespace. However, this benefit can be realized only in the smallest and simplest data warehouses. As soon as fact tables become situated in multiple tablespaces, multiple DBMSs, or multiple remote machines, the dimension manager must exercise the full set of responsibilities described in the previous paragraph, in order to support drilling across multiple data sets.

It is worth mentioning one more time that the roles described for the dimension manager and the fact table provider apply not only to geographically distributed and autonomous data warehouse environments but also to highly centralized warehouses on a single machine administered by a single set of DBAs. As soon as fact tables reside in separate table spaces, all these issues are relevant because there must be multiple physical copies of the dimensions.

Detailed Delivery Steps for Conformed Dimensions

The creation of conformed dimensions is more than just reaching agreement on certain standard descriptive attributes in a dimension. In the following steps, the references to Type 1, 2, and 3 slowly changing dimensions (SCDs) are explained in detail in Chapter 5. The dimension manager must:

1. Add fresh new records to the conformed dimension, generating new surrogate keys.
2. Add new records for Type 2 changes to existing dimension entries (true physical changes at a point in time), generating new surrogate keys.
3. Modify records in place for Type 1 changes (overwrites) and Type 3 changes (alternate realities), without changing the surrogate keys. Update the version number of the dimension if any of these Type 1 or Type 3 changes are made.
4. Replicate the revised dimension simultaneously to all fact table providers.

The receiving fact table provider has a more complex task. This person must:

1. Receive or download dimension updates.
2. Process dimension records marked as new and current to update current key maps in the surrogate key pipeline.
3. Process dimension records marked as new but postdated. This triggers a complex alternative to the normal surrogate key pipeline processing (described in Chapters 5 and 6).
4. Add all new records to fact tables after replacing their natural keys with correct surrogate keys.
5. Modify records in all fact tables for error correction, accumulating snapshots, and postdated dimension changes. You probably do this on a partition by partition basis. See comment in Step 9.
6. Remove aggregates that have become invalidated. An existing historical aggregate becomes invalidated only when a Type 1 or Type 3 change occurs on the attribute that is the target of the aggregation or if historical fact records have been modified in Step 5. Changes to other attributes do not invalidate an aggregate. For instance, a change in the Flavor attribute of a product does not invalidate aggregates based on the Category attribute.
7. Recalculate affected aggregates. If the new release of a dimension does not change the version number, aggregates have to be extended to handle only newly loaded fact data. If the version number of the dimension has changed, the entire historical aggregate may have to

be recalculated if it was removed in Step 6. OLAP systems may handle these steps automatically.

8. Quality-assure all base and aggregate fact tables. Be satisfied that the aggregate tables are correctly calculated.

9. Bring updated fact and dimension tables on line. The detailed strategy for taking a fact table (or more likely a partition of a fact table) offline for the briefest possible duration can be found in the *Lifecycle Toolkit* book starting on page 645.

10. Inform end users that the database has been updated. Tell users if major changes have been made, including dimension version changes, postdated records being added, and changes to historical aggregates.

Implementing the Conforming Modules

To implement conformed dimensions and facts, the conforming subsystem needs reference metadata that captures the relationships between explicitly valid values from source systems to conformed dimension attribute values and conformed fact values.

Many ETL tools support these types of domain mappings, either with prebuilt metadata attributes or by allowing the ETL team to use extensible metadata attributes for the source table objects. Figure 4.11 shows an example of metadata tables that support data conforming. The table and column

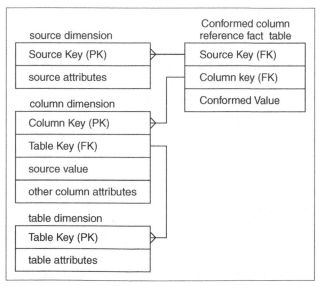

Figure 4.11   Conformed column support schema.

entities capture metadata about each table and its associated columns, re-spectively. The fact table records the officially defined conformed values from each source system. The identities of the overall source systems are captured in the source system table. The column dimension contains the source value mapped into the official conformed value. Thus, in the simple example cited earlier, if Male and Female were the target conformed values for gender, the fact table would associate M with Male, F with Female from source system A; and M with Male but W with Female from source system B; and Man with Male and Woman with Female from source system C.

Columns in records that contain invalid values—that is, values that are not in the set of explicit valid values in the column dimension table—should be replaced with a predefined value like Unknown from the standardized value reference table; replacement should be noted in the error event fact table.

> ☀ It is important that bogus or invalid data that cannot be standardized be removed from the visibility of downstream ETL processes (like matching) and the end user community.

More complex forms of standardization are now routinely used to deal with cleansing of names and addresses. Specialized software tools provide support in this area that would be very difficult for ETL teams to attempt to duplicate. By all means, have a look at the leading players in this arena listed in Chapter 7. In some cases, the standardized value is arrived at *probabilistically* by a technique that uses statistical techniques to align im-perfect data with some known universe of common names or geographies. Be aware that some probabilistic standardization tools also have self-tuning integration engines that learn over time more about the distribution of data specific to the particular application and adjust their processing algorithms appropriately. This is a powerful feature but one that can challenge the ETL architect's ability to test a data-integration engine whose behavior changes/evolves as it gets smarter. Most standardization tools produce feedback on their success in reengineering data and in exceptions/errors encountered in processing of the data. It is important to capture, retain, and mine data-integration lineage observations—using the log tables left behind to generate error event facts.

Matching Drives Deduplication

Matching, or deduplication, involves the elimination of duplicate standard-ized records. In some cases, the duplicate can be easily detected through the appearance of identical values in some key column—like social security number, telephone number, or charge card number. This happy situation is all-too rare, unfortunately. In other cases, no such definitive match is found, and the only clues available for deduplicating are the similarity of several columns that almost match. In still tougher cases, more than one definitive-match columns are found to be identical, but they contradict one another.

Specialized data integration matching tools are now mature and in widespread use and deal with these very specialized data-cleansing issues. Often, these tools are closely associated with data-standardization tools and are sold together.

The matching software must compare the set of records in the data stream to the universe of conformed dimension records and return:

- A numeric score that quantifies the likelihood of a match
- A set of match keys that link the input records to conformed dimension instances and/or within the standardized record universe alone

Thus, an input record running through the match processes can be a match to zero or one conformed dimension records *and* zero, one, or more other input records in the batch process queue. In either case, the matching software's job is to associate match keys to these input records that detail these derived match relationships. These match keys are used by the survivorship module described in the next section in figuring which records have been matched to one another and are therefore candidates for distillation into a single integrated record.

Many data-matching tools also include a *match score*, or matching confidence metric, that describes the likelihood of match obtained. Often, these match scores are derived by creating several matching approaches, or passes, scoring match probabilities from each pass and then distilling results into a recommended set of match keys and an overall weighted score.

Organizations with a need for very robust deduplication capabilities can choose also to maintain a persistent library of previously matched data, each still associated with a single data provider, and use this consolidated library to improve their matching results. In this way, the matching engine can apply its match passes not just to the conformed dimension records but also to the complete set of previously matched dimension records that it has from all source systems. This approach might result in better matches, because the universe of match candidates is richer, and it is far more resilient to gracefully handling matching rule changes, which can now be satisfied without having to run every source system's data through the entire data-integration process. But this approach complicates match processing because matches can occur within and across the source and fully conformed data universes.

💡 As of this writing, matching tools are far from turn-key implementations that plug into ETL streams and somehow know what to do. On the contrary, they require much profiling and training based on the organization's data, the establishing of matching strategies for deciding which combinations of attributes (matching passes or perspectives) are most predictive of duplication, the tuning to distill these different perspectives into a matching policy, and the setting of *match* and *no match* thresholds based on the organization's tolerance for over (aggressive) and under (conservative) matching. ETL tool-suite vendors have recently been targeting this application, however, and you should examine their plug-in matching transformers.

Surviving: Final Step of Conforming

Survivorship refers to the process of distilling a set of matched (deduplicated) records into a unified image that combines the highest-quality column values from each of the matched records to build conformed dimension records. This entails establishing business rules that define a hierarchy for column value selections from all possible sources and capturing the source-to-target mapping to be applied when writing out for survived (conformed) records.

In addition, survivorship must be capable of distilling combinations of columns together, rather than individually. This is needed for situations where the combining of individually survived columns could result in a nonsensical mishmash, such as combining address lines 1, 2, and 3 from three different source systems and ending up with a distilled address that is less credible than all three. It is far better in situations like this to create rules that mandate that certain combinations of columns (survivorship blocks) must be survived together: all or nothing. The metadata tables shown in Figure 4.12 support the most common requirements of survivorship.

- The **Survivorship Source to Target Map table** captures data-integration mappings between source columns (input data that has been cleaned but not conformed) and target columns (conformed dimension table columns). For both flexibility and simplicity, it allows any combination of columns to be used as sources into any combination of targets—thus placing a burden on the ETL architect (rather than referential integrity that might have been included in a more complex structure) to populate it properly.

- The **Survivorship Block table** groups mapped source and target columns into blocks that must be survived together (to properly address the address 1, 2, 3 types of issues described earlier). Survivorship blocks are allowed to be of one source and one target,

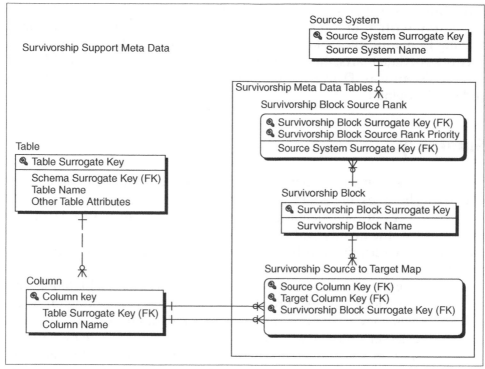

Figure 4.12   Survivorship support metadata.

too, so by forcing all survivorship to be performed by block, you can simplify both the metadata model and survivorship processing. This table includes a rank that allows the priority of source system blocks of fields to be determined with dynamic SQL, which looks for non-null values in each block ordered by survivorship block source rank priority, and builds an appropriate INSERT or UPDATE statement depending on whether the match key already exists as a conformed record surrogate key (UPDATE) or not (INSERT).

> In cases where the deduplication process successfully coalesces separate source entities (such as customers) into a single entity, if the source entities have been assigned separate primary keys in the source system, a table of those obsolete primary keys should be maintained to speed subsequent deduplication runs using data from that source system.

Delivering

Delivering is the final essential ETL step. In this step, cleaned and conformed data is written into the dimensional structures actually accessed by the end users and application systems. In the smallest data warehouses consisting of a single tablespace for end user access, dimensional tables are simply written to this table space. But in all larger data warehouses, ranging from multiple table spaces to broadly distributed and autonomous networks of data marts, the dimensional tables must be carefully published in a consistent way. Delivering is so important that we devote Chapters 5 and 6 to its details.

Summary

Stepping back from all the detail, this chapter covered four big topics: objectives, techniques, metadata, and measurements.

The *objectives* of data cleaning and conforming are to reduce errors in data, improve the quality and usefulness of the contents of data, and standardize key descriptive attributes and numerical measures shared across the organization.

Data-quality techniques range from examining individual field definitions at the data-base level (column property enforcement), to checking for field-to-field consistency (structure enforcement), and finally to business-rule specific checks on data (data and value rule enforcement). The final phase of data-quality processing (conforming and deduplicating) is the most far reaching, since in this phase we resolve differences across separate data sources.

Data-quality metadata contains declarations and business rules that hold our techniques together. We described a methodology for building a family of screens, each representing a data-quality investigation. Some of the screens are run routinely as part of every ETL episode, and some are run occasionally as periodic sanity checks or special investigations. The routine screens supply diagnostic indicators and measurements that we store in a detailed error event fact table and in audit dimensions attached to our fact tables. These audit dimensions are interesting because in a sense they elevate metadata to real data. Data-quality indicators can participate in *instrumented* end user queries just as if they were normal data.

Finally, *data-quality measurements* we proposed are a starter set of measurements that the ETL team needs in order to build a comprehensive data-quality processing pipeline.

When data has made it through data-quality processing pipeline, it is ready for the final delivering step, laid out in detail in Chapters 5 and 6.

Delivering Dimension Tables

Dimension tables provide the context for fact tables and hence for all the measurements presented in the data warehouse. Although dimension tables are usually much smaller than fact tables, they are the heart and soul of the data warehouse because they provide entry points to data. We often say that a data warehouse is only as good as its dimensions. We think the main mission of the ETL team is the handoff of the dimension tables and the fact tables in the delivery step, leveraging the end user applications most effectively.

PROCESS CHECK Planning & Design:
Requirements/Realities → *Architecture* → *Implementation* → Test/Release

Data Flow: Extract → Clean → Conform → *Deliver*

Chapters 5 and 6 are the pivotal elements of this book; they describe in a highly disciplined way how to deliver data to end users and their analytic applications. While there is considerable variability in the data structures and delivery-processing techniques leading up to this handoff, the final ETL step of preparing the dimensional table structures is much more constrained and disciplined.

Please keep in mind that our insistence on using these highly constrained design techniques is not adherence to a foolish consistency of a dimensional modeling methodology but rather is the key to building data warehouse systems with replicable, scalable, usable, and maintainable architectures. The more a data warehouse design deviates from these standardized dimensional modeling techniques, the more it becomes a custom programming job. Most IT developers are clever enough to take on a custom programming job, and most find such development to be intellectually stimulating. But custom programming is the kiss of death for building replicable, scalable, usable, and maintainable systems.

The Basic Structure of a Dimension

All dimensions should be physically built to have the minimal set of components shown in Figure 5.1. The *primary key* is a single field containing a meaningless, unique integer. We call a meaningless integer key a *surrogate*. The data warehouse ETL process should always create and insert the surrogate keys. In other words, the data warehouse owns these keys and never lets another entity assign them.

The primary key of a dimension is used to join to fact tables. Since all fact tables must preserve referential integrity, the primary dimension key is joined to a corresponding *foreign key* in the fact table. This is shown in our insurance example in Figure 2.3 in Chapter 2. We get the best possible performance in most relational databases when all joins between dimension tables and fact tables are based on these single field integer joins. And finally, our fact tables are much more compact when the foreign key fields are simple integers.

All dimension tables should possess one or more other fields that compose the *natural key* of the dimension. We show this in Figure 5.1 as an *ID* and

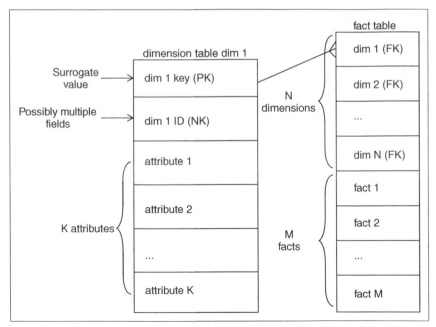

Figure 5.1   The basic structure of a dimension.

designate the natural key field(s) with *NK*. The natural key is not a meaningless surrogate quantity but rather is based on one or more meaningful fields extracted from the source system. For instance, a simple static (nonchanging) employee dimension would probably have the familiar EMP_ID field, which is probably the employee number assigned by the human resources production system. EMP_ID would be the natural key of this employee dimension. We still insist on assigning a data warehouse surrogate key in this case, because we must insulate ourselves from weird administrative steps that an HR system might take. For instance, in the future we might have to merge in bizarrely formatted EMP_IDs from another HR system in the event of an acquisition.

When a dimension is static and is not being updated for historical changes to individual rows, there is a 1-to-1 relationship between the primary surrogate key and the natural key. But we will see a little later in this chapter that when we allow a dimension to change slowly, we generate many primary surrogate keys for each natural key as we track the history of changes to the dimension. In other words, in a slowly changing dimension, the relationship between the primary surrogate key and the natural key is many-to-1. In our employee dimension example, each of the changing employee profile snapshots would have different and unique primary surrogate keys, but the profiles for a given employee would all have the same natural key (EMP_ID). This logic is explained in detail in the section on slowly changing dimensions in this chapter.

The final component of all dimensions, besides the primary key and the natural key, is the set of *descriptive attributes*. Descriptive attributes are predominately textual, but numeric descriptive attributes are legitimate. The data warehouse architect probably will specify a very large number of descriptive attributes for dimensions like employee, customer, and product. Do not be alarmed if the design calls for 100 descriptive attributes in a dimension! Just hope that you have clean sources for all these attributes. More on this later.

The data warehouse architect should not call for numeric fields in a dimension that turn out to be periodically measured quantities. Such measured quantities are almost certainly facts, not descriptive attributes. All descriptive attributes should be truly static or should only change slowly and episodically. The distinction between a measured fact and a numeric descriptive attribute is not as difficult as it sounds. In 98 percent of the cases, the choice is immediately obvious. In the remaining two percent, pretty strong arguments can be made on both sides for modeling the quantity either as a fact or as a dimensional attribute. For instance, the standard (catalog) price of a product is a numeric quantity that takes on both roles. In the final analysis, it doesn't matter which choice is made. The requesting applications will look different depending on where this numeric quantity is located, but the information content will be the same. The difference between these two choices will start to become important if it turns out that the standard price is actually slowly changing. As the pace of the change accelerates, modeling the numeric quantity as a measured fact becomes more attractive.

 Generating Surrogate Keys for Dimensions

Creating surrogate keys via the DBMS is probably the most common technique used today. However, we see this trend changing. In the past, it was common practice to have surrogate keys created and inserted by database triggers. Subsequently, it has been determined that triggers cause severe bottlenecks in the ETL process and should be eliminated from any new processes being created. Even though it is still acceptable for the integers for a surrogate key to be maintained by the DBMS, these integers should be called by the ETL process directly. Having the ETL process call the database sequence will produce a significant improvement in ETL performance over the use of database triggers.

Also, using the database to generate surrogate keys almost guarantees that the keys will be out of sync across the different environments of the data warehouse—development, test, and production. As each environment gets loaded at different intervals, their respective database could generates different surrogate key values for the same incoming dimension records. This lack of synchronization will cause confusion during testing for developers and users alike.

For ultimate efficiency, consider having an ETL tool or third-party application generate and maintain your surrogate keys. Make sure that efficient generation and maintenance of surrogate keys are in your ETL proof-of-concept success criteria.

A tempting solution seen repeatedly during design reviews is concatenating the natural key of the source system and a date stamp that reflects when the record was either created in the source system or inserted into the data warehouse. Giving the surrogate key intelligence—the exact time of its creation—may be useful in some situations, but it is not an acceptable alternative to a true integer-based surrogate key. Intelligent or smart keys fail as an acceptable surrogate key for the following reasons:

- *By definition.* Surrogate keys, by definition, are supposed to be meaningless. By applying intelligence to the surrogate key, their responsibility is broadened, making them need to be maintained. What happens if a primary key in the source system changes—or gets corrected in some way? The concatenated smart key would need to be updated, as will all of its associated records in fact tables throughout the entire data warehouse.

- *Performance.* Concatenating the source system key with a date stamp degrades query performance. As part of the data warehouse team, you have no control over the content of source system keys and must be able to handle any data type. This fact forces you to use the CHAR or VARCHAR data types to accommodate alpha, numeric, or alphanumeric keys coming from the source systems. Moreover, by appending the date stamp to the key, potentially 16 characters or more, the field can become unwieldy. What's worse, this key will need to be propagated into huge fact tables throughout the entire warehouse. The space to store the data and indexes would be excessive, causing ETL and end user query performance to diminish. Additionally, joining these large VARCHAR concatenated columns during query time will be slow when compared to the same join using INTEGER columns.

- *Data type mismatch.* Veteran data warehouse data modelers will know to build the dimensional model surrogate keys with the NUMBER or INTEGER data type. This data type prevents alpha characters from being inserted, thwarting the use of the concatenated date stamp method.

- *Dependency on source system.* The use of the smart-key approach is dependent on the source system revealing exactly when an attribute in a dimension changed. In many cases, this information is simply not available. Without reliable maintenance of some kind of audit columns, attaining the exact timestamp of a change can be impossible.

- *Heterogeneous sources.* The concatenation of the natural key and date stamp supports only a homogeneous environment. In virtually all enterprise data warehouses, common dimensions are sourced by many different source systems. These source systems each have their own purpose and can uniquely identify the same values of a dimension differently. The concatenated natural key, date-stamp approach falls short with the introduction of a second source system. Natural keys from each system must be stored equally, in dedicated nonkey columns in the dimension. Imagine attempting to concatenate each natural key and their respective timestamps—a maintenance nightmare.

The attractive characteristic of using this forbidden smart-key strategy is its simplicity at ETL development time when building the first data mart, when it is quite simple to implement a smart key by appending the SYSDATE to the natural key upon insertion. Avoid the temptation of this prohibited shortcut. This approach doesn't scale to your second data mart.

The Grain of a Dimension

Dimensional modelers frequently refer to the *grain* of a dimension. By this they mean the definition of the key of the dimension, in business terms. It is then a challenge for the data warehouse architect and the ETL team to analyze a given data source and make sure that a particular set of fields in that source corresponds to the definition of the grain. A common and notorious example is the commercial customer dimension. It is easy to say that the grain of the dimension is the commercial customer. It is often quite another thing to be absolutely sure that a given source file always implements that grain with a certain set of fields. Data errors and subtleties in the business content of a source file can violate your initial assumptions about the grain. Certainly, a simple test of a source file to demonstrate that fields A, B, and C implement the key to the candidate dimension table source is the query:

```
Select A, B, C, count(*)
From dimensiontablesource
Group by A, B, C
Having Count(*) > 1
```

If this query returns any rows, the fields A, B, and C do not implement the key (and hence the grain) of this dimension table. Furthermore, this query is obviously useful, because it directs you to exactly the rows that violate your assumptions.

It's possible that the extract process itself can be the culprit for exploding the rows being extracted, creating duplicates. For example, in a denormalized Orders transaction system, instead of referring to a source table that stores the distinct *Ship Via* values for the Order, the textual values of the attribute may very well be stored repeatedly directly in the Orders transaction table. To create the dimensional model, you build the Ship Via dimension by performing a SELECT DISTINCT on the Orders table. Any data anomalies in the original Orders table will create bogus duplicate entries in the Ship Via dimension.

The Basic Load Plan for a Dimension

A few dimensions are created entirely by the ETL system and have no real outside source. These are usually small lookup dimensions where an operational code is translated into words. In these cases, there is no real ETL processing. The little lookup dimension is simply created directly as a relational table in its final form.

But the important case is the dimension extracted from one or more outside sources. We have already described the four steps of the ETL data flow thread in some detail. Here are a few more thoughts relating to dimensions specifically.

Dimensional data for the big, complex dimensions like customer, supplier, or product is frequently extracted from multiple sources at different times. This requires special attention to recognizing the same dimensional entity across multiple source systems, resolving the conflicts in overlapping descriptions, and introducing updates to the entities at various points. These topics are handled in this chapter.

Data *cleaning* consists of all the steps required to clean and validate the data feeding a dimension and to apply known business rules to make the data consistent. For some simple, smaller dimensions, this module may be almost nonexistent. But for the big important dimensions like employee, customer, and product, the data-cleaning module is a very significant system with many subcomponents, including column validity enforcement, cross-column value checking, and row deduplication.

Data *conforming* consists of all the steps required to align the content of some or all of the fields in the dimension with fields in similar or identical dimensions in other parts of the data warehouse. For instance, if we have fact tables describing billing transactions and customer-support calls, they probably both have a customer dimension. In large enterprises, the original sources for these two customer dimensions could be quite different. In the worst case, there could be no guaranteed consistency between fields in the billing-customer dimension and the support-customer dimension. In all cases where the enterprise is committed to combining information across multiple sources, like billing and customer support, the conforming step is required to make some or all of the fields in the two customer dimensions *share the same domains*. We describe the detailed steps of conforming dimensions in the Chapter 4. After the conforming step has modified many of the important descriptive attributes in the dimension, the *conformed data* is staged again.

Finally, the *data-delivering module* consists of all the steps required to administer slowly changing dimensions (SCDs, described in this chapter) and write the dimension to disk as a physical table in the proper dimensional format with correct primary keys, correct natural keys, and final descriptive attributes. Creating and assigning the surrogate keys occur in this module. This table is definitely staged, since it is the object to be loaded into the presentation system of the data warehouse. The rest of this chapter describes the details of the data-delivering module in various situations.

Flat Dimensions and Snowflaked Dimensions

PROCESS CHECK Planning & Design:
Requirements/Realities → **Architecture** → *Implementation* → **Test/Release**

Data Flow: Extract → **Clean** → **Conform** → *Deliver*

Dimension tables are denormalized flat tables. All hierarchies and normalized structures that may be present in earlier staging tables should be flattened in the final step of preparing the dimension table, if this hasn't happened already. All attributes in a dimension must take on a single value in the presence of the dimension's primary key. Most of the attributes will be of medium and low cardinality. For instance, the gender field in an employee dimension will have a cardinality of three (male, female, and not reported), and the state field in a U.S. address will have a cardinality of 51 (50 states plus Washington, DC). If earlier staging tables are in third normal form, these flattened second normal form dimension tables are easily produced with a simple query against the third normal form source. If all the proper data relationships have been enforced in the data-cleaning step, these relationships are preserved perfectly in the flattened dimension table. This point is consistently misunderstood by proponents of delivering data to end users via a normalized model. In the dimensional-modeling world, the data-cleaning step is separated from the data-delivery step, in such a way that all proper data relationships are delivered to the end user, without the user needing to navigate the complex normalized structures.

It is normal for a complex dimension like store or product to have multiple simultaneous, embedded hierarchical structures. For example, the store dimension could have a normal geographic hierarchy of location, city, county, and state and also have a merchandising-area hierarchy of location, district, and region. These two hierarchies should coexist in the same store dimension. All that is required is that every attribute be single valued in the presence of the dimension table's primary key.

If a dimension is normalized, the hierarchies create a characteristic structure known as a snowflake, if indeed the levels of the hierarchies obey perfect many-to-1 relationships. See Figure 5.2. It is important to understand that there is no difference in the information content between the two versions of dimensions in this figure. The difference we do care about is the negative impact the normalized, snowflaked model has on the end user environment. There are two problems. First, if the strict many-to-1 relationships in a hierarchical model change, the normalized table schema and the declared joins between the tables must change, and the end user environment must be recoded at some level for applications to continue working. Flat versions of the dimension do not have this problem. Second, complex schemas are notorious for confusing end users, and a normalized schema requires *masking* this complexity in the presentation area of the data warehouse. Generally, flat dimension tables can appear directly in user interfaces with less confusion.

Having railed against snowflaked dimensions, there are nevertheless some situations where a kind of snowflaking is recommended. These are best described as subdimensions of another dimension. Please refer to the section with this name later in this chapter.

If an attribute takes on multiple values in the presence of the dimension's primary key, the attribute cannot be part of the dimension. For example, in a retail-store dimension, the cash register ID attribute takes on many values for each store. If the grain of the dimension is the individual store, the cash register ID cannot be an attribute in that dimension. To include the

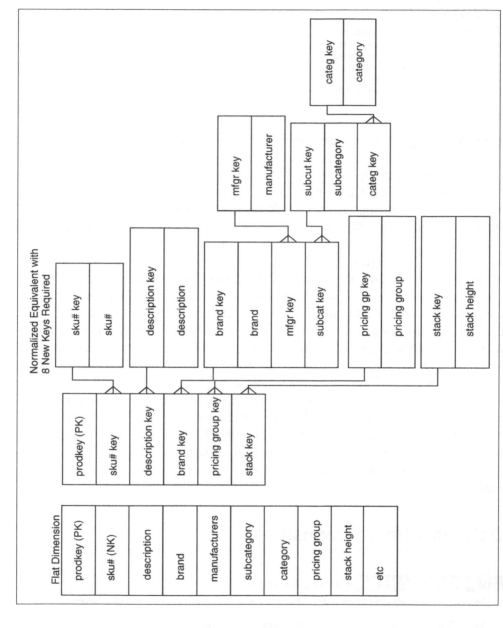

Figure 5.2 Flat and snowflaked versions of a dimension.

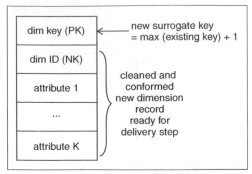

Figure 5.3 Assigning the surrogate key in the dimensionalizing step.

cash register attribute, the grain of the dimension must be redeclared to be cash register, not store. But since cash registers roll up to stores in a perfect many-to-1 relationship, the new cash-register dimension contains all of the store attributes, since they are all single valued at the cash-register level.

Each time a new dimension record is created, a fresh surrogate key must be assigned. See Figure 5.3. This meaningless integer is the primary key of the dimension. In a centralized data warehouse environment, the surrogate keys for all dimensions could be generated from a single source. In that case, a master metadata element contains the highest key used for all the dimensions simultaneously. However, even in a highly centralized data warehouse, if there are enough simultaneous ETL jobs running, there could be contention for reading and writing this single metadata element. And of course, in a distributed environment, this approach doesn't make much sense. For these reasons, we recommend that a surrogate key counter be established for each dimension table separately. It doesn't matter whether two different surrogate keys have the same numeric value; the data warehouse will never confuse the separate dimensional domains, and no application ever analyzes the value of a surrogate key, since by definition it is meaningless.

Date and Time Dimensions

PROCESS CHECK Planning & Design:
Requirements/Realities → Architecture → *Implementation* → Test/Release

Data Flow: Extract → Clean → Conform → *Deliver*

Virtually every fact table has one or more time-related dimension foreign keys. Measurements are defined at specific points and most measurements are repeated over time.

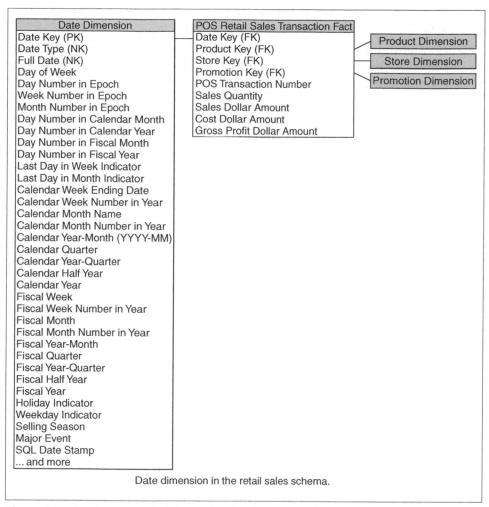

Date dimension in the retail sales schema.

Figure 5.4 Attributes needed for a calendar date dimension.

The most common and useful time dimension is the calendar date dimension with the granularity of a single day. This dimension has surprisingly many attributes, as shown in Figure 5.4. Only a few of these attributes (such as month name and year) can be generated directly from an SQL date-time expression. Holidays, work days, fiscal periods, week numbers, last day of month flags, and other navigational attributes must be embedded in the calendar date dimension and all date navigation should be implemented in applications by using the dimensional attributes. The calendar date dimension has some very unusual properties. It is one of the only dimensions completely specified at the beginning of the data warehouse project. It also doesn't have a conventional source. The best way to generate the calendar date dimension is to spend an afternoon with a spreadsheet and build it by hand. Ten years worth of days is fewer than 4000 rows.

Every calendar date dimension needs a date type attribute and a full date description attribute as depicted in Figure 5.4. These two fields compose the natural key of the table. The date type attribute almost always has the value *date*, but there must be at least one record that handles the special nonapplicable date situation where the recorded date is inapplicable, corrupted, or hasn't happened yet. Foreign key references in fact tables referring to these special data conditions must point to a nondate date in the calendar date table! You need at least one of these special records in the calendar date table, but you may want to distinguish several of these unusual conditions. For the inapplicable date case, the value of the date type is *inapplicable* or *NA*. The full date attribute is a full relational date stamp, and it takes on the legitimate value of null for the special cases described previously. Remember that the foreign key in a fact table can never be null, since by definition that violates referential integrity.

The calendar date primary key ideally should be a meaningless surrogate key, but many ETL teams can't resist the urge to make the key a readable quantity such as 20040718, meaning July 18, 2004. However, as with all smart keys, the few special records in the time dimension will make the designer play tricks with the smart key. For instance, the smart key for the inapplicable date would have to be some nonsensical value like 99999999, and applications that tried to interpret the date key directly without using the dimension table would always have to test against this value because it is not a valid date.

Even if the primary surrogate key of the calendar date dimension table is a true meaningless integer, we recommend assigning date surrogate keys in numerical order and using a standard starting date for the key value of zero in every date dimension table. This allows any fact table with a foreign key based on the calendar date to be physically partitioned by time. In other words, the oldest data in a fact table could be on one physical medium, and the newest data could be on another. Partitioning also allows the DBA to drop and rebuild indexes on just the most recent data, thereby making the loading process faster, if only yesterday's data is being loaded. Finally, the numeric value of the surrogate key for the special inapplicable time record should probably be a high number so that the inapplicable time-stamped records are in the most active partition. This assumes that these fact records are more likely to be rewritten in an attempt to correct data.

Although the calendar date dimension is the most important time dimension, we also need a calendar month dimension when the fact table's time grain is a month. In some environments, we may need to build calendar week, quarter, or year dimensions as well if there are fact tables at each of these grains. The calendar month dimension should be a separate physical table and should be created by physically eliminating selected rows and columns from the calendar day dimension. For example, either the first or the last day of each month could be chosen from the day dimension to be the basis of the month dimension. It is possible to define a view on a calendar day dimension that implements a calendar month dimension, but this is not recommended. Such a view would drag a much larger table into every month-based query than if the month table were its own physical table. Also, while this view technique can be made to work for calendar dimensions, it cannot be made to work for dimensions like customer or product, since individual customers and products come and go. Thus, you couldn't build a brand table with a view on the base product table, for instance, because you wouldn't know which individual product to choose to permanently represent a brand.

In some fact tables, time is measured below the level of calendar day, down to minute or even second. One cannot build a time dimension with every minute or every second represented. There are more than 31 million seconds in a year! We want to preserve the powerful calendar date dimension and simultaneously support precise querying down to the minute or second. We may also want to compute very precise time intervals by comparing the exact time of two fact table records. For these reasons, we recommend the design shown in Figure 5.5. The calendar day component of the precise time remains as a foreign key reference to our familiar calendar day dimension. But we also embed a full SQL date-time stamp directly in the fact table for all queries requiring the extra precision. Think of this as special kind of fact, not a dimension. In this interesting case, it is not useful to make a dimension with the minutes or seconds component of the precise time stamp, because the calculation of time intervals across fact table records becomes too messy when trying to deal with separate day and time-of-day dimensions. In previous *Toolkit* books, we have recommended building such a dimension with the minutes or seconds component of time

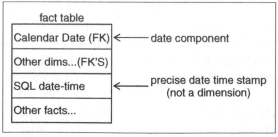

Figure 5.5 Fact table design for handling precise time measurements.

as an offset from midnight of each day, but we have come to realize that the resulting end user applications became too difficult when trying to compute time spans that cross daily boundaries. Also, unlike the calendar day dimension, in most environments there are very few descriptive attributes for the specific minute or second within a day.

If the enterprise does have well-defined attributes for time slices within a day, such as shift names or advertising time slots, an additional time-of-day dimension can be added to the design where this dimension is defined as the number of minutes (or even seconds) past midnight. Thus, this time-of-day dimension would either have 1440 records if the grain were minutes or 86,400 records if the grain were seconds. The presence of such a time-of-day dimension does not remove the need for the SQL date-time stamp described previously.

Big Dimensions

PROCESS CHECK Planning & Design:

Requirements/Realities → **Architecture** → *Implementation* → **Test/Release**

Data Flow: Extract → **Clean** → **Conform** → *Deliver*

The most interesting dimensions in a data warehouse are the big, wide dimensions such as customer, product, or location. A big commercial customer dimension often has millions of records and a hundred or more fields in each record. A big individual customer record can have tens of millions of records. Occasionally, these individual customer records have dozens of fields, but more often these monster dimensions (for example, grocery store customers identified by a shopper ID) have only a few behaviorally generated attributes.

The really big dimensions almost always are derived from multiple sources. Customers may be created by one of several account management systems in a large enterprise. For example, in a bank, a customer could be created by the mortgage department, the credit card department, or the checking and savings department. If the bank wishes to create a single customer dimension for use by all departments, the separate original customer lists must be de-duplicated, conformed, and merged. These steps are shown in Figure 5.6.

In the deduplication step, which is part of the *data-cleaning module*, each customer must be correctly identified across separate original data sources so that the total customer count is correct. A master natural key for the customer may have to be created by the data warehouse at this point. This

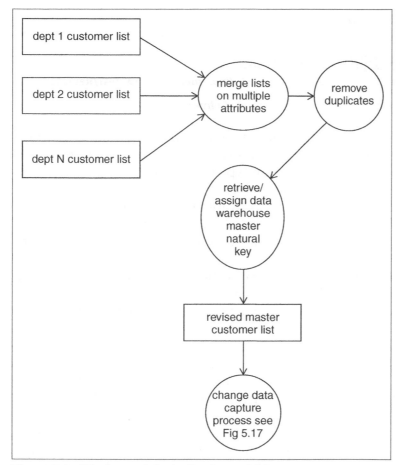

Figure 5.6   Merging and de-duplicating multiple customer sets.

would be a kind of enterprise-wide customer ID that would stay constant over time for any given customer.

In the conforming step, which is part of the *data-conforming module*, all attributes from the original sources that try to describe the same aspect of the customer need to be converted into single values used by all the departments. For example, a single set of address fields must be established for the customer. Finally, in the merge (survival) step, which is part of the *delivery-module*, all the remaining separate attributes from the individual source systems are unioned into one big, wide dimension record.

Later in this chapter, when we discuss slowly changing dimensions, we will see that the biggest dimensions are very sensitive to change, if it means that we generate new dimension records for each change. Hold that thought for a moment.

Small Dimensions

PROCESS CHECK Planning & Design:
Requirements/Realities → Architecture → *Implementation* → Test/Release

Data Flow: Extract → Clean → Conform → *Deliver*

Many of the dimensions in a data warehouse are tiny lookup tables with only a few records and one or two columns. For example, many transaction-grained fact tables have a transaction type dimension that provides labels for each kind of transaction. These tables are often built by typing into a spreadsheet and loading the data directly into the final physical dimension table. The original source spreadsheet should be kept because in many cases new records such as new transaction types could be introduced into the business.

Although a little dimension like transaction type may appear in many different data marts, this dimension cannot and should not be conformed across the various fact tables. Transaction types are unique to each production system.

In some cases, little dimension tables that serve to decode operational values can be combined into a single larger dimension. This is strictly a tactical maneuver to reduce the number of foreign keys in a fact table. Some data sources have a dozen or more operational codes attached to fact table records, many of which have very low cardinalities. Even if there is no obvious correlation between the values of the operational codes, a single *junk dimension* can be created to bring all these little codes into one dimension and tidy up the design. The ETL data flow for a typical junk dimension is shown in Figure 5.7. The records in the junk dimension should probably be created as they are encountered in the data, rather than beforehand as the Cartesian product of all the separate codes. It is likely that the incrementally produced junk dimension is much smaller than the full Cartesian product of all the values of the codes. The next section extends this kind of junk-dimension reasoning to much larger examples, where the designer has to grapple with the problem of one dimension or two.

One Dimension or Two

In dimensional modeling, we normally assume that dimensions are independent. In a strictly mathematical sense, this is almost never true. Although you may sell many products in many stores, the product dimension and the store dimension are probably not truly independent. Some products are sold in only selected stores. A good statistician would be able to demonstrate

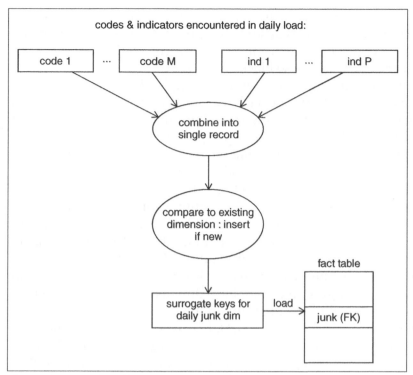

codes & indicators encountered in daily load:

code 1 ··· code M ind 1 ··· ind P

combine into single record

compare to existing dimension : insert if new

surrogate keys for daily junk dim

load

fact table

junk (FK)

Figure 5.7 ETL data flow for a typical junk dimension.

a degree of correlation between the product dimension and the store dimension. But such a finding normally does not deter us from creating separate product and store dimensions. The correlation that does exist between these dimensions can be faithfully and accurately depicted in the sales fact table.

Modeling the product dimension with the store dimension in this example would be a disaster. If you had a million-row product dimension and a 100-row store dimension, a combined dimension might approach 100 million rows! Bookkeeping the cross-correlations between dimensions solely in the fact table is an example of a powerful dimensional-modeling step: *demoting the correlations between dimensions* into a fact table.

A final nail in the coffin for combining product and store is that there may be more than one independent type of correlation between these two dimensions. We have discussed the merchandising correlation between these two dimensions, but there could be a pricing-strategy correlation, a warehousing correlation, or a changing-seasonality correlation. In general, tracking all of these complex relationships must be handled by leaving the dimensions simple and independent and by bookkeeping the cross-dimensional relationships in one or more fact tables.

At this point, you may be convinced that all dimensions can be independent and separate. But that's because we have been discussing a somewhat extreme example of two big dimensions where the correlation is statistically weak. Are other situations not so black and white?

First, let us immediately dispense with the completely correlated overlap of two dimensions. We should never have a single fact table with both a product dimension and a brand dimension if product rolls up to brand in a perfect many-to-1 relationship. In this case, product and brand are part of a hierarchy, and we should always combine these into a single dimension.

There are other cases where two candidate dimensions do not form a perfect hierarchy but are strongly correlated. To jump to the bottom line, if the correlation is reasonably high and the resulting combined dimension is reasonably small, the two dimensions should be combined into one. Otherwise, the dimensions should be left separate. The test for a reasonably high correlation should be made from the end user's perspective. If the pattern of overlap between the two dimensions is interesting to end users and is constant and unchanging, the combined dimension may be attractive. Remember that the combined dimension in this case serves as an efficient target for queries, independent of any fact table. In our opinion, a dimension is no longer reasonably small when it becomes larger than 100,000 rows. Over time, perhaps technology will relax this arbitrary boundary, but in any case a 100,000 row dimension will always present some user-interface challenges!

Dimensional Roles

The data warehouse architect will frequently specify a dimension to be attached multiple times to the same fact table. These are called *dimensional roles*. Probably the most common role-playing dimension is the calendar date dimension. Many fact tables, especially the accumulating snapshot fact tables, have multiple date foreign keys. We discuss accumulating snapshot fact tables in Chapter 6. See Figure 5.8. Another common example of a role-playing dimension is the employee dimension, where different foreign keys in the fact table represent different types of employees being involved in a single transaction. See Figure 5.9.

In all role-playing dimension implementations, we recommend first building a generic single dimension table and then implementing each of the roles with a view on this generic table. See Figure 5.10. For instance, if we have an order-date, a shipment-date, a payment-date, and a return-date on an orders transaction accumulating snapshot fact table, we would first build a generic calendar date dimension and the create four views corresponding to the four dates needed. If the fields in each view are identically named,

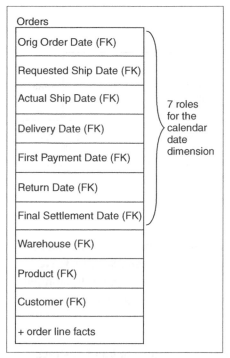

Figure 5.8 A typical accumulating snapshot fact table.

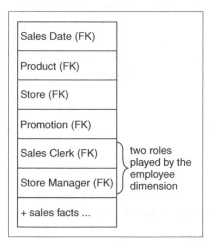

Figure 5.9 Two employee role playing dimensions.

the application developer and possibly the end user will need to see the fully qualified names to distinguish similar fields from the different views in the same query. For that reason, we recommend creating distinguishable field names in the original view definitions so that every tool, even those not supported by metadata, will display the fields unambiguously.

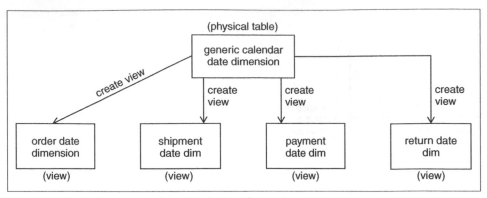

Figure 5.10   Multiple calendar role playing dimensions.

💡 The recommended design of dimensional roles described previously makes the impact of dimensional roles on the ETL team equal to zero. So why do we discuss it? Our objective is to make sure the ETL team doesn't generate multiple physical tables in cases where view definitions (roles) accomplish the same purpose.

💡 Don't use the dimensional-role techniques as an excuse to build abstract, super-large dimensions. For instance, in a telco environment, nearly everything has a location. If every possible location of every entity is represented in a single location dimension, this dimension could have millions of rows. Using a view on a multimillion row dimension in every application with a location dimension is probably a performance killer. In this case, actual physical dimensions created as extracted subsets of the big location dimension are probably better.

Dimensions as Subdimensions of Another Dimension

PROCESS CHECK Planning & Design:
Requirements/Realities → Architecture → *Implementation* → Test/Release

Data Flow: Extract → Clean → Conform → *Deliver*

Usually, we think of a reference to a dimension as a foreign key in a fact table. However, references to dimensions occasionally appear in other dimensions, and the proper foreign key should be stored in the parent dimension in the same way as a fact table. In other writings, we have sometimes referred to these subdimensions as *outriggers*. Let's discuss two common examples.

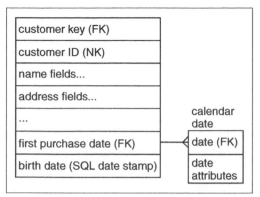

Figure 5.11   Customer dimension showing two date treatments.

Many dimensions have calendar dates embedded in them. Customer dimension records often have a first purchase date attribute. This should be modeled as a foreign key reference to the calendar date dimension, not as an SQL date stamp. See Figure 5.11. In this way, applications have access to all the extended calendar attributes when constraining on the first purchase date. This foreign key reference is really another kind of dimensional role played by the calendar date dimension. A separate view, in this case on the calendar date dimension, must be defined for each such reference.

Note that not all dates stored in dimensions can be modeled as foreign key references to the calendar date dimension, since the calendar date dimension has a bounded duration. A customer's birth date may well precede the first entry in the calendar date dimension. If that could happen, the customer birth date attribute must always be a simple SQL date stamp, not a foreign key reference. This is also shown in Figure 5.11.

A second common example of a dimension attached to a dimension is attaching an individual customer dimension to a bank account dimension. Although there might be many account holders in an account, usually a single customer is designated as the primary account holder. This primary account holder should be modeled as a foreign key reference in the account dimension to the customer dimension. See Figure 5.12.

In this banking example, we have not handled the problem of many customers being associated with an account. We have dealt only with the single primary account holder customer. We will associate an open-ended number of customers to an account later in this chapter when we discuss multivalued dimensions and bridge tables.

To summarize this section, the ETL dimensional delivery module must convert selected fields in the input data for the dimension to foreign key references.

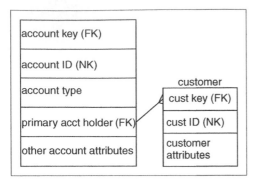

Figure 5.12   A customer dimension used as a subdimension.

Degenerate Dimensions

PROCESS CHECK Planning & Design:
Requirements/Realities → Architecture → *Implementation* → Test/Release

Data Flow: Extract → Clean → Conform → *Deliver*

Whenever a parent-child data relationship is cast in a dimensional frame-work, the natural key of the parent is left over as an orphan in the design process. For example, if the grain of a fact table is the line item on an order, the dimensions of that fact table include all the dimensions of the line it-self, as well as the dimensions of the surrounding order. Remember that we attach all single-valued dimensional entities to any given fact table record. When we have attached the customer and the order date and other dimen-sions to the design, we are left with the original order number. We insert the original order number directly into the fact table as if it were a dimension key. See Figure 5.13. We could have made a separate dimension out of this or-der number, but it would have turned out to contain only the order number, nothing else. For this reason, we give this natural key of the parent a special

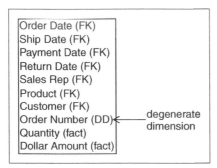

Figure 5.13   An order line accumulating snapshot fact table.

status and call it a *degenerate* (or empty) dimension. This situation arises in almost every parent-child design, including order numbers, shipment numbers, bill-of-lading numbers, ticket numbers, and policy numbers.

💡 **There is a danger that these source-system-generated numbers can get reused by different ERP instances installed in separate business units of an overall organization. For this reason, it may be a good idea to make a smart degenerate key value in these cases by prepending an organization ID onto the basic order number or sales ticket number.**

Slowly Changing Dimensions

PROCESS CHECK Planning & Design:
Requirements/Realities → Architecture → *Implementation* → Test/Release

Data Flow: Extract → Clean → Conform → *Deliver*

When the data warehouse receives notification that an existing row in a dimension has in some way changed, there are three basic responses. We call these three basic responses Type 1, Type 2, and Type 3 slowly changing dimensions (SCDs).

Type 1 Slowly Changing Dimension (Overwrite)

The Type 1 SCD is a simple overwrite of one or more attributes in an existing dimension record. See Figure 5.14. The ETL processing would choose the Type 1 approach if data is being corrected or if there is no interest in keeping the history of the previous values and no need to run prior reports. The Type 1 overwrite is always an UPDATE to the underlying data, and this overwrite must be propagated forward from the earliest permanently stored staging tables in the ETL environment so that if any of them are used to recreate

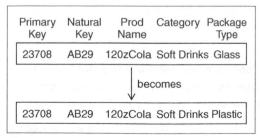

Figure 5.14 Processing a Type 1 SCD.

the final load tables, the effect of the overwrite is preserved. This point is expanded in Chapter 8.

Although inserting new records into a Type 1 SCD requires the generation of new dimension keys, processing changes in a Type 1 SCD never affects dimension table keys or fact table keys and in general has the smallest impact on the data of the three SCD types. The Type 1 SCD can have an effect on the storage of aggregate fact tables, if any aggregate is built directly on the attribute that was changed. This issue will be described in more detail in Chapter 6.

> Some ETL tools contain *UPDATE else INSERT* functionality. This functionality may be convenient for the developer but is a performance killer. For maximum performance, existing records (UPDATEs) should be segregated from new ones (INSERTs) during the ETL process; each should be fed to the data warehouse independently. In a Type 1 environment, you may not know whether an incoming record is an UPDATE or an INSERT. Some developers distinguish between a VERY SCD (very slowly changing dimension) where INSERTs predominate and a Fastly Changing Dimension (FCD?). They use INSERT else UPDATE logic for VERY SCDs and UPDATE else INSERT logic for the FCDs. We hope this terminology doesn't catch on.

In most data warehouse implementations, the size of the majority of dimensions is insignificant. When you are loading small tables that do not warrant the complexity of invoking a bulk loader, Type 1 changes can be applied via normal SQL DML statements. Based on the natural key extracted from the source system, any new record is assigned a new surrogate key and appended to the existing dimension data. Existing records are updated in place. Performance of this technique may be poorer as compared with being loaded via a bulk loader, but if the tables are of reasonable size, the impact should be negligible.

Some ETL tools offer specialized transformations that can detect whether a record needs to be inserted or updated. However, this utility must *ping* the table using the primary key of the candidate record to see if it exists. This approach is process intensive and should be avoided. To minimize the performance hit when using SQL to load a Type 1 dimension, the ETL process should explicitly segregate existing data that requires UPDATE statements from data that requires INSERT.

> Type 1 SCD changes can cause performance problems in ETL processing. If this technique is implemented using SQL data-manipulation language (DML), most database management systems will *log* the event, hindering performance.
>
> A database log is implicitly created and maintained by the DBMS. Database logging is constructive for transaction processing where data is entered by many users

in an uncontrolled fashion. *Uncontrolled* is used because in the on-line transaction processing (OLTP) environment, there is no way to control unpredicted user behavior, such as closing a window midway through an update. The DBMS may need to ROLLBACK, or undo, a failed update. The database log enables this capability.

Conversely, in the data warehouse, all data loading is controlled by the ETL process. If the process fails, the ETL process should have the capability to recover and pick-up where it left off, making the database log superfluous.

With database logging enabled, large dimensions will load at an unacceptable rate. Some database management systems allow you to turn logging off during certain DML processes, while others require their bulk loader to be invoked for data to be loaded without logging.

Bulk Loading Type 1 Dimension Changes

Because Type 1 overwrites data, the easiest implementation technique is to use SQL UPDATE statements to make all of the dimension attributes correctly reflect the current values. Unfortunately, as a result of database logging, SQL UPDATE is a poor-performing transaction and can inflate the ETL load window. For very large Type 1 changes, the best way to reduce DBMS overhead is to employ its bulk loader. Prepare the new dimension records in a separate table. Then drop the records from the dimension table and reload them with the bulk loader.

Type 2 Slowly Changing Dimension (Partitioning History)

The Type 2 SCD is the standard basic technique for accurately tracking changes in dimensional entities and associating them correctly with fact tables. The basic idea is very simple. When the data warehouse is notified that an existing dimension record needs to be changed, rather than overwriting, the data warehouse issues a new dimension record at the moment of the change. This new dimension record is assigned a fresh surrogate primary key, and that key is used from that moment forward in all fact tables that have that dimension as a foreign key. As long as the new surrogate key is assigned promptly at the moment of the change, no existing keys in any fact tables need to be updated or changed, and no aggregate fact tables need to be recomputed. The more complex case of handling late-arriving notifications of changes is described later in this chapter.

We say that the Type 2 SCD *perfectly partitions history* because each detailed version of a dimensional entity is correctly connected to the span of fact table records for which that version is exactly correct. In Figure 5.15, we illustrate

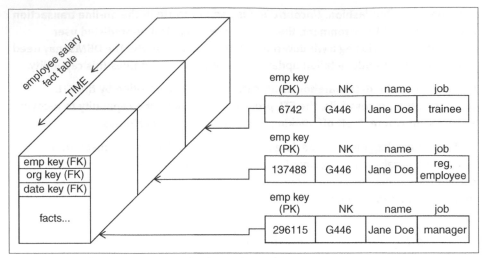

Figure 5.15 The Type 2 SCD perfectly partitions history.

this concept with a slowly changing employee dimension where a particular employee named Jane Doe is first a trainee, then a regular employee, and finally a manager. Jane Doe's natural key is her employee number and that remains constant throughout her employment. In fact, the natural key field always has the unique business rule that it cannot change, whereas every other attribute in the employee record can change. Jane Doe's primary surrogate key takes on three different values as she is promoted, and these surrogate primary keys are always correctly associated with contemporary fact table records. Thus, if we constrain merely on the employee Jane Doe, perhaps using her employee number, we pick up her entire history in the fact table because the database picks up all three surrogate primary keys from the dimension table and joins them all to the fact table. But if we constrain on *Jane Doe, manager*, we get only one surrogate primary key and we see only the portion of the fact table for which Jane Doe was a manager.

> If the natural key of a dimension can change, from the data warehouse's point of view, it isn't really a natural key. This might happen in a credit card processing environment where the natural key is chosen as the card number. We all know that the card number can change; thus, the data warehouse is required to use a more fundamental natural key. In this example, one possibility is to use the original customer's card number forever as the natural key, even if it subsequently changes. In such a design, the customer's current contemporary card number would be a separate field and would not be designated as a key.

The Type 2 SCD requires a good *change data capture system* in the ETL environment. Changes in the underlying source data need to be detected as soon as they occur, so that a new dimension record in the data warehouse can be created. We discuss many of the issues of change data capture at extract time in Chapter 3. In the worst scenario, the underlying source system does not notify the data warehouse of changes and does not date-stamp its own updates. In this case, the data warehouse is forced to download the complete dimension and look record by record and field by field for changes that have occurred since the last time the dimension was downloaded from the source. Note that this requires the prior extract (the master dimension cross reference file) from the dimension's source to be explicitly staged in the ETL system. See Figure 5.16.

For a small dimension of a few thousand records and a dozen fields, such as a simple product file, the detection of changes shown in Figure 5.16 can be done by brute force, comparing every field in every record in today's download with every field in every record from yesterday. Additions, changes, and deletions need to be detected. But for a large dimension, such as a list of ten million insured health care patients with 100 descriptive fields in each record, the brute-force approach of comparing every field in every record is too inefficient. In these cases, a special code known as a CRC is

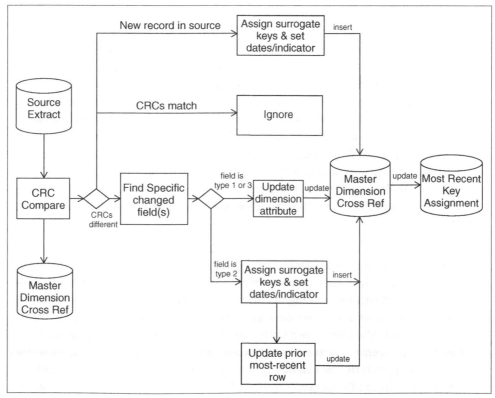

Figure 5.16   Dimension table surrogate key management.

computed and associated with every record in yesterday's data. The CRC (cyclic redundancy checksum) code is a long integer of perhaps 20 digits that is exquisitely sensitive to the information content of each record. If only a single character in a record is changed, the CRC code for that record will be completely different. This allows us to make the change data capture step much more efficient. We merely compute the CRC code for each incoming new record by treating the entire record as a single text string, and we compare that CRC code with yesterday's code for the same natural key. If the CRCs are the same, we immediately skip to the next record. If the CRCs are different, we must stop and compare each field to find what changed. The use of this CRC technique can speed up the change data capture process by a factor of 10. At the time of this writing, CRC calculation modules are available from all of the leading ETL package vendors, and the code for implementing a CRC comparison can be readily found in textbooks and on the Internet.

Once a changed dimension record has been positively identified, the decision of which SCD type is appropriate can be implemented. Usually, the ETL system maintains a policy for each column in a dimension that determines whether a change in that attribute triggers a Type 1, 2, or 3 response, as shown in Figure 5.16.

To identify records deleted from the source system, you can either read the source transaction log file (if it is available) or note that the CRC comparison step described previously cannot find a record to match a natural key in the ETL system's comparison file. But in either case, an explicit business rule must be invoked to deal with the deletion. In many cases, the deleted entity (such as a customer) will have a continuing presence in the data warehouse because the deleted entity was valid in the past. If the business rule conclusively states that the deleted entity can no longer appear in subsequent loads from the dimension-table source, the deleted entity can be removed from the daily comparison step, even though in the historical dimension tables and fact tables it will live on.

Without transaction log files, checking for deleted data is a process- intensive practice and usually is implemented only when it is demanded. An option that has proven to be effective is utilizing the MINUS set operator to compare the natural keys from the dimension in the data warehouse against the natural keys in the source system table. UNION and MINUS are SET operators supported by most database management systems used to compare two sets of data. These operators are extremely powerful for evaluating changes between the source and target. However, for these SET operators to work, the two tables need to be in the same database, or a database link must be created. Some ETL tools support SET operations between heterogeneous systems. If this is a critical requirement for your environment, be sure it is included in your proof-of-concept criteria when selecting your ETL toolset.

Notice in Figure 5.16 that when we have created the new surrogate key for a changed dimension entity, we update a two-column lookup table, known as the *most recent key lookup table* for that dimension. These little tables are of immense importance when loading fact table data. Hold this thought until you read the surrogate key pipeline section in Chapter 6.

The same benefits that the lookup-table solution offers can be accomplished by storing all of the relevant natural keys directly in the dimension table. This approach is probably the most common for determining whether natural keys and dimension records have been loaded. This approach makes the associated natural keys available to the users, right in the dimension. The major benefit of this strategy over the lookup table is that the surrogate key exists only in one place, eliminating the risk of the dimension and the mapping table becoming out of sync. During the ETL, the process selects the natural key from the appropriate column within the dimension where it equals the incoming natural key. If a match is found, the process can apply any of the SCD strategies described later in this chapter. If the key is not found, it can generate a surrogate key using any of the methods discussed in the next section and insert a new record.

Looking directly to dimensions is favored by many data warehouse designers because it exposes the data lineage to users. By having the natural keys directly in the dimension, users know exactly where the data in the dimension came from and can verify it in the source system. Moreover, natural keys in the dimension relieve the ETL and DBA teams from having to maintain a separate mapping table for this purpose. Finally, this approach makes a lot of sense in environments where there is a large fraction of late-arriving data where the *most recent* advantages of a lookup table cannot be used.

In this section, we have described a change-data-capture scenario in which the data warehouse is left to guess if a change occurred in a dimension record and why. Obviously, it would be preferable if the source system handed over only the changed records (thereby avoiding the complex comparison procedure described previously) and ideally accompanied the changed records with *reason codes* that distinguished the three SCD responses. What a lovely dream.

Our approach allows us to respond to changes in the source for a dimension as they occur, even when the changes are not marked. A more difficult situation takes place when a database is being loaded for the first time from such an uncooperative source. In this case, if the dimension has been overwritten at the source, it may be difficult to reconstruct the historical changes that were processed unless original transaction log files are still available.

Precise Time Stamping of a Type 2 Slowly Changing Dimension

The discussion in the previous section requires only that the ETL system generate a new dimension record when a change to an existing record is detected. The new dimension record is correctly associated with fact table records automatically because the new surrogate key is used promptly in all fact table loads after the change takes place. No date stamps in the dimension are necessary to make this correspondence work.

Having said that, it is desirable in many situations to *instrument* the dimension table to provide optional useful information about Type 2 changes. We recommend adding the following five fields to dimension tables processed with Type 2 logic:

- Calendar Date foreign key (date of change)
- Row Effective DateTime (exact date-time of change)
- Row End DateTime (exact date-time of next change)
- Reason for Change (text field)
- Current Flag (current/expired)

These five fields make the dimension a powerful query target by itself, even if no fact table is mentioned in the query. The calendar date foreign key allows an end user to use the business calendar (with seasons, holidays, paydays, and fiscal periods) to ask how many changes of a particular type were made in certain business-significant periods. For instance, if the dimension is a human resources employee table, one could ask how many promotions occurred in the last fiscal period.

The two SQL date-time stamps define an exact interval in which the current dimension record correctly and completely describes the entity. When a new change is processed, the Row Effective DateTime is set to the current date and time, and the Row End DateTime is set to an arbitrary time far in the future. When a subsequent change to this dimension entity is processed, the previous record must be revisited and the Row End DateTime set to the proper value. If this procedure is followed, the two date-time stamps always define an *interval of relevance* so that queries can specify a random specific date and time and use the SQL BETWEEN logic to immediately deliver records that were valid at that instant. We need to set the Row End DateTime to a real value, even when the record is the most current, so that the BETWEEN logic doesn't return an error if the second date is represented as null.

> It is seems to be universal practice for back-end scripts to be run within the transaction database to modify data without updating respective metadata fields, such as the last_modified_date. Using these fields for the dimension row effective_datetime will cause inconsistent results in the data warehouse. Do not depend on metadata fields in the transaction system. Always use the system or *as of* date to derive the row effective_datetime in a Type 2 slowly changing dimension.

The Reason for Change field probably needs to come from the original data-entry process that gave rise to the changed dimension record. For instance, in the human resources example, you would like a promotion to be represented as a single new record, appropriately time stamped, in the employee dimension. The Reason for Change field should say *promotion*. This may not be as easy as it sounds. The HR system may deliver a number of change records at the time of an employee's promotion if several different employee attributes (job grade, vacation benefits, title, organization and so on) change simultaneously. The challenge for the data warehouse is to coalesce these changes into a single new dimension record and correctly label this new record with *promotion*. Such a coalescing of underlying transaction records into a kind of aggregated *super-transaction* may be necessary with some source systems, even if no attempt is made to ascribe a reason code to the overall change. We have seen relatively simple updates such as employee promotions represented by dozens of micro transactions. The data warehouse should not carry these microtransactions all the way to the final end user tables, because the individual microtransactions may not have real business significance. This processing is depicted in Figure 5.17. Finally, the Current Flag is simply a convenient way to retrieve all the most-current records in a dimension. It is indeed redundant with the two SQL date-time

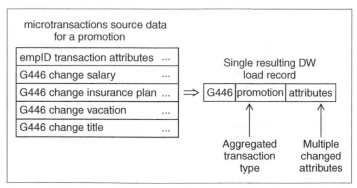

Figure 5.17 Consolidating source system microtransactions.

stamps and therefore can be left out of the design. This flag needs to be set to EXPIRED when a superceding change to the dimension entity takes place.

Type 3 Slowly Changing Dimension (Alternate Realities)

The Type 3 SCD is used when a change happens to a dimension record but the old value of the attribute remains valid as a second choice. The two most common business situations where this occurs are changes in sales-territory assignments, where the old territory assignment must continue to be available as a second choice, and changes in product-category designa-tions, where the old category designation must continue to be available as a second choice. The data warehouse architect should identify fields that require Type 3 administration.

In a Type 3 SCD, instead of issuing a new row when a change takes place, a new column is created (if it does not already exist), and the old value is placed in this new field before the primary value is overwritten. For the example of the product category, we assume the main field is named Category. To implement the Type 3 SCD, we alter the dimension table to add the field Old Category. At the time of the change, we take the original value of Category and write it into the Old Category field; then we overwrite the Category field as if it were a Type 1 change. See Figure 5.18. No keys need to be changed in any dimension table or in any fact table. Like the Type 1 SCD, if aggregate tables have been built directly on the field undergoing

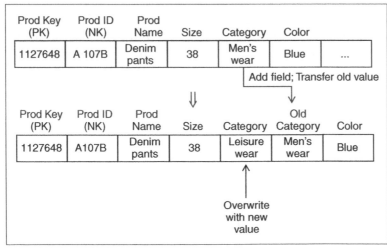

Figure 5.18 Implementing the Type 3 SCD for a product-category description.

the Type 3 change, these aggregate tables need to be recomputed. This procedure is described in Chapter 6.

> 💡 **Type 3 changes often do not come down the normal data-flow pipeline. Rather, they are executive decisions communicated to the ETL team, often verbally. The product-category manager says, "Please move Brand X from Mens Sportswear to Leather Goods, but let me track Brand X optionally in the old category." The Type 3 administration is then kicked off by hand, and can even involve a schema change, if the changed attribute (in this case, *brand*) does not have an *alternate* field.**

When a new record is added to a dimension that contains Type 3 fields, a business rule must be invoked to decide how to populate the old value field. The current value could be written into this field, or it could be NULL, depending on the business rule.

We often describe the Type 3 SCD as supporting an *alternate reality*. In our product-category example, the end user could choose between two versions of the mapping of products to categories.

The Type 3 SCD approach can be extended to many alternate realities by creating an arbitrary number of alternate fields based on the original attribute. Occasionally, such a design is justified when the end user community already has a clear vision of the various interpretations of reality. Perhaps the product categories are regularly reassigned but the users need the flexibility to interpret any span of time with any of the category interpretations. The real justification for this somewhat awkward design is that the user interface to this information *falls out* of every query tool with no programming, and the underlying SQL requires no unusual logic or extra joins. These advantages trump the objections to the design using positionally dependent attributes (the alternate fields).

Hybrid Slowly Changing Dimensions

The decision to respond to changes in dimension attributes with the three SCD types is made on a field-by-field basis. It is common to have a dimension containing both Type 1 and Type 2 fields. When a Type 1 field changes, the field is overwritten. When a Type 2 field changes, a new record is generated. In this case, the Type 1 change needs to be made to all copies of the record possessing the same natural key. In other words, if the ethnicity attribute of an employee profile is treated as a Type 1, if it is ever changed (perhaps to correct an original erroneous value), the ethnicity attribute must be overwritten in all the copies of that employee profile that may have been spawned by Type 2 changes.

Figure 5.19 A hybrid SCD showing all three types.

It is possible to combine all the SCD types in a single dimension record. See Figure 5.19. In this example, the district assignment field for the sales team is a Type 2 attribute. Whenever the district assignment changes, a new record is created, and the beginning and effective dates are set appropriately. The set of yearly old district assignments are Type 3 fields, implementing many alternate realities. And finally, the current district assignment is a Type 1 field, and it is overwritten in all copies of the sales team dimension records whenever the current district is reassigned.

Late-Arriving Dimension Records and Correcting Bad Data

PROCESS CHECK Planning & Design:
Requirements/Realities → Architecture → *Implementation* → Test/Release

Data Flow: Extract → Clean → Conform → *Deliver*
   Late-arriving data may need to be extracted via a different application or different constraints compared to normal contemporary data. Bad data obviously is picked up in the data-cleaning step.

A late-arriving dimension record presents a complex set of issues for the data warehouse. Suppose that we have a fictitious product called Zippy Cola. In the product dimension record for Zippy Cola 12-ounce cans, there is a formulation field that has always contained the value *Formula A*. We have a number of records for Zippy Cola 12-ounce cans because this is a Type 2 slowly changing dimension and other attributes like the package type and the subcategory for Zippy Cola 12-ounce cans have changed over the past year or two.

Today we are notified that on July 15, 2003 (a year ago) the formulation of Zippy Cola 12-ounce cans was changed to *Formula B* and has been Formula B ever since. We should have processed this change a year ago, but we failed to do so. Fixing the information in the data warehouse requires the following steps:

1. Insert a fresh new record with a new surrogate key for Zippy Cola 12-ounce cans into the Product dimension with the formulation field set to *Formula B*, the row effective datetime set to July 15, 2003, and the row end datetime set to the row effective datetime of the next record for Zippy Cola in the product dimension table. We also need to find the closest previous dimension record for Zippy Cola and set its row end datetime to the datetime of our newly inserted record. Whew!

2. Scan forward in the Product dimension table from July 15, 2003, finding any other records for Zippy Cola 12-ounce cans, and destructively overwrite the formulation field to *Formula B* in all such records.

3. Find all fact records involving Zippy Cola 12-ounce cans from July 15, 2003, to the first next change for that product in the dimension after July 15, 2003, and destructively change the Product foreign key in those fact records to be the new surrogate key created in Step 1.

💡 **Updating fact table records (in Step 3) is a serious step that should be tested carefully in a test environment before performing it on the production system. Also, if the update is protected by a database transaction, be careful that some of your updates don't involve an astronomical number of records. For operational purposes, such large updates should be divided into chunks so that you don't waste time waiting for an interrupted update of a million records to roll back.**

There are some subtle issues here. First, we need to check to see if some other change took place for Zippy Cola 12-ounce cans on July 15, 2003. If so, we need only to perform Step 2. We don't need a new dimension record in this special case.

In general, correcting bad data in the data warehouse can involve the same logic. Correcting a Type 1 field in a dimension is simplest because we just have to overwrite all instances of that field in all the records with the desired natural key. Of course, aggregate tables have to be recalculated if they have specifically been built on the affected attribute. Please see the aggregate updating section for fact tables in Chapter 6. Correcting a Type 2 field requires thoughtful consideration, since it is possible that the incorrect value has a specific time span.

💡 **This discussion of late-arriving dimension records is really about late-arriving *versions* of dimension records. In real-time systems (discussed in Chapter 11), we deal with true late-arriving dimension records that arrive after fact records have already been loaded into the data warehouse. In this case, the surrogate key in the fact table must point to a special temporary placeholder in the dimension until the real dimension record shows up.**

Multivalued Dimensions and Bridge Tables

PROCESS CHECK Planning & Design:
Requirements/Realities → Architecture →*Implementation* → Test/Release

Data Flow: Extract → Clean → Conform → *Deliver*

Occasionally a fact table must support a dimension that takes on multiple values at the lowest level of granularity of the fact table. Examples described in the other Toolkit books include multiple diagnoses at the time of a billable health care treatment and multiple account holders at the time of a single transaction against a bank account.

If the grain of the fact table is not changed, a multivalued dimension must be linked to the fact table through an associative entity called a *bridge table*. See Figure 5.20 for the health care example.

To avoid a many-to-many join between the bridge table and the fact table, one must create a *group entity* related to the multivalued dimension. In the health care example, since the multivalued dimension is diagnosis, the group entity is diagnosis group. The diagnosis group becomes the actual normal dimension to the fact table, and the bridge table keeps track of the many-to-many relationship between diagnosis groups and diagnoses. In the bank account example, when an account activity record is linked to the multivalued customer dimension (because an account can have many customers), the group entity is the familiar account dimension.

The challenge for the ETL team is building and maintaining the group entity table. In the health care example, as patient-treatment records are presented to the system, the ETL system has the choice of either making

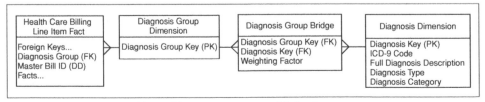

Figure 5.20   Using a bridge table to represent multiple diagnoses.

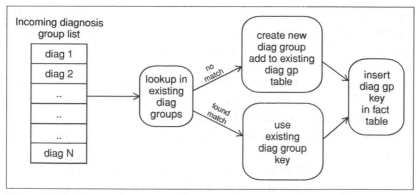

Figure 5.21   Processing diagnosis groups in an outpatient setting.

each patient's set of diagnoses a unique diagnosis group or reusing diagnosis groups when an identical set of diagnoses reoccurs. There is no simple answer for this choice. In an outpatient setting, diagnosis groups would be simple, and many of the same ones would appear with different patients. In this case, reusing the diagnosis groups is probably the best choice. See Figure 5.21. But in a hospital environment, the diagnosis groups are far more complex and may even be explicitly time varying. In this case, the diagnosis groups should probably be unique for each patient and each hospitalization. See Figure 5.22 and the discussion of time-varying bridge tables that follows. The admission and discharge flags are convenient attributes that allow the diagnosis profiles at the time of admission and discharge to be easily isolated.

Administering the Weighting Factors

The diagnosis group tables illustrated in Figures 5.20 and 5.22 include weighting factors that explicitly prorate the additive fact (charge dollars) by each diagnosis. When a requesting query tool constrains on one or more

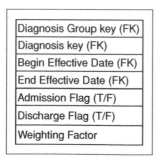

Figure 5.22   A time-varying diagnosis group bridge table appropriate for a hospital setting.

diagnoses, the tool can chose to multiply the weighting factor in the bridge table to the additive fact, thereby producing a *correctly weighted* report. A query without the weighting factor is referred to as an *impact* report. We see that the weighting factor is nothing more than an explicit allocation that must be provided in the ETL system. These allocations are either explicitly fetched from an outside source like all other data or can be simple computed fractions depending on the number of diagnoses in the diagnosis group. In the latter case, if there are three diagnoses in the group, the weighting factor is $1/3 = 0.333$ for each diagnosis.

In many cases, a bridge table is desirable, but there is no rational basis for assigning weighting factors. This is perfectly acceptable. The user community in this case cannot expect to produce correctly weighted reports. These front-room issues are explored in some depth in the *Data Warehouse Toolkit, Second Edition* in the discussion of modeling complex events like car accidents.

Time-Varying Bridge Tables

If the multivalued dimension is a Type 2 SCD, the bridge table must also be time varying. See Figure 5.23 using the banking example. If the bridge table were not time varying, it would have to use the natural keys of the customer dimension and the account dimension. Such a bridge table would potentially misrepresent the relationship between the accounts and customers. It is not clear how to administer such a table with natural keys if customers are added to or deleted from an account. For these reasons, the bridge table must always contain surrogate keys. The bridge table in Figure 5.23 is quite sensitive to changes in the relationships between accounts and customers. New records for a given account with new begin-date stamps and end-date stamps must be added to the bridge table whenever:

- The account record undergoes a Type 2 update
- Any constituent customer record undergoes a Type 2 update
- A customer is added to or deleted from the account or
- The weighting factors are adjusted

Account key (FK)
Customer key (FK)
Begin effective date (FK)
End effective date (FK)
Primary Account Holder Flag (T/F)
Weighting factor

Figure 5.23 A time-varying bridge table for accounts and customers.

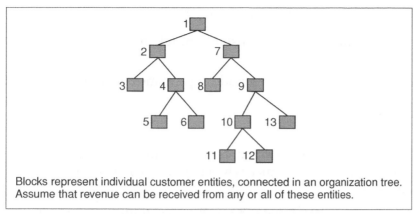

Blocks represent individual customer entities, connected in an organization tree. Assume that revenue can be received from any or all of these entities.

Figure 5.24 A representative ragged organization hierarchy.

Ragged Hierarchies and Bridge Tables

PROCESS CHECK Planning & Design:
Requirements/Realities → Architecture → *Implementation* → Test/Release

Data Flow: Extract → Clean → Conform → *Deliver*

Ragged hierarchies of indeterminate depth are an important topic in the data warehouse. Organization hierarchies such as depicted in Figure 5.24 are a prime example. A typical organization hierarchy is unbalanced and has no limits or rules on how deep it might be.

There are two main approaches to modeling a ragged hierarchy, and both have their pluses and minuses. We'll discuss these tradeoffs in terms of the customer hierarchy shown in Figure 5.24.

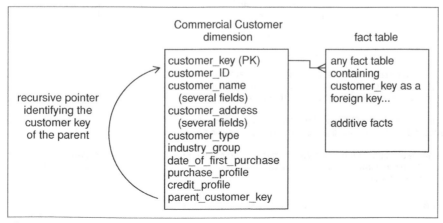

Figure 5.25 A customer dimension with a recursive pointer.

The *recursive pointer* approach shown in Figure 5.25.

- (+) embeds the hierarchy relationships entirely in the customer dimension
- (+) has simple administration for adding and moving portions of the hierarchy

but

- (−) requires nonstandard SQL extensions for querying and may exhibit poor query performance when the dimension is joined to a large fact table
- (−) can only represent simple trees where a customer can have only one parent (that is, disallowing shared ownership models)
- (−) cannot support switching between different hierarchies
- (−) is very sensitive to time-varying hierarchies because the entire customer dimension undergoes Type 2 changes when the hierarchy is changed

The *hierarchy bridge table* approach shown in Figure 5.26:

- (+) isolates the hierarchy relationships in the bridge table, leaving the customer dimension unaffected

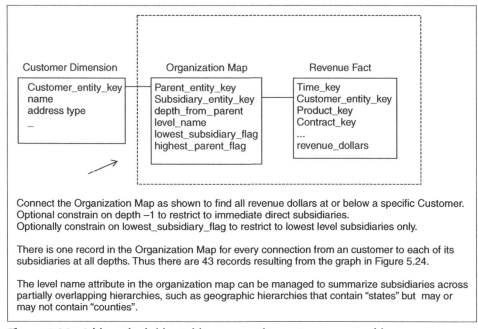

Connect the Organization Map as shown to find all revenue dollars at or below a specific Customer. Optional constrain on depth −1 to restrict to immediate direct subsidiaries.
Optionally constrain on lowest_subsidiary_flag to restrict to lowest level subsidiaries only.

There is one record in the Organization Map for every connection from an customer to each of its subsidiaries at all depths. Thus there are 43 records resulting from the graph in Figure 5.24.

The level name attribute in the organization map can be managed to summarize subsidiaries across partially overlapping hierarchies, such as geographic hierarchies that contain "states" but may or may not contain "counties".

Figure 5.26 A hierarchy bridge table representing customer ownership.

- (+) is queried with standard SQL syntax using single queries that evaluate the whole hierarchy or designated portions of the hierarchy such as just the leaf nodes
- (+) can be readily generalized to handle complex trees with shared ownership and repeating subassemblies
- (+) allows instant switching between different hierarchies because the hierarchy information is entirely concentrated in the bridge table and the bridge table is chosen at query time
- (+) can be readily generalized to handle time-varying Type 2 ragged hierarchies without affecting the primary customer dimension

but

- (−) requires the generation of a separate record for each parent-child relationship in the tree, including second-level parents, third-level parents, and so on. Although the exact number of records is dependent on the structure of the tree, a rough rule of thumb is three times the number of records as nodes in the tree. Forty-three records are required in the bridge table to support the tree shown in Figure 5.24.
- (−) involves more complex logic than the recursive pointer approach in order to add and move structure within the tree
- (−) requires updating the bridge table when Type 2 changes take place within the customer dimension

Technical Note: POPULATING HIERARCHY BRIDGE TABLES

In February 2001, the following technical note on building bridge tables for ragged hierarchies was published as one of Ralph Kimball's monthly design tips. Because it is so relevant to the ETL processes covered in this book, we reproduce it here, edited slightly, to align the vocabulary precisely with the book.

This month's tip follows on from Ralph's September 1998 article "Help for Hierarchies" (http://www.dbmsmag.com/9809d05.html), which addresses hierarchical structures of variable depth which are traditionally represented in relational databases as recursive relationships. Following is the usual definition of a simple company dimension that contains such a recursive relationship between the foreign key PARENT_KEY and primary key COMPANY_KEY.

```
Create table COMPANY (
COMPANY_KEY INTEGER NOT NULL,
COMPANY_NAME        VARCHAR2(50),
(plus other descriptive attributes... ),
PARENT_KEY          INTEGER);
```

While this is efficient for storing information on organizational structures, it is not possible to navigate or rollup facts within these hierarchies using the nonprocedural SQL that can be generated by commercial query tools. Ralph's original article describes a bridge table similar to the one that follows that contains one record for each separate path from each company in the organization tree to itself and to every subsidiary below it that solves this problem.

```
Create table COMPANY_STRUCTURE (
  PARENT_KEY              INTEGER NOT NULL,
  SUBSIDIARY_KEY          INTEGER NOT NULL,
  SUBSIDIARY_LEVEL        INTEGER NOT NULL,
  SEQUENCE_NUMBER       INTEGER NOT NULL,
  LOWEST_FLAG           CHAR(1),
  HIGHEST_FLAG           CHAR(1),
  PARENT_COMPANY         VARCHAR2(50),
  SUBSIDIARY_COMPANY VARCHAR2(50));
```

The last two columns in this example, which denormalize the company names into this table, are not strictly necessary but have been added to make it easy to see what's going on later.

The following PL/SQL stored procedure demonstrates one possible technique for populating this *hierarchy explosion* bridge table from the COMPANY table on Oracle:

```
CREATE or Replace procedure COMPANY_EXPLOSION_SP as
CURSOR Get_Roots is
select  COMPANY_KEY ROOT_KEY,
     decode(PARENT_KEY, NULL,'Y','N') HIGHEST_FLAG,
     COMPANY_NAME ROOT_COMPANY
from COMPANY;
BEGIN
For Roots in Get_Roots
LOOP
     insert into COMPANY_STRUCTURE
     (PARENT_KEY,
     SUBSIDIARY_KEY,
     SUBSIDIARY_LEVEL,
     SEQUENCE_NUMBER,
     LOWEST_FLAG,
     HIGHEST_FLAG,
     PARENT_COMPANY,
     SUBSIDIARY_COMPANY)
```

```
      select
        roots.ROOT_KEY,
        COMPANY_KEY,
        LEVEL - 1,
        ROWNUM,
        'N',
        roots.HIGHEST_FLAG,
        roots.ROOT_COMPANY,
        COMPANY_NAME
      from
        COMPANY
        Start with COMPANY_KEY = roots.ROOT_KEY
        connect by prior COMPANY_KEY = PARENT_KEY;
END LOOP;
update COMPANY_STRUCTURE
    SET LOWEST_FLAG = 'Y'
where not exists (select * from COMPANY
where PARENT_KEY = COMPANY_STRUCTURE.SUBSIDIARY_KEY);
COMMIT;
END; /* of procedure */
```

This solution takes advantage of Oracle's CONNECT BY SQL extension to walk each tree in the data while building the bridge table. While CONNECT BY is very useful within this procedure, it could not be used by an ad-hoc query tool for general-purpose querying. If the tool can generate this syntax to explore the recursive relationship, it cannot in the same statement join to a fact table. Even if Oracle were to remove this somewhat arbitrary limitation, the performance at query time would probably not be too good.

The following fictional company data will help you understand the COMPANY_STRUCTURE table and COMPANY_EXPLOSION_SP procedure:

```
/* column order is Company_key,Company_name,Parent_key */
insert into company values (100,'Microsoft',NULL);
insert into company values (101,'Software',100);
insert into company values (102,'Consulting',101);
insert into company values (103,'Products',101);
insert into company values (104,'Office',103);
insert into company values (105,'Visio',104);
insert into company values (106,'Visio Europe',105);
insert into company values (107,'Back Office',103);
insert into company values (108,'SQL Server',107);
insert into company values (109,'OLAP Services',108);
insert into company values (110,'DTS',108);
insert into company values (111,'Repository',108);
insert into company values (112,'Developer Tools',103);
insert into company values (113,'Windows',103);
insert into company values (114,'Entertainment',103);
insert into company values (115,'Games',114);
```

```
insert into company values (116,'Multimedia',114);
insert into company values (117,'Education',101);
insert into company values (118,'Online Services',100);
insert into company values (119,'WebTV',118);
insert into company values (120,'MSN',118);
insert into company values (121,'MSN.co.uk',120);
insert into company values (122,'Hotmail.com',120);
insert into company values (123,'MSNBC',120);
insert into company values (124,'MSNBC Online',123);
insert into company values (125,'Expedia',120);
insert into company values (126,'Expedia.co.uk',125);
/* End example data */
```

The procedure will take the 27 COMPANY records and create 110 COMPANY_STRUCTURE records make up of one big tree (Microsoft) with 27 nodes and 26 smaller trees. For large datasets, you may find that performance can be enhanced by adding a pair of concatenated indexes on the CONNECT BY columns. In this example, you could build one index on COMPANY_KEY,PARENT_KEY and the other on PARENT_KEY, COMPANY_KEY.

If you want to visualize the tree structure textually, the following query displays an indented subsidiary list for Microsoft:

```
select LPAD( ' ', 3*(SUBSIDIARY_LEVEL)) ||  SUBSIDIARY_COMPANY from
COMPANY_STRUCTURE order by SEQUENCE_NUMBER
```

where PARENT_KEY = 100.

The SEQUENCE_NUMBER has been added since Ralph's original article; it numbers nodes top to bottom, left to right. It allows the correct level-2 nodes to be sorted below their matching level-1 nodes.

For a graphical version of the organization tree, take a look at Visio 2000 Enterprise Edition, which has a database or text-file-driven organization chart wizard. With the help of VBA script, a view on the COMPANY_STRUCTURE table, and a fact table, it might automate the generation of just the HTML pages you want.

Using Positional Attributes in a Dimension to Represent Text Facts

The SQL interface to relational databases places some severe restrictions on certain kinds of analyses that need to perform complex comparisons across dimension records. Consider the following example of a *text fact*.

Suppose that we measure numeric values for recency, frequency, and intensity (RFI) of all our customers. We call in our data-mining colleagues and ask them to identify the natural clusters of customers in this abstract cube labeled by recency, frequency, and intensity. We really don't want all the numeric results; we want behavioral clusters that are meaningful to our marketing department. After running the cluster identifier data-mining step, we find, for example, eight natural clusters of customers. After studying where the centroids of the clusters are located in our RFI cube, we are able to assign behavior descriptions to the eight behavior clusters:

- A: High-volume repeat customer, good credit, few product returns
- B: High-volume repeat customer, good credit, but many product returns
- C: Recent new customer, no established credit pattern
- D: Occasional customer, good credit
- E: Occasional customer, poor credit
- F: Former good customer, not seen recently
- G: Frequent window shopper, mostly unproductive
- H: Other

We can view the tags A through H as *text facts* summarizing a customer's behavior. There aren't a lot of text facts in data warehousing, but these behavior tags seem to be pretty good examples. We can imagine developing a time series of behavior-tag measurements for a customer over time with a data point each month:

```
John Doe: C C C D D A A A B B
```

This little time series is pretty revealing. How can we structure our data warehouse to pump out these kinds of reports? And how can we pose interesting constraints on customers to see only those who have gone from cluster A to cluster B in the most recent time period? We require even more complex queries such as finding customers who were an A in the 5th, 4th, or 3rd previous time period and are a B or a C in either the 2nd or 1st previous period.

We can model this time series of textual behavior tags in several different ways. Each approach has identical information content but differs significantly in ease of use. Let's assume we generate a new behavior tag for each customer each month. Here are three approaches:

1. Fact table record for each customer for each month, with the behavior tag as a textual fact

2. Slowly changing customer dimension record (Type 2) with the behavior tag as a single attribute (field). A new customer record is

created for each customer each month. Same number of new records each month as choice #1.

3. Single customer dimension record with a 24 month time series of behavior tags as 24 attributes, a variant of the Type 3 SCD many alternate realities approach

The whole point of this section is that choices 1 and 2, which create separate records for each behavior tag, leave the data warehouse with a structure that is effectively impossible to query. SQL has no direct approach for posing constraints across records. A sufficiently clever programmer can, of course, do anything, but each complex constraint would need to be programmed by hand. No standard query tool can effectively address design choices 1 or 2.

Design choice 3, shown in Figure 5.27, elegantly solves the query problem. Standard query tools can issue extremely complex *straddle constraints* against this design involving as many of the behavior tags as the user needs, because all the targets of the constraints are in the same record. Additionally, the resulting dimension table can be efficiently indexed with bitmap indexes on each of the low-cardinality behavior tags, so that performance can be excellent, even for complex queries.

There are several ways to maintain this positionally dependent set of text facts over time. Depending on how the applications are built, the attributes could be moved backward each sampling period so that a specific physical field is always the most current period. This makes one class of applications simple, since no changes to a query would have to take place to track the current behavior each month. An additional field in the dimension should identify which real month is the most current, so end users will understand when the time series has been updated. Alternatively, the fields in the dimension can have fixed calendar interpretations. Eventually, all the fields originally allotted would be filled, and a decision would be made at that time to add fields.

Using positionally dependent fields in a dimension to represent a time series of text facts has much of the same logic as the *many alternate realities* design approach for the Type 3 SCD.

Cust key PK	Cust ID NK	Cust name	Period 1 cluster	Period 2 cluster	Period 3 cluster	Period 4 cluster	...	Period 24 cluster
12766	A23X	John Doe	C	C	D	A	...	B

Figure 5.27 Using positional attributes to model text facts.

Summary

This chapter has presented the state-of-the-art design techniques for building the dimensions of a data warehouse. Remember that while there are many different data structures in the ETL back room, including flat files, XML data sets, and entity-relation schemas, we transform all these structures into dimensional schemas to prepare for the final data-presentation step in the front room.

Although dimension tables are almost always much smaller than fact tables, dimension tables give the data warehouse its texture and provide the entry points into the universe of fact table measurements.

The dimension-table designs given here are both practical and universal. Every one of the techniques in this chapter can be applied in many different subject areas, and the ETL code and administrative practices can be reused. The three types of slowly changing dimensions (SCDs), in particular, have become basic vocabulary among data warehouse designers. Merely mentioning Type 2 SCD conveys a complete context for handling time variance, assigning keys, building aggregates, and performing queries.

Having exhaustively described the techniques for building dimensions, we now turn our attention to fact tables, the monster tables in our data warehouse containing all of our measurements.

Delivering Fact Tables

Fact tables hold the measurements of an enterprise. The relationship between fact tables and measurements is extremely simple. If a measurement exists, it can be modeled as a fact table row. If a fact table row exists, it is a measurement. What is a measurement? A common definition of a measurement is *an amount determined by observation with an instrument or a scale*.

In dimensional modeling, we deliberately build our databases around the numerical measurements of the enterprise. Fact tables contain measurements, and dimension tables contain the context surrounding measurements. This simple view of the world has proven again and again to be intuitive and understandable to the end users of our data warehouses. This is why we package and deliver data warehouse content through dimensional models.

PROCESS CHECK Planning & Design:
Requirements/Realities → Architecture → Implementation → Test/Release

Data Flow: Extract → Clean → Conform → *Deliver*

Chapter 5 describes how to build the dimension tables of the data warehouse. It might seem odd to start with the dimension tables, given that measurements and therefore fact tables are really what end users want to see. But dimension tables are the entry points to fact table data. Facts make no sense unless interpreted by dimensions. Since Chapter 5 does a complete job of describing dimensions, we find this chapter to be simpler in some ways.

The Basic Structure of a Fact Table

Every fact table is defined by the *grain* of the table. The grain of the fact table is the definition of the measurement event. The designer must always state the grain of the fact table in terms of how the measurement is taken in the physical world. For example, the grain of the fact table shown in Figure 6.1 could be *an individual line item on a specific retail sales ticket*. We will see that this grain can then later be expressed in terms of the dimension foreign keys and possibly other fields in the fact table, but we don't start by defining the grain in terms of these fields. The grain definition must first be stated in physical-measurement terms, and the dimensions and other fields in the fact table will follow.

All fact tables possess a set of foreign keys connected to the dimensions that provide the context of the fact table measurements. Most fact tables also possess one or more numerical measurement fields, which we call *facts*. See Figure 6.1. Some fact tables possess one or more special dimension-like fields known as *degenerate dimensions*, which we introduce Chapter 5. Degenerate dimensions exist in the fact table, but they are not foreign keys,

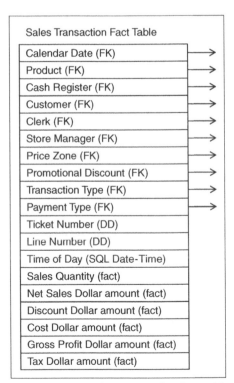

Figure 6.1 A sales transaction fact table at the lowest grain.

and they do not join to a real dimension. We denote degenerate dimensions in Figure 6.1 with the notation *DD*.

In practice, fact tables almost always have at least three dimensions, but most fact tables have more. As data warehousing and the surrounding hardware and software technology has matured over the last 20 years, fact tables have grown enormously because they are storing more and more granular data at the lowest levels of measurement. Ironically, the smaller the measurement, the more dimensions apply. In the earliest days of retail-sales data warehouses, data sets were available only at high levels of aggregation. These early retail databases usually had only three or four dimensions (usually product, market, time, and promotion). Today, we collect retail data at the atomic level of the individual sales transaction. An individual sales transaction can easily have the ten dimensions shown in Figure 6.1 (calendar date; product; cash register, which rolls up to the store level; customer; clerk; store manager; price zone; promotional discount; transaction type; and payment type). Even with these ten dimensions, we may be tempted to add more dimensions over time including store demographics, marketplace competitive events, and the weather!

Virtually every fact table has a primary key defined by a subset of the fields in the table. In Figure 6.1, a plausible primary key for the fact table is the combination of the ticket number and line number degenerate dimensions. These two fields define the unique measurement event of a single item being run up at the cash register. It is also likely that an equivalent primary key could be defined by the combination of cash register and the date/time stamp.

It is possible, if insufficient attention is paid to the design, to violate the assumptions of the primary key on a fact table. Perhaps two identical measurement events have occurred on the same time period, but the data warehouse team did not realize that this could happen. Obviously, every fact table should have a primary key, even if just for administrative purposes. If two or more records in the fact table are allowed to be completely identical because there is no primary key enforced, there is no way to tell the records apart or to be sure that they represent valid discrete measurement events. But as long as the ETL team is sure that separate data loads represent legitimate distinct measurement events, fact table records can be made unique by providing a unique sequence number on the fact record itself at load time. Although the unique sequence number has no business relevance and should not be delivered to end users, it provides an administrative guarantee that a separate and presumably legitimate measurement event occurred. If the ETL team cannot guarantee that separate loads represent legitimate separate measurement events, a primary key on the data must be correctly defined before any data is loaded.

💡 **The preceding example illustrates the need to make all ETL jobs *reentrant* so that the job can be run a second time, either deliberately or in error, without updating the target database incorrectly. In SQL parlance, UPDATES of constant values are usually safe, but UPDATES that increment values are dangerous. INSERTS are safe if a primary key is defined and enforced because a duplicate INSERT will trigger an error. DELETES are generally safe when the constraints are based on simple field values.**

Guaranteeing Referential Integrity

In dimensional modeling, referential integrity means that every fact table is filled with legitimate foreign keys. Or, to put it another way, no fact table record contains corrupt or unknown foreign key references.

There are only two ways to violate referential integrity in a dimensional schema:

1. Load a fact record with one or more bad foreign keys.

2. Delete a dimension record whose primary key is being used in the fact table.

If you don't pay attention to referential integrity, it is amazingly easy to violate it. The authors have studied fact tables where referential integrity was not explicitly enforced; in every case, serious violations were found. A fact record that violates referential integrity (because it has one or more bad foreign keys) is not just an annoyance; it is dangerous. Presumably, the record has some legitimacy, as it probably represents a true measurement event, but it is stored in the database incorrectly. Any query that references the *bad dimension* in the fact record will fail to include the fact record; by definition, the join between the dimension and this fact record cannot take place. But any query that omits mention of the bad dimension may well include the record in a dynamic aggregation!

In Figure 6.2, we show the three main places in the ETL pipeline where referential integrity can be enforced. They are:

1. Careful bookkeeping and data preparation just *before loading* the fact table records into the final tables, coupled with careful bookkeeping before deleting any dimension records

2. Enforcement of referential integrity in the database itself *at the moment* of every fact table insertion and every dimension table deletion

3. Discovery and correction of referential integrity violations *after loading* has occurred by regularly scanning the fact table, looking for bad foreign keys

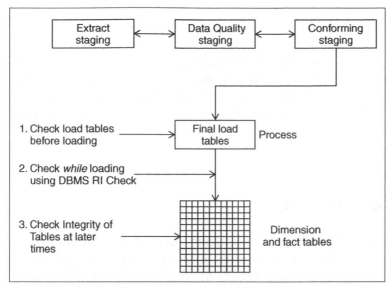

Figure 6.2   Choices for enforcing referential integrity.

Practically speaking, the first option usually makes the most sense. One of the last steps just before the fact table load is looking up the natural keys in the fact table record and replacing them with the correct contemporary values of the dimension surrogate keys. This process is explained in detail in the next section on the surrogate key pipeline. The heart of this procedure is a special lookup table for each dimension that contains the correct value of the surrogate key to be used for every incoming natural key. If this table is correctly maintained, the fact table records will obey referential integrity. Similarly, when dimension table records are to be deleted, a query must be done attempting to join the dimension record to the fact table. Only if the query returns null should the dimension record be deleted.

The second option of having the database enforce referential integrity continuously is elegant but often too slow for major bulk loads of thousands or millions of records. But this is only a matter of software technology. The Red Brick database system (now sold by IBM) was purpose-built to maintain referential integrity at all times, and it is capable of loading 100 million records an hour into a fact table where it is checking referential integrity on all the dimensions simultaneously!

The third option of checking for referential integrity after database changes have been made is theoretically capable of finding all violations but may be prohibitively slow. The queries checking referential integrity must be of the form:

```
select f.product_key
from fact_table f
```

```
where f.product_key not in (select p.product_key from
product_dimension p)
```

In an environment with a million-row product dimension and a billion-row fact table, this is a ridiculous query. But perhaps the query can be restricted only to the data that has been loaded today. That assumes the time dimension foreign key is correct! But this is a sensible approach that probably should be used as a sanity check even if the first approach is the main processing technique.

Surrogate Key Pipeline

When building a fact table, the final ETL step is converting the natural keys in the new input records into the correct, contemporary surrogate keys. In this section, we assume that all records to be loaded into the fact table are current. In other words, we need to use the most current values of the surrogate keys for each dimension entity (like customer or product). We will deal with late-arriving fact records later in this chapter.

We could theoretically look up the current surrogate key in each dimension table by fetching the most recent record with the desired natural key. This is logically correct but slow. Instead, we maintain a special surrogate key lookup table for each dimension. This table is updated whenever a new dimension entity is created and whenever a Type 2 change occurs on an existing dimension entity. We introduce this table in the Chapter 5 when we discuss Figure 5.16.

The dimension tables must all be updated with insertions and Type 2 changes before we even think of dealing with the fact tables. This sequence of updating the dimensions first followed by updating the fact tables is the usual sequence when maintaining referential integrity between the dimension tables and fact tables. The reverse sequence is used when deleting records. First, we remove unwanted fact table records; then we are free to remove dimension records that no longer have any links to the fact table.

> 💡 **Don't necessarily delete dimension records just because a fact table has no references to such records. The entities in a dimension may well exist and should be kept in the dimension even if there is no *activity* in the fact table.**

When we are done updating our dimension tables, not only are all the dimension records correct; our surrogate key lookup tables that tie the natural keys to the current values of the data warehouse keys have been updated correctly.

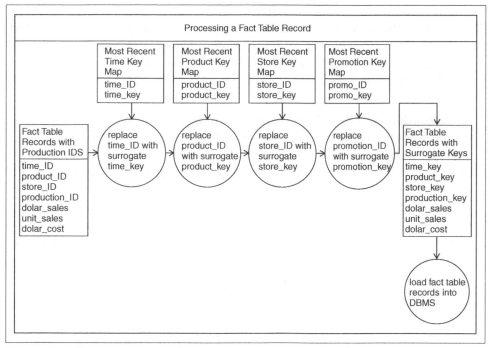

Figure 6.3   The surrogate key pipeline.

Our task for processing the incoming fact table records is simple to understand. See Figure 6.3. We take each natural dimension key in the incoming fact table record and *replace* it with the correct current surrogate key. Notice that we say *replace*. We don't keep the natural key value in the fact record itself. If you care what the natural key value is, you can always find it in the associated dimension record.

If we have between four and 12 natural keys, every incoming fact record requires between four and twelve separate lookups to get the right surrogate keys. First, we set up a multithreaded application that streams all the input records through all the steps shown in Figure 6.3. When we say *multithreaded,* we mean that as input record #1 is running the gantlet of successive key lookups and replacements, record #2 is simultaneously right behind record #1, and so on. We do not process all the incoming records in the first lookup step and then pass the whole file to the next step. It is essential for fast performance that the input records are not written to disk until they have passed though all the processing steps. They must literally *fly* through memory without touching ground (the disk) until the end.

If possible, all of the required lookup tables should be pinned in memory so that they can be randomly accessed as each incoming fact record presents its natural keys. This is one of the reasons for making the lookup tables separate from the original data warehouse dimension tables. Suppose we have a million-row lookup table for a dimension. If the natural key is 20 bytes and the surrogate key is 4 bytes, we need roughly 24 MB of RAM to hold the lookup table. In an environment where we can configure the data-staging machine with 4 to 8 GB of RAM, we should easily get all of the lookup tables in memory.

> The architecture described in the previous paragraph is the highest-performance configuration we know how to design. But let's keep things in perspective. If you are loading a few hundred-thousand records per day, and your load windows are forgiving, you don't need to emphasize performance to this degree. You can define a star join query between your fact tables and your dimension tables, swapping out the natural keys for the surrogate keys, and run the whole process in SQL. In this case, you would also define outer joins on certain dimensions if there were a possibility that any incoming fact records could not be matched to the dimensions (a referential integrity failure).

> The programming utility *awk* can also be used in this situation because it supports the creation of in-memory arrays for the natural key to surrogate key translation by allowing the natural key itself to serve as the array index. Thus, if you define Translate_Dimension_A[natural_key] = surrogate_key, processing each fact record is simply: print Translate_Dimension_A($1), Translate_Dimension_B($2), and so on.

In some important large fact tables, we may have a *monster dimension*, like residential customer, that might have a hundred-million members. If we have only one such huge dimension, we can still design a fast pipelined surrogate key system, even though the huge dimension lookup table might have to be read off the disk as it is being used. The secret is to presort both the incoming fact data and the lookup table on the natural key of this dimension. Now the surrogate key replacement is a single pass sort-merge through the two files. This should be pretty fast, although nothing beats in-memory processing. If you have two such monster lookup tables in your pipeline that you cannot pin in memory, you will suffer a processing penalty because of the I/O required for the random accesses on the nonsorted dimension key.

> It is possible for incoming fact records to make it all the way to the surrogate key pipeline with one or more bad natural keys because we may or may not be checking referential integrity of the underlying source system. If this happens, we recommend creating a new surrogate key and a new dimension record appropriately labeled *Unknown*. Each such incoming bad natural key should get a unique fresh surrogate key if there is any hope of eventually correcting the data. If

your business reality is that bad natural keys must remain forever unresolved, a single well-known surrogate key value (and default Unknown record) can be used in all these cases within the affected dimension.

Using the Dimension Instead of a Lookup Table

The lookup table approach described in the previous section works best when the overwhelming fraction of fact records processed each day are *contemporary* (in other words, completely current). But if a significant number of fact records are late arriving, the lookup table cannot be used and the dimension must be the source for the correct surrogate key. This assumes, of course, that the dimension has been designed as described in Chapter 5, with begin and end effective date stamps and the natural key present in every record.

Avoiding the separate lookup table also simplifies the ETL administration before the fact table load because the steps of synchronizing the lookup table with the dimension itself are eliminated.

Certain ETL tool suites offer a high-speed, in-memory cache created by looking at the natural keys of the incoming fact records and then linking these natural keys to the right surrogate keys by querying the dimension table in real time. If this works satisfactorily, it has the advantage that the lookup table can be avoided entirely. A possible downside is the startup overhead incurred in dynamically creating this cache while accessing the possibly large dimension. If this dynamic lookup can successfully search for old values of surrogate keys by combining a given natural key with the time stamp on the incoming fact record, this technique could be very effective for handling late-arriving fact table records. You should ask your ETL vendor specific questions about this capability.

Fundamental Grains

Since fact tables are meant to store all the numerical measurements of an enterprise, you might expect that here would be many flavors of fact tables. Surprisingly, in our experience, fact tables can always be reduced to just three fundamental types. We recommend strongly that you adhere to these three simple types in every design situation. When designers begin to mix and combine these types into more complicated structures, an enormous burden is transferred to end user query tools and applications to keep from making serious errors. Another way to say this is that every fact table should have one, *and only one*, grain.

The three kinds of fact tables are: the transaction grain, the periodic snapshot, and the accumulating snapshot. We discuss these three grains in the next three sections.

Transaction Grain Fact Tables

The transaction grain represents an instantaneous measurement at a specific point in space and time. The standard example of a transaction grain measurement event is a retail sales transaction. When the product passes the scanner and the scanner beeps (and only *if* the scanner beeps), a record is created. Transaction grain records are created only if the measurement events take place. Thus, a transaction grain fact table can be virtually empty, or it can contain billions of records.

We have remarked that the tiny atomic measurements typical of transaction grain fact tables have a large number of dimensions. You can refer to Figure 6.1, which shows the retail scanner event.

In environments like a retail store, there may be only one transaction type (the retail sale) being measured. In other environments, such as insurance claims processing, there may be many transaction types all mixed together in the flow of data. In this case, the numeric measurement field is usually labeled generically as *amount*, and a transaction type dimension is required to interpret the amount. See Figure 6.4. In any case, the numeric measures in the transaction grain tables must refer to the instant of the measurement event, not to a span of time or to some other time. In other words, *the facts must be true to the grain*.

Transaction grain fact tables are the largest and most detailed of the three kinds of fact tables. Since individual transactions are often carefully time

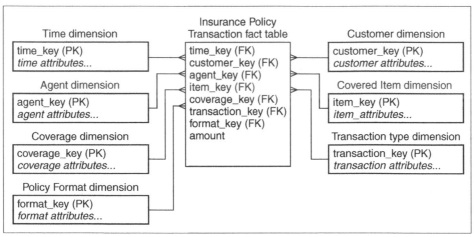

Figure 6.4 A standard transaction grain fact table drawn from insurance.

stamped, transaction grain tables are often used for the most complex and intricate analyses. For instance, in an insurance claims processing environment, a transaction grain fact table is required to describe the most complex sequence of transactions that some claims undergo and to analyze detailed timing measurements among transactions of different types. This level of information simply isn't available in the other two fact-table types. However, it is not always the case that the periodic snapshot and the accumulating snapshot tables can be generated as routine aggregations of the transaction grain tables. In the insurance environment, the operational premium processing system typically generates a measure of *earned premium* for each policy each month. This earned premium measurement must go into the monthly periodic snapshot table, not the transaction grain table. The business rules for calculating earned premium are so complicated that it is effectively impossible for the data warehouse to calculate this monthly measure using only low-level transactions.

Transactions that are time stamped to the nearest minute, second, or microsecond should be modeled by making the calendar day component a conventional dimension with a foreign key to the normal calendar date dimension, and the full date-time expressed as a SQL data type in the fact table, as shown in Chapter 5 in Figure 5.5.

Since transaction grain tables have unpredictable sparseness, front-end applications cannot assume that any given set of keys will be present in a query. This problem arises when a customer dimension tries to be matched with a demographic behavior dimension. If the constraints are too narrow (say, a specific calendar day), it is possible that no records are returned from the query, and the match of the customer to the demographics is omitted from the results. Database architects aware of this problem may specify a *factless* coverage table that contains every meaningful combination of keys so that an application is guaranteed to match the customer with the demographics. See the discussion of factless fact tables later in this chapter. We will see that the periodic snapshot fact table described in the next section neatly avoids this sparseness problem because periodic snapshots are perfectly dense in their primary key set.

In the ideal case, contemporary transaction level fact records are received in large batches at regular intervals by the data warehouse. The target fact table in most cases should be partitioned by time in a typical DBMS environment. This allows the DBA to drop certain indexes on the most recent time partition, which will speed up a bulk load of new records into this partition. After the load runs to completion, the indexes on the partition are restored. If the partitions can be renamed and swapped, it is possible for the fact table to be offline for only minutes while the updating takes place. This is a complex subject, with many variations in indexing strategies and physical data storage. It is possible that there are indexes on the fact table

Reporting Month (FK)
Account (FK)
Branch (FK)
Household (FK)
Ending Balance (fact)
Change in Balance (fact)
Average Daily Balance (fact)
Number of Deposits (fact)
Total of Deposits (fact)
Number of Withdrawal (fact)
Total of Withdrawals (fact)
Total of Penalties (fact)
Total Interest Paid into (fact)
Daily Average Backup Reserve amount (fact)
Number of ATM Withdrawals (fact)
Number Foreign System ATM Withdrawal (fact)
Number PayPal Withdrawals (fact)
Total PayPal Withdrawals (fact)

Figure 6.5 A periodic snapshot for a checking account in a bank.

that do not depend on the partitioning logic and cannot be dropped. Also, some parallel processing database technologies physically distribute data so that the most recent data is not stored in one physical location.

When the incoming transaction data arrives in a streaming fashion, rather than in discrete file-based loads, we have crossed the boundary into real-time data warehouses, which are discussed in Chapter 11.

Periodic Snapshot Fact Tables

The periodic snapshot represents a span of time, regularly repeated. This style of table is well suited for tracking long-running processes such as bank accounts and other forms of financial reporting. The most common periodic snapshots in the finance world have a monthly grain. All the facts in a periodic snapshot must be true to the grain (that is, they must be measures of activity during the span). In Figure 6.5, we show a periodic snapshot for a checking account in a bank, reported every month. An obvious feature in this design is the potentially large number of facts. Any numeric measure of the account that measures activity for the time span is fair game. For this reason, periodic snapshot fact tables are more likely to be *gracefully modified* during their lifetime by adding more facts to the basic grain of the table. See the section on graceful modifications later in this chapter.

The date dimension in the periodic snapshot fact table refers to the period. Thus, the date dimension for a monthly periodic snapshot is a dimension of calendar months. We discuss generating such aggregated date dimensions in Chapter 5.

An interesting question arises about what the exact surrogate keys for all the nontime dimensions should be in the periodic snapshot records. Since the periodic snapshot for the period cannot be generated until the period has passed, the most logical choice for the surrogate keys for the nontime dimensions is their value at the exact end of the period. So, for example, the surrogate keys for the account and branch dimensions in Figure 6.5 should be those precise values at the end of the period, notwithstanding the possibility that the account and branch descriptions could have changed in complicated ways in the middle of the period. These intermediate surrogate keys simply do not appear in the monthly periodic snapshot.

Periodic snapshot fact tables have completely predictable sparseness. The account activity fact table in Figure 6.5 has one record for each account for each month. As long as an account is active, an application can assume that the various dimensions will all be present in every query.

⚓ **The final tables delivered to end user applications will have completely predictable sparseness, but your original sources may not! You should outer join the primary dimensions of your periodic snapshot fact table to the original data source to make sure that you generate records for every valid combination of keys, even when there is no reported activity for some of them in the current load.**

Periodic snapshot fact tables have similar loading characteristics to those of the transaction grain tables. As long as data is promptly delivered to the data warehouse, all records in each periodic load will cluster in the most recent time partition.

However, there are two somewhat different strategies for maintaining periodic snapshot fact tables. The traditional strategy waits until the period has passed and then loads all the records at once. But increasingly, the periodic snapshot maintains a special *current hot rolling period*. The banking fact table of Figure 6.5 could have 36 fixed time periods, representing the last three years of activity, but also have a special 37th month updated incrementally every night during the current period. This works best if the 37th period is correctly stated when the last day has been loaded in normal fashion. This strategy is less appealing if the final periodic snapshot differs from the last day's load, because of behind-the-scenes ledger adjustments during a month-end-closing process that do not appear in the normal data downloads.

When the hot rolling period is updated continuously throughout the day by streaming the data, rather than through periodic file-based loads, we have crossed the line into real-time data warehouse systems, which we discuss in Chapter 11.

> 💡 **Creating a contunuously updated periodic snapshot can be difficult or even impossible if the business rules for calculating measures at period end are very complex. For example, in insurance companies, the calculation of earned premium at the end of the period is handled by the transaction system, and these measures are available only at the end of the period. The data warehouse cannot easily caluclate earned premium at midpoints of the reporting periods; the business rules are extraordinarily complex and are far beyond the normal ETL transformation logic.**

Accumulating Snapshot Fact Tables

The accumulating snapshot fact table is used to describe processes that have a definite beginning and end, such as order fulfillment, claims processing, and most workflows. The accumulating snapshot is not appropriate for long-running continuous processes such as tracking bank accounts or describing continuous manufacturing processes like paper mills.

The grain of an accumulating snapshot fact table is the complete history of an entity from its creation to the present moment. Figure 6.6 shows an accumulating snapshot fact table whose grain is the line item on a shipment invoice.

Accumulating snapshot fact tables have several unusual characteristics. The most obvious difference seen in Figure 6.6 is the large number of calendar date foreign keys. All accumulating snapshot fact tables have a set of dates that implement the *standard scenario* for the table. The standard scenario for the shipment invoice line item in Figure 6.6 is order date, requested ship date, actual ship date, delivery date, last payment date, return date, and settlement date. We can assume that an individual record is created when a shipment invoice is created. At that moment, only the order date and the requested ship date are known. The record for a specific line item on the invoice is inserted into the fact table with known dates for these first two foreign keys. The remaining foreign keys are all *not applicable* and their surrogate keys must point to the special record in the calendar date dimension corresponding to Not Applicable. Over time, as events unfold, *the original record is revisited and the foreign keys corresponding to the other dates are overwritten* with values pointing to actual dates. The last payment date may well be overwritten several times as payments are stretched out. The

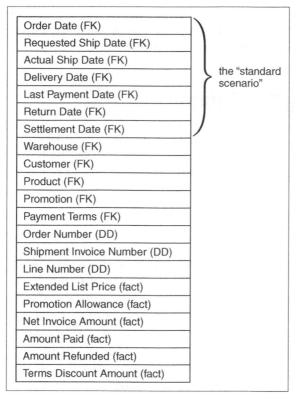

Order Date (FK)
Requested Ship Date (FK)
Actual Ship Date (FK)
Delivery Date (FK)   } the "standard
Last Payment Date (FK)   scenario"
Return Date (FK)
Settlement Date (FK)
Warehouse (FK)
Customer (FK)
Product (FK)
Promotion (FK)
Payment Terms (FK)
Order Number (DD)
Shipment Invoice Number (DD)
Line Number (DD)
Extended List Price (fact)
Promotion Allowance (fact)
Net Invoice Amount (fact)
Amount Paid (fact)
Amount Refunded (fact)
Terms Discount Amount (fact)

Figure 6.6 An accumulating snapshot fact table where the grain is the shipment invoice line item.

return date and settlement dates may well never be overwritten for normal orders that are not returned or disputed.

The facts in the accumulating snapshot record are also revisited and over-written as events unfold. Note that in Oracle, the actual width of an individual record depends on its contents, so accumulating snapshot records in Oracle will always grow. This will affect the residency of disk blocks. In cases where a lot of block splits are generated by these changes, it may be worthwhile to drop and reload the records that have been extensively changed, once the changes settle down, to improve performance. One way to accomplish this is to partition the fact table along two dimensions such as date and current status (Open/Closed). Initially partition along current status, and when the item is closed, move it to the other partition.

An accumulating snapshot fact table is a very efficient and appealing way to represent finite processes with definite beginnings and endings. The more the process fits the standard scenario defined by the set of dates in the fact table, the simpler the end user applications will be. If end users occasionally need to understand extremely complicated and unusual situations, such as a shipment that was damaged or shipped to the wrong customer, the best recourse is a companion transaction grain table that can be fully exploded to see all the events that occurred for the unusual shipment.

Preparing for Loading Fact Tables

In this section, we explain how to build efficient load processes and overcome common obstacles. If done incorrectly, loading data can be the worst experience for an ETL developer. The next three sections outline some of the obstructions you face.

Managing Indexes

Indexes are performance enhancers at query time, but they are performance killers at load time. Tables that are heavily indexed bring your process to a virtual standstill if they are not handled correctly. Before you attempt to load a table, drop all of its indexes in a preload process. You can rebuild the indexes after the load is complete in a post-load process. When your load process includes updates, separate the records required for the updates from those to be inserted and process them separately. In a nutshell, perform the steps that follow to prevent table indexes from causing a bottleneck in your ETL process.

1. Segregate updates from inserts.
2. Drop any indexes not required to support updates.
3. Load updates.
4. Drop all remaining indexes.
5. Load inserts (through bulk loader).
6. Rebuild the indexes.

Managing Partitions

Partitions allow a table (and its indexes) to be physically divided into *mini-tables* for administrative purposes and to improve query performance. The ultimate benefit of partitioning a table is that a query that requires a month of data from a table that has ten years of data can go directly to the partition of the table that contains data for the month without scanning other data. Table partitions can dramatically improve query performance on large fact tables. The partitions of a table are *under the covers*, hidden from the users. Only the DBA and ETL team should be aware of partitions.

The most common partitioning strategy on fact tables is to partition the table by the date key. Because the date dimension is preloaded and static, you know exactly what the surrogate keys are. We've seen designers add a timestamp to fact tables for partitioning purposes, but unless the timestamp is constrained by the user's query, the partitions are not utilized by the optimizer. Since users typically constrain on columns in the date dimension, you need to partition the fact table on the key that joins to the date dimension for the optimizer to recognize the constraint.

Tables that are partitioned by a date interval are usually partitioned by year, quarter, or month. Extremely voluminous facts may be partitioned by week or even day. Usually, the data warehouse designer works with the DBA team to determine the best partitioning strategy on a table-by-table basis. The ETL team must be advised of any table partitions that need to be maintained.

Unless your DBA team takes a proactive role in administering your partitions, the ETL process must manage them. If your load frequency is monthly and your fact table is partitioned by month, partition maintenance is pretty straightforward. When your load frequency differs from the table partitions or your tables are partitioned on an element other than time, the process becomes a bit trickier.

Suppose your fact table is partitioned by year and the first three years are created by the DBA team. When you attempt to load any data after December, 31, 2004, in Oracle you receive the following error:

```
ORA-14400: inserted partition key is beyond highest legal partition key
```

At this point, the ETL process has a choice:

- Notify the DBA team, wait for them to manually create the next partition, and resume loading.
- Dynamically add the next partition required to complete loading.

Once the surrogate keys of the incoming data have been resolved, the ETL process can proactively test the incoming data against the defined partitions in the database by comparing the highest date_key with the high value defined in the last partition of the table.

```
select max(date_key) from 'STAGE_FACT_TABLE'
```

compared with

```
select high_value from all_tab_partitions
where table_name = 'FACT_TABLE'
and partition_position = (select max(partition_position)
from all_tab_partitions where table_name = 'FACT_TABLE')
```

If the incoming data is in the next year after the defined partition allows, the ETL process can create the next partition with a preprocess script.

```
ALTER TABLE fact_table
ADD PARTITION year_2005 VALUES LESS THAN (1828)
   --1828 is the surrogate key for January 1, 2005.
```

The maintenance steps just discussed can be written in a stored procedure and called by the ETL process before each load. The procedure can produce the required ALTER TABLE statement, inserting the appropriate January 1 surrogate key value as required, depending on the year of the incoming data.

Outwitting the Rollback Log

By design, any relational database management system attempts to support midtransaction failures. The system recovers from uncommitted transaction failures by recording every transaction in a log. Upon failure, the database accesses the log and *undoes* any transactions that have not been committed. To *commit* a transaction means that you or your application explicitly tells the database that the entry of the transaction is completely finished and that the transaction should be permanently written to disk.

The rollback log, also known as the redo log, is invaluable in transaction (OLTP) systems. But in a data warehouse environment where all transactions are managed by the ETL process, the rollback log is a superfluous feature that must be dealt with to achieve optimal load performance. Reasons why the data warehouse does not need rollback logging include:

- All data is entered by a managed process—the ETL system.
- Data is loaded in bulk.
- Data can easily be reloaded if a load process fails.

Each database management system has different logging features and manages its rollback log differently.

Loading the Data

The initial load of a new table has a unique set of challenges. The primary challenge is handling the one-time immense volume of data.

- **Separate inserts from updates.** Many ETL tools (and some databases) offer *update else insert* functionality. This functionality is very convenient and simplifies data-flow logic but is notoriously slow. ETL processes that require updates to existing data should include logic that separates records that already exist in the fact table from new ones. Whenever you are dealing with a substantial amount of data, you want to bulk-load it into the data warehouse. Unfortunately, many bulk-load utilities cannot update existing records. By separating the update records from the inserts, you can first process the updates and then bulk-load the balance of the records for optimal load performance.

- **Utilize a bulk-load utility.** Using a bulk-load utility rather than SQL INSERT statements to load data substantially decreases database overhead and drastically improves load performance.

- **Load in parallel.** When loading volumes of data, physically break up data into logical segments. If you are loading five years of data, perhaps you can make five data files that contain one year each. Some ETL tools allow you to partition data based on ranges of data values dynamically. Once data is divided into equal segments, run the ETL process to load all of the segments in parallel.

- **Minimize physical updates.** Updating records in a table requires massive amounts of overhead in the DBMS, most of which is caused by the database populating the rollback log. To minimize writing to the rollback log, you need to bulk-load data in the database. But what about the updates? In many cases, it is better to delete the records that would be updated and then bulk-load the new versions of those records along with the records entering the data warehouse for the first time. Since the ratio of records being updated versus the number of existing rows plays a crucial factor in selecting the optimal technique, some trial-and-error testing is usually required to see if this approach is the ultimate load strategy for your particular situation.

- **Build aggregates outside of the database.** Sorting, merging, and building aggregates outside of the database may be more efficient than using SQL with COUNT and SUM functions and GROUP BY and ORDER BY keywords in the DBMS. ETL processes that require sorting and/or merging high volumes of data should perform these functions before they enter the relational database staging area. Many ETL tools are adequate at performing these functions, but dedicated tools to perform sort/merges at the operating-system level are worth the investment for processing large datasets.

💡 **Your ETL process should minimize updates and insert all fact data via the database bulk-load utility. If massive updates are necessary, consider truncating and reloading the entire fact table via the bulk loader to obtain the fastest load strategy. When minimal updates are required, segregate the updates from the inserts and process them separately.**

Incremental Loading

The incremental load is the process that occurs periodically to keep the data warehouse synchronized with its respective source systems. Incremental processes can run at any interval or continuously (real-time). At the time of this writing, the customary interval for loading a data warehouse is daily, but no hard-and-fast rule or best practice exists where incremental load intervals are concerned. Users typically like daily updates because they leave data in the warehouse static throughout the day, preventing *twinkling* data, which would make the data ever-changing and cause intraday reporting inconsistencies.

ETL routines that load data incrementally are usually a result of the process that initially loaded the historic data into the data warehouse. It is a preferred practice to keep the two processes one and the same. The ETL team must parameterize the begin_date and end_date of the extract process so the ETL routine has the flexibility to load small incremental segments or the historic source data in its entirety.

Inserting Facts

When you create new fact records, you need to get data in as quickly as possible. Always utilize your database bulk-load utility. Fact tables are too immense to process via SQL INSERT statements. The database logging caused by SQL INSERT statements is completely superfluous in the data warehouse. The log is created for failure recovery. If your load routine fails, your ETL tool must be able to recover from the failure and pick up where it left off, regardless of database logging.

> **Failure recovery is a feature prevalent in the major ETL tools. Each vendor handles failures, and recovering from them, differently. Make sure your ETL vendors explain exactly how their failure-recovery mechanism works and select the product that requires minimal manual intervention. Be sure to test failure-recovery functionality during your ETL proof-of-concept.**

Updating and Correcting Facts

We've participated in many discussions that address the issue of updating data warehouse data—especially fact data. Most agree that dimensions, regardless of the slowly changing dimension strategy, must exactly reflect the data of their source. However, there are several arguments against making changes to fact data once it is in the data warehouse.

Most arguments that support the notion that the data warehouse must reflect all changes made to a transaction system are usually based on theory, not reality. However, the data warehouse is intended to support analysis of the *business*, not the system where the data is derived. For the data warehouse to properly reflect business activity, it must accurately depict its factual events. Regardless of any opposing argument, a data-entry error is not a business event (unless of course, you are building a data mart specifically for analysis of data-entry precision).

Recording unnecessary records that contradict correct ones is counterproductive and can skew analytical results. Consider this example: A company sells 1,000 containers of soda, and the data in the source system records that the package type is 12-ounce cans. After data is published to the data warehouse, a mistake is discovered that the package type should have been 20-ounce bottles. Upon discovery, the source system is immediately updated to reflect the true package type. The business never sold the 12-ounce cans. While performing sales analysis, the business does not need to know a data error occurred. Conversely, preserving the erroneous data might misrepresent the sales figures of 12-ounce cans. You can handle data corrections in the data warehouse in three essential ways.

- Negate the fact.
- Update the fact.
- Delete and reload the fact.

All three strategies result in a reflection of the actual occurrence—the sale of 1,000 20-ounce bottles of soda.

Negating Facts

Negating an error entails creating an exact duplicate of the erroneous record where the measures are a result of the original measures multiplied by -1. The negative measures in the reversing fact table record *cancel out* the original record.

Many reasons exist for negating an error rather than taking other approaches to correcting fact data. The primary reason is for audit purposes. Negating errors in the data warehouse is a good practice if you are specifically looking to capture data-entry errors for analytical purposes. Moreover, if capturing actual erroneous events is significant to the business, the transaction system should have its own data-entry audit capabilities.

Other reasons for negating facts, instead of updating or deleting, involve data volume and ETL performance. In cases where fact table rows are in the hundreds of millions, it could be argued that searching and affecting existing records makes ETL performance deteriorate. However, it is the responsibility of the ETL team to provide required solutions with optimum efficiency. You cannot dictate business policies based on technical criterion. If the business prefers to eliminate errors rather than negate them, it is your responsibility to fulfill that request. This chapter discusses several options to ensure your processes are optimal.

Updating Facts

Updating data in fact tables can be a process-intensive endeavor. In most database management systems, an UPDATE automatically triggers entries in the database log for ROLLBACK protection. Database logging greatly reduces load performance. The best approach to updating fact data is to REFRESH the table via the bulk-load utility. If you must use SQL to UPDATE fact tables, make sure you have the column(s) that uniquely identify the rows in the table indexed and drop all other indexes on the table. Unessential indexes drastically degrade performance of the updates.

Deleting Facts

Most agree that deleting errors is most likely the best solution for correcting data in your fact tables. An arguable drawback is that current versions of previously released reports will not reconcile. But if you accept that you are changing data, any technique used to achieve that goal amends existing reports. Most do not consider changing data a bad thing if the current version represents the truth.

Academically, deleting facts from a fact table is forbidden in data warehousing. However, you'll find that deleting facts is a common practice in most data warehouse environments. If your business requires deletions, two ways to handle them exist:

- **Physical deletes.** In most cases, the business doesn't want to see data that no longer exists in the source transaction systems. When physical deletes are required, you must adhere to the business rules and delete the unwanted records.

- **Logical deletes.** Logically deleting fact records is considered by some to be the *safe* deletion practice. A logical delete entails the utilization of an additional column aptly named *deleted*. It is usually a Bit or Boolean data type and serves as a flag in fact tables to identify deleted records. The caveat to the logical delete approach is that every query that includes the fact table must apply a constraint on the new Boolean field to filter out the logically deleted records.

Physically Deleting Facts

Physically deleting facts means data is permanently removed from the data warehouse. When you have a requirement to physically delete records, make sure the user completely understands that the data will never be able to be retrieved once it is deleted.

Users often carry a misconception that once data enters the data warehouse, it is there forever. So when users say they will *never* have a reason to *see* deleted data, *never* and *see* need to be clarified. Make sure they say exactly what they mean and mean what they say.

- **Never.** It is quite common for users to think in terms of today's requirements because it is based on their current way of thinking about the data they use. Users who've never been exposed to a data warehouse may not be used to having certain types of history available to them. There's an old aphorism: You can't miss what you've never had. In most cases, when a user says *never*, he or she means *rarely*. Make sure your users are well aware that physical deletion is a permanent removal of the record.

- **See.** When a user says *see*, most likely he or she is referring to the appearance of data in reports. It's quite common that users have no idea what exists in raw data. All data is usually delivered through some sort of delivery mechanism such as business-intelligence tools or reports that may be automatically filtering unwanted data. It's best to check with the team responsible for data presentation to confirm such requirements. If no such team exists, make sure your users are well aware that physical deletion is a permanent removal of the record in the data warehouse.

Once the requirement for permanent physical deletion is confirmed, the next step is to plan a strategy for finding and deleting unwanted facts. The simplest option for resolving deleted records is to truncate and reload the fact tables. Truncating and reloading is usually a viable option only for smaller data warehouses. If you have a large data warehouse consisting of many fact tables, each containing millions or billions of records, it's not recommended to truncate and reload the entire data warehouse with each incremental load.

> If the source system doesn't contain audit tables to capture deleted data, you must store each data extraction in a staging area to be compared with the next data load—looking for any missing (deleted) records.

If you are lucky, the source system contains audit tables. Audit tables are common in transaction databases where deleted or changed data may have significance or may need to be traced in the future. If audit tables are not available in the source system, another way to detect deleted facts is to compare the source data to a staging table that contains the last data extraction prior to the current data being loaded, which means each day (or whatever your ETL interval is), you must leave a copy of the data extraction in your staging area.

During your ETL process, after both the prior day's extract and the current extract are in the staging area, perform a SQL MINUS on the two tables.

```
Insert into deleted_rows nologging
select * from prior_extract
MINUS
select * from current_extract
```

The result of the MINUS query reveals rows that have been deleted in the source system but have been loaded into the data warehouse. After the process is complete, you can drop the prior_extract table, rename the current_extract table to prior_extract, and create a new current_extract table.

Logically Deleting Facts

When physical deletions are prohibited or need to be analyzed, you can logically delete the record, physically leaving it in place. A logical delete entails the utilization of an additional column named *deleted*. It is usually a Bit or Boolean data type and serves as a flag in fact tables to identify deleted records. The caveat to the logical delete approach is that every query that includes the fact table must apply a constraint on the new Boolean field to filter the logically deleted records.

Factless Fact Tables

The grain of every fact table is a measurement *event*. In some cases, an event can occur for which there are no measured values! For instance, a fact table can be built representing car-accident events. The existence of each event is indisputable, and the dimensions are compelling and straightforward, as shown in Figure 6.7. But after the dimensions are assembled, there may well be no measured fact. Event tracking frequently produces factless designs like this example.

Actually, the design in Figure 6.7 has some other interesting features. Complex accidents have many accident parties, claimants, and witnesses. These are associated with the accident through bridge tables that implement accident party groups, claimant groups, and witness groups. This allows this design to represent accidents ranging from solo fender benders all the way to complex multicar pileups. In this example, it is likely that accident parties, claimants, and witnesses would be added to the groups for a given accident as time goes on. The ETL logic for this application would have

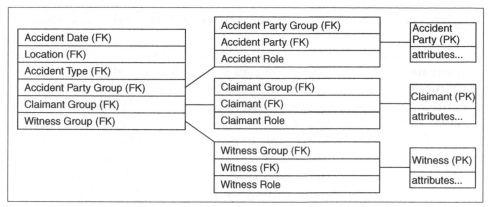

Figure 6.7   A factless fact table representing automobile-accident events.

to determine whether incoming records represent a new accident or an existing one. A master accident natural key would need to be assigned at the time of first report of the accident. Also, it might be very valuable to deduplicate accident party, claimant, and witness records to investigate fraudulent claims.

Another common type of factless fact table represents a *coverage*. The classic example is the table of products on promotion in certain stores on certain days. This table has four foreign keys and no facts, as shown in Figure 6.8. This table is used in conjunction with a classic sales table in order to answer the question, *What was on promotion that did not sell?* The formulation of *what did not happen* queries is covered in some detail in *Data Warehouse Toolkit, Second Edition*, pages 251–253. Building an ETL data pipeline for promoted products in each store is easy for those products with a price reduction, because the cash registers in each store know about the special price. But sourcing data for other promotional factors such as special displays or media ads requires parallel separate data feeds probably not coming from the cash register system. Display utilization in stores is a notoriously tricky data-sourcing problem because a common source of this data is the manufacturing representative paid to install the displays. Ultimately, an unbiased third party may need to walk the aisles of each store to generate this data accurately.

Calendar Day (FK)
Product (FK)
Store (FK)
Promotion (FK)

Figure 6.8   A factless coverage table.

Augmenting a Type 1 Fact Table with Type 2 History

Some environments are predominately Type 1, where, for example, the complete history of customer purchases is always accessed through a Type 1 customer dimension reflecting the most current profiles of the customers. In a pure Type 1 environment, historical descriptions of customers are not available. In these situations, the customer dimension is smaller and simpler than in a full-fledged Type 2 design. In a Type 1 dimension, the natural key and the primary key of the dimension have a 1-to-1 relationship.

But in many of these Type 1 environments, there is a desire to access the customer history for specialized analysis. Three approaches can be used in this case:

1. Maintain a full Type 2 dimension off to the side. This has the advantage of keeping the main Type 1 dimension clean and simple. Query the Type 2 dimension to find old customer profiles valid for certain spans of time, and then constrain the fact table using those time spans. This works pretty well for fact tables that represent *immediate actions* like retail sales where the customer is present at the measurement event. But there are some fact tables where the records represent *delayed actions* like a settlement payment made months after a disputed sale. In this case, the span of time defined by a specific customer profile does not overlap the part of the fact table it logically should. The same weird time-synchronization problem can arise when a product with a certain time-delimited profile is sold or returned months later, after the profile has been superceded. This is another example of a delayed-action fact table. If your fact table represents delayed action, you cannot use this option.

2. Build the primary dimension as a full Type 2 dimension. This has the disadvantage that the dimension is bigger and more complicated than a Type 1 dimension. But you can simulate the effect of a Type 1 dimension by formulating all queries with an embedded SELECT statement on the dimension that fetches the natural keys of only the current Customer dimension records; then you can use these natural keys to fetch all the historical dimensional records for the actual join to the fact table.

3. Build the primary dimension as a full Type 2 dimension and simultaneously embed the natural key of the dimension in the fact table alongside the surrogate key. This has the disadvantage that the dimension is bigger and more complicated than a Type 1 dimension. But if the end user application carefully constrains on just the most

current customer records, the natural key can be used to join to the fact table, thereby fetching of the entire history. This eliminates the embedded SELECT of approach #2.

Graceful Modifications

One of the most important advantages of dimensional modeling is that a number of significant changes can be made to the final delivered schemas without affecting end user queries or applications. We call these *graceful modifications*. This is a powerful claim that distinguishes the dimensional modeling world from the normalized modeling world, where these changes are often not graceful and can cause applications to stop working because the physical schema changes.

There are four types of graceful modifications to dimensional schemas:

1. Adding a fact to an existing fact table at the same grain
2. Adding a dimension to an existing fact table at the same grain
3. Adding an attribute to an existing dimension
4. Increasing the granularity of existing fact and dimension tables.

These four types are depicted in Figure 6.9. The first three types require the DBA to perform an ALTER TABLE on the fact table or the dimension table. It is highly desirable that this ALTER TABLE operation be performed on populated tables, rather than requiring that the fact table or dimension table be dropped, redefined, and then reloaded.

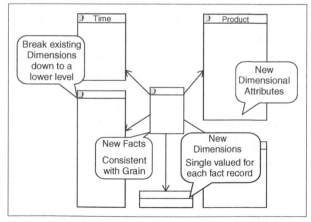

Figure 6.9 The four types of graceful modification.

The first three types raise the issue of how to populate the old history of the tables prior to the addition of the fact, dimension, or attribute. Obviously, it would be nice if old historical values were available. But more often, the fact, dimension, or attribute is added to the schema because it has just become available today. When the change is valid only from today forward, we handle the first three modifications as follows:

1. *Adding a Fact.* Values for the new fact prior to its introduction must be stored as nulls. Null is generally treated well by calculations that span the time during which the fact has been introduced. Counts and averages are correct.

2. *Adding a Dimension.* The foreign key for the new dimension must point to the Not Applicable record in the dimension, for all times in the fact table prior to the introduction of the dimension.

3. *Adding a Dimension Attribute.* In a Type 1 dimension, nothing needs to be done. The new attribute is simply populated in all the dimension records. In a Type 2 dimension, all records referring to time spans preceding the introduction of the attribute need to represent the attribute as null. Time spans that include the introduction of the new attribute are tricky, but probably a reasonable approach is to populate the attribute into these records even though part of their time spans predate the introduction of the attribute.

The fourth type of graceful modification, increasing the granularity of a dimensional schema, is more complicated. Imagine that we are tracking individual retail sales, as depicted in Figure 6.1. Suppose that we had chosen to represent the location of the sale with a store dimension rather than with the cash register dimension. In both cases, the number of fact table records is exactly the same, since the grain of the fact table is the individual retail sale (line item on a shopper ticket). The only difference between a cash-register view of the retail sales and a store view of the retail sales given the same fundamental grain is the choice of the location dimension. But since cash registers roll up to stores in a perfect many-to-1 relationship, the store attributes are available for both choices of the dimension. If this dimension is called location, with some care, no changes to the SQL of existing applications are needed if the design switches from a store-location perspective to a cash-register-location perspective.

It is even possible to increase the granularity of a fact table without changing existing applications. For example, weekly data could change into daily data. The date dimension would change from week to day, and all applications that constrained or grouped on a particular week would continue to function.

Multiple Units of Measure in a Fact Table

PROCESS CHECK Planning & Design:
Requirements/Realities → Architecture → *Implementation* → Test/Release

Data Flow:Extract → Clean → Conform → *Deliver*

Sometimes in a value chain involving several business processes monitoring the flow of products through a system, or multiple measures of inventory at different points, a conflict arises in presenting the amounts. Everyone may agree that the numbers are correct but different parties along the chain may wish to see the numbers expressed in different units of measure. For instance, manufacturing managers may wish to see the entire product flow in terms of car loads or pallets. Store managers, on the other hand, may wish to see amounts in shipping cases, retail cases, scan units (sales packs), or consumer units (individual sticks of gum). Similarly, the same quantity of a product may have several possible economic valuations. We may wish to express the valuation in inventory-valuation terms, in list-price terms, in original-selling-price terms, or in final-selling-price terms. Finally, this situation may be exacerbated by having many fundamental quantity facts in each fact record.

Consider a situation where we have ten fundamental quantity facts, five unit-of-measure interpretations, and four valuation schemes. It would be a mistake to present just the 13 quantity facts in the fact table and then leave it up to the user or application developer to seek the correct conversion factors in remote dimension tables, especially if the user queries the product table at a separate time from the fact table without forcing the join to occur. It would be equally bad to try to present all the combinations of facts expressed in the different units of measure in the main fact table. This would require ten times five quantity facts, plus ten times four valuation facts or 90 facts in each fact table record! The correct compromise is to build an underlying physical record with ten quantity facts, four unit-of-measure conversion factors, and four valuation factors. We need only four unit-of-conversion factors rather than five, since the base facts are already expressed in one of the units of measure, preferably either the smallest unit of measure or the largest so that all the calculations to derive the other units of measure are consistently either multiplications or divisions. Our physical design now has ten plus four plus four, or 18 facts, as shown in Figure 6.10.

The packaging of these factors in the fact table reduces the pressure on the product dimension table to issue new product records to reflect minor changes in these factors, especially the cost and price factors. These items, especially if they routinely evolve, are much more like facts than dimension attributes.

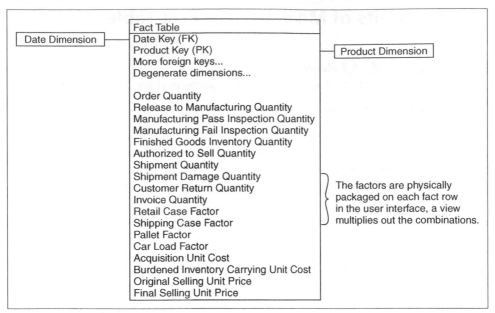

Figure 6.10 A physical fact table design showing ten facts, five units of measure, and four valuation schemes.

We now actually deliver this fact table to users through one or more views. The most comprehensive view could actually show all 90 combinations of units of measure and valuations, but obviously we could simplify the user interface for any specific user group by only making available the units of measure and valuation factors that the group wanted to see.

Collecting Revenue in Multiple Currencies

Multinational businesses often book transactions, collect revenues, and pay expenses in many different currencies. A good basic design for all of these situations is shown in Figure 6.11. The primary amount of the sales transaction is represented in the local currency. In some sense, this is always the *correct* value of the transaction. For easy reporting purposes, a second field in the transaction fact record expresses the same amount in a single standard currency, such as the euro. The equivalency between the two amounts is a basic design decision for the fact table and probably is an agreed upon daily spot rate for the conversion of the local currency into the global currency. Now all transactions in a single currency can be added up easily from the fact table by constraining in the currency dimension to a single currency type. Transactions from around the world can easily be added up by summing the global currency field. Note that the fact table contains a currency

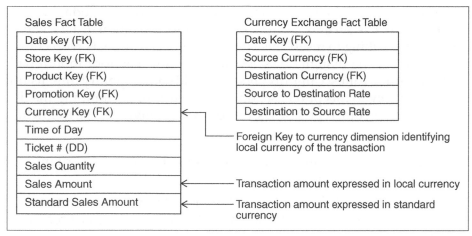

Figure 6.11   A Schema Design For Dealing With Multiple Currencies.

dimension separate from the geographic dimension representing the store location. Currencies and countries are closely correlated, but they are not the same. Countries may change the identity of their currency during periods of severe inflation. Also, the members of the European Monetary Union must be able to express historical transactions (before Jan 1, 2002) in both their original native currencies and in the euro.

But what happens if we want to express the value of a set of transactions in a third currency or in the same currency but using the exchange rate at a different time, such as the last day of a reporting period? For this, we need a currency exchange table, also shown in Figure 6.11. The currency exchange table typically contains the daily exchange rates both to and from each the local currencies and one or more global currencies. Thus, if there are 100 local currencies and three global currencies, we need 600 exchange-rate records each day. It is probably not practical to build a currency exchange table between each possible pair of currencies, because for 100 currencies, there would be 10,000 daily exchange rates. It is not likely, in our opinion, that a meaningful market for every possible pair of exchange rates actually exists.

Late Arriving Facts

PROCESS CHECK Planning & Design:
Requirements/Realities → Architecture → *Implementation* → Test/Release

Data Flow:Extract → Clean → Conform → *Deliver*

Using a customer-purchase scenario, suppose we receive today a purchase record that is several months old. In most operational data warehouses, we are willing to insert this late-arriving record into its correct historical position, even though our sales summary for this prior month will now change. But we must carefully choose the old contemporary dimension records that apply to this purchase. If we have been time-stamping the dimension records in our Type 2 SCDs, our processing involves the following steps:

1. For each dimension, find the corresponding dimension record in effect at the time of the purchase.

2. Using the surrogate keys found in the each of the dimension records from Step 1; replace the natural keys of the late-arriving fact record with the surrogate keys.

3. Insert the late-arriving fact record into the correct physical partition of the database containing the other fact records from the time of the late-arriving purchase.

There are a few subtle points here. We assume that our dimension records contain two time stamps, indicating the beginning and end of the period of validity of the detailed description. This makes the search for the correct dimension records simple.

A second subtle point goes back to our assumption that we have an *operational data warehouse* willing to insert these late-arriving records into old months. If your data warehouse has to *tie to the books*, you can't change an old monthly sales total, even if the old sales total was incorrect. Now you have a tricky situation in which the date dimension on the sales record is for a *booking date*, which may be today, but the other customer, store, and product dimensions should nevertheless refer to the old descriptions in the way we have described. If you are in this situation, you should have a discussion with your finance department to make sure that they understand what you are doing. An interesting compromise we have used in this situation is to carry two sets of date dimensions on purchase records. One refers to the actual purchase date, and the other refers to the booking date. Now you can roll up the sales either operationally or by the books.

The third subtle point is the requirement to insert the late-arriving purchase record into the correct physical partition of the database containing its contemporary *brothers and sisters*. This way, when you move a physical partition from one form of storage to another, or when you perform a backup or restore operation, you will be affecting all the purchase records from a particular span of time. In most cases, this is what you want to do. You can guarantee that all fact records in a time span occupy the same physical partition if you declare the physical partitioning of the fact table to be based on the date dimension. Since you should be using surrogate keys for the date dimension, this is the one case where the surrogate keys of a dimension should be assigned in a particular logical order.

Aggregations

PROCESS CHECK Planning & Design:
Requirements/Realities → Architecture → *Implementation* → Test/Release

Data Flow:Extract → Clean → Conform → *Deliver*

The single most dramatic way to affect performance in a large data warehouse is to provide a proper set of aggregate (summary) records that coexist with the primary base records. Aggregates can have a very significant effect on performance, in some cases speeding queries by a factor of a hundred or even a thousand. No other means exist to harvest such spectacular gains. Certainly, the IT owners of a data warehouse should exhaust the potential for performance gains with aggregates before investing in major new hardware purchases. The benefits of a comprehensive aggregate-building program can be realized with almost every data warehouse hardware and software configuration, including all of the popular relational DBMSs such as Oracle, Red Brick, Informix, Sybase, and DB2, and uniprocessor, SMP and MPP parallel processing architectures. This section describes how to structure a data warehouse to maximize the benefits of aggregates and how to build and use those aggregates without requiring complex accompanying metadata.

Aggregate navigation is a standard data warehouse topic that has been discussed extensively in literature. Let's illustrate this discussion with the simple dimensional schema in Figure 6.12.

The main points are:

- In a properly designed data warehouse environment, multiple sets of aggregates are built, representing common grouping levels within the key dimensions of the data warehouse. Aggregate navigation has been defined and supported only for dimensional data warehouses. There is no coherent approach for aggregate navigation in a normalized environment.

- An aggregate navigator is a piece of middleware that sits between the requesting client and the DBMS. See Figure 6.13.

- An aggregate navigator intercepts the client's SQL and, wherever possible, transforms base-level SQL into aggregate aware SQL.

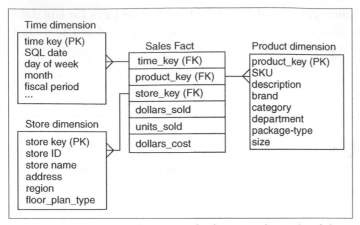

Figure 6.12 A simple dimensional schema at the grain of day, product, and store.

- The aggregate navigator understands how to transform base-level SQL into aggregate-aware SQL because the navigator uses special metadata that describes the data warehouse aggregate portfolio.

The goals of an aggregate program in a large data warehouse need to be more than just improving performance. A good aggregate program for a large data warehouse should:

1. Provide dramatic performance gains for as many categories of user queries as possible

2. Add only a reasonable amount of extra data storage to the warehouse. *Reasonable* is in the eyes of the DBA, but many data

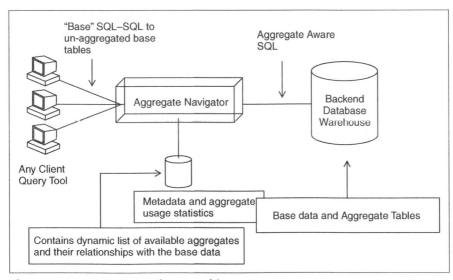

Figure 6.13 Aggregate navigator architecture.

warehouse DBAs strive to increase the overall disk storage for the data warehouse by a factor of two or less.

3. Be completely transparent to end users and to application designers, except for the obvious performance benefits. In other words, no end user application SQL should reference the aggregates directly! Aggregates must also benefit all users of the data warehouse, regardless of which query tool they are using.

4. Affect the cost of the data-extract system as little as possible. It is inevitable that a lot of aggregates will have to be built every time data is loaded, but the specification of these aggregates should be as automated as possible.

5. Affect the DBA's administrative responsibilities as little as possible. In particular, the metadata supporting aggregates should be very limited and easy to maintain. Much of the metadata should be automatically created by monitoring user queries and suggesting new aggregates to be created.

A well-designed aggregate environment can achieve all these objectives. A poorly designed aggregate environment can fail all of the objectives! Here is a series of design requirements, which, if adhered to, will achieve our desired objectives.

Design Requirement #1

Aggregates must be stored in their own fact tables, separate from base-level data. Each distinct aggregation level must occupy its own unique fact table.

The separation of aggregates into their own fact tables is very important and has a whole series of beneficial side effects. First, the aggregate navigation scheme described in this section is much simpler when the aggregates occupy their own tables, because the aggregate navigator can learn almost everything it needs from the DBMS's ordinary system catalog, rather than needing additional metadata. Second, an end user is much less likely to accidentally double-count additive fact totals when the aggregates are in separate tables, because every query against a given fact table will by definition go against data of a uniform granularity. Third, the small number of giant numerical entries representing, for instance, national sales totals for the entire year do not have to be shoehorned into the base table. Often, the presence of these few giant numbers forces the database designer to increase the field with of all entries in the database, thereby wasting disk storage. Since the base table is huge and occupies perhaps half of the entire database, it is very helpful to keep its field widths as tight as possible. And fourth, the administration of aggregates is more modular and segmented when the aggregates occupy separate tables. Aggregates can be built at separate times, and with an aggregate navigator, individual aggregates can be taken off-line and placed back on-line throughout the day without affecting other data.

Design Requirement #2

The dimension tables attached to the aggregate fact tables must, wherever possible, be shrunken versions of the dimension tables associated with the base fact table.

> 💡 **The MOST shrunken version of a dimension is a dimension removed altogether!**

In other words, assuming the base-level fact table as shown in Figure 6.12, we might wish to build category-level aggregates, representing the product dimension rolled up from the individual product to the category. See Figure 6.14. We call this the one-way category aggregate schema.

Notice that in this case we have not requested aggregates in either the time dimension or the store dimension. The table in Figure 6.14 represents how much of a category of a product has sold in each store each day. Our design requirement tells us that the original product table must now be replaced with a shrunken product table, which we might as well call *category*. A simple way to look at this shrunken product table is to think of it as containing only fields that survive the aggregation from individual product up to the category level. Only a few fields will still be uniquely defined.

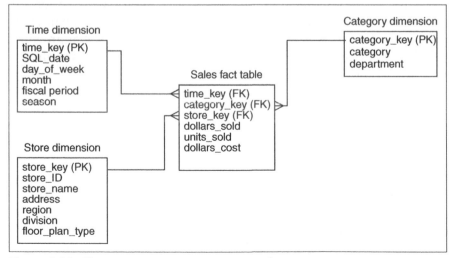

Figure 6.14 The one-way category aggregate schema.

For example, both the category description and the department description would be well defined at the category level, and these must have the same field names they have in the base product dimension table. However, the individual UPC number, the package size, and the flavor would not exist at this level and must not appear in the category table.

Shrunken dimension tables are extremely important for aggregate navigation because the scope of any particular aggregation level can be determined by looking in the system catalog description of the shrunken table. In other words, when we look in the category table, all we find is category description and department description. If a query asks for product flavor, we know immediately that this aggregation level cannot satisfy the query, and thus the aggregate navigator must look elsewhere.

Shrunken dimension tables are also attractive because they allow us to avoid filling the original dimension tables with weird null values for all the dimension attributes that are not applicable at higher levels of aggregation. In other words, since we don't have flavor and package size in the category table, we don't have to dream up null values for these fields, and we don't have to encode user applications with tests for these null values.

Although we have focused on shrunken dimension tables, it is possible that the number of measures in the fact table will also shrink as we build ever-higher levels of aggregation. Most of the basic additive facts such as dollar sales, unit sales, and dollar cost will survive at all levels of aggregation, but some dimensions such as promotion and some facts such promotion cost may make sense only at the base level and need to be dropped in the aggregate fact tables.

A simplification of requirement #2 builds aggregate fact tables only where specific dimensions are completely eliminated rather than just shrunk. For example, in a retail sales fact table, the location (or store) dimension could be eliminated, effectively creating a national total sales fact table. This approach, when it can be used, has the advantage that the aggregate fact table is now impervious to changes in the dropped dimension. Thus, you could change the definitions of your geographic regions and the table in our example would not change, whereas a partially shrunken location dimension that rolled up to region would need to be recalculated. This approach is not a panacea; in our example, the only queries that could use the proposed aggregate table would be ones that requested the national sales totals.

Design Requirement #3

The base fact table and all its related aggregate fact tables can be associated together as a *family of schemas* so that the aggregate navigator knows which tables are related to each other. Any single schema in the family consists of a fact table and its associated dimension tables. There is always exactly one base schema that is the unaggregated data, and there will be one or more aggregate schemas, representing computed summary data. Figure 6.12 is a base schema, and Figure 6.14 is one of perhaps many aggregate schemas in our family.

The registration of this family of fact tables, together with the associated full-size and shrunken dimension tables, is the sole metadata needed in this design.

Design Requirement #4

Force all SQL created by any end user or application to refer exclusively to the base fact table and its associated full-size dimension tables.

This design requirement pervades all user interfaces and all end user applications. When a user examines a graphical depiction of the database, he or she should see only the equivalent of Figure 6.12. The user should not be aware that aggregate tables even exist! Similarly, all hand-coded SQL embedded in report writers or other complex applications should only reference the base fact table and its associated full-size dimension tables.

Administering Aggregations, Including Materialized Views

There are a number of different physical variations of aggregations, depending on the DBMS and the front-end tools. From our design requirements in the previous section, we see that the correct architecture of an aggregate navigator is a middleware module sitting in front of the DBMS intercepting all SQL and examining it for possible redirection. The wrong architecture is an aggregate navigation scheme embedded in a single proprietary front-end tool, where the aggregation benefit is not available to all SQL clients.

There are two fundamental approaches to aggregating navigation at the time of this writing. One is to support a variation of the explicit shrunken fact and dimension tables described in the previous section. The other is to dynamically create these tables by designating certain ephemeral queries to be *materialized* as actual data written to the disk so that subsequent queries can immediately access this data without recomputing the query. Oracle's Materialized Views are an example of the second approach.

Both the explicit-table approach and the materialized-view approach require the DBA to be aware of the effects on the aggregates of updating the underlying base fact tables. Immediately after updating the base tables, the aggregates are invalid and must not be used. In most environments, the base tables must be published to the user community immediately, before all of the aggregates have been recomputed.

Routine daily additions to fact tables may allow the aggregates to be updated by just adding into the various aggregate buckets. But significant changes to the content or logic of a dimension table may require aggregates to be completely dropped and recomputed. For example, Type 1 corrections to historical dimension data will require aggregates to be recomputed if the aggregate is based on the attribute that changed. But the converse is true! If the changed attribute is not the target of an aggregate, the aggregate can be left alone. For example, one could completely remap the flavor attributes of a big product file and the Category aggregate would not be affected. Visualizing these dependencies is a critical skill in managing the portfolio of aggregates.

Note that Type 2 changes to a dimension generally will not require any aggregates to be rebuilt, as long as the change is administered promptly and does not involve the late-arriving data scenario. Type 2 changes do not affect the existing aggregates; they were correct when they were written.

Generally, a given aggregate fact table should be at least ten-times smaller than the base fact table in order to make the tradeoff between administrative overhead and performance gain worthwhile. Roughly speaking, the performance gain of an aggregate is directly proportional to the storage-shrinkage factor. In other words, an aggregate fact table ten-times smaller than the base table will be about ten-times as fast.

If the overall aggregate table portfolio occupies only 1 percent of the total fact table storage, not enough aggregates have been built. A total aggregate overhead approaching 100 percent (that is, a doubling of the total storage) is reasonable.

Large hardware-based, parallel-processing architectures gain exactly the same performance advantages from aggregates as uniprocessor systems with conventional disk storage, since the gain comes simply from reducing total I/O. However, the salesperson and system engineers of these hardware-intensive systems will deny this because their business is based on selling more hardware, not on improving the performance of the system with clever data structures. Beware!

Delivering Dimensional Data to OLAP Cubes

Server-based OLAP (online analytic processing) products are an increasingly popular component of the data warehouse infrastructure. OLAP servers deliver two primary functions:

- **Query performance.** Using aggregates and specialized indexing and storage structures. The OLAP servers automatically manage aggregates and indexes, a benefit whose value may become clear by reviewing the previous section that discusses how to manage aggregate tables.

- **Analytic richness.** Using languages that, unlike SQL, were designed for complex analytics. OLAP servers also have mechanisms for storing complex calculations and security settings on the server, and some are integrated with data-mining technologies.

In all cases, the best source for an OLAP cube is a dimensional data warehouse stored in an RDBMS. The language of the dimensional data warehouse, dimensions, keys, hierarchies, attributes, and facts, translates exactly to the OLAP world. OLAP engines are developed primarily to support fast and complex querying of dimensional structures. OLAP engines, unlike relational databases and ETL tools, are not designed primarily to cleanse data or ensure referential integrity. Even if your OLAP technology provides features that let you build a cube directly from transactional sources, you should seldom plan to use those features. Instead, you should design a relational data warehouse and populate it using the techniques described in this book. That relational store should feed data to the cube.

Cube Data Sources

The various server-based OLAP products and versions have different features. One area of significant difference is the proximate source of the data that flows into a cube. Some products require that data be sourced from a text file; others require that data be sourced from a single brand of relational database; others permit data to be loaded from practically any source.

If you are sourcing your cube from flat files, one of the last steps in your ETL process is, obviously, to write out the appropriate datasets. Though sourcing from flat files is inelegant and slower than sourcing directly from the relational database, it's not a terrible performance hit: All relational databases and ETL tools can efficiently write the results of a query to files.

Analyze any queries that your cube processing issues against the relational data warehouse. Ensure that such queries are well tuned. If necessary, add indexes or materialized views to improve the performance of these processing queries.

Processing Dimensions

Just as relational dimensions are processed before the fact tables that use them, so must OLAP dimensions be processed before facts. Depending on which OLAP tool you use, you may have the option of processing dimensions and facts in a single transaction, which rolls back if an error is encountered. This is appealing in theory but tends not to scale very well for a large OLAP database. Most large OLAP systems process dimensions one by one, often as the last step in the ETL module that populates the corresponding relational dimension table.

Your ETL system design needs to be aware of a few characteristics of OLAP dimensions. First, recall that OLAP systems are designed for ease of use and good query performance for queries that navigate up and down the strong dimensional hierarchy or hierarchies (such as Product to Brand to Category). With a classic relational data warehouse, you should ensure referential integrity between hierarchy levels (that is, that a product rolls up to one and only one brand, and so on). But with OLAP tools, you absolutely must ensure referential integrity. The OLAP server will insist on referential integrity between the levels of a strong hierarchy. If a violation is found, the dimension processing will either fail, or, at best, the OLAP server will make an assumption about how to proceed. You don't want either of these events to occur: Thoroughly clean your data before OLAP processing is launched.

Changes in Dimension Data

OLAP servers handle different kinds of dimension-data changes completely differently. Most OLAP servers handle new dimension rows, such as adding a new customer, as gracefully as the relational dimensional model does. Updating attribute values that do not participate in strong hierarchies and thus do not have permanent aggregations built on them is usually graceful as well. With changes in dimension attributes where attributes are part of the OLAP dimension hierarchy, the ETL designer needs to be very careful.

Let's get the easy case out of the way first. Type 2 slowly changing dimensions, where a new dimension row with a new surrogate key is added for the changed member, is consumed gracefully by the OLAP servers. From the OLAP server's point of view, this is simply a new customer, indistinguishable from a completely new customer.

A Type 1 slowly changing dimension that updates in place the strong hierarchical attributes is much harder for OLAP servers to manage. The OLAP servers' challenges are exactly analogous to those faced by relational data warehouses with aggregate tables built on the same dimension attributes. When the dimension hierarchy is restructured, the existing aggregations are invalidated. The OLAP servers handle this problem with a wide variety of gracefulness, from not noticing the change, to simply throwing away the aggregations and rebuilding them as a background process, to invalidating the dimension and all cubes that use that dimension, forcing a full OLAP database reprocessing. You should look to your OLAP server vendor for detailed information about how this problem is handled in your technology.

Vendors are improving this area with each release, so it's important to use the latest software or validate the conditions for your version.

You should test before OLAP dimension processing to verify that no changes have been made that would put your OLAP database into an invalid or inconsistent state. Depending on the costs and system usage, you could decide to design your system to:

- Let the OLAP and relational data warehouse databases diverge: Defer any further OLAP processing until a convenient time (typically the next weekend).

- Keep the OLAP cubes in synch with the relational data warehouse by halting relational processing as well (typically accumulating changes in the staging area).

- Keep the OLAP cubes in synch with the relational data warehouse by accepting the expensive reprocessing operation during a nightly load. This option would be more palatable if the OLAP cubes were *mirrored* or otherwise remain available to business users during reprocessing.

In any case, the extraordinary event should be logged into the ETL error event table and the operator e-mailed or paged.

Processing Facts

Many people think of cubes as containing only aggregated data. This perception is becoming as old fashioned as the notion that the data warehouse contains only aggregated data. Server-based OLAP products are capable of managing very large volumes of data and are increasingly used to hold data at the same grain as the relational data warehouse. This distinction is important for the design of the cube-processing portion of the ETL system.

Most server-based OLAP products support some form of incremental processing; others support only full processing. Full cube processing is most appropriate for aggregate cubes or small detailed cubes. For good processing performance on a large volume of detailed data, it is vital to use incremental processing for fact data. Two types of cube incremental processing may be available in your OLAP technology: partition-based and incremental facts.

Loading into a partition is an appealing way to load a subset of the cube's data. If your OLAP technology supports partitions, and your cube is partitioned by time, usually weekly or monthly, you can easily load only that time period. If you process daily into weekly partitions, your Monday data will actually be dropped and reloaded seen times during the week until the Sunday load closes down the partition. Certainly, this technique doesn't maximize load efficiency, but it is perfectly acceptable for many applications. It is common to design OLAP cube partitions with the same periodicity as their corresponding relational partitions and to extend the script that manages the relational partitions to also manage the OLAP partitions.

Partitioning the OLAP cube can provide significant benefits for both query and processing performance. Queries against cubes partitioned by one or more dimensions can be executed only against the partitions included in the query rather than the whole cube. The advantages of processing are both to support a simple pseudo-incremental processing as described previously and also to support the processing of multiple partitions in parallel. If your cubes use a complex partition design, your ETL system should be designed to launch multiple partition processing jobs in parallel. If your OLAP server doesn't manage parallel processing on your behalf, you should design this part of your ETL system so you can process a configurable number of partitions in parallel. This is a parameter to optimize during the system-testing phase.

Some OLAP servers also support true incremental fact processing. You supply a way to identify the new data (usually Date Processed), and the OLAP server will add it to the cube or cube partition. If you have late-arriving facts, incremental processing will almost surely be a better approach for you than reprocessing the current partition.

An alternative to full or incremental processing is for the OLAP engine to monitor the source databases for new transactions and to automatically populate the cube with new data. This is a complex process that requires close integration between OLAP engine and relational engine. At the time of this writing, some rudimentary examples of such a feature are available; more functional features are under development.

Common Errors and Problems

One of the most common errors during fact processing is a referential integrity failure: A fact row being processed does not have a corresponding dimension member. If you follow the advice in this and other Toolkit books and use surrogate keys, you should not confront a fact referential integrity failure in the normal course of processing. Nonetheless, you should educate yourself about how your OLAP server will handle this event should an extraordinary event occur.

OLAP servers are not a natural fit with fact data that is updated in place. On the relational side, the preferred design is to use ledgered fact tables that have entries for fact *changes* as positive or negative transaction amounts. The ledger design enables auditing of fact changes and for that reason alone is preferred. An OLAP cube built on a ledgered fact table can accept changes gracefully, though the processing logic may need to be complex enough to support late-arriving fact data if the cube is partitioned by time.

By contrast, an OLAP cube built on a fact table that supports in-place updates is very likely to need full processing each time an update occurs. If the cube is small, this may not be a problem. If the cube is large, you should investigate whether it is acceptable to business users to group updates into weekly or monthly batches or else forgo incorporating the updateable subject area into the OLAP database. Note also that the OLAP processing, which is designed to consume new fact rows, will not identify that fact rows have been updated. The ETL system must trigger the extraordinary processing.

Occasional Full Processing

OLAP technology is not, at the time of this writing, as reliable as relational technology. We believe firmly that the relational dimensional data warehouse should be managed as the data warehouse system-of-record. OLAP cubes should be regarded as ephemeral. Many companies go six months, a year, or more without having to fully reprocess their cubes. However, all installations should develop and test procedures for fully reprocessing the OLAP database. A corollary to this stricture is that you should not design an OLAP cube to contain data that is not in the relational data warehouse or is not easily recoverable into the data warehouse. This includes *writeback* data (most common in budgeting applications), which should be populated directly or indirectly into a relational database.

Until OLAP servers are as reliable and open as their relational brethren, they should be considered secondary systems. OLAP vendors are focusing on reliability and recoverability in versions currently under development, so we hope this second-class status will soon be unnecessary.

Integrating OLAP Processing into the ETL System

If your data warehouse includes OLAP cubes, they should be as professionally managed as any other part of the system. This means that you should have service agreements with business users about data currency and system uptime. Although we generally prefer cubes to be published on the same schedule as relational data, it may be acceptable to refresh cubes on a slower schedule than the relational database. The most important thing is to negotiate an agreement with business users, stick to it, and notify them promptly when the inevitably unexpected occurs.

Although the OLAP server vendors haven't done a great job of providing tools to manage OLAP databases in a professional way, they have all at the very least provided a command-line tool in addition to the more familiar cube management wizard. If you can launch OLAP processing from a command line, you can integrate it, however weakly, into your ETL system.

Technologies that include ETL and OLAP offerings from a single vendor provide more elegant integration.

Many systems can fully process the entire OLAP database on a regular schedule, usually weekly or monthly. In this case, the OLAP processing needs merely to verify that week-end or month-end processing of the relational data warehouse has completed successfully. The ETL system can check the system metadata for that successful condition and, if encountered, kick off the cube processing.

For larger systems, a common integration structure includes adding the OLAP dimension processing as the final step in each dimension table processing branch, module, or package in your ETL system. As described previously, you should test for dangerous data operations that might invalidate a cube before launching the OLAP dimension processing script or command. Similarly, the fact table processing module or branch should be extended to include the OLAP processing. The ultimate step of all processing should update metadata of timing and success (or failure) and post this information to the business community.

OLAP Wrap-up

If an OLAP database is part of your data warehouse system, it should be managed rigorously. The ETL team should be expert in the processing features and quirks of the corporate OLAP technology and ideally should have input into the choice of that technology. This is especially true if you are following the current trend of including most or all data warehouse data, including fine-grained data, in the OLAP cubes. To truly reap the benefits of fine-grained cubes, the data warehouse team must own and integrate OLAP processing with the more familiar relational-focused ETL system.

Summary

In this chapter, we defined the fact table as the vessel that holds all numeric measurements of the enterprise. All fact table records have two main parts: the keys that describe the context of the measurements and the measurements themselves which we call facts. We then described the essential role of the fact table provider, who publishes the fact table to the rest of the community.

We saw that referential integrity is hugely important to the proper functioning of a dimensional schema, and we proposed three places where referential integrity can be enforced.

We then showed how to build a surrogate key pipeline for data warehouses that accurately track the historical changes in their dimensional entities.

We described the structure of the three kinds of fact tables: transaction grain, periodic snapshot grain, and accumulating snapshot grain. In our experience, these three grains suffice to model all possible measurement conditions. This simple result is made possible by never mixing the grain of measurements in a single fact table. Adhering to this approach simplifies application development and makes it far less likely that the end user will make mistakes by not understanding the structure of the data.

We then proposed a number of specific techniques for handling graceful modifications to fact and dimension tables, multiple units of measurement, late-arriving fact data, and building aggregations.

We finished the chapter with a specialized section on loading OLAP cubes, which are legitimate first cousins of relational dimensional schemas.

With this chapter, we have described the four main steps of the ETL system in a data warehouse: extraction, quality assurance, conforming, and structuring data as a series of dimensional schemas ready to be consumed by end users. In the next Chapters 7 and 8, we'll dive into the software tools most commonly used in building ETL systems, and we'll figure out how to schedule the operations of such a complicated system.

Implementation and Operations

Development

"By failing to prepare, you are preparing to fail."
Benjamin Franklin

If you have been reading this book in sequence, you now have a detailed model of the challenges you face building your ETL system. We have described the data structures you need (Chapter 2), the range of sources you must connect to (Chapter 3), a comprehensive architecture for cleaning and conforming the data (Chapter 4), and all the target dimension tables and fact tables that constitute your final delivery (Chapters 5 and 6). We certainly hope that you can pick and choose a subset of all this for your ETL system!

Hopefully, you are at the point where you can draw a process-flow diagram for your proposed ETL system that clearly identifies at a reasonable level of detail the extracting, cleaning, conforming, and delivering modules.

Now it's time to decide what your ETL system development platform is and how to go about the development. If you have the luxury of starting fresh, you have a big fork in the road: Either purchase a professional ETL tool suite, or plan on rolling your own with a combination of programming and scripting languages. We tried to give you an even handed assessment of this choice in Chapter 1. Maybe you should go back and read that again.

PROCESS CHECK Planning & Design:
Requirements/Realities → **Architecture** → *Implementation* → **Test/Release**

Data Flow : *Extract* → *Clean* → *Conform* → *Deliver*

In the next section, we give you a brief listing of the main ETL tool suites, data-proofing systems, data-cleansing systems, and scripting languages available as of this writing, but in writing a book intended to have a useful shelf life of several years, please understand that we intend this only as a general guide. We invite you to perform an Internet search for each of these vendors and scripting languages to get their latest offerings.

The first half of this chapter is a spirited and we hope entertaining tour through a number of basic low-level transforms you must implement. We have chosen to illustrate these with simple UNIX utilities like ftp, sort, gawk, and grep, keeping in mind that the professional ETL tool suites would have proprietary data-flow modules that would replace these examples.

The second half of this chapter focuses on DBMS specific techniques for performing high-speed bulk loads, enforcing referential integrity, taking advantage of parallelization, and troubleshooting performance problems.

Current Marketplace ETL Tool Suite Offerings

In Chapter 1, we discussed the pros and cons of purchasing a vendor's ETL tool suite or rolling your own ETL system with hand-coding. From the data warehouse point of view, the ETL marketplace has three categories: mainline ETL tool, data profiling, and data cleansing.

In alphabetical order, the main ETL tool suite vendors as of this writing, with product names where the company has products in other categories, are:

- Ab Initio
- Ascential DataStage
- BusinessObjects Data Integrator
- Cognos DecisionStream
- Computer Associates Advantage Data Transformation
- CrossAccess eXadas
- Data Junction Integration Studio (acquired by Pervasive)
- DataHabitat ZeroCode ETL
- DataMirror Transformation Server
- Embarcadero DT/Studio
- ETI (Evolutionary Technologies International)
- Hummingbird ETL
- IBM DB2 Data Warehouse Manager

- Informatica (PowerCenter and SuperGlue)
- Information Builders iWay
- Mercator Inside Integrator (acquired by Ascential)
- Microsoft SQL Server DTS (Data Transformation Services)
- Oracle9i Warehouse Builder
- Sagent Data Flow Server (acquired by Group 1)
- SAS Enterprise ETL Server
- Sunopsis

Most of the names in these lists are copyright, their owners.
The main data-profiling vendors at the time of this writing are:

- Ascential (ProfileStage)
- Evoke Software
- SAS
- Trillium/Harte Hanks (with the Avelino acquisition)

The main data cleansing vendors at the time of this writing are:

- Ascential (acquisition of Vality)
- First Logic
- Group 1
- SAS DataFlux
- Search Software America
- Trillium (acquired Harte Hanks)

If you perform an Internet search for each of these products, you will get a wealth of information and their current statuses.

ETL tool suites typically package their functionality as a set of *transforms*. Each performs a specific data manipulation. The inputs and outputs of these transforms are compatible so that the transforms can easily be strung together, usually with a graphical interface. Typical categories of transforms that come built with dozens of examples in each category include:

- Aggregators
- General expressions
- Filters
- Joiners
- Lookups

- Normalizers
- Rankers
- Sequence generators
- Sorters
- Source readers (adapters)
- Stored procedures
- Updaters
- XML inputers and outputers
- Extensive facilities for writing your own transforms in a variety of languages

Current Scripting Languages

Interesting scripting languages available on a variety of platforms (typically UNIX, Linux, Windows, and, in some cases, IBM mainframes) include:

- JavaScript
- Perl
- PHP
- Python
- Tcl

All of these scripting languages excel at reading and writing text files and invoking sort routines including native OS sorting packages as well as commercial packages like SyncSort and CoSort. Several have good interfaces to commercial DBMSs as well.

Of course, one can always drop down to C or C++ and *do anything*. While all the ETL alternatives eventually allow escapes into C or C++, it would be unusual to build the entire ETL system at such a low level.

Time Is of the Essence

PROCESS CHECK Planning & Design:
Requirements/Realities → **Architecture** → *Implementation* → **Test/Release**

Data Flow: *Extract* → Clean → Conform → *Deliver*

Throughout the ETL system, time or, more precisely, throughput, is the primary concern. Mainly, this translates to devising processing tasks that ultimately enable the fastest loading of data into the presentation tables and then the fastest end user response times from those tables. Occasionally, throughput rears its head when cleaning up unwieldy or dirty data.

Push Me or Pull Me

In every data warehouse, there inevitably is data that originates from flat-file systems. The first step to incorporating this data into the data warehouse is moving it from its host server to the ETL server. Flat files can either be pushed from the source host systems or pulled by the ETL server.

Which approach works best? The honest answer to this question is, well, *both*. However, the more important question to ask is *when?*—as in "When is the source file available to be moved?"

In many cases, the source files that must be moved are from operational business systems, and the files are often not available to be moved to the ETL server until after the operational systems nightly batch processes are completed. If the ETL server attempts to *pull* the file, it risks attempting to start the file transfer before the file is ready, in which case the data loaded into the warehouse might be incorrect or incomplete. In these situations, having the host system *push* the source files has the following advantages:

- The FTP step to push the source file can be embedded into the operational system's batch process so that the file is pushed as soon as it is prepared by the host system, thereby starting the ETL process at the earliest possible time and minimizing idle time during the load window.

- Errors in the process of preparing the source file can prevent the file transfer from being initiated, thereby preventing incorrect or incomplete data from being loaded into the data warehouse.

The ETL server must have an FTP host service running in order to support pushing source files from the host systems.

In many cases, an interrupted FTP process must be restarted. The larger the download file and the tighter the batch window, the riskier relying on *simple* FTP becomes. If this is important to you, you should try to find a resumable FTP utility and/or verify the capabilities of your ETL tool suite to resume an interrupted transfer. Also, when looking at these added-value, higher-end, FTP-like capabilities, you may be able to get compression and encryption at the same time.

It is equally likely that some of the files needed by the ETL process are available at any time the ETL process needs them. In these cases, the ETL server can *pull* the files when it needs them. The ETL server must establish an FTP connection to the host file server. Running FTP from a Unix shell script or Windows batch file is quite simple. On both platforms, the file-transfer commands can be passed to FTP via an external command file, as in the following example.

> In the following pages, we describe many low-level data-manipulation commands including sorting, extracting subsets, invoking bulk loaders, and creating aggregates. For clarity, we show command-line versions of each of these commands. Obviously, in a commercial ETL tool suite, all of these commands would be invoked graphically by clicking with the mouse. Keep that in mind!

You can embed the following command in a Windows batch file:

```
ftp -n -v -s:transfer.ftp
```

```
-n options turns off login prompting
-v turns off remote messages
-s: specifies the command file, In this case "transfer.ftp"
```

The content of command file transfer.ftp might be something like:

```
open hostname
user userid password
cd /data/source
lcd /etl/source
ascii
get source_1.dat
get source_2.dat
get source_3.dat
... ... ...
get source_n.dat
bye
```

> On a UNIX system, the commands are the same, but the syntax for passing a command file is slightly different.

Ensuring Transfers with Sentinels

Whether you are pushing or pulling your flat-file sources, you need to be sure that your file transfer completes without any errors. Processing a partially transferred file can lead to corrupt or incomplete data being loaded into the data warehouse.

An easy way to ensure your transfers are complete is to use *sentinel* (or signal) files. The sentinel file has no meaningful content, but its mere existence signifies the readiness of the file(s) to which it relates.

- In the push approach, a sentinel file is sent after the last true source file is pushed. When the ETL receives the sentinel file, it signifies that all of the source files have been completely received and that the ETL process can now safely use the source files. If the transfer of the source files is interrupted, the sentinel file is not sent, and the ETL process suspends until the error is corrected and the source files are resent.

- Sentinel files can also be used in a pull environment. In this case, the source host sends a sentinel file only to notify the ETL server that the source files are available. Once the ETL server receives the sentinel, it can initiate the FTP process to pull the source files to begin the ETL process.

Either way, the ETL process must include a method to *poll* the local file system to check for the existence of the sentinel file. Most dedicated ETL tools include this capability. If you are manually developing the ETL process, a Windows NT/2000 server scheduled task or Unix cron job can accomplish this task.

Sorting Data during Preload

PROCESS CHECK Planning & Design:
Requirements/Realities → **Architecture** → *Implementation* → **Test/Release**

Data Flow: Extract → *Clean* → **Conform** → *Deliver*

Certain common ETL processes call for source data to be sorted in a particular order to achieve the desired outcome. Such ETL processes as aggregating and joining flat-file sources require the data to be presorted. Some ETL tools can handle these tasks in memory; however, aggregating or joining unsorted data is significantly more resource-intensive and time-consuming than doing so on sorted data.

When the source data is contained in a database, sorting is easily accomplished by including an `order by` clause in the SQL that retrieves the data from the database. But if the source data is from flat files, you need to use a sort utility program to arrange the data in the correct order prior to the ETL process.

Sorting on Mainframe Systems

Every mainframe system includes either IBM's DFSORT or SyncSort's SORT utility program. Syncsort and DFSORT commands are virtually identical and are quite simple. With few exceptions, mainframe data files are formatted in fixed widths, so most sorts are accomplished by simply specifying the positions and lengths of the data elements on which the data are to be sorted. We use the sample sales file that follows to show how mainframe sorts are accomplished.

```
20000405026Discount Electronics          00014SUBWOOFER
^^^^000001500001980000297000
20000406005City Electronics              00008AMPLIFIER
^^^^000003500002610000913500
20000407029USA Audio and Video           00017KARAOKE MACHINE
^^^^000002000000882000176400
20000410010Computer Audio and Video      00017KARAOKE MACHINE
^^^^000001000000882000088200
20000411002Computer Audio and Video      00017KARAOKE MACHINE
^^^^000003500000882000308700
20000411011Computer Audio and Video      00008AMPLIFIER
^^^^000001000002610000261000
20000415019Computer Discount             00018CASSETTE PLAYER/RECORDER
^^^^000002000000684000136800
20000418013Wolfe''s Discount             00014SUBWOOFER
^^^^000002500001980000495000
20000418022USA Audio and Video           00008AMPLIFIER
^^^^000001500002610000391500
20000419010Computer Audio and Video      00023MP3 PLAYER
^^^^000001000001764000176400
20000419014Edgewood Audio and Video      00006CD/DVD PLAYER
^^^^000002000004410000882000
20000419016Computer Audio and Video      00014SUBWOOFER
^^^^000003000001980000594000
20000419021Computer Audio and Video      00014SUBWOOFER
^^^^000003500001980000693000
20000419028Bayshore Electronics          00020CD WALKMAN
^^^^000001500000414000062100
```

The COBOL copybook for this file would be:

```
01 SALES-RECORD.
      05 SALE-DATE          PIC 9(8).
      05 CUSTOMER-ID         PIC X(3).
      05 CUSTOMER-NAME       PIC X(27).
      05 PRODUCT-ID          PIC X(5).
      05 PRODUCT-NAME        PIC X(28).
      05 UNIT-COST           PIC 9(4)V99 COMP-3.
           (this takes up only 4 physical bytes)
      05 UNITS               PIC 9(7).
```

```
05 UNIT-PRICE          PIC 9(7)V99.
05 SALE-AMOUNT         PIC 9(7)V99.
```

The basic structure of the SORT command is:

```
SORT FIELDS=(st,len,dt,ad)
```

where st denotes the starting position, len denotes the length, dt denotes the data type, and ad denotes the sort order (ascending or descending). So, sorting our sales file by customer-id is coded as follows:

```
SORT FIELDS=(9,3,BI,A)
```

meaning, sort on positions 9 to 11 in ascending order, treating the data as *binary*. To perform sorts on multiple fields, simply supply the st, len, dt, ad parameters for each additional sort field.

For example, suppose your ETL task is to aggregate this sale data by year, product, and customer. The source data is at a daily grain, and its natural order is also by day. Aggregating data from its natural order would be a quite complex task, requiring creating, managing, and navigating arrays of memory variables to hold the aggregates until the last input record is processed and again navigating the memory arrays to load the aggregates into the warehouse. But by presorting the source data by the aggregate key (year + product-id + customer-id), the ETL task to aggregate the data becomes fairly simple. The command for sorting the data by the aggregate key is as follows:

```
SORT FIELDS=(1,4,BI,A,39,5,BI,A,9,3,BI,A)
```

Once sorted in this way, the ETL process to aggregate the data can be made extremely efficient. As source records are read, the values of the key fields year, product-id, and customer-id are compared to the key values of the preceding record, which are held in memory variables. As long as the keys are the same, the units and sales amounts are added to cumulative memory variables. When the keys change, the aggregate values for the preceding key are loaded to the warehouse from the memory variables, and the memory variables are reset to begin accumulating the aggregates for the new keys.

As discussed in earlier chapters, mainframe data often poses certain challenges unique to mainframes. The SORT utility has a rich set of data types to help you handle these challenges. While using BI (binary) as the data type works in many situations, there are a number of alternate data types that handle special situations, including those listed in Table 7.1.

Table 7.1 Alternate Mainframe Data Types

DATA TYPE	USAGE
PD	Use to properly sort numeric values stored in *packed decimal* (or COMP-3) format.
ZD	Use to properly sort numeric values stored in *zoned decimal* format.
AC	Use to properly sort data by the ASCII codes associated with the data, rather than by the mainframe native EBCDIC codes. Use this format for mixed (alphanumeric) fields when the data is transferred from a mainframe to an ETL process on a Unix or Windows system.
dates	Believe it or not, you will likely encounter legacy system files with dates still in pre-Y2K formats (that is, without explicit centuries). SORT has a rich set of data types for handling such dates and assigning them to the proper century.

This table represents just a small subset of the available data types. Many others are available for the multitude of numeric and other data formats you might encounter.

You can also mix data formats on a compound index. So, for example, sorting sales file by year and descending unit-cost uses the following command:

```
SORT FIELDS = (1,4,BI,A,72,4,PD,D)
```

Sorting on Unix and Windows Systems

Flat files on Unix and Windows systems, which are ASCII character-based, are not plagued by the antiquated data formats (packed-decimal, and so on) concocted on the mainframe systems of old to save disk space. But these systems present challenges of their own.

Among the most common sorting challenge you'll face is sorting delimited or other unstructured data files. In this context, *unstructured* refers to the fact that the data is not arranged in neat columns of equal width on every record. As such, unlike the mainframe examples, you can't specify the sort keys positionally.

Instead, the `sort` utility must be able to parse the records using the delimiters. (Of course, the mainframe utilities SyncSort and CoSort are available on Unix and Windows platforms, too.) The following extract shows the same sales data used earlier in the chapter now formatted as a comma delimited file.

```
04/05/2000,026,Discount Electronics,
00014,SUBWOOFER,124.74,15,198.00,2970.00
04/06/2000,005,City Electronics,00008,AMPLIFIER,164.43,35,261.00,9135.00
04/07/2000,029,USA Audio and Video,00017,KARAOKE MACHINE,
55.57,20,88.20,1764.00
04/10/2000,010,Computer Audio and Video,00017,KARAOKE MACHINE,
55.57,10,88.20,882.00,
04/11/2000,002,Computer Audio and Video,00017,KARAOKE MACHINE,
55.57,35,88.20,3087.00,
04/11/2000,011,Computer Audio and
Video,00008,AMPLIFIER,164.43,10,261.00,2610.00
04/15/2000,019,Computer Discount,00018,CASSETTE
PLAYER/RECORDER,43.09,20,68.40,1368.00
04/18/2000,013,Wolfe''s Discount,
00014,SUBWOOFER,124.74,25,198.00,4950.00
04/18/2000,022,USA Audio and
Video,00008,AMPLIFIER,164.43,15,261.00,3915.00
04/19/2000,010,Computer Audio and Video,00023,MP3
PLAYER,111.13,10,176.40,1764.00
04/19/2000,014,Edgewood Audio and Video,00006,CD/DVD
PLAYER,277.83,20,441.00,8820.00
04/19/2000,016,Computer Audio and
Video,00014,SUBWOOFER,124.74,30,198.00,5940.00
04/19/2000,021,Computer Audio and
Video,00014,SUBWOOFER,124.74,35,198.00,6930.00
04/19/2000,028,Bayshore Electronics,00020,CD WALKMAN,
16.08,15,21.40,621.00
```

The basic syntax for the Unix `sort` command is as follows:

```
sort +start_field_number -stop_field_number file
```

Fields are numbered beginning from zero, so in the sales file, the field numbers are as follows:

```
(0) SALE-DATE
(1) CUSTOMER-ID
(2) CUSTOMER-NAME
(3) PRODUCT-ID
(4) PRODUCT-NAME
(5) UNIT-COST
(6) UNITS
(7) UNIT-PRICE
(8) SALE-AMOUNT
```

The default delimiter for the sort program is white space. The `--t` option allows you to specify an alternate delimiter. To replicate the first example again, sorting by customer-id, the `sort` command would be:

```
sort -t, +1 -2 sales.txt > sorted _sales.txt
```

which means, begin sorting on column 1 (customer-id) and stop sorting on column 2 (customer-name). The sort output is currently directed to standard output (terminal), so you redirect the output to a new file: `sorted_sales.txt`.

If the stop column is not specified, sort sorts on a compound key consisting of every column beginning with the start column specified.

Look at how to perform the aggregate key sort (year + product-id + customer-id) used earlier in the chapter to prepare the data for an aggregation ETL process. Year is last part of the field 0, product-id is field 3, and customer-id is field 1. The main challenge is limiting the sort to use only the year portion of the date. Here's how:

```
sort -t, +0.6 -1 +3 -4 +1 -2 sales.txt > sorted_sales.txt
```

To sort on the year portion of the date (field 0), you specify the starting byte within the field following a period. As with the field numbers, byte numbers start with 0, so +0.6 means to sort on the seventh byte of the date.

Up to this point, these Unix sort examples have used alphabetic sorts. However, alphabetic sorts won't yield the desired results on quantitative numeric fields. For example, sorting the sales-file unit cost alphabetically would yield incorrect results—the CD WALKMAN, with a cost of 16.08, would be placed after the SUBWOOFER, with a cost of 124.74. To solve this problem, you need to specify that the unit-cost field is numeric, as follows:

```
sort -t, +5n -6 sales.txt > sorted_sales.txt
```

To change the sort order from ascending to descending, use the `--r` (reverse) option. For example, sorting the sale data by descending year + unit cost is specified by the following:

```
sort -t, +0.6r -1 +5n -6 sales.txt > sorted_sales.txt
```

Other useful sort options are listed in Table 7.2.

Table 7.2 Switches for the UNIX sort command

DATA TYPE	USAGE
-f	Ignore case in alphabetic sort fields
-b	Ignore leading blanks in sort fields
-d	Ignore punctuation characters
-i	Ignore nonprintable characters
-M	Sort 3-letter month abbreviations (for example, JAN precedes FEB, and so on)

💡 A rich set of Unix utility commands, including `sort`, `grep`, and `gawk` to name few key utilities, have been *ported* to the Windows operating system and are available as freeware. There are many Web sites from which you can obtain these utilities. We found a relatively complete set in a zipped file at http://unxutils .sourceforge.net/.

Trimming the Fat (Filtering)

PROCESS CHECK Planning & Design:
Requirements/Realities → Architecture → *Implementation* → Test/Release

Data Flow: *Extract* → *Clean* → Conform → *Deliver*

Source files often contain loads of data not pertinent to the data warehouse. In some cases, only a small subset of records from the source file is needed to populate the warehouse. Other times, only a few data elements from a wide record are needed. One sure way to speed up the ETL process is to eliminate unwanted data as early in the process as possible. Creating extract files on the source host system provides the greatest performance gain, because, in addition to the improvement in the ETL process itself, the time spent on file transfers is reduced in proportion to the reduction in file size. Whether you shrink a source file by picking, say, half the records in the file or half the fields on each record, you save time transferring the data to the ETL server and save I/O time and memory processing the smaller file during the ETL process.

The easiest extract files to create are those where only a subset of the source file records is needed. This type of extract can generally be created using utility programs, which are also typically the most efficient running programs on the system.

The following sections discuss creating extracts on mainframe systems and Windows and Unix systems.

Extracting a Subset of the Source File Records on Mainframe Systems

On mainframe systems, the SORT utility happens to be perhaps the fastest and easiest way to create extract files without writing COBOL or fourth-generation language (SAS, FOCUS, and so on) programs.

The simplest case is to create an extract in which only a subset of the records is needed. SORT allows to you specify source records to either include or omit from the extract file.

```
INCLUDE COND=(st,len,test,dt,val)
OMIT COND=(st,len,test,dt,val)
```

The `st` indicates the start position of the input field, `len` is its length, `test` is the Boolean test to perform, `dt` is the data type of the input field, and `val` is the value to compare against. For this example, we use the sample sales file from the prior sort examples in the chapter. Here's how to extract only records for sales from the year 2000 and higher.

```
SORT FIELDS=COPY
INCLUDE COND=(1,4,GE,CH,C'2000')
```

This could also be coded with an EXCLUDE as:

```
SORT FIELDS=COPY
OMIT COND=(1,4,LT,CH,C'2000')
```

Compound conditions are created by joining condition sets with AND or OR clauses. To select only records from the year 2000 and later for customer-ids over 010, use the following:

```
SORT FIELDS=COPY
INCLUDE COND=(1,4,GE,CH,C'2000', AND,9,3,GT,CH,C'010')
```

More complex conditions can be created using a combination of ANDs, Ors, and parentheses to control the order of execution. You can even search for fields containing a certain value. For example, to choose customers with the word *Discount* in their names, code the INCLUDE statement as follows:

```
SORT FIELDS=COPY
INCLUDE COND=(12,27,EQ,CH,C'Discount')
```

Because the 27-byte input field specified is longer than the constant `Discount`, SORT searches through the entire input field for an occurrence of the constant. (This is equivalent to coding a SQL `where` clause of LIKE '%Discount%')

Extracting a Subset of the Source File Fields

Creating an extract file containing only the fields necessary for the data warehouse ETL process can have an enormous impact on the size of the ETL source files. It is not at all uncommon to have source files with dozens and dozens of data elements of which only a small handful are needed for the ETL process. The impact of extracting only the required fields can have an enormous impact on file size even when the source file record is relatively small. Considering that some source files have millions of records, extracting only the required fields can shave tens or hundreds of megabytes off the data to be transferred to and processed by the ETL server.

Lo and behold, SORT can also handle the task of selecting a subset of the fields in a source file to shrink the amount of data that must be transferred to the ETL server using the OUTFIL OUTREC statement. The sales file we have used in the examples thus far has a record length of 100 bytes. Suppose your ETL process required only the sale-date, customer-id, product-id, unit-cost, units, and sale-amount fields, which total 36 bytes. An extract with only these fields would be about one-third the size of the full source file. To shrink it further, you can choose only records from the year 2000 and later.

```
SORT FIELDS=COPY
INCLUDE COND=(1,4,CH,GE,C'2000')
OUTFIL OUTREC=(1,8,9,3,39,5,72,4,76,7,92,9)
```

In this simplest form, the OUTREC clause comprises simply pairs of starting positions and lengths of the fields to copy to the extract file. However, this still leaves you with some undesirable remnants of mainframe days. The unit-cost, units, and sale-amount are still in their mainframe storage formats. These fields are not usable in these native mainframe formats when transferred to the ETL server. To be usable on the Unix or Windows ETL server, you must reformat these numeric fields to *display* format.

```
SORT FIELDS=COPY
INCLUDE COND=(1,4,CH,GE,C'2000')
OUTFIL OUTREC=(1,8,9,3,39,5,
    72,4,PD,EDIT=IT.TT,LENGTH=7,
    76,7,ZD,EDIT=IT,LENGTH=7,
    92,9,ZD,EDIT=IT.TT,LENGTH=10)
```

In this format, the unit-cost, which is stored in *packed numeric* format on the source file, is exploded to a 7-byte display field taking the form *9999.99*. Likewise, the units and sale-amount are reformatted to display as *9999999* and *9999999.99*, respectively.

Clearly, the mainframe SORT utility is a powerful ally in your pursuit of mainframe data. The techniques cited in the preceding examples demonstrate just a subset of its rich functionality. Proficiency with SORT can be your ticket to self-sufficiency when you need to acquire mainframe data.

Extracting a Subset of the Source File Records on Unix and Windows Systems

Now let's look at how to accomplish these same extract tasks on Unix and Windows systems. Again, we use a Unix utility, gawk, that has been ported to Windows. Gawk is the GNU version of the programming language awk. The basic function of awk is to search files for lines (or other units of text) that contain certain patterns.

The syntax we use for gawk is as follows:

```
gawk -fcmdfile infile > outfile
```

The --f option specifies the file containing the gawk commands to execute. The infile specifies the input source file, and outfile specifies the file to which the gawk output is redirected.

The first extract task is to select only the sales from 2000 and later. The gawk command would be something like the following:

```
gawk -fextract.gawk sales.txt > sales_extract.txt
```

The extract.gawk command file contains the following:

```
BEGIN {
FS=",";
OFS=","}
substr($1,7,4) >= 2000 {print $0}
```

The BEGIN {..} section contains commands to be executed before the first source record is processed. In this example, FS="," and OFS="," stipulate that fields in the input and output files are delimited by commas. If not specified, the default delimiters are spaces.

The extract logic is contained in the statement substr($1,7,4) >= 2000. It says to select records where the seventh through tenth bytes of the first ($1) field are greater than or equal to 2000.

The {print $0} statement says to output the entire source record ($0) for the selected records.

Compound conditions are created by joining condition sets with && (and) or || (or) clauses. To select only records from the year 2000 and later for customer-ids over 010, use the following:

```
BEGIN {
FS=",";
OFS=","}
substr($1,7,4) >= 2000 && $1 > "010" {print $0}
```

And to find the records where the customer-name contains *Discount*:

```
BEGIN {
FS=",";
OFS=","}
$3~/Discount/ {print $0}
```

As you can see, with a bit of knowledge of the gawk command, you can very easily create these time-saving and space-saving extracts.

Extracting a Subset of the Source File Fields

You can also use gawk to create field extracts. As before, suppose you want to create an extract containing only the sale-date, customer-id, product-id, unit-cost, units, and sale-amount fields. Again, you want only to extract records from 2000 and later. Here's how:

```
BEGIN {
FS=",";
OFS=","}
substr($1,7,4) >= 2000 {print $1,$2,$4,$6,$7,$9}
```

The print statement specifies the columns to include in the output.

> Take note that in gawk, the fields are numbered starting with $1, and $0 refers to the entire input record. This differs from the sort command, where $0 connotes the first field.

Now suppose you want to create an extract file that has fixed field widths rather than a delimited file. Well, gawk can do that as well. Here's how you make the prior extract into a fixed-width file:

```
BEGIN {
FS=",";
OFS=","}
{substr($1,7,4) >= 2000
{printf "%-11s%-4s%-6s%07.2f%08d%010.2f\ n", $1,$2,$4,$6,$7,$9}}
```

Here, the printf command (formatted print) takes the place of the regular print command. printf is followed by a format string. The % sign denotes the beginning of a format, and the number of formats must match the number of output fields. The formats you commonly use are:

- **%*n*s:** For text strings, n is the minimum output length
- **%0*n*d:** For decimal numbers, n is the minimum output length
- **%0*n.m*f:** For floating point numbers, n is the total number of digits, m the decimal digits.

By default, data is right-justified. To left-justify data (as you would for most text fields), precede the field length with a dash as in the preceding example. To left-pad numeric formats with zeros, precede the length with a zero, (for example, %07.2f) The newline indicator \n at the end of the format string tells gawk to put each output record on a new line.

Creating Aggregated Extracts on Mainframe Systems

Suppose you want to summarize the sample sales files by month, customer, and product, capturing the aggregate units and sales-amounts. Here's the mainframe SORT commands to accomplish this:

```
INREC FIELDS=(1,4,5,2,9,3,39,5,3Z,76,7,3Z,91,9)
SORT FIELDS=(1,14,CH,A)
SUM FIELDS=(15,10,ZD,25,12,ZD)
```

You can see two new commands here—INREC and SUM. INREC work the same way as OUTREC, except that it operates on the input records before any sort operations are processed. In this case, the input records are reformatted to include only the fields needed for the aggregate—year, month, customer-id, product-id, units, and sale-amount. Take note as well of the two 3Z entries. These left-pad units and sale-amount with zeros prevent arithmetic overflows from occurring from the SUM operation. The effect is to increase the size of these fields by three bytes each.

Next, the SORT command specifies the fields used to sort the file. The SORT FIELDS act as the key for the SUM operation, essentially acting like a SQL GROUP BY clause. But note that the SORT FIELDS use the reformatted record layout—so the SORT FIELDS can be simply defined as positions 1 through 14, which now contain year, month, customer-id, and product-id.

Finally, the SUM command specifies the quantitative fields to be summed (or aggregated). Again, the reformatted field positions (and lengths, in this case) are used. So whereas units occupied positions 76–82 (a total of 7 bytes) in the source file, in the reformatted records, units occupies positions 15–24 (10 bytes).

Using this technique, the output file is only 36 bytes wide (versus the original 100 byte source records) and contains only one record per combination of year, month, customer-id, and product-id in the file. The network and ETL server will thank you for shrinking the size of the source file in this way.

Note, however, that transaction systems are often configured with minimal temp space available. This may affect your decision to compress data at the source during extraction. See the discussion on this topic later in this chapter under "Using Aggregates and Group Bys."

Creating Aggregated Extracts on UNIX and Windows Systems

Accomplishing the same aggregation using the UNIX/Windows utilities is a bit more complex but not much. You need to use both the sort and gawk utilities together. The sort output is *piped* to the gawk command using the |pipe character. Here's the command:

```
sort -t, +0.6 -1 +0.0 -0.2 +1 -2 +3 -4 |  gawk -fagg.gawk > agg.txt
```

First, review the sort.

```
+0.6 -1      = year
+0.0 -0.2    = month
+1 -2        = customer-id
+3 -4        = product-id
```

The agg.gawk command file follows. We've added comments (preceded by #) to explain how it works:

```
# set delimiters
BEGIN {
FS=",";
OFS=","}
#initialize variables for each record
{inrec += 1}
{next_year=substr($1,7,4) substr($1,1,2)}
{next_cust=$2}
{next_product=$4}


#after a new year and month record
#write out the accumulated total_units and total_sales for the
prior year
inrec > 1 && ( \
   next_year != prev_year \
   || next_cust != prev_cust \
   || next_product != prev_product ) \
   {print prev_year,prev_cust,prev_product,total_units,total_sales}
#accumulate the total_sales sales and count of records
{total_units += $7}
{total_sales += $9}
#if the year changed reinitialize the aggregates
next_year != prev_year {
   total_units = $7;
   total_sales = $9}
#store the year (key) of the record just processed
{prev_year = next_year}
{prev_cust = next_cust}
{prev_product = next_product}
#after the last record, print the aggregate for the last year
END {print prev_year,prev_cust,prev_product,total_units,total_sales}
```

It's a bit more complex than the mainframe sort but not very much. It is simply a matter of keeping track of the key values as records are processed and writing out records as the keys change. Note also the END command.

This command ensures that the last aggregate record is output. Once you get familiar with the operators and learn how the flow of control works, you'll be aggregating in no time.

Using Database Bulk Loader Utilities to Speed Inserts

PROCESS CHECK Planning & Design:
Requirements/Realities → Architecture → *Implementation* → Test/Release

Data Flow: Extract → Clean → Conform → *Deliver*

If after using sorting, extracting, and aggregating techniques to get your source data to the ETL server as quickly as possible, you still face a daunting amount of data that needs to be loaded into the data warehouse regularly, it's time to master the bulk-load functionality of your database management system. Bulk loaders can interact with the database system in a more efficient manner than plain old SQL can and give your ETL a tremendous performance boost. We use Oracle's SQL*LOADER utility to discuss the benefits of bulk loaders. You can find similar bulk-load functionalities in most other database management systems.

One important caveat is that many bulk loaders are limited to handling inserts into the database. As such, they can provide a real benefit for inserting large volumes of data, but if your process involves updating existing records, you may be out of luck. Depending on the number of rows you need to insert and update, you may find that with careful preprocessing of your input data, you can separate the updates from the inserts so that at least the inserts can be run in pure *bulk-loader mode*. Note that IBM's Red Brick system supports UPDATE else INSERT logic as part of its bulk loader.

In its basic *conventional path* method, SQL*LOADER uses INSERT statements to add data to tables, and the database operates in the same manner as if the inserts were part of a regular SQL procedure. All indexes are maintained; primary key, referential integrity, and all other constraints are enforced; and insert triggers are fired. The main benefit to using SQL*LOADER in this mode is that it provides a simple way to load data from a flat file with minimal coding.

A variety of syntax styles for invoking SQL*LOADER exist. Here's an example for loading the sales file we used in the previous examples into an Oracle table with SQL*LOADER.

```
sqlldr userid=joe/etl control=sales.ctl data=sales.txt log=sales.log
bad=sales.bad rows=1000
```

The control file sales.ctl would contain the following:

```
LOAD DATA
APPEND INTO TABLE SALES
FIELDS TERMINATED BY "," OPTIONALLY ENCLOSED BY '"'
(SALE_DATE DATE(20) "MM/DD/YYYY",
CUSTOMER_ID,
CUSTOMER_NAME,
PRODUCT_ID,
PRODUCT_NAME,
UNIT_COST,
UNITS,
UNIT_PRICE,
SALE_AMOUNT)
```

Of course, the target table SALES would have to already exist in Oracle. Again, this simple example uses conventional SQL INSERT functionality to load data into the database. Next, we want to look at ways to improve performance.

The second, performance-enhancing mode for SQL*LOADER is *direct* mode. Changing the prior load to use direct mode is achieved by simply adding the direct=true clause to the sqlldr command, as shown in the following.

```
sqlldr userid=joe/etl control=sales.ctl data=sales.txt log=sales.log
bad=sales.bad rows=1000 direct=true
```

Here's how direct mode increases performance:

1. SQL*LOADER places an exclusive lock on the table, preventing all other activity.
2. Database constraints (primary and unique key constraints, foreign key constraints, and so on) are not enforced during direct loads. If violations occur, the associated indices are left in an unstable state and require manual clean up before rebuilding the indices.
3. Foreign key constraints are disabled by the direct load and must be re-enabled after the load. All rows are checked for compliance with the constraint, not just the new rows.

4. Insert triggers do not fire on rows inserted by direct loads, so a separate process must be developed to perform the actions normally handled by the triggers if necessary.

So the efficiencies of direct load don't come free. We'd be particularly wary of using direct loads if you expect dirty data that will prevent your primary and foreign key constraints from being re-enabled after the load. But if you have robust processes for ensuring that the data to be loaded is clean, direct loads of large source files is the way to go.

Whether you are using conventional or *direct path* mode, SQL*LOADER has a fairly rich set of functionality beyond the simple example shown previously. Some key functions include the following:

- Handles fixed-width, delimited, and multiline input
- Accepts input from multiple files
- Loads to multiple target table
- Loads partitioned tables
- Manages and updates indexes efficiently

A number of other, more programmatic features allow conditional processing, value assignments, and so on. However, these features should be avoided, since they generally operate on each input row and can considerably degrade the performance of the bulk load. After all, performance is what using the bulk loader is all about.

Preparing for Bulk Load

Many of the ETL tools on the market today can stream data directly from their tool through the database bulk-load utility into the database table. But not all of the tools utilize the bulk-load utilities the same way. Some are more efficient than others, and some require extra plug-ins to make them compatible with bulk loaders. Regardless of how you pass data, as an ETL developer, it is important that you understand how to prepare your data to be processed by a bulk-load utility.

Bulk loading is the most efficient way to get data into your data warehouse. A bulk loader is a utility program that sits outside of the database and exists for the sole purposes of getting large amounts of data into the database very quickly. Each database management system has a different, proprietary, bulk-load utility program. The popular ones are listed in Table 7.3.

Generally speaking, the various bulk-load utilities work in the same way. For the purpose of illustrating the functionality of a bulk-load utility, we'll discuss Oracle's SQL*Loader; at the time of this writing, we believe it is the common denominator of bulk loaders in the domain of data warehouses.

Table 7.3 Bulk Load Utilities

DBMS	BULK LOAD UTILITY NAME	COMMENTS
Oracle	SQL*Loader	Requires a control file that describes the data file layout. Two important parameters for optimal performance are: DIRECT={TRUE | FALSE} PARALLEL={TRUE | FALSE}
Microsoft SQL Server	Bulk Copy Program (BCP)	Microsoft also offers BULK INSERT that can be faster than BCP. It saves a significant amount of time because it doesn't need to utilize the Microsoft NetLib API.
IBM DB2	DB2 Load Utility	DB2 accepts Oracle Control and Data files as input sources.
Sybase	Bulk Copy Program (BCP)	Also supports DBLOAD with the parameter BULKCOPY = 'Y'.

Once you understand the general concepts of bulk loading, the similarities among the loaders makes learning each specific utility a breeze.

Bulk loaders typically need two files to function properly:

- **Data file.** The data file contains the actual data to be loaded into the data warehouse. Data can be in various file formats and layouts, including a variety of delimiters. All of these parameters are defined in the control file.
- **Control file.** The control file contains the metadata for the data file. The list of the various parameters is extensive. Following is a list of the basic elements of SQL*Loader control file.
    - The location of the source file
    - Column and field layout specifications
    - Data-type specifications
    - The data mapping from the source to the target
    - Any constraints on the source data
    - Default specifications for missing data
    - Instructions for trimming blanks and tabs
    - Names and locations of related files (for example, event log, reject, and discarded record files)

For a comprehensive guide to SQL*Loader command syntax and usage, refer to *Oracle SQL*Loader: The Definitive Guide*, by Jonathan Gennick and Sanjay Mishra (O'Reilly & Associates, 2001).

> 💡 **Even if you must pay the penalty for the I/O of writing data to a physical file before it is bulk loaded into the data warehouse, it is still likely to be faster than accessing the database directly and loading the data with SQL INSERT statements.**

Many ETL tools can *pipe* data directly into the database via the bulk-load utility without having to place data on disk until it hits its final destination—the data warehouse fact table. Others can create the required control and data files on your files system. From there, you need to write a command-line script to invoke the bulk loader and load the data into the target data warehouse.

The main purpose of purchasing an ETL tool is to minimize hand-coding any routines, whether extracting, transforming, or loading data. But no tool on the market can solve every technical situation completely. You'll find that seamlessly pipelining data through bulk loaders or any third-party load utilities will be a bit of a challenge. Experiment with tool plug-ins and other application extenders such as *named pipes*, and exhaust all options before you determine bulk loading is not feasible.

If you have not yet purchased your ETL tool, make sure to test potential products for their compatibility with your DBMS bulk-load utility during your proof-of-concept. If you already own an ETL tool and it cannot prepare your data for bulk loading, do not throw it away just yet. You need to prepare the data manually. Configure your ETL tool to output your data to a flat file, preferably comma delimited. Then, create a control file based on the specifications of the output file and required load parameters. The control file should need to be changed only when physical attributes change within the source or target, like when new columns are added or data types are modified.

Managing Database Features to Improve Performance

PROCESS CHECK Planning & Design:
Requirements/Realities → Architecture → *Implementation* → Test/Release

Data Flow:Extract → Clean → Conform → *Deliver*

As we all know, there's more to the database than tables and the data contained therein. Powerful features like indexes, views, triggers, primary and foreign key constraints, and column constraints are what separate a database management system from a flat-file system. Managing these features can consume significant amounts of system resources as your database grows and, as a result, can drag down the performance of the ETL load process.

With this in mind, the first thing to do is review the database design and remove any unnecessary indexes, constraints, and triggers. Then consider the following options to improve load performance:

1. Disable foreign key (referential integrity) constraints before loading data. When foreign key constraints are enabled, for each row loaded the database system compares the data in foreign key columns to the primary key values in the parent table. Performance can be enhanced considerably by disabling foreign key constraints on fact tables having several foreign key constraints.

   Remember, though, that the database validates every row in the table (not just new ones) when you enable foreign key constraints after the load. Make sure your foreign key columns are indexed to ensure that the re-enabling the constraints does not become a bottleneck in itself.

2. Keep database statistics up to date. Database statistics managed by the database management system track the overall sizes of tables, the sizes and number of unique values in indexes, and other facts about the efficiency of how data is stored in the database. When an SQL SELECT statement is submitted to the database management system, it uses these statistics to determine the fastest access path to supply the requested data. Optimally, you should update the statistics after each load. However, if your load process is frequent (daily) and the daily percentage change in the size of the database is relatively small, updating statistics weekly or monthly should be sufficient to keep performance levels high. Partitioning large tables decreases the time it takes to update statistics, since the statistics need not be refreshed on the static (or near-static) partitions but only on the *current* partition.

3. Reorganize fragmented data in the database. Tables become fragmented when rows are frequently updated and/or deleted, and response time degrades as a result.

   When dealing with large fact tables, one way to minimize the occurrence of such fragmentation is to create *partitioned* tables. Partitioned tables are typically organized by time period (for example, a sales table with separate partitions for each year). Once a year is complete, the partition containing the sales data for that year will in all likelihood remain static and thus no longer be susceptible to fragmentation. ETL tools have the ability to automatically streamline loads based on the partition scheme specified in the DBMS dictionary.

Data for the current year, though, is constantly being deleted and reloaded, and so the current partition becomes fragmented. Reorganizing a fragmented table rewrites the data in the table in contiguous storage blocks and eliminates dead space that arises when rows are updated and deleted. If your load process performs updates and deletes on large (fact) tables, consider reorganizing the table every month or so or more frequently if warranted. The reorganization can be set to run each time data is loaded, if significant fragmentation occurs with each load.

Again, partitioning reduces the time it takes to reorganize tables. The older, static partitions will rarely, if ever, need to be reorganized. Only the current partition will need reorganizing.

The Order of Things

PROCESS CHECK Planning & Design:
Requirements/Realities → Architecture → *Implementation* → Test/Release

Data Flow:Extract → Clean → Conform → *Deliver*

The ordinal position of jobs within a batch is crucial when you are loading a data warehouse, primarily because the ETL needs to enforce referential integrity in the data warehouse. Referential integrity (RI) means that a primary key must exist for every foreign key. Therefore, every foreign key, which is known as the child in a referential relationship, must have a parent primary key. Foreign keys with no associated parents are called orphans. It is the job of the ETL process to prevent the creation of orphans in the data warehouse.

In transaction systems, RI is usually enforced within the database management system. Database-level RI enforcement is required in a transaction environment because humans enter data one row at a time—leaving a lot of room for error. Errors or actions that create RI violations cause data to become corrupt and of no use to the business. Users find amazing ways to unintentionally corrupt data during data entry. Once data is corrupt, it is worthless—a cost that cannot be overturned.

Enforcing Referential Integrity

Unlike transaction systems vulnerable to volatile data-entry activity, the data warehouse has its data loaded in bulk via a controlled process—the ETL system. The ETL process is tested and validated before it ever actually loads production data. The entry of data into the data warehouse is in a controlled and managed environment. It's common practice in the data warehouse to have RI constraints turned off at the database level, because it depends on the ETL to enforce its integrity.

Another reason RI is typically disabled in the DBMS is to minimize overhead at the database level to increase load performance. When RI is turned on within the database, every row loaded is tested for RI—meaning every foreign key has a parent in the table that it references—before it is allowed to be inserted.

RI in the data warehouse environment is much simpler than in transaction systems. In transaction systems, any table can essentially be related to any other table, causing a tangled web of interrelated tables. In a dimensional data warehouse, the rules are simple:

- Every foreign key in a fact table must have an associated primary key in a dimension.
- Every primary key in a dimension does not need an associated foreign key on a fact table.

Those trained in normalization know this is called a zero-to-many relationship. If you already have a dimensional data warehouse implemented, or have read any of the *Toolkit* books, you know that not all dimensional models are that straightforward. In reality, a fact can be associated to many records in a dimension (with a bridge table as described in Chapters 5 and 6) and dimensions can be snowflaked. In addition to facts and dimensions, the ETL must contend with outriggers and hierarchy tables. The ETL team must understand the purpose and functions of each of the types of tables in the dimensional data model to effectively load the data warehouse. Review Chapter 2 for more information on the different types of tables found in a dimensional model.

The following list is offered as a guide to the ordinal position of load processes for a given data mart.

1. Subdimensions (outriggers)
2. Dimensions
3. Bridge tables
4. Fact tables
5. Hierarchy mappings

6. Aggregate (shrunken) dimensions

7. Aggregate fact tables

Subdimensions

A subdimension, as discussed in Chapter 5, is simply a dimension attached to another dimension, when the design is *permissibly snowflaked*. A subdimension may play the role of a primary dimension in some situations. The calendar date dimension is a good example of an entity that is frequently a primary dimension as well as a subdimension.

Subdimensions are usually the first to be loaded in the data warehouse because the chain of dependency starts with the outermost tables, namely the subdimensions. Facts depend on dimensions, and dimensions depend on subdimensions. Therefore, subdimensions must be loaded, and their keys defined, before any other table downstream in the structure can be populated. The caveat is that depending on business requirements and your particular environment, it's possible that some subdimensions are rarely used and not considered mission critical. That means if a failure occurs to prevent the subdimension from loading successfully, it may be acceptable to continue with the load process of its associated dimension anyway.

Dimensions

Once the subdimensions are loaded, you can load the dimensions. Dimensions that have subdimensions need to lookup the surrogate key in the subdimension so it can be inserted into the dimension during the load process. Naturally, dimensions that do not have subdimensions can be loaded at once, without waiting for anything else to complete.

> **Smaller dimensions without dependencies should be loaded concurrently and utilize parallel processing. Larger dimensions can also be loaded in this fashion, but test their performance for optimal results before you commit to this strategy. Sometimes, it is faster to load large dimensions individually to alleviate contention for resources. Unfortunately, trial and error is the best rule for action in these cases.**

Dimension loads must complete successfully before the process continues. If a dimension load fails, the scheduler must halt the load process from that point forward to prevent the rest of the jobs from loading. If the process continues to load without the dimension information populated, the data warehouse will be incomplete and viewed as corrupt and unreliable. Enforcing the dependencies between jobs is crucial for the data warehouse to maintain a respectable reputation.

Bridge Tables

A bridge table sits between a dimension and a fact table when a single fact record can be associated to many dimension records. Bridge tables are also used between a dimension and a multivalued subdimension. For example, a bridge table is needed when a fact is at the grain of a patient treatment event in a medical billing database and many patient diagnoses are valid at the moment of the treatment. After the patient diagnosis dimension is loaded, the treatment transaction table is scanned to determine which diagnoses occur together. Then the bridge table is loaded with a surrogate key to assemble the diagnoses ordered together into groups.

Not all data marts contain bridge tables, but when they do, the tables must be loaded immediately after the dimensions but before the fact table load starts. If a fact table depends on a bridge table, the bridge table load must complete successfully before the fact table load can be executed. If you attempt to load the fact table with the bridge table partially loaded, groups will be missing from the table, and data from the fact table will become suppressed when it is joined to the bridge table.

CROSS-REFERENCE Information on loading bridge tables can be found in Chapter 5; techniques for using a bridge table to find the groups while loading facts are found in Chapter 6.

Fact Tables

Fact tables are dependent on virtually all other tables in the dimensional data model and are usually loaded last. Once the subdimensions, dimensions, and bridge tables are loaded, the fact table has all of the look-ups it needs and is ready to be loaded. Remember, RI is enforced here, so you must ensure that every foreign key in the fact table has an associated primary key in its relative dimension or bridge table.

Fact tables typically take longest of all the different types of tables in the data warehouse to load; you should begin the fact table load process as soon as all of its related tables are loaded. Do not wait for all of the dimensions in the data warehouse to load before kicking off the fact load. Only the dimensions and bridge tables directly related to the fact table need to complete before the associated fact table load can begin.

Because of the extreme volume of data usually stored in fact tables, it's a good idea to process their loads in parallel. The scheduler should spawn the ETL process into multiple threads that can run concurrently and take advantage of parallel processing. The next chapter discusses more about optimizing your fact table loads.

Hierarchy Mapping Tables

Hierarchy mapping tables are specially designed to traverse a hierarchy that lives within a dimension. See Chapter 5. Hierarchy mapping tables are not dependent on facts or bridge tables (unless, of course, the fact table itself contains the hierarchy). Technically, hierarchy tables can be loaded immediately following their relative dimension load, but we recommend loading them at the end of the data-mart process to enable the long-running fact table loads to begin, and finish, sooner.

Regardless of where the hierarchy is physically placed in a batch, its success or failure should have no bearing on the other processes in the batch. Don't kill the launch of a fact table process because of a failure in a hierarchy mapping table. The mapping table can be restarted independently of any fact table load.

The Effect of Aggregates and Group Bys on Performance

Aggregate functions and the `Group By` clause require databases to utilize a tremendous amount of *temp space.* Temp space is a special area managed by the DBMS to store working tables required to resolve certain queries that involve sorting. Most DBMSs attempt to perform all sorting in memory and then continue the process by writing the data to the temp space after the allocated memory is full. If you attempt to build aggregates for the data warehouse with SQL, you have a few issues to address.

SQL is processed on the server where it is executed. That means that if you attempt to aggregate data in your extract query, you will likely blow-out the allocated temp space in the source transaction system. By design, transaction systems keep their temp space very small compared to the space allocated on data warehouses. When you need to build aggregate tables, it's good practice to utilize the ETL engine or a third-party tool specifically dedicated to sorting data at lightning-fast speeds.

You should adjust your aggregates incrementally with a dedicated tool that supports incremental updates to aggregates.

💡 **Do not attempt to execute aggregating SQL with a `Group By` clause in your data extraction query. The `Group By` clause creates an implicit sort on all of the columns in the clause. Transaction systems are typically not configured to handle large sort routines, and that type of query can crash the source database. Extract the necessary atomic-level data and aggregate later in the ETL pipeline utilizing the ETL engine or a dedicated sort program.**

Performance Impact of Using Scalar Functions

Scalar functions return a single value as output for a single input value. Scalar functions usually have one or more parameters. As a rule, functions add overhead to query performance, especially those that must evaluate values character by character. The following functions are known performance inhibitors:

- SUBSTR()
- CONCAT()
- TRIM()
- ASCII()
- TO_CHAR()

This list is not exhaustive. It is served as an example to get you thinking about the different types of functions available in your database. For example, TO_CHAR() is a data-type conversion function. If TO_CHAR() inhibits performance, you can imagine that TO_DATE() and TO_NUMBER() also do. Try to substitute database functions with operators. For example, in Oracle, the CONCAT() function can be replaced with the double pipe || to concatenate two strings.

💡 **Databases are getting better at handling functions. Oracle has introduced function-based indexes that speed up response time for function-based constraints on queries. Look for more advanced functionality from the database vendors as they integrate the ETL with their base products.**

Avoiding Triggers

Database triggers are stored procedures executed by the occurrence of an event in the database. Events such as deleting, inserting, or updating data are common events related to database triggers. The problem is that each event is the occurrence of a record trying to get into the database, and the database must fire off the stored procedure between each record. Triggers are notorious for slowing down transactions as well.

If you should need event-based execution of a process, use the ETL engine to accomplish the task, especially for performing such tasks as appending audit metadata to records or enforcing business rules. ETL engines can perform such tasks in memory without requiring I/O.

Overcoming ODBC the Bottleneck

Chapter 3 offers insight into the layers within the Open Database Connectivity (ODBC) manager, but it's worth mentioning again here that ODBC is usually an unnecessary layer in your communication between the ETL engine and the database that can—and should—be avoided. ODBC adds layers of code to each SQL statement. It is equivalent to using a translator while teaching a class. The message eventually gets across but is a much slower process. And at times, things do get lost in translation.

Try to obtain native drivers to communicate between the ETL engine and the databases in that participate in process. Remember, just as a chain is only as strong as its weakest link, the ETL is only as fast as its slowest component. If you include ODBC in your ETL solution, you will not achieve optimal performance.

Benefiting from Parallel Processing

Processing the ETL in parallel is probably the most powerful way to increase performance. Each time you add another process, the throughput proportionally increases. This section does not discuss the technical architecture options (SMP, MPP, NUMA, and so on). Instead, we offer the benefits of processing the ETL in parallel versus sequential processing.

Parallel processing, in its simplest definition, means that more than one operation is processed at a time. As you can imagine, three major operations exist in any given ETL process—extract, transform, and load. You can, and should, take advantage of parallel processing in as many of them as possible.

Parallelizing Extraction Queries

The effective way to parallelize extraction queries is to logically partition the data set into subsets of equal size. We say *logically partition* because partitioning data is usually a physical database function. In this case, you divide the data based on ranges of an attribute. For example, you can divide the effective_date by year. Therefore, if you have ten years of data, you have ten logical partitions. Each partition is retrieved by a separate SQL statement and executed concurrently. The potential problem with this approach is that the database identifies each SQL statement as a separate process and attempts to maximize the memory allocated to each. Therefore, if you have very memory-intensive extraction queries, you can bring the server to its knees by replicating and executing such intensive processes.

Fortunately, most DBMSs have the capability to process a query in parallel, realizing it is the same process and managing memory accordingly. Optimal parallel solutions usually combine the two techniques—spawn several extract queries, each with a different range of values, and then parallelize each of those processes with database-specific parallel query techniques.

Each database—those that support it—has its own syntax for executing queries in parallel. In Oracle, you enable parallelization by setting the *degree* parameter when you create a table, or you can alter the table after it's created to enable parallelized queries. Run the following query to check to see what the parallel parameters for a table are:

```
Select table_name, degree, instances from all_tables where
table_name = '<TABLE_NAME>'
```

The preceding query returns three columns:

- **Table Name.** The name of the table being checked for parallelism
- **Degree.** The number of concurrent threads that would be used on each instance to resolve a query
- **Instances.** The number of database instances that the query can span to resolve a query

> 💡 **You do not need Oracle Parallel Server to run parallel processes. As long as you have the parallel degree set greater than 1, the query runs in as many processes as are indicated. However, to span instances, you must have multiple instances active and have Oracle Parallel Server running.**

Unfortunately, most transaction tables have the parallel degree set to 1 by default. And as you have probably found out, the source system DBA is not about to alter tables for the data warehouse team. Luckily, you don't need them to. Since the extraction query is a static, reusable SQL statement, it is permissible to insert a *hint* to override the physical parallel degree to tell the DBMS to parallelize the query on the fly! Dynamic parallelization is a robust mechanism invaluable for speeding up extract queries.

To dynamically parallelize a query, insert a hint that specifies the number of threads that you want to run concurrently and the number of instances you want to span.

```
select /*+ full(products) parallel(products,4,1) */
  product_number, product_name, sku, unit_price from products
where product_status = 'Active'
```

The hint in the query is marked by a proceeding /*+ and is terminated with */. Notice that the hint made the query execute on four different threads on a single instance dynamically. By quadrupling the execution threads, you can usually come awfully close to quadrupling the total throughput for the process. Obviously, other variables, such as memory and the physical attributes on the source system and tables, which the ETL team has no control over, also affect performance. So, don't expect performance increases to be 100-percent proportional to the number of parallel degrees specified. Refer to your DBMS user's manual for the calculation to determine the optimal parallel degree setting for your specific situation.

Parallelizing Transformations

If you are using SQL for your transformation logic, you can use the hint offered in the last section for any SQL DML statement. However, if you are using a dedicated ETL tool, and by now you probably are, you have two options to parallelize your transformations:

1. Purchase a tool that can natively parallelize an operation.
2. Manually replicate a process, partition the input data, and execute the processes in parallel.

Obviously, you want to strive for the first option. However, some tools do not natively support parallelism within jobs. If you have very large data sets, parallelism is not a nice option but a requirement. Luckily, the ETL vendors realize that data volumes are growing at a rapid pace, and they are quickly adding parallelization functionality to their tool sets.

If you have a tool (or an add-on to a tool) that enables transformations to be processed in parallel, simply follow the guidelines set by the vendor to achieve optimal results.

On the other hand, if you need to replicate processes manually, you should take the following steps:

1. Analyze the source system to determine the best way to partition data. If the source table is partitioned, use the column that the partition is based on. If it is not partitioned, examine the date fields, that is, effective_date, add_date, and so on. Usually, partitioning by date makes a nice, even distribution of volume across partitions. Often, in cases such as Orders, the volume can increase across partitions over time (a sign that business is good). In those cases, consider range partitioning the primary key or creating a hash partition, perhaps doing MODs on the primary key, which is a simple way to split data evenly.

2. The next step is to replicate the ETL process as many times as you want parallel threads to run concurrently. Look for a tool that minimizes the amount of redundant code. Remember, if you have four copies of an ETL process, all four copies need to be maintained. It's better to utilize a tool that can execute the same job with different batches that feed the job different data sets.

3. Finally, set up several batch jobs, one for each process, to collect and feed the appropriate data sets based on the ranges of values determined in step one. If you have an extremely volatile source system, we recommend that you run a preprocess that scans the source data and determines the best ranges to evenly distribute the data sets across the replicated ETL jobs. Those ranges (start value and end value) should be passed to the ETL jobs as parameters to make the process a completed automated solution.

If you have a substantial amount of data being fed into your data warehouse, processing all of your ETL operations sequentially will not suffice. Insist on an ETL tool that can natively process multiple operations in parallel to achieve optimal throughput (where parallelization is built directly into the transformation engine, not implemented as *parallel extenders*).

Parallelizing the Final Load

In the earlier section discussing parallelizing extraction queries, we assume that you do not have control over the structures in the database and that you need to add a database hint to have your query spawn multiple threads that run concurrently. However, in the target, the presentation area of the data warehouse, you do—or at least should—have some say in how the structures are built. It's in the best interest of the data warehouse team to architect the tables to have multiple degrees of parallelization when they are created.

Earlier in this chapter, we recommend that you minimize SQL inserts, updates, and deletes and utilize the bulk-load utility. Furthermore, when using Oracle's SQL Loader, you should make sure to set the DIRECT parameter to TRUE to prevent unnecessary logging.

Now we want to introduce one more technique to extend the extract and transform parallel processing: Spawn multiple processes of SQL Loader—one for each partition—and run them in parallel. When you run many SQL Loader processes concurrently, you must set the PARALLEL parameter to TRUE. No faster way exists—at least at the time of this writing—to load a data warehouse than following these three rules:

1. Utilize the bulk loader.

2. Disable logging.

3. Load in parallel.

More information about using bulk loaders can be found in Chapter 8. For an exhaustive reference for the Oracle SQL Loader utility, read *Oracle*

SQL*Loader: The Definitive Guide by Jonathan Gennick and Sanjay Mishra (O'Reilly & Associates 2001).

Troubleshooting Performance Problems

No matter how efficient you make your ETL system, you still stand a chance of having performance issues. However, as Robin Williams says so eloquently in the film *Good Will Hunting*, "It's not your fault." When you are dealing with very large data sets, sometimes they decide to make their own rules. On more than one occasion, we've come across a situation where everything is configured correctly, but for some unexplainable reason, it just doesn't work!

When a job catches you by surprise and performs with lackluster results, don't fight it. Simply take a pragmatic approach to find the operation within the process causing the bottleneck and address that specific operation. Monitor areas such as CPU, memory, I/O, and network traffic to determine any high-level bottleneck.

If no substantial bottlenecks are detected outside of the actual ETL process, you need to dive inside the code. Use the process of elimination to narrow down potential bottlenecks. To eliminate operations, you must have the ability to isolate each operation and test it separately. Code isolation tends to be quite difficult if you are hand-coding the entire process in SQL or another procedural language. Virtually all of the ETL tools provide a mechanism to isolate components of a process to determine undesired bottlenecking.

The best strategy is to start with the extraction process; then work your way through each calculation, look-up, aggregation, reformatting, filtering, or any other component of the transformation process; and then finally test the I/O of the actual data load into the data warehouse.

To begin the isolation process for detecting bottlenecks, copy the ETL job and modify the copy of the job to include or exclude appropriate components as needed. As you step through the process, you will likely need to delete the copy and recopy the job to restore changes made to test preceding components. Follow these steps to isolate components of the ETL process to identify bottlenecks:

1. **Isolate and execute the extract query.** Usually, the extraction query is the first operation in the process and passes the data directly into the next transformation in the pipeline. To isolate the query, temporarily eliminate all transformations and any interaction with databases downstream from the extract query and write the result of the query directly to a flat file. Hopefully, the ETL tool can provide the duration of the query. If not, use an external monitoring tool, or, in Oracle, use

the SET TIMING ON command before you execute the process. That setting automatically displays the elapsed time of the query once it completes. If the extract query does not return the rows substantially faster than when the whole process is enabled, you've found your bottleneck, and you need to tune your SQL; otherwise, move on to Step 2.

NOTE In our experience, badly tuned SQL is by FAR the most common reason for slowness.

2. **Disable filters.** Believe it or not, sometimes feeding data in an ETL job and then filtering the data within the job can cause a bottleneck. To test this hypothesis, temporarily disable or remove any ETL filters downstream from the extract query. When you run the process, watch the *throughput*. Keep in mind that the process might take longer, but its how much data is processed during that time that's important. If the throughput is substantially faster without the filter, consider applying a constraint in the extract query to filter unwanted data.

3. **Eliminate look-ups.** Depending on your product, reference data is cached into memory before it is used by the ETL process. If you retrieve a lot of data in your look-ups, the caching process can take an inordinate amount of time to feed all of the data into memory (or to disk). Disable each look-up, one at a time, and run the process. If you notice an improvement in throughput with one or more look-ups disabled, you have to minimize the rows and columns being retrieved into cache. Note that even if you are not caching your look-up, you may still need to minimize the amount of data that the look-up query returns. Keep in mind that you need only the column being referenced and the column being selected in your look-ups (in most cases, the natural key and surrogate key of a dimension). Any other data is usually just unnecessary I/O and should be eliminated.

4. **Watch out for sorters and aggregators.** Sorters and aggregators tend to hog resources. Sorters are especially bad because they need the whole dataset in memory to do their job. Disable or remove any resource-intensive transformations such as sorters and aggregators and run the process. If you notice a substantial improvement without the components, move those operations to the operating system. Quite often, it's much faster to sort or presort for aggregates outside of the database and ETL tool.

5. **Isolate and analyze each calculation or transformation.** Sometimes the most innocent transformations can be the culprit that causes ETL

performance woes. Remove each remaining transformation, one at a time, and run the process. Look for things such as implicit defaults or data-type conversions. These seemingly harmless operations can have substantial impact on the ETL process. Address each operation independently for the best bottlenecking detection and remedy.

6. **Eliminate any update strategies.** As a general rule, the update strategies that come packaged in ETL tools are notoriously slow and are not recommended for high-volume data loads. The tools are getting better, so test this process before removing it. If the update strategy is causing a bottleneck, you must segregate the inserts, updates, and deletes and run them in dedicated streams.

7. **Test database I/O.** If your extraction query and the rest of the transformations in your ETL pipeline are running efficiently, it's time to test the target database. This is a simple test. Redirect the target to load to a flat file instead of a database. If you see a noticeable improvement, you must better prepare your database for the load. Remember to disable all constraints, drop all indexes, and utilize the bulk loader. If you still cannot achieve desired performance, introduce a parallel process strategy for the data-load portion of the ETL.

Increasing ETL Throughput

This section is a summary of sorts. It can be used as a quick reference and a guideline for building new processes. The ETL development team is expected to create ETL jobs that obtain the maximum possible throughput. We recommend the following ten rules, which are applicable for hand-coded solutions as well as for various ETL tools for boosting throughput to its highest level:

1. **Reduce I/O.** Minimize the use of staging tables. Pipeline the ETL to keep the data in memory from the time it is extracted to the time it is loaded.

2. **Eliminate database reads/writes.** When staging tables are necessary, use flat files instead of database tables when you must touch the data down to disk.

3. **Filter as soon as possible.** Reduce the number of rows processed as far upstream in the process as you can. Avoid transforming data that never makes its way to the target data warehouse table.

4. **Partition and parallelize.** The best way to increase throughput is to have multiple processes process the data in parallel.

   - Parallelize the source system query with parallel DML.

   - Pipeline and parallelize transformations and staging.

   - Partition and load target tables in parallel.

5. **Update aggregates incrementally.** Rebuilding aggregates from scratch is a process-intensive effort that must be avoided. You should process deltas only and add those records to existing aggregates.

6. **Take only what you need (columns and rows).** Similar to the filtering recommendation, do not retrieve rows unessential to the process. Likewise, do not select unessential columns.

7. **Bulk load/eliminate logging.**

   - Utilize database bulk-load utility.

   - Minimize updates; delete and insert instead.

   - Turn off logging.

   - Set `DIRECT=TRUE`.

8. **Drop database constraints and indexes.** Foreign key (FK) constraints are unnecessary overhead; they should be dropped—permanently (unless they are required by your aggregate navigator). If FKs are required, disable them before the ETL process and enable them as a post-process. Leave indexes for updates and deletes to support `WHERE` clauses only. Drop all remaining indexes for inserts. Rebuild all indexes as a post-process.

9. **Eliminate network traffic.** Keep working files on local disk drives. Also, place the ETL engine on the data warehouse server.

10. **Let the ETL system do the work.** Minimize any dependency on DBMS functionality. Avoid stored procedures, functions, database key generators, and triggers; determine duplicates.

Many of the top ten rules have already been discussed in previous chapters in this book. For a more comprehensive examination, you'll find that Chapters 5, 6, and 7 offer especially great details on optimal design strategies.

Each of the top ten rules for boosting ETL productivity is discussed briefly in the following sections.

TIP Rebuilding indexes can take a lot of time. It's recommended that you partition high-volume target tables. Not only can you truncate and reload the data in a partition, while leaving the rest of the table intact, but indexes local to a partition can be dropped and rebuilt, regardless of how data is maintained. Rebuilding the subset of the index can save a substantial amount of time during the post-load process.

Reducing Input/Output Contention

Because databases and operating systems each interact with input and output so differently, we don't attempt to explain the technical operations of I/O in this section. However, we do maintain the stance that I/O must be reduced to an absolute minimum. Obviously, you may need to touch down data for various reasons. The number-one permissible reason to touch down data is when you need to minimize access to the source system or if your source system allows only one-shot to retrieve the data you need from it. In those cases, it's good practice to write the extraction result set to disk as soon as it is retrieved. That way, in case of failure, you can always reprocess data from the saved copy instead of penetrating the source system again.

Excessive I/O is a remarkably common offender. In most cases, intermediary tables or files can be omitted without any loss of functionality while their respective processes benefit from increased throughput. If you find yourself creating staging tables and many jobs to read and write to them, stop! Step back and analyze the total solution. By eliminating staging tables, you not only reduce I/O—the biggest performance hit—but also you reduce the number of jobs that need to be maintained and simplify the batch and scheduling strategy.

Eliminating Database Reads/Writes

The ETL process often requires data to be touched down to disk for various reasons. It can be to sort, aggregate, or hold intermediate calculations or just retain for safekeeping. The ETL developer has a choice of using a database for these purposes of flat files. Databases require much more overhead than simply dumping data into a flat file. And ETL tools can manipulate data from a flat file just as easily as database data. Therefore, it's a preferred practice to utilize sequential or flat files in the data-staging area whenever possible.

The irony of this recommendation is that the ultimate goal of the data warehouse is to present data in a way that it has optimal query response time and that the solution is a relational database management system. However, even though the ETL may need to read intermediary data, it does not *query* data in the same sense end users do in the data warehouse's presentation layer. ETL staging processes are static and repeated, whereas the data warehouse must support unpredictable, ad-hoc queries.

Dramatic performance improvements can be obtained by simply redirecting the staging database tables to flat files. The downside to eliminating the database in the staging area is that the associated metadata that comes for *free* by the nature of the database is lost. By choosing to use flat files, you must maintain any metadata related to the files manually (unless your ETL tool can capture the metadata).

Filtering as Soon as Possible

This tip addresses what is possibly the most common mistake in ETL design. Whenever we conduct design reviews of existing ETL processes, one of the first things we look for is the placement of filters. A filter is a component that exists in most ETL products that applies constraints to the data after it's been retrieved. Filters are extremely useful because in many cases you need to constrain on fields from the source system that are not indexed. If you were to apply the constraint in the extraction SQL on a nonindexed field, the source database would need to perform a full table scan, a horrendously slow process. Conversely, if the source system indexes the field you want to constrain, this would be the preferred place for filtering because you eliminate extracting unwanted records.

We often notice that filters are placed downstream of very complex calculations or process-intensive and I/O-intensive data look-ups. Granted, at times you must perform certain calculations before filters are applied. For example, when you have to figure the dwell time of a Web page, you must calculate the difference between the current page hit and the next before you dispose of the unwanted pages.

As a general rule, you should keep and apply ETL filters as far upstream in the process as requirements permit. Typically, filtering advantages are best achieved when they are placed immediately following the initial SQL statement that extracts data from the source system and before any calculations or look-ups occur. Precious processing is wasted if you transform data and then throw it away.

> 💡 Apply ETL filters to reduce the number of rows to process instead of applying constraints to the extraction SQL only if the source system database does not have the appropriate indexes to support your constraints. Because other factors such as table size, SQL complexity, network configuration, and so on play a role in data-retrieval performance, it makes sense to test both strategies before deciding on the optimal solution.

Partitioning and Parallelizing

Partitioning and parallelizing your ETL process is more than a design issue; it requires specific hardware and software and software solutions as well. One can partition data without executing its ETL in parallel and visa versa. But if you attempt to parallelize without partitioning, you can incur bottlenecking. An effective partition and parallelization strategy for unpredictable source data is to create hash partitions on your target tables and apply that same partition logic to the ETL process. Be careful though—hash partitions may not be an optimal solution for the data warehouse ad-hoc queries. Work closely with the data warehouse architect to implement the most appropriate partition strategy. Refer to earlier in this chapter for techniques and advantages concerning parallel processing.

Updating Aggregates Incrementally

Aggregates are summary tables that exist in the data warehouse specifically designed to reduce query time. Aggregates make a dramatic performance gain in the data warehouse because queries that had to scan through hundreds of millions of rows now can achieve the same results by scanning a few hundred rows. This drastic reduction in rows is attributable to the ETL process combining additive facts in a mechanical rollup process. More complex summaries that depend on complex business rules are not what we call aggregates in the dimensional world. Remember that an aggregate is used in conjunction with a query rewrite capability that applies a fairly simple rule to judge whether the aggregate can be used rather than a dynamic aggregation of atomic data at query time.

Aggregates are computed in several different ways in a mature data warehouse environment:

- **Calculating aggregate records that depend only on the most recent data load.** Product rollups and geographic rollups (for instance) generated entirely from the most recent data load should be calculated by sorting and summarizing the data outside the DBMS. In other words, don't use the DBMS's sort routines when native OS sorts are much faster. Remember that the computation of aggregates is merely a process of sorting and summarizing (creating *break rows*).

- **Modifying an existing aggregate in place by adding or subtracting data.** This option is called *tweaking* the aggregate. An existing aggregate spanning an extended period of time may be modified when that period of time includes the current load. Or an existing aggregate may be modified when the criteria for the aggregate are changed. This can happen, for example, if the definition of a product category is modified and an aggregate exists at the category level, or a rollup above the category level. If the tweak to the category is sufficiently complicated, a quality-assurance check needs to be run, explicitly checking the aggregate against the underlying atomic data.

- **Calculating an aggregate entirely from atomic data.** This option, called a *full rollup*, is used when a new aggregate has been defined or when the first two options are too complex to administer.

Taking Only What You Need

It doesn't make much sense to retrieve hundreds of thousands or millions (or even billions) of rows if only a few hundred of the records are new or have been modified since the last incremental ETL process. You must select a mechanism for retrieving deltas from the source system only. There are several ways to approach change-data capture depending on what's available in the source transaction system. Refer to Chapter 6 for a display of the many different techniques for capturing changed data in the source system and techniques for determining the most appropriate for your particular situation.

Once you have the rows trimmed down to a manageable size for your incremental loads, you must next ensure that you don't return more columns than necessary. Returning excessive columns is commonly encountered in look-ups in ETL tools. Some ETL tools automatically select all of the columns in a table whether they are needed or not when it is used for a look-up. Pay special attention to explicitly *unselect* columns that are not vital to the process. When you are looking up surrogate keys, you typically need only the natural and surrogate keys from a dimension. Any other column in a dimension is superfluous during a surrogate key look-up process.

Bulk Loading/Eliminating Logging

Bulk loading is the alternative to inserting data into the data warehouse one row at a time, as if it were a transaction system. The biggest advantage of utilizing a bulk loader is that you can disable the database logging and load in parallel. Writing to the rollback log consumes overhead as well as I/O and is unnecessary in the data warehouse. Specific bulk-load techniques and advantages to bulk loading are offered throughout this book.

Dropping Databases Constraints and Indexes

Another certain way to have a positive impact on loading your data warehouse is to drop all of the constraints and indexes from the target of the ETL process. Remember, the data warehouse is not transactional. All data is entered via a controlled, managed mechanism—ETL. All RI should be enforced by the ETL process, making RI at the database level redundant and unnecessary. After a table is loaded, the ETL must run a post-process to rebuild any dropped indexes.

Eliminating Network Traffic

Whenever you have to move data across *wires*, the process is vulnerable to bottlenecking and performance degradation.

Depending on your infrastructure, it sometimes makes sense to run the ETL engine on the data warehouse server to eliminate network traffic. Furthermore, benefits can also be achieved by storing all of the staging data on internal disk drives, rather than by having the data travel over the network just to touch down during the ETL process.

This recommendation can be a Catch-22, meaning that in your situation, putting the ETL engine on your data warehouse database server might actually make your performance worse, not better. Work with your ETL, database, and hardware vendor to achieve the best solution for your specific requirements.

Letting the ETL Engine Do the Work

ETL products are specifically designed to extract, transform, and load massive amounts like no other nondata warehousing solution. With minimal exception, most databases are designed to support transactional and operational applications. Database-procedural programming is good for supporting data-entry applications but is not optimal for processing large data sets at once. The use of cursors—where each record is analyzed individually before moving on to the next—is notoriously slow and usually results in unacceptable performance while processing very large data sets. Instead of using procedures stored within the database, it's beneficial to utilize the ETL engine for manipulating and managing the data.

Summary

This chapter has provided an overview and some examples of the technologies you need to choose to develop your ETL system. You must start by choosing a development environment: either a dedicated ETL tool suite from one of the vendors we have listed or a development environment based on operating system commands driven by scripting languages, with occasional escapes into a low-level programming language.

In the second half of this chapter, we have given you some guidance on DBMS-specific techniques for performing high-speed bulk loads, enforcingRI, taking advantage of parallelization, calculating dimensional aggregates, and troubleshooting performance problems.

Now we're ready to *get operational* in Chapter 8 and manage this wonderful technology suite we have built.

Operations

"Overall system speed is governed by the slowest component."
—Gene Amdahl

Developing ETL processes that load the data warehouse is just part of the ETL development lifecycle. The remainder of the lifecycle is dedicated to precisely executing those processes. The timing, order, and circumstances of the jobs are crucial while loading the data warehouse, whether your jobs are executed real-time or in batch. Moreover, as new jobs are built, their execution must integrate seamlessly with existing ETL processes. This chapter assumes that your ETL jobs are already built and concentrates on the operations strategy of the ETL.

In this chapter, we discuss how to build an ETL operations strategy that supports the data warehouse to make its data reliably on time. In the first half of this chapter, we discuss ETL schedulers as well as tips and techniques for supporting ETL operations once the system has been designed.

The second half of this chapter discusses the many ways in which you can measure and control ETL system performance at the job or system level. (We discuss database software performance in Chapter 7.) You have more than a dozen *knobs* for controlling performance, and we give you a balanced perspective on which are most important in your environment.

At the end of this chapter, we recommend a simple but effective approach to ETL system security at the database, development environment, QA-environment, production-environment, and basic file-system levels.

PROCESS CHECK Planning & Design:
Requirements/Realities → Architecture → Implementation → *Test/Release*

Data Flow: Extract → Clean → Conform → Deliver

This chapter describes best practices for running your ETL operations. Operations includes initial data loads, execution and monitoring the daily flow of data, capacity planning, performance monitoring, maintenance of the metadata repository, and controlling access to the back room databases.

Scheduling and Support

The ETL execution strategy falls into two major categories:

- **Scheduling.** ETL scheduling is a comprehensive application that does much more than arrange for jobs to execute at a given time. In reality, the time of day that a job executes is almost insignificant. Instead, an effective scheduler involves the designation of relationships and dependencies between ETL jobs and acts as a reliable mechanism to manage the physical implementation of the execution strategy.

- **Support.** Once the data warehouse is deployed, it invariably becomes a mission-critical application. Users, as well as other downstream applications, depend on the data warehouse to provide them with the information they need to function properly. If the data warehouse is not loaded consistently, it is deemed a failure. To make certain that the ETL process runs and completes, it must be actively monitored and supported by a production-support team.

Reliability, Availability, Manageability Analysis for ETL

A data warehouse can have the best dimensional data model, a best-of-breed business-intelligence tool, and sponsorship from the highest executives. But it is not a proven solution until it is considered a dependable source for corporate analytical information.

The goal of a new data warehouse is to build a reputation for being a consistent, reliable data source to support corporate data analysis to empower the business. To be a success, the ETL and the data warehouse teams must fulfill three key criteria:

- **Reliability.** The ETL process must run consistently, without fail. The data within must be trustworthy at any level of granularity.

- **Availability.** The data warehouse must be up, running, and available for use as promised by the data warehouse manager during initial kick-off meetings with the sponsors and users. ETL jobs must execute and complete within the allocated load window.

- **Manageability.** Remember that the data warehouse is never finished. It must have the capability to change and expand as your company grows. The ETL processes must evolve gracefully with the data warehouse. To achieve extensibility, keep processes as simple as possible; break down complex routines into smaller, simpler components. At the same time, avoid an upsurge of jobs to carry out processes. Moreover, a crucial part of designing the execution strategy is ensuring the ability to support the ETL. The ETL team must provide metadata for all components of the ETL and document recovery procedures for every failure scenario. If you are hand-coding your system, make sure you have the management skills and perspectives to control a long-term software development environment.

The ETL manager must appraise each phase of the data warehouse by using the Reliability, Availability, and Manageability (RAM) criteria to score the project. The jobs and scheduling approach must pass each of the three criteria to get a perfect score and earn the right to deploy. If no metadata or recovery documentation exists, points are deducted and the processes must be revisited and enhanced or corrected. Jobs that are overly complex making them virtually impossible to maintain must be streamlined to progress to the next stage of the lifecycle. Each deployment of the data warehouse must achieve a perfect RAM score before it is rolled into production.

ETL Scheduling 101

Scheduling ETL processes is an obvious necessity to get them to run, so why write nearly a whole chapter about it? This chapter explains not just execution but execution *strategy*. A strategy is an elaborate and systematic plan of action. Anyone can execute a program, but developing an execution strategy requires skill.

For example, during a data warehouse and ETL design review, a user was complaining that the data warehouse was not available until 11:00 a.m. With this information, we immediately started to review ETL jobs to find where the bottleneck was so we could recommend a remedy. We shortly discovered the jobs were efficient and should not have taken three full hours to process from execution to completion. "That's correct!" claimed an ETL developer on the project. "I kick them off as soon as I arrive at work, around 8:00 a.m., and they complete in three hours—by 11 o'clock." In disbelief, we interrogated the developer about automation—and the lack of it in his implementation. He claimed he was never trained in the ETL tool's scheduler, so he had to kick the jobs off manually.

Even though you execute your programs, it is imperative that you do so systematically. It is crucial that the ETL team understand the tools in your environment and have the ability to properly schedule and automate the ETL process to consistently load the data warehouse.

Scheduling Tools

Any enterprise data warehouse must have a robust enterprise ETL scheduler. Major ETL vendors package schedulers with their core ETL engine offerings. Some offer little more than a way to execute your ETL jobs depending on the time of the day, while others offer comprehensive ETL execution solutions that can trigger ETL jobs based on a variety of vital criteria.

If you are not satisfied with the packaged scheduler bundled with your ETL product or you opted to venture the ETL without a dedicated product, you have a few alternatives. Regardless of whether you buy a dedicated ETL scheduler, use your existing production-scheduling system, or manually code your ETL jobs to execute, a production ETL scheduler should meet certain criteria to be a viable enterprise solution.

Required Functionality of an ETL Scheduler

The next sections examine some of the options available to automate the ETL process. Many options are available, and each varies in cost and ease of use. Certain functionality is required in production ETL environments. When you select (or build) your ETL scheduling solution, make sure it contains the functionality discussed in the following sections.

Token Aware

Often, the data warehouse requires data acquired from an external source. External data providers are common, and your ETL solution must be able to accommodate their data. External data sources are usually provided as a flat file or in XML format. Reading and processing this data is by and large quite simple; the challenge is to make the ETL process aware of data's existence. Unlike database sources, where you can look in tables' audit columns to recognize new rows, external sources typically dump data files into a directory on the file system via FTP. As long as the format is correct each time, the ETL process can handle the data. But how does the ETL system know when an externally sourced data file has arrived and should begin its process? The ETL system must be able to recognize that the file has appeared in the file system and execute automatically. This process is called *token aware*.

Tokens are files created in the file system to trigger an ETL event. Applications that are token aware can poll a directory (or database table) for the arrival of a token file (or a row). When you handle flat files, Web logs, or external sourced data, you must avoid processing the same file repeatedly and also ensure that you don't miss running the ETL process if the file arrives late. The token file is considered a token because it is not necessarily the actual file processed; it can be an indicator file that tells a process to execute merely by its arrival.

Intra-Day Execution

Daily processing is becoming less acceptable in today's society, where expectations for immediate action are set so high. ETL processes must have the ability to run multiple times throughout the day and even on demand. Where monthly or daily incremental loads used to suffice, there are now calls for 12-hour, six-hour and four-hour increments; even hourly updates are becoming more common where real-time technology does not exist. These aggressive requirements mean that not only must your ETL jobs be efficient, but your scheduling system must be steadfast to manage the exorbitant number of processes that run throughout the day.

Moreover, your process must be able to span over the stroke of midnight—and restart outside of its allocated window. The practice of hard-coding *SYSDATE-1* to look for *yesterday's* data is not adequate for launching and selecting data from your source systems. The ETL system must be able to capture new data from source systems, regardless of when it was created or when the process is executed.

Real-Time Capability

Real-time execution is a reality of data warehousing that cannot be ignored. It is so important that we dedicate an entire chapter to the subject. Chapter 11 discusses several techniques for achieving real-time ETL execution. Real-time ETL is becoming more commonplace in most enterprises. More and more users now expect the data warehouse to be continuously updated and are growing impatient with *stale* data. Soon, real-time ETL will not be a luxury but a standing requirement.

Furthermore, as the data warehouse evolves, its value is realized by the most unexpected users. Because it offers clean, consistent, and reliable data, the data warehouse is becoming a source system itself. Transaction applications are increasingly becoming dependent on the data warehouse to be a standardized source for common reference data elements. To fulfill this so-called *closed-loop* movement, the data warehouse must update continuously to support operational applications.

Command-Line Execution

ETL products have dedicated so much energy toward creating slick graphical user interfaces (GUI) for their scheduling packages to reduce the learning curve for beginning developers and to expedite development time for seasoned ETL experts. But most enterprise system operations environments need the ability to execute ETL jobs from a command-line interface. The reality is that the team that supports the daily operations also supports many other applications and cannot be expected to learn a different interface to support each. Therefore, your ETL application must allow processes to be executed from a command-line interface for the data warehouse ETL to be supported by your system-operations staff. Note that the major ETL tool suites all allow command-line execution as an option for these reasons.

Notification and Paging

Once the ETL has been developed and deployed, its execution must be a hands-off operation. It should run like clockwork, without any human intervention and without fail. If a problem with the process does occur, the support group must be notified electronically. Your ETL solution must have the ability to notify different groups or people depending on the job or the type of failure. As we write this book, wireless PDAs and smart phones are exploding. These devices seem likely to be standard equipment for operational personnel. The displays on these devices can display complex text and graphical information, and the operator can issue commands to the ETL system remotely. See the warning that follows!

E-mail notification and paging must be completely automated. There is simply not enough time to wait for the key support personnel to be notified manually. Automated notification can be achieved in one of three ways:

- **Integrated ETL tool.** Some of the major ETL products offer paging and notification features natively in their scheduling application. Features are usually not very robust, but they are getting better. At a minimum, you need to differentiate between successful loads and failures and page-appropriate personnel accordingly. Also, messages should automatically send vital information about the failure (for example, job name, time of failure, rows loaded, rows failed, and last error message dynamically).

- **Third-party messaging application.** A number of companies offer urgent messaging products dedicated to supporting 24/7 system operations to minimize downtime. Additionally, operations management/monitoring tools often include notification features that can be utilized if your operations-support team utilizes such a tool.

- **Custom scripts.** You have the option of manually scripting the e-mail notification portion of the execution strategy at the operating-system level. The scripts must interact with the ETL jobs and be triggered as necessary.

💡 **When designing your custom e-mail notification system, use scripts with embedded e-mail addresses with extreme caution. Scripts can be read on the file system as simply as a text file. Scripts are vulnerable to having e-mail addresses hijacked by spammers who can saturate the e-mail recipients with junk mail. Use encryption techniques or a solution from a secure product whenever possible.**

Nested Batching

A batch is a group of jobs or programs that run together as a single operation. Usually, ETL jobs are grouped together—or batched—to load a single data mart. And the data warehouse, composed of a collection of data marts, is loaded with a batch of data mart load batches. The technique of loading batches of batches is known as *nested* batching. Nested batching can involve several layers of ETL jobs. For example, a single dimension can require several ETL jobs to load it due to severe complexity within the data or business rules. Those dimension jobs are grouped together to run in a single batch. That batch is included in another batch to load the rest of the dimensions for the data mart. The data mart batch is then incorporated into the data warehouse batch, making the batch three layers deep. No logical limit to the depth of nested batching exists.

ETL jobs are typically executed in nested batches. You will rarely run a single, standalone ETL job in a production environment. A data mart usually requires at least one job for every dimension and the fact table. As you can see, multiple levels of nested batching are common while loading the data warehouse. Therefore, your solution must be able to manage nested batches. Batch management includes the following:

- **Graphical interface.** ETL batches typically become quite complex due to the nature of the nesting required to load the data warehouse. Select a batch-management tool that has the capability to navigate through your nested batches as easily as navigating through a directory structure in Windows Explorer. Without a graphical representation of the nested batches, management can become unwieldy. Developers should be able to create, delete, edit, and schedule batches through a GUI, as well as move jobs and nested batches among outer batches by dragging and dropping them. Batch management is best achieved graphically, although a logical naming standard must accompany the graphics. Visualization of the dependencies between batches is crucial to maintaining a clear understanding of which jobs belong in each batch and also to identifying dependencies between batches.

- **Dependency management.** A dependency occurs when the execution of one job is contingent upon the successful completion of another. Rules of dependencies between jobs are defined in the execution strategy and must be enforced at runtime by the ETL scheduling system. Your batch-management tool must have the ability to stop a batch dead in its tracks upon a failed job if business rules so require. For example, if a dimension job fails, you must not proceed to load the fact table. Not all scenarios require such a strict batch-halt policy. For example, if an outrigger fails, it is usually still okay to load its associated dimension. The batch-management tool should be robust enough to set dependencies on a batch-by-batch basis as business rules dictate.

- **Parameter sharing.** Values of parameters might need to be passed from one job to another or set once at the outermost batch and used globally throughout the nested batches. The batch manager must include parameter-management functionality. More information regarding parameter management is discussed in a section dedicated to that topic later in this chapter.

- **Graceful restart.** What happens if a job fails in the middle of its execution? How do you know exactly what has been loaded and what has not? Upon restart, the batch-management tool must be able to systematically identify which rows have been processed and loaded and process only the rest of the input data. Special attention must be paid to the load process at times of midprocess failure. In general, the ETL system should have a number of staging points (steps in the process where data has been written to the disk) if for no other reason than to support a restart scenario. Also, special care should be taken if one of the ETL steps involves manual intervention and correction of data. These manual steps must at least be preserved in a log so that they can be reapplied if the ETL processing step must be rerun.

- **Sequential/Concurrent execution.** In some cases, it is necessary to load tables sequentially. For instance, when tables have dependencies between them, you must load the parent before you can load child tables. Outriggers associated with specific dimensions are a good example of this parent-child sequencing, as well as normal dimensions and facts. You cannot load a fact until all dimensions are loaded. Also, sometimes you need to load tables in sequence rather than concurrently to distribute server resources. If you attempt to load all dimensions in a data mart at once, you might bring the ETL server to its knees by overloading its resources. Conversely, in cases of long-running processes, you can separate a job into several smaller jobs run concurrently to improve load performance. Assuming appropriate resources are available, run as many independent processes concurrently as possible to maximize processing and minimize the load window. More information on concurrent and parallel processing is detailed later in this chapter.

■ **Pre/Post-execution activity.** Simply launching scripts before or after an ETL process is not execution management. The batch manager must be able to realize that a preprocess script has executed successfully before it launches the core ETL job. Moreover, it must trigger only post-process scripts if the core ETL job completes without failure. Lastly, scripts must be able to be executed at the batch level as well as the job level. This is especially important for batches run concurrently, because a different job might complete last each time the batch is executed. Nevertheless, you might need a post-process script to fire off only after *all* jobs are complete.

■ **Metadata capture.** All metadata within the control of the batch manager must be captured, stored, and published. In a best-case scenario, metadata should be stored in an open repository that can be shared with other applications. Each ETL job has a scheduled execution time and frequency, its parameters, and recovery procedures, which are all forms of metadata that must be presented and easily obtained by those who need to support the load processes as well as business users. At a minimum, metadata must have reporting abilities so users and developers have insight into the operational aspects of the data warehouse ETL. Refer to Chapter 9 for an in-depth view of ETL metadata.

💡 **ETL tools are becoming better at failure recovery, but graceful restart is an extremely difficult requirement that we have not yet seen perfected. In many cases, it is still safest to truncate or delete the information that has been partially loaded as a result of midprocess failures and begin the failed ETL process from the beginning. If you entrust your tool set to automatically pick up where it left off, it is recommended that extra time be spent auditing the data of the completed process to ensure data quality and integrity.**

Parameter Management

The ETL system moves through different environments throughout its development lifecycle. Since the lifecycle includes testing the code within the ETL system, you cannot alter the code between environments. Therefore, hard-coded parameters are not acceptable while coding variables in the ETL system. Parameters are a way to substitute values in code that would otherwise be constant. A robust ETL scheduling system must have the ability to manage and pass parameters to ETL jobs as they are executed. Parameters add flexibility to ETL jobs so they can gracefully change environments or extraction criteria without reprogramming the application. For example, the natural course of an ETL job is to be developed in a development environment, tested in a test environment, and ultimately migrated to a production environment where it supports the production data warehouse.

Each of the environments in the ETL lifecycle has dedicated source, staging, and target databases; file systems; and directory structures. By making each of these environment changes parameter driven, the ETL system can pass the jobs through the environments without changing code to point to relevant files or databases. You must parameterize environment variables and allow the scheduler to pass the applicable values to those variables at run time.

A good list of items to parameterize includes:

- Server name
- Database or instance name
- Schema description file name
- Database connection information (without the password in plain text!)
- The root directory or folder in which to find useful control files
- Metadata database-connection information

Your scheduler must be able to manage two kinds of parameters:

- **Global parameters.** A global parameter is a single parameter that supports many ETL jobs. Naturally, ETL jobs can have many global parameters. For example, the target database name should be set globally; otherwise, you are forced repeatedly to maintain the parameter for each job that loads the data warehouse.
- **Local parameters.** Local parameters live only within an ETL job. Local parameters can be set to change variables within a single job without affecting other jobs in its batch. An example of a local parameter is the setting of the earliest date that should be retrieved from the source table.

Native ETL tool schedulers are the best bet to obtain a robust parameter-management system because the scheduler is usually natively integrated with the ETL engine. Native integration of the ETL engine and the scheduler makes communication between the two components remarkably efficient. Architectures that involve parameter management by a third-party vendor are not as efficient but might provide more flexibility. ETL solutions that do not support parameters that can be set at runtime fail the Manageability criteria of RAM.

In an enterprise environment, it's important to produce metadata for the parameters in your ETL jobs. If you don't have a robust parameter-management system, parameters can be maintained in flat files on your files system. By utilizing flat files, the operations teams can simply update a parameter file without at all invading the ETL system.

ETL Scheduler Solution Options

In the previous section, we describe the functionality that one should expect of an enterprise ETL scheduling system. A few options that achieve the same functionally exist. In this section, we offer five options to select from when you are building your ETL scheduler solution:

1. Integrated ETL tool
2. Third-party scheduler
3. Operating system
4. Real-time execution
5. Custom application

The key is to select a solution robust enough to meet all the criteria you think you'll need based on your knowledge of the jobs that have been created to load your data warehouse thus far, yet fits within the budget of the data warehouse initiative. The final criterion is to consider in-house expertise. The next sections evaluate each of the five options.

Integrated ETL Tool

Virtually all of the dedicated ETL tools incorporate a scheduling system to execute ETL jobs created within their toolset. Some tools offer minimal functionality, while others are robust scheduling applications. If you are not forced into using a tool that your operations-support team has already established as the *standard* scheduling tool and your ETL tool contains a robust scheduler, it is most beneficial to use your integrated ETL scheduler. Benefits of an integrated solution include:

- **Product support by your ETL vendor.** Utilize a single Service Level Agreement (SLA) for both applications. Those with IT experience are familiar with the passing of the buck that occurs with multivendor solutions. Funny how problems are never the fault of the vendor on the phone. (*It must be a compatibility issue caused by the other product.*)

Using a single vendor or product suite can improve vendor support and expedite the resolution of technical issues.

- **Integration of scheduler and ETL engine.** Integrated suites are designed to pass parameters between components and natively enforce dependencies between jobs. Dependency between jobs, meaning the execution of one job depends on the successful completion of another job or set of jobs, is a crucial to properly loading the data warehouse and recovering from ETL failures.

- **Knowledge of toolset within ETL group.** Since the ETL toolset is the specialty of the ETL team, they can set up the execution strategy without learning another application. Moreover, once an ETL job has been thoroughly tested, it is rare that it fails in production. When jobs do fail, the ETL team usually needs to get involved at some level of capacity. By keeping ETL scheduling within the domain of the ETL toolset, the team can easily jump into the support role and help recover any failed ETL processes.

Third-Party Scheduler

Many production-support departments standardize on a single scheduling system that all applications must adapt to. In some enterprise environments, the data warehouse is treated like any other application and must abide by the rules set by the production-support team. In these cases, the ETL is triggered by a scheduling system that supports all applications throughout the enterprise. Operating an enterprise-scheduling system is a specialty beyond the scope of the ETL team's knowledge. The ETL team needs to work closely with the production-support team in cases where failure recovery is not straightforward.

> If your production-support team insists that they execute ETL jobs via their standardized enterprise scheduling application, make sure it has the required functionality to properly support your ETL execution strategy, including dependencies between jobs, parameter management, and notification and alerts.

Operating System

It's not uncommon for the ETL process to be executed by native operating system scheduling systems such as Unix Crontab or the Windows Scheduler. Even if you have a state-of-the-art ETL product, many production-support groups require scripts to execute the ETL jobs in production because it is a common denominator of all applications throughout the enterprise. Virtually any application can be executed via a line command or script at the operating-system level. In the Windows world, very elaborate batch or .BAT or VBScript or JScript files can be constructed to manage the execution of ETL processes. On Unix, Crontab is used to launch jobs. Operating-system schedulers can execute the ETL job directly or by way of a script.

As most programmers know, the power of scripting is not trivial. One can build very robust application-type logic with scripting languages. Most of the RAM criteria can be met with scripting. Moreover, Perl, VBScript, or JavaScript can be run on Unix or Windows to handle complex business logic while executing jobs that load the data warehouse. In fact, scripting languages can most likely provide the functionality of the logic within the jobs, too. However, we still recommend a robust ETL tool for building and maintaining ETL jobs. The shortfall of using scripting instead of a dedicated ETL scheduling tool is its lack of metadata. Any useful information regarding the ETL schedule lies within the scripts. One needs to be a programmer to decipher the information within the script. Two techniques can be utilized to maintain metadata within the execution scripts.

- **Spreadsheets.** The ETL manager or programmer must maintain a spreadsheet that contains important metadata, including parameters, jobs within the batch, timing of the execution, and so on.
- **Tables.** A dynamic scripting solution is metadata driven. All pertinent metadata is stored in tables (either database or flat) and is passed to scripts at runtime. Metadata-driven scripts are an achievable goal that should be built and utilized when integrated ETL schedulers are not an option.

Real-Time Execution

If part of your data warehouse is real-time enabled, you need to select one of the mechanisms detailed in Chapter 11 to support your real-time requirements. It is rare that an entire enterprise data warehouse is loaded in real time. Often, some segments of the data warehouse are loaded real-time, while others are batched and processed periodically. Special attention must be paid to the integration of the two types of ETL techniques to ensure a seamless, cohesive solution.

Custom Application

Building a custom scheduling solution is always an option. However, we have not come across a reasonable justification for a custom scheduling application—but that doesn't stop some from building them anyway. If you choose to execute all of your jobs via scripts, it might be worthwhile to build an application to manage them, but building a custom GUI for this purpose would be overkill. Usually, scripting programs, along with metadata tables, are a viable solution for custom ETL scheduling.

Load Dependencies

Defining dependencies between jobs is perhaps the most important aspect of batching ETL jobs. If a subdimension load job fails, perhaps you can continue to load a dimension, but if a dimension load fails, should you continue to load the fact table? It's usually not recommended. A dependency set between jobs is metadata that the load process must be aware of. Operational metadata of this sort is needed for the operation of the ETL to function properly. A fact table ETL process will load erroneously—missing key data—if it is executed before all of its dimensions are successfully loaded. Moreover, if the fact table is not designed to perform updates, all of the erroneous data must be manually *backed out* or deleted before the process can restart. Manual intervention is the costliest approach to rectifying failed ETL loads. Much of that cost can be avoided by declaring enforceable dependency rules between ETL jobs.

Dependency holds true between bridge tables and dimensions—and hierarchy mapping tables and dimensions. Use the preceding list as a reference for job-dependency definitions. In a nutshell:

- Do not load dimensions without successfully completing their subdimensions.
- Do not load bridge tables without successfully completing their dimensions.
- Do not load fact tables without loading all parents, including bridge tables and dimensions.

However, keep this clever data warehouse aphorism in mind: For each rule of thumb, there are four more fingers to consider. For example, if a dimension is designed to update the foreign key that associates itself to a subdimension, it is not necessary to stop loading the data mart because a subdimension load has failed, as long as the scheduler issues a warning whenever a job does not complete as expected.

Metadata

Imagine if your local railroad ran its service without publishing its train schedule. How would anyone know when to catch the train? Running an execution strategy without publishing its metadata is equally detrimental to its users. Earlier in this chapter, we told you that your scheduler must capture metadata for the contents and schedule of batches and nested batches and that this metadata must be available to business users as well as to the data warehouse team. Batch metadata serves as the train schedule for the data warehouse. It should predict when users should expect data to arrive and become available for use.

The scheduling system should also let users know when data will be arriving late. This notification is different from the failure notification discussed earlier in this chapter. Data-availability metadata is a crucial aspect of communication and a key mechanism for setting user expectations. Metadata used to notify users of data arrival falls under the category of *process metadata*. Process metadata captures the operational statistics on the ETL process. It typically includes measures such as the count of rows loaded successfully, rows rejected, elapsed time, rows processed per second, and the row's estimated time of completion. It is important process metadata because it helps to set user expectations—just like giving announcements at the train station.

Metadata collected during the cleaning and conforming steps serves several operational roles. It serves to advise the ETL team whether the data is fit to be delivered to the end user community. The data in the audit dimension is meant to be combined with normal data in specially instrumented data-quality reports, both for instilling confidence in the reported results and supporting compliance reporting. Finally, the cleaning and conforming metadata is a direct indicator of action items for improving the data quality of the original sources.

All metadata within control of the batch manager must be captured, stored, and published. In a best-case scenario, metadata should be stored in an open repository that can be shared with other applications. At a minimum, metadata must have reporting capabilities so users and developers have insight into the operational aspects of the data warehouse ETL.

Migrating to Production

The migration process can vary depending on many variables, including politics, technical infrastructure, and the ETL toolset. In general, the ETL team is usually part of the development side of things and should avoid the distractions associated with providing first-level production support for the data warehouse, unless your organization is large enough to warrant a dedicated production-support ETL team.

For the purpose of this chapter, assume that the ETL team exists only in development and hands its work over to a production-support team when the jobs are ready for production. Again, these processes can vary depending on your organizational structure and the tools employed in your environment. This section should be used as a guide to the finishing touches of the ETL lifecycle.

Operational Support for the Data Warehouse

It's interesting how many books and articles talk about how the data warehouse team needs to maintain the data warehouse. In reality, at least in our experience, the data warehouse team—including the ETL team—are analysts as well as developers. They gather all of the business requirements, analyze the findings, and build the data warehouse. Once it is built, they usually hand it off to another team that monitors and maintains the production environment.

The data warehouse architect and data modelers are responsible for the dimensional data model, and the ETL manager is responsible for populating the dimensionally designed data warehouse.

The ETL development team builds the processes to load the data warehouse, and the quality-assurance (QA) team thoroughly tests them according to the written test plans. The data warehouse needs to be transitioned to the group within your organization that can support its day-to-day operations. If you are a small company or the data warehouse is still in its infancy, the development team may in fact support the operation of the ETL in production. But as the data warehouse grows—more data marts are added to it—the development team needs to be alleviated from the distractions of supporting the operational aspects of the production environment.

> Once the ETL process is developed and tested, the first level of operational support for the data warehouse and ETL should be provided by a group dedicated to monitoring production operations—not the data warehouse development team. The data warehouse team should be called only if the operational support team has exhausted all troubleshooting procedures without resolution.

Bundling Version Releases

Once the ETL team gets past the terrific challenges of developing the ETL process and manages to complete the creation of the jobs required to load the data warehouse or data mart, the jobs must be bundled and migrated to the next environment according to the lifecycle that has been implemented by your data warehouse management team.

> Have a discussion with your ETL tool vendor about exactly this step of your ETL deployment. Does the tool support incremental scripting of all edits, so that you can migrate your test system into development in a single command? Or do all the files have to be opened, examined, closed, and transferred one at a time?

With each data warehouse release, the development team should produce a release procedures document similar to the one displayed in Figure 8.1.

Environments: From QA to Production
Server names: Migrate from na-dwqasvr-01 to na-dwprdsvr-01
ETL Programs: Migrate from /DWQA to /DWPRD
Database Name: Migrate fromDWQA to DWPROD

File Name: DW_Release_5.0_SALES_PROD.doc
Last Modified Date: 16-Feb-04 7:10:00 AM
Change Type: Major Release
DW Release #: 5.0

Following System Change Requests (SCRs) are addressed in this Release/Build.

Change Request#	Subject Area /Table	Change type	Description	Lineage Report Name	PVCS Script Name	PVCS Version
10845	Sales	Data Model/ETL code	New star schemais added for Sales analysis	Sales_mart_data Lineage.xls	Sales_By_Month_Release_5_Build1.zip	

System Operations needs to follow below procedures for moving the Datamart from one environment to another.

☑ **Standard Release Procedures**

☐	**Procedure**
☐	**Project Code**
	• The DDL, and ETL scripts are in PVCS as **Sales_By_Month_Release_5_Build1.zip**.
☐	**Tables/Views**
	• **Execute the following DDL scripts in order** : in DW_PROD database. Get The DDL script from the PVCSProject:/DWQA/sql DW_SALES_MART_STEP1_CreateTablesIndexes.sql Version 1.0 DW_SALES_MART_STEP2_CreateStagingTables.sql Version 1.0 DW_SALES_MART_STEP3_CreatePubSynonyms.sql Version 1.0
☐	**Security View Changes**
	Not Applicable
☐	**SQL Packages**
	• **The following Package needs to be migrated to DWPROD :** Get the scripts from PVCS: DWQA/packages/PKG_SALES.sql Version 1.0
☐	**Configuration Changes**
	• **Include below entries intnsnames.ora on ETL server.** -Not Applicable -
☐	**ETL Jobs Migration**
	• **Migrate all of the below jobsfromPVCS or use the zip file.** Import all the jobs into DWROD from the following file: DW_SALES_MART_Release_5.0_ETL_Jobs.zip Version 1.0
☐	**Copy Shell Scripts**
	• **Copy below mentioned files from /dw/sales/qa/shellto /dw/sales/prod/shell** - Not Applicable -
☐	**Copy SQL Scripts**
	• **Copy below mentioned files from /dsprojects/DWDEV /sql to /dsprojects/DWQA /sql** - Not Applicable -
☐	**Copy Source Flat Files**
	- Not Applicable -
☐	**Copy/Edit Parameter file**
	• **Change below mentioned parameters in /dsprojects/DWQA/paramfile/param.ini.** If the following parameters do not exist in the param.,ini file, then set the value as follows: TgtStageUserName : Set this to dwetluser TgtStagePassword: Set this to the password for the DB user resultewd.
☐	**Additional Comments**
☐	**Execution Steps**
	• **Follow below mentioned steps to do current Release/Build.** 1. Do all the Migration steps as mentioned above. 2. Run BatchSalesLoad.sh

Figure 8.1 Data mart release document.

The data mart release document introduces the release and provides technical details required to migrate and support the release. The document includes the following:

- **Environment.** This section contains the source and the target environment. Environment migrations are usually Development to Test or Test to Production. If you have more environments such as dedicated User Acceptance or QA, those will also be included in this section, depending on where your project is in its lifecycle.

- **Server name.** The physical names of the servers in the environments participating in the migration. This can list the ETL and DW servers.

- **ETL Programs.** Lists the directory where the programs reside. If you are using an ETL tool, use the component to identify the correct programs or jobs for the release.

- **Database Name.** The database the migration is coming from and going to. This is usually Development to QA or QA to Production.

- **Documentation File Name.** The name of the file that contains information about the migration, including step-by-step recovery procedures

- **Last Modified Date.** The last time the Release Document has been modified

- **Change Type.** The description of the type of release. Types include major, minor, or patch. See Chapter 2 for a complete explanation of release types.

- **Release Number.** This is the version that the data warehouse becomes as a result of the release.

- **Change Request Numbers.** This corresponds to the requests addressed and included in the deployment as a result of your scope-management procedures.

- **Procedures.** The procedure is a step-by-step guide to migrate the jobs. The standard information usually provided on the release document includes:

  - **Project Code.** The area in the version-management tool to find the code to build the release in the data warehouse

  - **Tables/Views.** The Data Definition Language (DDL) that created the new structures and indexes for the new data mart

  - **Security.** Any new security policies or requirements to support the release

  - **SQL Packages.** Database store procedures used by the ETL

■ **Configuration Changes.** Global settings or entries required for the release, such as TNSNames (Oracle's aliases for remote database names) or Object Database Connectivity (ODBC) connections.

■ **ETL Jobs.** Where to get the ETL jobs required for the release. Usually specifies an area in your version-control manager or ETL tool.

■ **Shell Scripts.** Preprocess and post-process OS shell scripts that the ETL depends on

■ **SQL Scripts.** Preprocess and post-process SQL scripts that the ETL depends on

■ **Flat Files.** A list of flat files, including their path for new source or staging files

■ **Edits to Parameter File.** For environments with managed parameters, this is where you list the new source system databases or any new changed parameters for the ETL process to utilize.

■ **Additional Comments.** Any further instructions or comments about the release to help the system operations team with the migration

■ **Execution Steps.** Explicit instructions for the execution of the job. For new data marts or independent ETL processes, you can specify the schedule and frequency of the run.

Once the data mart release document is complete, the ETL team walks through the document with the implementation team. During the migration, the ETL team should be on standby for any emergency issues that might affect production. Immediate response by the ETL team might not be a key requirement for the first release of the data warehouse. But as the data warehouse becomes recognized as a mission-critical application, any downtime can be detrimental to the organization and must be avoided. Once the migration is complete, the ETL team can return to their regular development tasks for the next phase of the data warehouse. Ongoing support for the production environment should be provided by a dedicated production-support team. The next section walks you through the different support levels required for a data warehouse.

Supporting the ETL System in Production

The beginning of this chapter explains how to get the ETL processes running and shared recommendations on several techniques for scheduling, batching, and migrating ETL jobs. This section of the chapter concentrates on supporting the ETL once it is in Production. Generally speaking, support for any software implementation essentially has three levels:

1. **First-level support.** First-level support is usually a Help Desk type of situation. If a failure occurs or a user notices an error in data, first-level support is notified. Armed with the appropriate procedures provided by the ETL team, the first-level support team makes every attempt to resolve the situation before escalating it to the next level.

2. **Second-level support.** If the Help Desk cannot resolve the support issue, the system administrator or DBA is usually notified. The second level of support is usually technically proficient and can support general infrastructure type failures.

3. **Third-level support.** If the production operations technical staff cannot resolve an issue, the ETL manager is the next to be called. The ETL manager should have the knowledge to resolve most issues that arise in production. Sometimes the ETL manager converses with developers or external vendors for advice on certain situations.

4. **Fourth-level support.** When all else fails, go directly to the source. Fourth-level support demands the expertise of the actual developer of the ETL job to analyze the code to find a bug or resolve an issue. If the issue involves a potential bug in a vendor application, the vendor is called in to support its product.

In smaller environments, it is acceptable—and common—to combine support levels three and four. However, that combination puts more of a burden and coordination factor on the second-level support team. It is not advised to call an ETL developer every time a job fails. First-level support should be more than merely a phone service and must make every effort to resolve production issues before they are escalated to the next service level.

Achieving Optimal ETL Performance

Okay, you've thoroughly read this book and implemented a luminous ETL solution. But wait; you are not done yet! As your data warehouse expands, you must ensure that your ETL solution can grow along with it. A scalable ETL solution means that the processes you've designed have the ability to process much larger volumes of data without requiring redesign. Your designs must execute efficiently to achieve the performance required to process loads far greater than the size of their current volume. Scalability and performance are attributes that cannot be overlooked when designing the data warehouse ETL.

ETL developers, DBAs, and the data warehouse management team will benefit from this chapter because it outlines strategies that monitor and improve existing ETL implementations. The chapter assumes you've already done your analysis, designed your logical data lineage, and implemented the physical ETL process. It dives right into the details and techniques that should be applied to new and existing ETL jobs to obtain optimal technical performance.

Toward the end of this chapter, you'll find tips on how to tackle security issues in the data-staging area. We specifically address vulnerability during File Transfer Protocol (FTP) and offer techniques for encrypting and decrypting data in-stream to provide a secure yet efficient environment.

Upon completion of this chapter, you'll be able to offer expert ETL tuning techniques to your data warehouse team. The techniques offered in this chapter are specific to the data-staging environment and are not intended to be used to optimize the presentation layer of the data warehouse.

> If you need information on optimizing the target data warehouse, we recommend that you read *Essential Oracle8i Data Warehousing: Designing, Building, and Maintaining Oracle Data Warehouses* by Gary Dodge and Tim Gorman (Wiley 2000).

Estimating Load Time

Estimating the initial load of the data warehouse to bring all history from the transaction system into the data warehouse can be overwhelming, especially when the time frame can run into weeks or even months. Throughout this book, we present the extract, transform, and load processes as a complete package, according to the goal of the ETL process in its entirety. However, when you estimate a large initial load, it is necessary to divide the sections of the ETL system into its three discrete processes.

- Extracting data from source systems
- Transforming data into the dimensional model
- Loading the data warehouse

Estimating Extraction Process Time

Surprisingly, extracting data from the source system can consume the greater part of the ETL process. The historic load for the data warehouse extracts an enormous amount of data in a single query and online transaction processing (OLTP) systems are just not designed to return those voluminous data sets. However, the breath-of-life historic database load is quite different from the daily incremental loads.

But in any case, transaction systems are not designed to pull data in the way required to populate fact tables. ETL extraction processes often require overhead-intensive methods such as views, cursors, stored procedures, and correlated subqueries. It is crucial to estimate how long an extract will take before it is kicked off. Estimating the extract time is a difficult metric to calculate. The following obstacles prevent straightforward estimation procedures:

- **Hardware in the test environment is usually substantially smaller than in production.** Estimates based on executions of the ETL processes on the test environment can be significantly skewed because of the hardware difference between the test and production servers.

- **Since the ETL jobs that extract historic data can take days to run, it is impractical to perform a test run of the complete data set.** We have seen projects where an extract job ran and ran until it eventually failed; then it would be restarted and run again until it failed again. Days to weeks went by without an ounce of productivity.

To overcome the difficulties of dealing with massive volumes of data, you need to break the extract process into two smaller components:

- **Query response time.** The time it takes from the moment the query is executed to the moment the data begins to be returned

- **Dataset retrieval time.** The measurement of time between the first and last record returned

Since the initial extract load is likely to be massive, it's recommended that you take a portion of the data for your estimation. In most cases, the fact table you are loading is partitioned. We recommend that you retrieve enough data to populate an entire fact table partition for your sample. Use a partition worth of data for your sample because database partitions should divide data—more or less—into equal portions and provide a clean benchmark. Once the time to extract one partition is obtained, multiply that number by the number of partitions allocated for the fact table to estimate the total extraction time. The caveat with this method is that it combines the query response time with the data retrieval time, which can skew estimates.

Calculating Query Response Time

The best approach to isolating the two processes is to utilize a query-monitoring tool. Most of the ETL tools have a monitoring tool built into their application. Keep in mind that if you are using an ETL tool, reference tables are loaded into memory before the main extraction begins. Therefore, you need to separate the cache process from the raw extract process as well.

Calculating Data Retrieval Time

Once the extract query starts to return data, begin timing exactly how long it takes to load a portion of the data. Select a portion that makes sense for your situation. If you've got 200 million rows to load, perhaps one million would be a good test. Stop the job when exactly one million rows have been loaded and check the elapsed time. Then multiply the elapsed time by 200 (200 million rows total/1 million test rows) to derive the data retrieval portion of the extraction estimate for the entire historic load.

> Once the extraction job has been thoroughly tested, insist that the sample job for the estimate is performed in the production environment to prevent skewed results that would occur by running the process in a smaller technical infrastructure.

Estimating Transformation Process Time

One would expect that manipulating data would be a time-intensive effort. Surprisingly, most of the actual transformations of data are done in memory at an amazing rate of speed. Relative to its sister processes, extraction and load, the time it takes to physically transform data can be inconsequential.

If you are using stored procedures that utilize cursors, consider redesigning your system. Depending on your circumstances, it might be best to utilize an ETL tool and minimize the use of database-stored procedures for your transformation processes. Most of the ETL process should be consumed by I/O (physically reading and writing to disk). If the transformation time is not significantly less than that of the extract and load processes, you might have a major bottleneck in your transformation logic.

The easiest way to estimate transformation time is to gather the extract estimate and the load estimate and then run the entire process. Once you have those statistics, subtract the duration of the extract and load processes from the complete process time. The difference is the time spent on the transformation process.

Estimating Loading Process Time

When you calculate the load time, you need to ensure that delays aren't being caused by the transformation of the data. Even though you may be pipelining the data from the transformation to the load process, for the purpose of the estimate, you need to touch down the data to a flat file after it's been transformed.

Many variables affect load time. The two most important factors to consider are indexes and logging. Make sure the environment during the test exactly matches the physical conditions that exist in production. Like data retrieval, the data load is processed proportionately. That means you can bulk load a sample data set—say 1 million of 200 million—and then multiply that duration by 200 to derive the complete load time estimate.

Vulnerabilities of Long-Running ETL processes

The purpose of an ETL process is to select data from a source transaction system, transform it, and load it into the data warehouse. The goal of the ETL team is to design efficient processes that are resilient against crashes and unexpected terminations while accomplishing those tasks.

Horizontal versus Vertical ETL System Flows

ETL systems are inherently organized either horizontally or vertically. In a horizontal organization, a given extract-clean-conform-deliver job runs from the start to completion with little or no dependency on other major data flows. Thus, a customer-orders ETL job could run to completion, but the inventory tracking ETL job could fail to complete. This may leave the decision makers in the organization with an inconsistent and unacceptable situation.

In a vertical ETL system organization, several ETL jobs are linked together so that comparable steps in each job run to completion and wait for the other jobs to get to the same point. Using our example, both customer orders and inventory tracking would need to complete the extract step before either would advance to the cleaning, conforming, and especially the delivery steps.

Determining whether your ETL system should be horizontally or vertically organized depends on two big variables in your environment:

1. Detailed data dependencies that require several ETL jobs to progress through the steps in parallel. (That is, if the inventory tracking job fails, maybe the customer-orders job could have undefined product codes.)

2. The sensitivity the end user community might have to partially updated data (for example, orders being updated but shipments lagging by a day)

Analyzing the Types of Failure

Unfortunately, to execute and complete successfully, the ETL process depends on many components. Once an ETL process is in production, failures are typically due to reasons beyond the control of the process itself. Leading causes for production ETL failures include:

- Network failure
- Database failure
- Disk failure
- Memory failure
- Data-quality failure
- Unannounced system upgrade

To familiarize you with the variables in your environment that may pose a threat to your ETL processes, this section discusses each of the ETL vulnerabilities and offers tips on minimizing your risks.

Network Failure

The network is the physical infrastructure that connects all components of the data warehouse. Each server, whether it is for a database or an application, connects via the internal corporate network. With the miles of cabling, routing, and nodes, the risk of network faults always exists. Network failures will never be completely unavoidable, but the ETL can take measures to minimize vulnerability to network failures.

A precaution to reduce your vulnerability is to put the ETL engine on the same server as the target data warehouse database. Obviously, this choice raises the issue of resource contention between ETL jobs and end user queries, but in the realm of minimizing network failures this practice eliminates 50 percent of network traffic because the data can pass from the ETL engine to the target data warehouse on the internal bus of the server. In many cases this co-residency makes sense if conventional data warehouse querying happens during the day while ETL processes take over most of the system resources at night.

Database Failure

Remember, the initial load does not only happen at the beginning of the data warehouse implementation. If you have an enterprise data warehouse implemented using the Data Warehouse Bus Architecture, each phase of the data warehouse requires an initial load. Each data mart needs to have historic data loaded into it before it is loaded incrementally.

A physical database failure is known as unscheduled downtime. With today's available technology, where virtually everything is redundant, unscheduled downtime can and should be avoided. Make sure you have a comprehensive Service Level Agreement (SLA) that specifies your unscheduled downtime rate requirements.

Moreover, a database does not have to be physically down to be perceived as down. One of the goals of the ETL team is to conduct the required processes to load the data warehouse yet remain transparent to users. If an ETL process has a table locked or has the temp space pegged, the experience by the user is a failure. Perceived database failures are as detrimental to the reputation of the data warehouse as physical failures.

Disk Failure

The storage of data in the data warehouse is perhaps the most vulnerable component of the data warehouse to all potential points of failure. Typically, three disk groups are involved in the ETL process:

- **Source system disk.** Typically, the ETL process merely reads data from the source system disk and risk of failure is minimal. However, use extra caution while extracting the initial history from the system. An extract with many years of history can be a quite large data set. If you run complex extract queries with multiple joins and order by or group by clauses, you may exceed the disk space allocated for these types of operations. To reduce your vulnerability, work with the source system DBA team to monitor temp-space usage while you perform test runs of the history load process. Make sure ample space is allocated before you run the whole process.

- **Staging area.** The staging area is the workbench of the ETL process. Generally, it contains a number of staged files representing different steps in the flow of data from the source to the final dimensional targets. Data would normally be staged immediately after each of the major steps of extracting, cleaning, conforming, and preparing for delivery. The process reads and writes to this area for several reasons, including for data persistence and safekeeping, as well as a holding cell for data in the midst of transition. The data-staging area can be the size of the source system and the data warehouse combined. However, this is rarely the case. But keep in mind that the possibility is there and that the data-staging database is often off the radar for the data warehouse and DBA teams. As a precaution, periodically check the available space in the data-staging environment to ensure you are not running too low.

- **Data warehouse storage.** The data warehouse can grow much faster than initially anticipated. Quite often, space for indexes and temp space is underestimated and allocated space is exceeded. When the ETL process tries to write to unallocated disk, the process crashes. It is very difficult to recover from errors that involve disk space. To prevent running out of space, you need to *lie* to your DBA team and exaggerate the volumetric estimate of the initial load and three-month size estimate of the data warehouse. We used to double our estimates, but now, after a few close calls, we triple our volumetric to be safe. We recommend tripling the estimate of your initial load to avoid potential catastrophe. Trust us; the space will not go to waste.

💡 **It is not enough to simply measure various storage capacities and utilizations. The ETL team should monitor these numbers regularly and do something when the alarm thresholds are reached. We have seen alarms set at 90 percent of capacity, but then the warning gets ignored for six weeks. Boom!**

Memory Failure

Memory can fail in any of the three environments:

- Source system
- Staging area
- Data warehouse

These environments are equally vulnerable to overloading their allocated memory and failing the ETL processes. A memory overload will not necessarily *crash* your process, but it will slow it down tremendously when it starts to utilize *virtual memory*—when the operating system writes data intended to be in random access memory (RAM) to disk. Make sure you consult with your ETL application vendor to obtain recommended cache settings for your particular history load.

If you have a hardware breakdown, you'll need to correct the problem and restart your process from the beginning (unless your ETL tool can recover gracefully).

Temp Space

Temp space is the area of the database used whenever you sort or join data. Temp space is often *blown out* when data warehouse type queries are run on a database environment set up for transactional processing. Fear of blowing out temp space is one of the primary reasons that historic data should be extracted from the source system into a staging area in its simplest form and then transformed further in the dedicated staging environment. If you fill up the temp space in any of your database environments, your process will stop dead.

When temp space failures arise, the DBA team needs to allocate more space, and the process must be restarted. Depending on where and when the temp space failure occurs, data cleanup is almost always required. Since the data warehouse is designed for queries, temp space should be plentiful. The issue typically occurs in the source system environment, where the ETL team unfortunately does not have any control.

Data Space

In the data warehouse, data should be stored separately from indexes to alleviate contention and lessen the burden of managing space. A practical solution to estimate the size of your historic load is to load a small sample of data. Loading a single partition of a partitioned table is a good benchmark. Then you can multiply the amount of space consumed by loaded data by the number of partitions in your table. Chapter 4 illustrates a volumetric worksheet that provides more information on estimating data space.

> **Make sure the data-staging databases and data warehouse databases have ample space available to load your historic data before the massive load is kicked off. Running out of disk space is an ungraceful failure that requires manual data cleanup and a restart of the load process.**

Index Space

Estimating space for indexes is a tricky science because indexes do not grow proportionately like table data. We won't go into too much detail on index space; the calculations are fairly complex, and the data warehouse architect, data modeler, and DBA should have the index space created appropriately in the data warehouse before you start. As a rule of thumb, make sure there is at least as much space allocated for the indexes as there is for the base table.

> **When you load voluminous historic data, drop the target table's indexes before the load begins; and rebuild them after the load completes. By dropping and rebuilding the indexes, not only does performance improve, but you are insulated from load failure if the index space runs out of room. Once the table is loaded, you can always allocate more space to the indexes and rebuild them without affecting the data in the table.**

Flat File Space

Just as the space allocated for data in a database can be exceeded, space on your file system must be monitored to avoid exceeding the space allocated to your flat files. Fortunately, the space requirement in the staging area is allocated according to the ETL team requirements, so if you've followed the recommendations for estimating file system requirements in Chapter 4, you should be in a safe position for processing your historic loads. Some robust ETL tools include a *checkpoint* feature that guarantees that any record to reach a certain point in the process is written to disk for safekeeping. But remember, those checkpoint files are written to the file system and might well be the culprit that is filling up your file space. Checkpoint, cache, hash, flat, temporary, or any intermediate data staging file can fill your disk space. If you exceed allocated space and your process crashes for any of these files, it is recommended that you begin the process from the beginning once additional space has been granted rather than attempt to salvage already processed data.

Data-Quality Failure

Data-quality failure in production can either be an easily detected catastrophic administrative failure, such as missing fields or referential integrity violations, or it can be a threshold of data-quality warnings reached gradually in the course of a long run. A data-quality failure in production should be an unusual event and generally requires expert intervention. Perhaps the job can run to completion with known unusual data or perhaps the job needs to be backed out and the source data fixed.

Unannounced System Upgrade

Perhaps the only good news about unannounced system upgrades is that they are usually dramatic and obvious. The ETL job hangs. There is often no simple fix at the scrimmage line. If the reason for the suspended job cannot be fixed quickly, provision must be made for rolling back the system upgrade. This situation is no different from any software change; for critical systems, you must perform the most robust regression tests on a test system before installing the changes on your production ETL systems.

Recovery Issues

Whenever a process fails, it is a knee-jerk reaction for the ETL team to try to salvage whatever has been processed up to the point of failure. If you are lucky and are using an ETL tool that has checkpoint functionality, you may be able to restart your process, and it will magically pick-up where it left off when it failed. Notwithstanding vendor claims, we'd be hesitant to rely on checkpoint technology. If a process fails midstream, it's good practice to clean up the data and begin the process from the beginning. Divide your processes into subsets of data to make recovery issues cleaner and more efficient; instead of reprocessing the entire history load, you merely have to reprocess a single subset of the data.

Minimizing the Risk of Load Failures

Here are some rules of thumb for processing historic data.

- **Break-up processes.** Use dates or ranges or the natural key to break up the process into smaller manageable chunks. In the event of a failure, only that portion of data needs to be reloaded.

- **Utilize points of recovery.** Write data to a flat file for safekeeping after every major intermediate process (for example, upon extract, significant transformation, or once surrogate keys are assigned).

- **Load in parallel.** Not only the data load but also all of the components of the ETL should run in parallel to reduce the time it takes to process data.

- **Maintain metadata.** Operational metadata (for example, the last date loaded or the number of rows loaded) is crucial to detecting the status of each of the components of the ETL during a failure.

Purging Historic Data

When any database application is designed, a matrix is created to track the processes that insert, update, delete, and select the data. The matrix is commonly referred to as a CRUD (Create, Read, Update, and Delete) Matrix. The CRUD Matrix ensures that every entity has a process to perform each of the four ways to manipulate data. While developing application software, it is most common that the *D* in the matrix is overlooked. That means that the data gets entered and can be changed and read but that there is no formal process for deletion. When no formal process is developed to purge history, one of two things usually happens: Back-end scripts are run against the system to delete the history, or the records stay in the system indefinitely. As you might imagine, neither of these solutions is suitable for a data warehouse.

A purge process must be laid out as each subject area is planned. If volume is relatively small and ten or more years of future data will not affect performance, the ETL need not be developed right away. However, the purge-policy metadata must still be collected and published with the initial implementation.

Archiving data warehouse data should be done by the DBA, not by the ETL team. However, the permanent deletion of data from the data warehouse must be executed by the ETL team. Business rules surrounding deleted data must be enforced by a thoroughly tested and quality-assured ETL process.

Monitoring the ETL System

The business depends on the data warehouse to be refreshed at an agreed interval (or continuously). Failure to fulfill that responsibility puts the reliability and dependability of the data warehouse in question. Therefore, the data warehouse cannot succeed without efficient and persistent data feeds. The ETL team must monitor and evaluate the ETL jobs to ensure they are operating efficiently and the data warehouse is being loaded in an effective manner.

ETL monitoring takes many aspects of the process into consideration. Resources outside the scope of the ETL system such as hardware and infrastructure administration and usage, as well as the source and target environments, play crucial parts in the overall efficiency of the ETL system. Here, we introduce several ETL performance indicators that tell you how well (or not so well) your processes are executing. The indicators are part of operational metadata and should be stored in a repository so they can be analyzed over time by the ETL team.

Measuring ETL Specific Performance Indicators

Those of you with exposure to system or database administration are aware that there are measurements specific to environments captured to ensure that they are performing properly. As you might expect, the ETL system has its own set of performance indicators. ETL indicators are specific to the physical movement and management of the actual data. They are a step below the typical performance indicators. By *below*, we mean they do not measure at the operating-system level or hardware-resource level but within the ETL process itself.

The measurement most indicative of ETL efficiency is the actual time it takes to process data. Remember: The goal of the ETL system, besides creating quality information, is to load the data warehouse within the allotted load window. But if a job takes 20 minutes to complete, is that good? There's really no way of knowing unless you know how many records were processed during that time. For example, 20 minutes is fantastic if you are processing 50 million rows but less than adequate if the job processes only 100 rows. Following are ETL-specific measurements that prove to be useful while investigating load performance.

- **Duration in seconds.** This straightforward calculation is the basis of all other calculations. The duration is the difference between the start time and the end time of an ETL process in seconds. For example, if a process is kicked off at 4:00 a.m. and completes at 4:15 a.m., its duration is 900 seconds.

- **Rows processed per second.** This is equivalent to the rows loaded per second calculation, except in cases where the source data is larger than the target, as in the case of aggregate loads. Then it is the same as the rows read per second. A sample calculation of rows per second is 1,000,000 rows processed in 15 minutes ($1000000 / (15 * 60)$) = 1111.11 rows/sec.

- **Rows read per second.** The row count of the result of the SQL that retrieves the data from the source system divided by the duration in seconds. The data is then fed through the downstream transformation processes in the ETL pipeline where the row count can increase or decrease depending on the process.

- **Rows written per second.** The count of rows committed to the target table after they have been transformed, divided by duration in seconds. In cases with multiple target tables, it is the sum of all rows inserted into all tables divided by duration in seconds. The rows written can be greater or less than the rows read.

- **Throughput.** Throughput is the rows processed per second multiplied by the number of bytes in each row. Throughput, as with all performance measurements, is an approximation that should be used as a baseline for improving processes.

Most of the major ETL tools provide the necessary metrics to measure the performance of the ETL. You should instrument your ETL system to trigger an alert for any ETL job that takes dramatically more or less time to run than the historical experience would predict.

> **Bottlenecking occurs when throughput of a process diminishes due to a component of a process not being able to handle the output volume sent by a prior component in the process stream. For example, a bulk loader can feed 1000 rows per second to disk, but the disk may write only 800 rows per second. Therefore, throughput bottlenecking occurs at the disk component of the process. As a result, the entire process can be only as fast as its slowest component.**

Measuring Infrastructure Performance Indicators

The next component to examine is the infrastructure of the data-staging area. Many process metrics are available through different monitoring software packages or can be written to logs in hand-coded ETL solutions. Only a few vendor solutions intentionally offer direct indications that ETL performance is being affected. The crucial measurements for ETL performance can be obtained only by monitoring the processes as they run. Measurements that offer a direct indication that there may be a bottleneck in the process include the following:

- CPU usage
- Memory allocation
- Server contention

Naturally, network traffic and other known infrastructure performance indicators can affect ETL performance. Unfortunately, their measurements are so volatile that they are not stable or consistent enough to use reliably. Moreover, the origin of network traffic is extremely hard to identify or duplicate in a test environment. If you suspect that you are experiencing network issues, contact your network administrator for assistance.

CPU Usage

The ETL process runs on the central processing unit (CPU) of its server. CPUs are processors or chips that actually facilitate the computations required to operate the computer, make software run, and accomplish the ETL goals. Most ETL servers contain more than one processor to handle the enormous amount of computations required for the extraction, transformation, and load of data warehouse data. You are not likely to find CPU-usage reporting within your ETL tool, as it is outside the scope of the ETL system. However, if you are running your process on Unix, you can use the SAR –u command to list the usage of each processor in your system.

On Windows-based operating systems, you can use the Performance Monitor, a graphical user interface that allows you to add new counters to the already available performance logs. In Windows XP, the Performance Monitor can be found in the Administrative Tools applet in the Control Panel. To add a new counter, open the Performance Monitor, right-click the System Monitor Details pane, and then click Add Counters. From there you can select *Processor* as the performance object and select the relevant counters. The Performance Monitor will create a log file that captures statistics of your CPU usage for analysis.

If you find that your CPUs are often reaching their capacity during the ETL process, you need to add possessors. These CPU monitoring utilities also help you to reveal if the ETL process is being distributed evenly across all available processes.

Memory Allocation

Random access memory (RAM) can be allocated to an ETL process in many different places. First of all, the memory has to be physically available on your server. If you are purchasing an ETL tool, your vendor should be able to provide hardware specifications and recommend how much RAM you are likely to need to process your load volume with their toolset. Once the RAM is installed in your server, the memory must be allocated to your processes. In most ETL tools, memory usage can be specified at the job or batch level as well.

You must have appropriate memory allocated to each ETL process for ultimate efficiency. If your process is constantly reading and writing to disk instead of processing data in memory, your solution will be much slower. Appropriate memory allocation in your process affects transformation performance more than any other setting, so take extra care to ensure the setting is correct.

Your ETL tools should be able to tell you how much memory is allocated to each process, how much the process actually uses, and also how much spills over to virtual memory (cached to disk). Make sure this operational metadata is provided by the ETL tool during your proof-of-concept. If much of the data that should be in RAM is getting written to disk, you need to allocate more memory to the process or to get more physical memory installed on your server.

Some ETL tools make memory management completely transparent to the development team, while others might require certain configurations to be set manually. Memory settings that can be found in some of the major ETL tools include:

- **Shared memory.** When ETL engines read and write data, they use a dedicated area in memory called *shared memory*. Shared memory is where data queues up before it enters or exits the physical transformation portion of the ETL process. If not enough shared memory is allocated to your job, excessive disk caching occurs. Conversely, if too much shared memory is allocated, an unnecessarily large amount of RAM is reserved and taken away from other processes. Your ETL vendor should provide guidelines on how to calculate optimal shared memory settings depending on the size of the data being processed. Some ETL engines may attempt to manage shared memory dynamically. Look for a tool that allows you to override the system-assigned setting for special situations that the engine may not be able to assess.

- **Buffer block size.** The buffer block setting is a key element to consider when allocating performance-related settings. The proper setting of buffer block size depends on the row size of the data in the transformation stream. If your tool requires or allows custom adjustments to the buffer block size, your ETL vendor can recommend calculations for optimal settings.

💡 When a program requires more RAM than is physically available, the operating system (or application) writes data that doesn't fit into memory onto disk. As the overflowed data is needed, the program must read from and write to disk instead of utilizing RAM. *Virtual memory* is commonly referred to as page swapping because memory is stored in pages and as more pages are required, they are swapped between disk and RAM. Page swapping is a performance killer and should be avoided during ETL processing. If continual page swapping is detected, more RAM must be added to the ETL server and process.

If you opt—at least for the time being—to hand-code the ETL, you can manually monitor memory usage with the vmstat command. Among other key measurements, the vmstat command reports virtual and real memory usage as well as paging activity and disk operations.

Server Contention

Another potential performance killer is server contention. Contention occurs when more than one process attempts to use the same resource. You can encounter contention for memory, disk access, or data access. The most common offender of contention is when two ETL processes try to access the same data. The ETL processes can cause deadlocks. A deadlock happens when process A attempts to lock out process B while process B attempts to lock out process A, and the system simply hangs. Usually, the DBMS does a good job at managing data-access contention, but it *will* happen at some point in an ETL developer's career. The ETL system is most vulnerable to server contention when ETL processes run concurrently but not in parallel. When this happens, the processes constantly compete for resources, and collision is imminent. Your best defense is to avoid concurrent processes unless each process has dedicated process streams and appointed data partitions.

Memory Contention

When many applications or processes are running on the same server, they each need physical RAM to operate. Unfortunately, RAM is a limited resource, and the individual processes must contend for it. If you are running ETL processes concurrently, you may run into memory-contention problems. The memory-allocating settings at the job level become crucial when they are processed concurrently. Each ETL product has its own recommendations for alleviating memory contention. As a rule of thumb, minimize the memory allocated to small jobs, leaving room for larger jobs such as Type 2 slowly changing dimensions, bridge tables, and facts.

The ETL tools should be able to manage memory usage within its tool and avoid memory contention. In any case, the tool should provide the operational metadata to expose memory contention. If it doesn't, the Unix SAR command can assist in detecting memory contention. The SAR command is especially useful to detect memory usage of processes running beside the ETL tool and competing for the same RAM. If your process warrants it (and the budget allows it), make sure that the ETL engine is the only process running on your server during the data warehouse load window.

The efficiency of an ETL processes is questioned when it does not complete within the load window. Effective monitoring can usually reveal that most load delays are not the result of ETL inefficiency but of external processes running at the same time as the ETL and competing for server resources.

Disk Contention

Most disks have a limit on the number of accesses and the amount of data they can read or write at any given time. When that limit is reached, the ETL processes have to wait in line to access the disk. If you place many tables loaded concurrently in the same data files on the same disk, hot spots can occur. A *hot spot* is an area on disk repeatedly accessed for reading or writing. If you are using Oracle, you can use the following SQL to detect hot spots in your source, staging, or target databases:

```
select d.name datafile_name, f.phyrds reads_count, f.phywrts
writes_count
from v$datafile d, v$filestat f
where f.file# = d.file#
order by greatest(f.phyrds, f.phywrts) desc
```

Since this query sorts the result set by the number of reads and writes in descending order, the data files hit the most rise to the top. If you have a few data files disproportionately larger than the rest, you need to reconfigure the physical attributes of your staging tables so they are distributed more evenly.

Disk contention occurs outside the database as well. ETL engines utilize temporary fields and implicitly create files to hold transient data. Furthermore, developers explicitly create staging tables, configuration, and parameter files on the file system. Constant reading and writing to these files can cause unwanted disk contention. For information about your disk activity from the operating system point of view, use the IOSTAT Unix command. The IOSTAT command lists each disk and pertinent information:

- Name of the disk
- Reads per second
- Writes per second

- Kilobytes read per second
- Kilobytes written per second
- Average number of transactions waiting for service (queue length)
- Average number of transactions actively being serviced (removed from the queue but not yet completed)
- Average service time, in milliseconds
- Percent of time there are transactions waiting for service (queue nonempty)
- Percent of time the disk is busy (transactions in progress)

Information about how to resolve disk contention is provided later in this chapter.

Database Contention

Database contention can be most problematic if the ETL processes attempt to update records in the same table at the same time. Essentially, managing database contention is the job of the DBMS, but at times processes that contend for the same resource can block each other out, causing them to wait indefinitely. Refer to your specific DBMS reference manual or contact your local DBA for the best procedure for detecting database contention.

Processor Contention

Sometimes, an attempt at parallel processing at the software level can cause problems if your hardware is not configured to run parallelized. When you have multiple processes—more than the number of processes available—attempting to run at the same time, you can overload the CPUs and cause critical performance issues. You can use the SAR command on Unix or PerfMon on Windows to capture statistics on the CPU usage.

Measuring Data Warehouse Usage to Help Manage ETL Processes

If you refer to the supply-chain analogy we provide earlier in this chapter, you'll notice that we've identified four key components that lend a hand in transforming raw data to the customer in a useful format for consumption. So far, we have described how to monitor the activity within the scope of the ETL system as well as in the hardware and infrastructure of the ETL environment. Now we outline important measures within the presentation layer of the data warehouse.

The measurements in this section indirectly affect the ETL system but are important to capture and analyze because the do have an impact on the load processes. Hopefully, the measurements in the list that follows soon are already being captured by the data warehouse team to help manage their user experience and prune the data warehouse of data stored but not used.

The ETL team should take advantage of data-warehouse usage reports and look for opportunities to rearrange the load schedule, modify the load frequency, or eliminate the maintenance of jobs that load dormant tables. For example, if a table is accessed only on the first of the month, it should not be updated daily. Another efficiency gain can be achieved by analyzing index usage. A large portion of ETL processing includes rebuilding indexes in the data warehouse after each load. If usage analysis determines that certain indexes are never utilized, their reconstruction should be dropped from the ETL process. Usage metrics that support ETL job management include:

- **Table usage.** The contents of a table-usage report can vary, but a useful report contains a list of each table, a timestamp to represent the first and last time the table is accessed, the count of queries that reference the table, and the count of distinct users that query the table. Tables accessed first should be made available first. Tables used only once a month can be dropped from the daily load process and switched to a monthly frequency. Tables that appear to have continuous usage, except for when the table is being refreshed, are candidates for *high availability* techniques. Tables highly available have a duplicate structure loaded in the background. Once the load is complete, the names of the two identical structures are switched. This technique leaves the table online while the refresh takes place.

- **Index usage.** Indexes are key performance enhancers for data warehouse tables but are a burden to the ETL because in many cases they must be dropped and rebuilt with each data load. When a data warehouse architect builds the dimensional structures for the presentation layer, he or she has a tendency to index as many columns as possible to prevent bad performance experiences by a user. The fact is that many indexed columns are never constrained on and the indexes are never utilized. An index-usage report reveals dormant indexes whose demise can be negotiated with the data warehouse team.

- **Aggregate usage.** Aggregates are typically built in the same vein as indexes—when in doubt, build it. But just as the case with indexes, some aggregates are built but never utilized. Or over time, they become less interesting and fall dormant. An aggregate-usage report can identify aggregates that are no longer used and should be dropped.

- **Dormant data.** The dormant-data report is always interesting because the data warehouse is created as a result of user interviews that find out what data elements are needed to perform the analysis required to do their job. Yet it's inevitable that tables refreshed by the ETL every day lay unused. Even if a table is used, certain columns may never be selected. We always find fact table column usage to be interesting because it's so common to find that the most complicated derived measures are not used because their definitions are not properly conveyed to the user community. A dormant data report can help the ETL team identify and question the effectiveness of measures and dimension attributes that are never selected.

You have several ways to gather statistics on the usage of the data warehouse. Some database management systems offer usage information natively. However, be sure to test performance with the usage-reporting functionality turned off versus having it turned on; it may affect query response and ETL load time. A noninvasive way to track usage statistics is to employ a middleware such as Teleran Technologies (www.teleran.com). These data warehouse monitoring tools capture SQL and data outside of the database at the network-packet level. We're sure there are other tools that provide database usage statistics. Try typing **data warehouse usage tracking** in www.google.com to find a list of vendors in this space. Also, a list of monitoring vendors is available at the companion Web site to this book.

Tuning ETL Processes

To best understand how to optimize ETL processes, you must be familiar with how databases work. Some functionality available in most database management systems should not be used in the data warehouse environment. And some features are hardly ever used in transaction systems that are not only applicable but also preferred in the data warehouse environment.

Many design decisions are based on the volume of data being moved by the process being developed. For example, if you have a very small dimension with minimal volatility, it is okay to have your incremental process update the existing data in the dimension with SQL UPDATE statements. But if the dimension is a monster with 20 million rows of highly volatile data, it is probably more efficient to truncate and bulk load the table.

Use the volumetric report created by the data warehouse architect or project manager that documents how much data will be loaded into the data warehouse initially and the planned growth to occur six months after implementation for capacity planning and to identify scalability expectations of the ETL system. Then follow up by documenting the actual growth over time.

The next few sections highlight the functionality of databases that are unnecessary overhead and should be avoided in a controlled ETL environment and provide faster but otherwise equivalent solutions for your implementation.

Explaining Database Overhead

Before relational databases were created, data was stored in sequential or flat files. Those files were known for having notoriously bad data quality. The bad data quality stemmed from repeating groups and elements, lack of primary keys, and no enforced relationships between tables. Everything was repeated throughout the database. Additionally, no validation of data existed at the database level. In those days, a database was nothing more than a collection of disconnected sequential files. In short, the situation was a mess.

In 1970, E. F. Codd invented the relational algebra that served as the basis for the design of relational database systems. Relational databases enforce referential integrity, data uniqueness, primary keys, check constraints, foreign keys, and so on. The result is much cleaner, more reliable data, but much slower operations. Each of the features of the relational database adds significant overhead to transactions. *Overhead* is additional processing by a program to perform behind-the-scenes error checking and controls.

In this section, we discuss different database features that you are likely to encounter as a member of an ETL team, and we offer suggestions to overcome database overhead. This is not a substitute for DBA training. In fact, the content of this section will not help you become a database administrator. The purpose of this chapter is to help the ETL team and those who are already DBAs to understand special considerations for optimizing ETL processes. Much of the work involved in optimizing the ETL is outside of the database. Portions of this chapter lend some insight into how databases handle large sets of data and offer tips and techniques for speeding up (or avoiding) those processes.

Inserts, Updates, Deletes

Data manipulation language (DML) has four main verbs: select, insert, update, and delete. Each of the four DML utilities has the ability to manipulate data in a database differently. Remember that DBMSs are primarily designed to survive transaction failures. Therefore, as a precaution, virtually every DBMS maintains a rollback log. A rollback log records DML transactions and provides a mechanism to *undo* changes that occur as a result of a DML submission. In the case of a midtransaction failure, the DBMS automatically rolls back the half-finished transaction, leaving the data in the exact state it was in before the transaction began.

The Effects of Logging

Each of the four types of DML affects the rollback log in a different way. Select statements don't get written to the log, because they don't alter the existing data. In most databases, insert statements are written to the log just in case data is inadvertently entered or the transaction fails midstream, the DBMS can simply rollback the entry instead of having to delete or clean it up. Updates and deletes both require writing to the rollback log. Deletes require some overhead because they store the *old* records before the deletes occur. Updates require the most overhead of all DML statements and are extremely slow to process.

The Effects of Indexes

The data warehouse is utilized because it is substantially faster and more reliable than the transaction system. The speed advantage that the data warehouse offers is due to a number of key features:

- Dimensional data model that allows purpose-built indexing of dimensions and facts
- Aggressive index strategy
- Physically stored aggregate records
- Query parallelism

Design techniques and benefits of dimensional data models are sprinkled throughout this book and are available in a wide range of others. In this section, we'd like to talk for a minute about indexes.

Indexes are the backbone of query-response time in the data warehouse. Every query that hits the database utilizes at least one index. Unfortunately, inasmuch as indexes help users query the data warehouse, the ETL team is burdened with managing the existing indexes during the ETL process. Index management accounts for a substantial portion of most ETL processes.

Before we dive into the techniques for managing indexes during the data warehouse load, it's important that we review the different types of indexes available in most databases. Primarily, you find two types of indexes, and it's important to understand the distinction between the two types:

- **B-tree indexes.** B-tree, or balanced tree, indexes store the key values and pointers in an inverted tree structure. B-tree indexes are optimal for columns with very high cardinality. By *high cardinality*, we mean the count of distinct values. Inverted tree structures utilize an extremely effective *divide and conquer* technique of sifting through data to find a specified value (or range of values). B-tree indexes are great for optimizing known queries but are fairly inflexible at supporting ad-hoc environments such as data warehouses. B-tree indexes are deemed inflexible because you cannot combine indexed columns on the fly to dynamically create compound indexes to resolve new, unexpected queries. All indexes must be made in advance. The DBA must attempt to guess which columns might be constrained. Moreover, the order in which the columns are positioned determines whether they are utilized or not. The result is the DBA team must make many, many compound B-tree indexes, many containing the same columns in different orders.

- **Bitmap indexes.** Bitmap indexes function completely different from B-tree indexes. Bitmap indexes are better suited for lower cardinality columns. Many single column bitmap indexes can dynamically join together to create necessary compound indexes to support ad-hoc queries. Because of their flexibility, it is common practice to create single-column bitmap indexes on each surrogate key in fact tables in the data warehouse.

Now we want to turn back to how indexes affect DML transactions. Every entry of a B-tree index contains one, and only one, rownum that points back to the corresponding record in the base table. Conversely, bitmap indexes contain a range of rownums for each value in the index. If a value is updated, every record that corresponds to the range of rownums is locked. Ultimately, each time a record is updated, a tremendous burden is put on the database to manage all of the row locking going on. Unfortunately, fact tables usually consist only of bitmap indexes, and doing massive updates creates massive headaches because of the excessive overhead and extremely poor performance.

In conclusion, it's recommended to drop all bitmap indexes before you begin to manipulate data in fact tables. It's further recommended to partition fact tables so you have to drop only the local index in the current partition (assuming the table is partitioned on the date key). B-tree indexes are not excluded from being dropped before the ETL process executes. Statistics show that in most cases, dropping data warehouse indexes, loading the tables, and rebuilding the indexes is substantially faster than loading tables with scores of indexes enabled.

Addressing Constraints and Foreign Keys

Foreign keys in relational DBMSs enforce integrity in data between tables. For example, you cannot enter an order status unless that status is an existing valid value in the order status table. But in the data warehouse, the transaction has already occurred and has been validated by the source system.

In a nutshell, all foreign keys and constraints should be disabled in the data warehouse, especially during the ETL process. Convincing the DBA team that it is okay to drop foreign keys can be a political challenge. You must walk through the ETL process with the DBA team and explain that fact records simply cannot exist without getting the surrogate keys from their associated dimensions. Also, point out that dimension natural keys are looked up to ensure they are not inserted more than once. Once the DBA team is convinced that the ETL is truly a controlled and managed environment, they realize that database constraints and foreign keys are superfluous elements that slow down the ETL process without offering much benefit.

The fastest way to load data into the data warehouse is to enable the database to bulk load it by following these four database-preparation steps:

1. Eliminate as many DML statements as possible.
2. Disable rollback logging.
3. Drop all existing indexes.
4. Eliminate database foreign keys and constraints.

Once the four steps are complete, you are ready to utilize the database bulk-load utility. A guide for utilizing bulk loaders can be found in Chapter 7.

ETL System Security

Database security in the data-staging area is much simpler to enforce than in the data warehouse presentation database. Generally speaking, no one is allowed to read or write to the data-staging area besides the ETL engine or program. Most databases utilize roles and users to enforce security at the database level. A *role* is a mechanism that allows a security administrator to group together many users that require the same database-access privileges. Each user has his or her own userID and authentication mechanism. When the user is authenticated to the system, he or she is handed the privileges associated with his or her role.

Without roles, a security administrator would have to explicitly grant every person appropriate privileges individually. A user is an individual that uses the database.

Typically, it is sufficient to create a single data warehouse administrative role with the following privileges:

- Select, Insert, Update, and Delete all objects
- TRUNCATE TABLE
- Utilize bulk loader
- Drop and create indexes

If there is highly sensitive data, such as compensation rates or sales leads, the data should be encrypted by the source system before it is extracted by the ETL team. Normally, column-level security is handled by the use of database views that sit on top of a table and conceal the sensitive columns. However, the ETL team must have the ability to select data from the source system and also be able to perform any DML required in the data warehouse. Therefore, views are not an appropriate mechanism for hiding sensitive data. Furthermore, the ETL team should not be responsible for encrypting sensitive data. Securing or encrypting sensitive data from the ETL team is the responsibility of the source system security administrator.

Securing the Development Environment

In the development environment, everyone on the ETL team is granted the privileges of the DWETL role (all DML and TRUNCATE on all objects and so forth). This is where all staging tables are created. Even though the data-staging area is owned by the ETL team, sometimes table creation is controlled by the data warehouse architect or DBA. In some cases the ETL architect has the authority to create tables in the data-staging area without further approval.

Furthermore, any ETL team member can add, delete, or modify files in the dedicated directories on the file system. No one outside ETL team should have access to data-staging environments.

Securing the Production Environment

The ETL team typically has read-only access to production. Sometimes, in very secure environments, such as banking, they have no access at all. The DWETL role exists in production, but the only the user ID and password used by the ETL engine is created in production. If for some extreme reason, an ETL team member must have write access to production, such as to fix a bug that exists only in production, it should be granted temporarily and revoked as soon as the fix is complete.

FTP Vulnerabilities

You must lock out everyone from the FTP *inbox*. Only the FTP process can write or delete within the specified directory. Moreover, only the ETL engine is allowed to read the directory. If there is an emergency situation, temporary access should be granted to a predetermined administrator whose privilege is revoked as soon as the issue is resolved.

Encryption/Decryption

The biggest performance inhibitor is writing to and reading from disk (I/O). However, you must encrypt data in movement for security purposes. Usually, the following steps are followed to secure data in movement:

1. Encrypt data and store encrypted data on disk.
2. Read and transfer encrypted data across networks.
3. Store encrypted data on data-staging server.
4. Decrypt data and store on disk.
5. Transform and load decrypted data into data warehouse.

It may be possible to reduce this to three steps by encrypting the source data as it is read into memory, then transferring the encrypted data, and finally decrypting the data as it enters the transformation and load routines.

As you can see, the second solution does not touch the disk from the time the data is read until it is loaded into the data warehouse. This process is known as *in-stream decryption*. Some ETL tools support in-stream decryption functionality. If you need to encrypt or decrypt in-stream to improve performance, make sure you select a tool that supports the functionality; otherwise, you can write your own applet in Java. In the case of the Java applet, make sure that your ETL toll can at least embed an external process, such as the in-stream decryption applet, without incurring more I/O.

Short-Term Archiving and Recovery

There are many reasons to keep the various data-staging results from the ETL system. In this book, we have identified needs for short-term restart capabilities, comparisons of day-to-day extracts to detect differences when you don't have a proper change data capture system, as well as legal and financial auditing requirements. All of these archiving and recovery scenarios should be familiar challenges to the IT staff. Back the data up to your current media and make sure it can be recovered. Make sure you have a believable audit trail that accounts for all accesses and alterations to the data. Make sure the data is physically secure, and protect the archived data as strongly as you protect the on line data.

But what if we are supposed to keep the data for many years?

Long-Term Archiving and Recovery

One of the oaths we take as data warehouse managers is that we will *preserve history*. In many ways, we have become the archivists of corporate information. We don't usually promise to keep all history on-line, but we often claim that we will store it somewhere for safekeeping. Of course, storing it for safekeeping means that we will be able to get history back out again when someone is interested in looking at it.

Most of us data warehouse managers have been so busy bringing up data warehouses, avoiding stovepipe data marts, adapting to new database technologies, and adapting to the explosive demands of the Web that we have relegated our archiving duties to backing up data on tapes and then forgetting about the tapes. Or maybe we are still appending data onto our original fact tables and we haven't really faced what to do with old data yet.

But across the computer industry there is a growing awareness that preservation of digital data is not being done yet, and that it is a serious problem and a hard problem.

Does a Warehouse Even Need To Keep Old Data?

Most data warehouse managers are driven by urgent needs of departments like marketing, who have very tactical concerns. Few marketing departments care about data that is more than three years old, because our products and our markets are changing so quickly. It is tempting to think only of these marketing clients and to discard data that no longer meets their needs.

But with a little reflection we realize we are sitting on a lot of other data in our warehouses that absolutely must be preserved. This data includes:

- Detailed sales records, for legal, financial, and tax purposes
- Trended survey data where long-term tracking has strategic value
- All records required for government regulatory or compliance tracking

- Medical records that in some cases must be preserved for 100 years!
- Clinical trials and experimental results that may support patent claims
- Documentation of toxic waste disposal, fuel deliveries, and safety inspections
- All other data that may have historical value to someone, sometime

Faced with this list, we have to admit that a plan is needed for retrieving these kinds of data five, ten, or maybe even 50 years in the future. It begins to dawn on us that maybe this will be a challenge. How long do mag tapes last, anyway? Are CD-ROMs or DVDs the answer? Will we be able to read the formats in the future? We have some eight-inch floppies from just a few years ago that are absolutely unrecoverable and worthless. All of a sudden, this is sounding like a difficult project.

Media, Formats, Software, and Hardware

As we begin to think about really long-term preservation of digital data, our world begins to fall apart. Let's start with the storage media. There is considerable disagreement about the practical longevity of physical media like mag tapes and CD-ROM disks, with serious estimates ranging from as little as five years to many decades. But, of course, our media may not be of archival quality, and they may not be stored or handled in an optimum way. We must counterbalance the optimism of vendors and certain experts with the pragmatic admission that most of the tapes and physical media we have today that are more than ten years old are of doubtful integrity.

Any debates about the physical viability of the media, however, pale when compared to the debates about formats, software, and hardware. All data objects are encoded on physical media in the *format of the day*. Everything from the density of the bits on the media, to the arrangement of directories, and finally to the higher-level application-specific encoding of the data is a stack of cards waiting to fall. Taking our eight-inch floppies as examples, what would it take to read the embedded data? Well, it would take a hardware configuration sporting a working eight-inch floppy drive, the software drivers for an eight-inch drive, and the application that originally wrote the data to the file.

Obsolete Formats and Archaic Formats

In the lexicon of digital preservationists, an obsolete format is no longer actively supported, but there is still working hardware and software extant that can read and display the content of the data in its original form. An archaic format has passed on to the nether realm. Our eight-inch floppies are, as far as we are concerned, an archaic format. We will never recover their data. The Phoenician writing system known as Linear A is also an archaic format that has apparently been lost forever. Our floppies may be only slightly easier to decipher than Linear A.

Hard Copy, Standards, and Museums

A number of proposals have been made to work around the format difficulties of recovering old data. One simple proposal is to reduce everything to hard copy. In other words, print all your data onto paper. Surely, this will side step all the issues of data formats, software, and hardware. While for tiny amounts of data this has a certain appeal, and is better than losing the data, this approach has a number of fatal flaws. In today's world, copying to paper doesn't scale. A gigabyte printed out as ASCII characters would take 250,000 printed pages at 4000 characters per page. A terabyte would require 250,000,000 pages! Remember that we can't cheat and put the paper on a CD-ROM or a mag tape, because that would just reintroduce the digital format problem. And finally, we would be seriously compromising the data structures, the user interfaces, and the behavior of the systems originally meant to present and interpret the data. In many cases, a paper backup would destroy the usability of the data.

A second proposal is to establish standards for the representation and storage of data that would guarantee that everything can be represented in permanently readable formats. In the data warehouse world, the only data that remotely approaches such a standard is relational data stored in an ANSI-standard format. But almost all implementations of relational databases use significant extensions of the data types, SQL syntax, and surrounding metadata to provide needed functionality. By the time we have dumped a database with all its applications and metadata onto a mag tape, even if it has come from Oracle or DB2, we can't be very confident that we will be able to read and use such data in thirty years or fifty years. Other data outside of the narrow ANSI-standard RDBMS definition is hopelessly fragmented. There is no visible market segment, for instance, that is coalescing all possible OLAP data storage mechanisms into a single physical standard that guarantees lossless transfer to and from the standard format.

A final somewhat nostalgic proposal is to support museums, where ancient versions of hardware, operating systems, and applications software would be lovingly preserved so that old data could be read. This proposal at least gets to the heart of the issue in recognizing that the old software must really be present in order to interpret the old data. But the museum idea doesn't scale and doesn't hold up to close scrutiny. How are we going to keep a Digital Data Whack 9000 working for 50 years? What happens when the last one dies? And if the person walking in with the old data has moved the data to a modern medium like a DVD ROM, how would a working Digital Data Whack 9000 interface to the DVD? Is someone going to write modern drivers for ancient pathetic machines? Maybe it has an eight-bit bus.

Refreshing, Migrating, Emulating, and Encapsulating

A number of experts have suggested that an IT organization should periodically refresh the storage of data by moving the data physically from old media onto new media. A more aggressive version of refreshing is migrating, where the data is not only physically transferred but is reformatted in order to be read by contemporary applications. Refreshing and migrating do indeed solve some of the short-term preservation crises because if you successfully refresh and migrate, you are free from the problems of old media and old formats. But taking a longer view, these approaches have at least two very serious problems. First, migrating is a labor-intensive, custom task that has little leverage from job to job and may involve the loss of original functionality. Second, and more serious, migrating cannot handle major paradigm shifts. We all expect to migrate from version 8 of an RDBMS to version 9, but what happens when the world is taken over by heteroschedastic database systems (HDS's)? The fact that nobody, including us, knows what an HDS is, illustrates our point. After all, we didn't migrate very many databases when the paradigm shifted from network to relational databases, did we?

Well, we have managed to paint a pretty bleak picture. Given all this, what hope do the experts have for long-term digital preservation? If you are interested in this topic and a serious architecture for preserving your digital data warehouse archives for the next 50 years, you should read Jeff Rothenberg's treatise *Avoiding Technological Quicksand, Finding a Viable Technical Foundation for Digital Preservation*. This is a report to the Council on Library and Information Resources (CLIR). The 41-page report can be retrieved as an Adobe PDF file by linking to www.clir.org/pubs/reports/rothenberg. Very well written and very highly recommended.

As a hint of where Jeff goes with this topic, he recommends the development of emulation systems that, although they run on modern hardware and software, nevertheless faithfully emulate old hardware. He chooses the hardware level for emulation because hardware emulation is a proven technique for recreating old systems, even ones as gnarly as electronic games. He also describes the need to encapsulate the old data sets along with the metadata needed for interpreting the data set, as well as the overall specifications for the emulation itself. By keeping all these together in one encapsulated package, the data will travel along into the future with everything that is needed to play it back out again in 50 years. All you need to do is interpret the emulation specifications on your contemporary hardware.

The library world is deeply committed to solving the digital-preservation problem. Look up *embrittled documents* on the Google search engine. Their techniques need to be studied and adapted to our warehouse needs.

Summary

In this chapter, we have provided an overview of the operations framework of typical ETL systems. The first half of the chapter was devoted to major scheduling approaches. Most of the second half dealt with managing performance issues as your system grows and gets more complicated. Finally, we proposed a simple framework for ETL system security.

Metadata

Metadata is an interesting topic because every tool space in the data warehouse arena including business intelligence (BI) tools, ETL tools, databases, and dedicated repositories claims to have a metadata solution, and many books are available to advise you on the best metadata strategies. Yet, after years of implementing and reviewing data warehouses, we've yet to encounter a true end-to-end metadata solution. Instead, most data warehouses have manually maintained pieces of metadata that separately exist across their components. Instead of adding to the metadata hoopla, this chapter simply covers the portions of metadata that the ETL team needs to be aware of—either as a consumer or a producer. We propose a set of metadata structures that you need to support the ETL team.

PROCESS CHECK Planning & Design:
Requirements/Realities → *Architecture* → *Implementation* → Release to Ops

Data Flow: *Extract* → *Clean* → *Conform* → *Deliver*

Because the ETL system is the center of your data warehouse universe, it often assumes the responsibility of managing and storing much of the metadata for the data warehouse. One might think that there is no better place than the ETL system for storing and managing metadata because the environment must already know the specifics of all data to function properly. And the ETL process is the creator of the most important metadata in the data warehouse—the data lineage. The *data lineage* traces data from its exact location in the source system and documents precisely what transformation is done to it before it is finally loaded. The data lineage includes the data definition of the source system database and also of the final resting place in the data warehouse. If you are using an ETL tool, attributes other than the data lineage can also live in the ETL environment. But can the ETL environment really capture and manage *all* metadata in the data warehouse? No way.

If you'd like to explore data warehouse metadata in more detail, a noteworthy text is *Metadata Solutions: Using Metamodels, Repositories, XML, and Enterprise Portals to Generate Information on Demand* by Adrienne Tannenbaum (Addison Wesley 2002). We want to start by trying to define exactly what is meant by *metadata*.

Defining Metadata

A leading cause for the difficulty behind metadata implementations is that the exact definition of metadata is ambiguous, and defining exactly what metadata is a very difficult task. In 1998 we tackled the definition of metadata in the *Data Warehouse Lifecycle Toolkit* book. In looking over those words, we still find them surprisingly relevant. Here's what we wrote:

Metadata—What Is It?

Metadata is an amazing topic in the data warehouse world. Considering that we don't know exactly what it is, or where it is, we spend more time talking about it, more time worrying about it, and more time feeling guilty that we aren't doing anything about it. Several years ago, we decided that metadata is any data about data. This wasn't very helpful, because it didn't paint a clear picture in our minds as to what exactly this darn stuff was. This fuzzy view gradually clarified and recently we have been talking more confidently about the *back room metadata* and *front room metadata*. Back room metadata is process related and guides the extraction, cleaning, and loading processes. Front room metadata is more descriptive and helps make our query tools and report writers function smoothly. Of course, process and descriptive metadata overlap, but it is useful to think about them separately.

Back room metadata presumably helps the DBA bring the data into the warehouse and is probably also of interest to business users when they ask where the data comes from. Front room metadata is mostly for the benefit of end user, and its definition has been expanded to not only be the oil that makes our tools function smoothly but a kind of dictionary of business content represented by all data elements.

Even these definitions, as helpful as they are, fail to give the data warehouse manager much of a feeling for what he or she is supposed to do. But one can apply a traditional IT perspective to metadata. At the very least, we should:

- Make a nice annotated list of all of it
- Decide just how important each part is
- Take responsibility for it or assign that responsibility to someone else
- Decide what constitutes a consistent and working set of it
- Decide whether to make it or buy it
- Store it somewhere for backup and recovery
- Make it available to people who need it
- Quality-assure it and make it complete and up to date
- Control it from one place
- Document all of these responsibilities well enough to hand this job off (soon)

The only trouble is that we haven't really said what metadata is yet. We do notice that the last item in the preceding list really isn't metadata; it's data about metadata. With a sinking feeling, we realize we probably need *meta meta data data*.

Source System Metadata

To understand this better, let's try to make a complete list of all possible types of metadata. We surely won't succeed at this first try, but we will learn a lot. First, let's go to the source systems, which could be mainframes, separate nonmainframe servers, users' desktops, third-party data providers, or even on-line sources. We will assume that all we do here is read source data and extract it to a data-staging area that could be on the mainframe or could be a downstream machine.

Source specifications:

- Repositories
- Source schemas
- Copy books
- Proprietary or third-party source schemas
- Print spool file sources
- Old format for archived mainframe data
- Relational source system tables and DDL
- Spreadsheet sources

- Lotus Notes databases
- Presentation graphics (for example, PowerPoint)
- URL source specifications:
- Source Descriptive Information:
    - Ownership descriptions of each source
    - Business descriptions of each source
    - Update frequencies of original sources
    - Legal limitations on the use of each source
    - Access methods, access rights privileges, and passwords for source access
- Process Information:
    - Mainframe or source system job schedules
    - The COBOL/JCL or C or Basic or other code to implement extraction
    - The automated extract-tool settings if we use such a tool
    - Results of specific extract jobs, including exact times content and completeness

Data-Staging Metadata

Now let's list all the metadata needed to get data into a data-staging area and prepare it for loading into one or more data marts. We may do this on the mainframe with hand-coded COBOL or by using an automated extract tool. Or we may bring the flat file extracts more or less untouched into a separate data-staging area on a different machine. In any case, we have to be concerned about metadata describing

Data Acquisition Information:

- Data transmission scheduling and results of specific transmissions
- File usage in the data-staging area, including duration volatility and ownership

Dimension Table Management:

- Definitions of conformed dimensions and conformed facts
- Job specifications for joining sources, stripping out fields, and looking up attributes

- Slowly changing dimension policies for each incoming descriptive attribute (for example, overwrite create new record or create new field)
- Current surrogate key assignments for each production key, including a fast lookup table to perform this mapping in memory
- Yesterday's copy of a production dimension to use as the basis for Diff Compare

Transformation and Aggregation:

- Data-cleaning specifications
- Data enhancement and mapping transformations (for example, expand abbreviations and provide detail)
- Transformations required for data mining (for example, interpret nulls and scale numerics)
- Target schema designs, source to target data flows, and target data ownership
- DBMS load scripts
- Aggregate definitions
- Aggregate usage statistics, base table usage statistics, and potential aggregates
- Aggregate modification logs

Audit, Job Logs, and Documentation:

- Data lineage and audit records (where *EXACTLY* did this record come from and when)
- Data transform run time logs, success summaries, and time stamps
- Data transform software version numbers
- Business descriptions of extract processing
- Security settings for extract files extract software and extract metadata
- Security settings for data transmission (that is, passwords certificates)
- Data-staging area archive logs and recovery procedures
- Data-staging archive security settings.

DBMS Metadata

Once we have finally transferred data to the data warehouse or data mart DBMS, another set of metadata comes into play:

- DBMS system table contents
- Partition settings
- Indexes
- Disk-striping specifications
- Processing hints
- DBMS-level security privileges and grants
- View definitions
- Stored procedures and SQL administrative scripts
- DBMS backup, status-backup procedures and backup security.

Front Room Metadata

In the front room, we have metadata extending to the horizon, including

- Business names and descriptions for columns tables groupings and so on
- Precanned query and report definitions
- Join specification tool settings
- Pretty print tool specifications (for relabeling fields in readable ways)
- End user documentation and training aids, both vendor supplied and IT supplied
- Network security user privilege profiles
- Network security authentication certificates
- Network security usage statistics, including log on attempts access attempts and user ID by location reports
- Individual user profiles with link to human resources to track promotions transfers resignations that affect access rights
- Link to contractor and partner tracking where access rights are affected
- Usage and access maps for data elements, tables, and views reports
- Resource charge-back statistics
- Favorite Web sites (as a paradigm for all data warehouse access)

Now we can see why we didn't know exactly what metadata was all about. It is everything, except for the data itself. All of a sudden, data seems like the simplest part. In a sense, metadata is the DNA of the data warehouse. It defines all elements and how they work together.

So, how do you capture and manage these forms of metadata? You don't. At least the ETL team doesn't. Over the past few decades, consortiums, alliances, committees, organizations, and coalitions have been formed to solve the metadata quandary. To this day, no universal solution exists. We have found that as an ETL team member you need certain metadata to do your job, and that it is convenient to focus on selected items from the preceding list and organize them into three major categories:

1. **Business metadata.** Describing the meaning of data in a business sense

2. **Technical metadata.** Representing the technical aspects of data, including attributes such as data types, lengths, lineage, results from data profiling, and so on

3. **Process execution metadata.** Presenting statistics on the results of running the ETL process itself, including measures such as rows loaded successfully, rows rejected, amount of time to load, and so on

In addition to the three categories of metadata, you need to consider another aspect of metadata: standards. Standards are another attempt by IT to make work throughout your organization consistent and maintainable. In Chapter 10, we define the role of the metadata librarian and propose a set of responsibilities for this person. Your organization most likely has many standards in place, and you can adopt specific data warehouse and ETL standards from the recommendations found throughout this book. If you seek to further investigate metadata standards, we've provided sources for your perusal in the next section.

As you read this chapter, please refer to Figure 9.1, showing the three main categories of ETL system metadata, together with each of the separate metadata tables discussed in the text.

Here is a comprehensive list of the places so far in this book where we have urged you to collect and use metadata:

- Origins and processing steps for each staged data set (Chapter 1)
- Metadata repository as an advantage of the vendor-supplied ETL tool (Chapter 1)
- Need for metadata architecture: source tables, cleaning, and processes (Chapter 1)
- Presenting useful metadata to end users (Chapter 1)
- Extract transformations applied (Chapter 2)
- Compliance metadata (Chapter 2)
- XML data descriptions of metadata (Chapter 2)

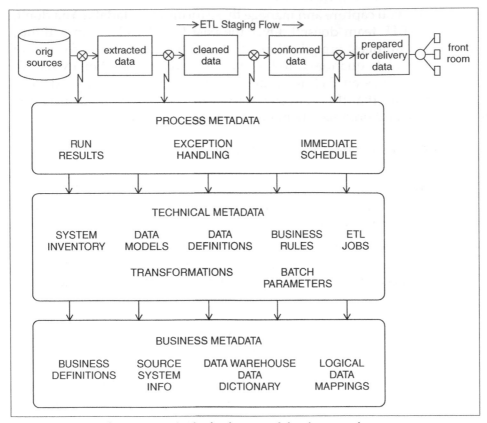

Figure 9.1 Metadata sources in the back room of the data warehouse.

- Lack of metadata in flat files (Chapter 2)
- Impact analysis metadata (Chapter 2)
- Planning for building metadata describing lineage, business definitions, technical definitions, and processes (Chapter 2)
- Logical data map (Chapter 3)
- Capturing calculations for derived data during extract (Chapter 3)
- Source database descriptions (Chapter 3)
- ETL tools reading ERP system metadata (Chapter 3)
- Results of data profiling (Chapter 4)
- Error event tracking fact table (Chapter 4)
- Audit dimension (Chapter 4)
- Column survivorship (conforming results) table (Chapter 4)
- Surrogate key highest value (Chapter 5)
- Aggregate navigator data (Chapter 6)

- Process data to kick off OLAP cube building (Chapter 6)
- Bulk loader control file (Chapter 7)
- Metadata supporting recovery processes (Chapter 8)
- Job schedule metadata (Chapter 8)
- Database connection information (Chapter 8)
- ETL system parameters (Chapter 8)
- Job dependencies (Chapter 8)
- Job operational statistics such as performance and resource use (Chapter 8)
- MetaData repository reporting (Chapter 8)
- Table purge policies (Chapter 8)

We hope you aren't too dismayed by these long lists. The rest of this chapter makes a serious attempt to propose specific metadata structures for tracking this kind of information!

Business Metadata

The assignment of who is responsible for business metadata in the data warehouse is often argued. Some say it is the responsibility of the data warehouse business analyst and should be created during the requirements-gathering process. Others believe the source system business analyst should create business terms because most data warehouse attributes originate in the source systems. Yet others think it is part of the data modeler's tasks to create and maintain business metadata because it is a natural part of the logical data model.

It's not up to you to settle those arguments, but there is some business metadata that the ETL team influences and must be maintained to accurately reflect reality. The ETL team should not be responsible for generating business metadata but must communicate changes that need to be applied to the appropriate personnel. From the ETL perspective, business metadata is *proxy* metadata. Proxy metadata is obtained from one system and made available to another without any explicit manipulation. Some business-intelligence tools are designed to look into ETL repositories to get business definitions to present to its users—making the tool a one-stop shop for data and data's metadata.

To keep things interesting, we must make you aware that the data warehouse can be in a situation where different business definitions are defined for the same attribute. Remember, by design, that data in the data warehouse is sourced from multiple systems, and each system can potentially have a different definition for the same attribute. For example, the marketing department defines a customer as anyone who has a registered account with the company, while the sales department might consider only persons who have actually made purchases to be customers. As a recommended practice, the data warehouse manager should bring all of the owners of an overlapping element into a room and have them agree on a single definition from an *enterprise* standpoint. We describe this process throughout the book as *conforming* business definitions, labels, and measures of the enterprise. That meaning might be from one of the source systems or an entirely new one. The enterprise definition is stored in the data warehouse and in ETL tool.

> The ETL team is part of the back room of the data warehouse and should not get involved in creating business metadata. However, you should understand the purpose of the data you are working with and review business definitions as you need them.

Business Definitions

Often, the data warehouse team gets caught up in designing the architectural database for query performance and optimizing the ETL process for load performance. Once the database is designed and loaded, the team concentrates on the business intelligence of the data warehouse, making elegant user interfaces and slick graphical reports. But to the business, the most important ingredient in the data warehouse recipe is the definition of the elements available to them. If the user cannot make sense of data, as sophisticated as it may be, it has absolutely no value to the organization.

Business definitions are a crucial requirement to the completion of the data warehouse. Not only are end users dependent on business definitions; the ETL team needs business definitions to give context to the data they are loading. You will notice how important the business definitions are to the ETL team if you attempt to present them with the data model and data lineage before the business definitions are complete. If you rush to complete the data lineage so the ETL development can begin, you'll be forced to continually explain the purpose of the main data elements in the data model to the ETL team before they have enough information to work on them. Therefore, shift the development priorities away from expediting the data lineage and to concentrating on the association of the business definitions with the data warehouse data elements before the data lineage is handed off to the ETL team. A simple business definition matrix includes three main components:

- **Physical table and column name.** The business interpretation of data elements in the data warehouse is based on the actual table and column names in the database. The physical names need not be presented to end users if the BI tool presents only the business names and completely hides the physical instance of the data structures. However, the ETL team deals only with physical names and needs this information to associate the business definitions to the appropriate data elements.

- **Business column name.** The database stores data elements in technical terms consisting of prefixes, suffixes, and underscores. The business community needs a translation of the technical names to names that make sense and provide context. For example, the business name for EMP_STTS_CD might be Employee Status Code or just Employee Status. We discourage the use of cryptic names. Remember, the business name is how the column is represented in the BI tool. Furthermore, the business name often becomes column and row headings in user reports.

- **Business definition.** A business definition is one or two sentences that describe the business meaning of an attribute. Each attribute in the data warehouse must have a business definition associated with it. If the business cannot define the attribute, it usually indicates that the attribute has no analytic value and probably does not need to be stored in the data warehouse. If the business demands that the attribute remain in the data warehouse, a business definition must be defined for it.

The business definition matrix can be as simple as a three-column spreadsheet. However, you should strive to make this particular metadata as centralized and sharable as your technical environment allows. Virtually all major ETL tools support capturing and storing business metadata. The ETL tool should work with your data-modeling tool and database to obtain business definitions and with your BI tool to present business names and definitions to your end users.

Source System Information

The ETL team needs to know every intimate detail of each table it accesses for the data warehouse. Imagine that you need to fill an open position on your team. Before you hire someone, you have your HR department find candidates, prescreen them, introduce them to you, and arrange for formal interviews so you can ensure they are the right fit for the position. During the interviews, you identify any weaknesses that might need some work before candidates are deemed satisfactory for the position.

When you populate a data warehouse, the data modeler creates the position; the data warehouse architect finds and prescreens the source. Then data must be analyzed thoroughly to identify its weaknesses, and a plan of action must be initiated to make data satisfactory enough to be included in the data warehouse. Some data will be perfect; other data elements will need some transformation or be rejected because of inadequate quality.

When you analyze source systems, you need certain pieces of metadata. At a minimum, you need the following metadata attributes:

- **Database or file system.** The name commonly used when referring to a source system or file. This is not the technical server or database instance. Names such as *Sales database* or *Inventory Management System* are common values for this piece of metadata.

- **Table specifications.** The ETL team needs to know the purpose of the table, its volume, its primary key and alternate key, and a list of its columns.

- **Exception-handling rules.** You must be informed of any data-quality issues and advised on how they should be handled by the ETL process.

- **Business definitions.** The infamous yet rarely available business definitions. Do your best to have these provided to you. These one-to-two-sentence definitions are invaluable when you are trying to make sense of data.

- **Business rules.** Every table should come with a set of business rules. Business rules are required to understand the data and to test for anomalies. Every business rule must be tested, and each exception to a rule must be documented and resolved by the source system or the ETL process. Forms of business rules include an account of when a table receives new rows, updates, or deletions. If you are lucky, business rules are enforced in the source database management system (DBMS) by way of referential integrity, check constraints, and triggers.

Investigating source systems takes a substantial amount of time during the data-analysis phase of the data warehouse project. A lack of source system metadata incurs excessive research and troubleshooting by the data warehouse team. To curb cost overruns, all source system metadata must be available to the ETL team before the development of any ETL process.

Data Warehouse Data Dictionary

When we refer to the data dictionary, we are not referring to the DBMS catalog. The data warehouse data dictionary is a list of all of the data elements in the data warehouse and their business descriptions. Similar to the source system business definitions, the data warehouse data dictionary contains the physical table and column names and the business names and definitions. In the case of data warehouse business metadata, spreadsheets are insufficient. Many data warehouse environments depend on the ETL repository to store the data dictionary because BI tools are designed to look there to obtain metadata for presentation.

> Many BI tools are designed to work cohesively with ETL metadata repositories. When you are selecting your toolset, make sure that your ETL tool has an open repository that can be read by any query tool or at least comes with an adapter or broker for this purpose.

Logical Data Maps

The logical data map is the lifeline of the ETL team. Read Chapter 3 for detailed information about logical data maps from an ETL work-specification perspective. From a metadata perspective, the logical data map consists of the source-to-target mapping that explains, logically, exactly what happens to the data from the moment it is extracted from its origin to when it is loaded into the data warehouse.

The logical data map is a crucial piece of metadata. The ETL team first uses the document as a functional specification to create the physical ETL jobs, then again to validate the work with the end users. The document provides guidance when questions arise during user-acceptance testing (UAT). It is also used when data goes through quality-assurance (QA) testing, when the ETL team provides a walkthrough of each mapping with the QA team. Finally, the ETL team reviews the document with the DBA team to provide information about the data transformations so they can support the processes in the event of a failure.

CROSS-REFERENCE Refer to Chapter 3 for the exact metadata elements created in the logical data map and recommendations on how to create, maintain, and utilize the information.

Technical Metadata

Technical metadata serves many purposes and is the most interesting type of metadata to the ETL team. Technical metadata can encompass everything from column names and data types to storage and the configuration of your RAID arrays. As a member of the ETL team, you needn't be too concerned with hardware configurations and the like. Most interesting are the physical attributes of the data elements in all databases involved in the data warehouse. To get essential metadata, seek out the physical data model of each of your source systems and the target data warehouse. If your sources include flat files, you need the file layouts for each file you will be working with.

System Inventory

The ETL team must have access to and thoroughly understand the technical metadata of each system in the data warehouse environment to accurately build the physical ETL jobs. The technical definition of data is probably what technicians think of first when they are asked about metadata. After all, that really is data about data—it is the container and the structure of the data. The ETL team must be aware of data definitions for at least three environments:

- Source databases
- Staging-area tables (for example, extracted, cleaned, conformed, prepared for delivery)
- Data warehouse presentation area

It is possible that an entity relationship diagram is provided for each environment. At a minimum, a listing that includes the following elements for each system is required.

- **Tables.** An exhaustive list of tables or files that are—or might be—required during the extract and load process. Often, only source system tables in the logical data mapping are provided. Yet, there are *associative* tables that are usually not specified but are required. Whenever the source system has many-to-many relationships, a well-designed system has associative tables to enable the relationship.

- **Columns.** For each table, you will need a list of the required columns for your data mapping. Hopefully, the source system DBA can provide a list of only the columns that you need. It works best if the column listing excludes unnecessary columns.

- **Data types.** Each column is defined with a data type. Data types vary among different database systems. Luckily, most dedicated ETL tools implicitly convert equivalent data types. For example, an INTEGER from SQL Server automatically becomes a NUMBER when it is loaded into Oracle. Be aware that a DBA can define custom data types known as User Defined Datatypes. User Defined Datatypes are based on the database's core data types but can extend their definition to include things such as column length, whether the data type can accept NULL values, or whether the data type contains special characters, for example, telephone numbers.

- **Relationships.** Relational databases are designed to support referential integrity (RI). RI is enforced by relationships designed between tables to ensure unique and consistent data entry. Relationships are outlined in data models by linking foreign keys (FK) in a table to primary keys (PK) in another.

Data Models

Data models in the form of physical schema diagrams (either normalized or dimensional) are really just a graphical display of metadata but not particularly metadata itself. However, they can be an invaluable asset to the ETL team arsenal because they enable you to quickly identify and confirm relationships at a glance. Even though table joins are depicted in logical data mapping, you cannot count on it being perfectly complete. We recommend that you hang the physical schema diagrams from all of the source systems (and the data warehouse) on the wall of your office. Having physical schema diagrams hung around you alleviates sifting through rolls of diagrams piled in a corner. Furthermore, the hung diagrams make an instant reference point that expedites the resolution of questions and issues—not to mention the positive impression it makes on managers!

Data Definitions

Data definitions must be consistent between each of their potential data stores. Each time your data *touches down* to a database or file, it is vulnerable to data truncation or corruption. If data definitions are not alike between environments, the ETL team must explicitly convert the data to avoid catastrophe. In addition to the attributes listed in the previous section, the following data-definition metadata elements must also be supplied to the ETL team.

- **Table name.** The physical name of the table or file that contains the data

- **Column name.** The physical name of the column within a table or file

- **Data type.** Data elements with a table are categorized into types. Common data types are Numeric, Character, Date, and Binary. You will find that custom data types are allowed in most DBMSs. Custom data types are based on common types and usually enforce formatting rules. Data types are mutually exclusive and cannot coexist within a single column.

- **Domain.** The set of values allowed to be entered into a column is known as its domain. The domain can be enforced by a foreign key, check constraints, or the application on top of the database. If the application enforces the domain, a list of allowed values must be provided by the programming team to the ETL team.

- **Referential integrity.** If your data comes from a database, you will most likely find foreign keys that point to a primary key of another table to ensure the data is unique. If referential integrity (RI) is enforced at the application level, the programming team must provide the RI rules. Typically, RI in the data warehouse is deemed unnecessary overhead because all data is entered in a controlled fashion—the ETL process—and does not have RI enforced at the database level.

- **Constraints.** Constraints are another form of a physical implementation of a business rule. Database constraints can eliminate NULL values, enforce foreign key look-ups, ensure compliance with allowed values, and so on.

- **Defaults.** A default in the context of ETL metadata is the assignment of a string, number, date, or bit, in the case when the actual value is not available. In your source system, column defaults are usually assigned at the database level. In the data warehouse, the defaults should be assigned in the ETL process. It is recommended that defaults in the data warehouse are used consistently.

- **Stored procedures.** Stored procedures, which store prewritten SQL programs in the database, offer great insight to how your source data is used. Each data warehouse project inevitably involves analyzing stored procedures that exist in the source systems.

- **Triggers.** A trigger is an SQL procedure automatically executed by the DBMS when a record is added, deleted, or updated. Like stored procedures, triggers offer information about how data is used. Triggers often enhance foreign key constraints by adding additional checks to records added to a table. Triggers also load audit tables when records are altered or deleted from a table. Audit tables loaded by triggers are a vital source of deleted data for the data warehouse.

Business Rules

Business rules can be categorized as business or technical metadata. We like to refer to business rules as *technical* because they are the essence of the ETL process—which is very technical. Each and every business rule must be coded in the ETL process. Business rules can include anything from allowed values to default values to calculations for derived fields. In source systems, business rules are enforced by stored procedures, constraints, or database triggers. But most often, business rules exist only in the application code. In older, especially mainframe, environments, the actual source code no longer exists and only the compiled portion of the application remains. In those cases, business rules are extremely difficult to obtain. It usually requires interviewing data analysts and programmers who support the application. The metadata for business rules varies between functional or technical documentation and source code in the native programming language of the application or pseudocode.

Business rules must be incorporated into logical data mapping. Sometimes business rules are omitted from logical data mapping and go unnoticed until the first attempt at the ETL process is complete and the exclusions are detected by users during UAT. As new business rules are learned, the metadata in the logical data mapping must be updated to reflect the new rules.

ETL-Generated Metadata

So far in this chapter, we have focused on metadata created outside of the ETL environment and provided to the ETL team from other sources. The remainder of this chapter addresses metadata generated by the ETL team and used either within the team to manage the ETL processes or by end users or other data warehouse members to better understand the data within the data warehouse.

As ETL physical processes are built, specific metadata must be generated to capture the inner workings of each process. ETL metadata falls into four main categories:

- **ETL job metadata.** The ETL job is a container that stores all of the transformations that actually manipulate the data. The job metadata is very valuable because it contains the data lineage of the elements in the data warehouse. Every ETL task—from extraction to load and all transformations in between—is captured in the ETL job metadata.

- **Transformation metadata.** Each job consists of many transformations. Any form of data manipulation within a job is performed by a dedicated transformation.

- **Batch metadata.** Batching is a technique used to run a collection of jobs together. Batches should have the ability to be configured to run sequentially or in parallel. Also, batches should be able to contain subbatches. Subbatches are common in data warehousing. You may have a batch that loads dimensions and a batch that loads facts. Those batches can be batched together to load a specific data mart. Batches are scheduled to run periodically or according to any triggering mechanism.

■ **Process metadata.** Each time a batch is executed, process metadata is generated. Process metadata is crucial for depicting whether the data warehouse was loaded successfully or not.

If you are not new to ETL, you've probably noticed that the metadata categories are not listed in container order but in the order that they are generally built or generated in the ETL process. For example, even though batches contain jobs, you must build your jobs before you can batch them. Each type of ETL metadata contains its own specific attributes that need to be created, maintained, and published. The subsequent sections examine the specifics of the technical metadata in the ETL environment.

For consistency throughout this book, we refer to the physical implementation of the data mapping as a *job* and their containers as *batches*. The terms may be consistent with some ETL tools but not others. Our generic designation of the terms does not infer any particular technology. If your technology calls your physical source-to-target mappings something other than *job*, substitute *job* with your own term for the purposes of capturing its metadata.

🔆 **If you implement your ETL solution without a dedicated tool, you are not excused from generating the metadata outlined in this chapter. Tools are meant to ease the burden of these tasks. Without them, you will have to produce and maintain metadata manually. If you must create ETL metadata by hand, use spreadsheets kept in a version-control system such as PVCS or SourceSafe.**

ETL Job Metadata

ETL metadata can be very technical, and end users tend to shy away from it. Source-to-target mapping usually contains programming code and can be cryptic to business users or nontechnical end users. However, source-to-target mapping is crucial for understanding the true data lineage of the data in the data warehouse. Metadata is sought after by the data warehouse team as well when credibility of the data is in question and its integrity needs to be proven.

🔆 **The optimal way to present source-to-target mappings is to utilize a dedicated ETL tool. These tools offer reports to present the information to users. Some tools are better at it than others. Make sure to ask your potential ETL vendor to show you how their tool handles the presentation of source-to-target mappings.**

Figure 9.2 illustrates the elements of ETL job metadata that need to be created, stored, and shared. The following elements must be tracked to

Job Name	Job Purpose	Source Tables/Files	Target Tables/Files
browser_platform_dim	Load the browser_platform_dim table.	stg_web_log	browser_platform_dim
claim_reason_dim	Load the claim_reason_dim table.	claim_reason	claim_reason_dim
claim_status_dim	Load the claim_status_dim table.	claim_status	claim_status_dim
claims_agent_dim	Load the claims_agent_dim table.	claims_agent	claims_agent_dim
claims_fact	Load the claims_fact table.	claims_fact	claims_fact
clickstream_customer_dim	Load the clickstream_customer_dim table.	weblogs, customer	clickstream_customer_dim
customer_credit_card_dim	Load the customer_credit_card_dim table.	customer_credit_card	customer_credit_card_dim
customer_dim	Load the customer_dim table.	stg_web_log	customer_dim
date_dim	Load the date_dim table.	date_dim.csv	date_dim
delivery_option_dim	Load the delivery_option_dim table.	delivery_option	delivery_option_dim
mktg_stg_tables	Load the mktg_stg_tables table.	campaigns.csv	mktg_stg_tables
page_dim	Load the page_dim table.	stg_web_log	page_dim
page_events_dims	Load the page_events_dims table.	stg_web_log	page_events_dims
page_events_fact	Load the page_events_fact table.	stg_web_log	page_events_fact
partner_promotion_dim	Load the partner_promotion_dim table.	partner, promotions	partner_promotion_dim
payment_status_dim	Load the payment_status_dim table.	payment_status	payment_status_dim
product_dim	Load the product_dim table.	product	product_dim
server_dim	Load the server_dim table.	weblogs, servers.csv	server_dim
stg_web_log	Load the stg_web_log table to utilize database functions.	weblogs	stg_web_log
time_dim	Load the time_dim table.	time_dim.csv	time_dim

Figure 9.2 ETL job metadata.

help manage your jobs and share their identity and functionality with your managers and users.

- **Job name.** The name of the physical ETL job
- **Job purpose.** Brief description of the primary focus of the process
- **Source tables/files.** The name and location of all source data
- **Target tables/files.** The name and location of all resulting data after it has been transformed
- **Reject file name.** The name and location of the file or table that stores any records intended to be loaded but are not in the ultimate target
- **Pre-processes.** Any other jobs or scripts on which the job is dependent to run before it can be executed
- **Post-processes.** Any other jobs or scripts that the job needs to run to complete its process

Jobs

A job is a collection of transformations that perform the physical extraction, transformation, and load routines. The metadata for a job is the physical source-to-target mapping. Jobs should be named after the target table or file that they are loading. If your ETL process has many segments, each job must contain a prefix that indicates its purpose. ETL jobs generally fall into one of three categories:

- **Extraction.** EXT_<table name>. Indicates that the job's primary purpose is to extract data from the source system.
- **Intermediate stage (for example, cleaning and conforming).** STG_<table name>. The STG prefix signifies that the job does not touch the source or the target. It is an intermediate process that lives only in the staging area. If your process touches down in the staging area more than once, append a counter to the prefix (for example, STG1, STG2, STG3, and so on).
- **Target.** TRG_<table name>. Indicates that the job loads the target data warehouse. Alternatively, we've seen these jobs named FAC_<table name> and DIM_<table name> to indicate if the target table is a fact or dimension, respectively. We don't see much value in that, but it is an acceptable convention if it provides value for your situation.

Transformation Metadata

Transformation metadata is information about the *construction* of the ETL process. The ETL developer spends most of his or her time constructing or reusing data transformations. Transformations are composed of custom functions, procedures, and routines that can include cursors, loops and memory variables, making them extremely difficult to document and offer as metadata. Any manipulation performed on your data during the ETL process is considered a transformation. If you are writing your ETL in SQL, you need to identify each of the distinct sections in your procedures and label them to be consistent with the common attributes of transformation metadata.

Dedicated ETL tools predefine transformations common to the data warehouse environment and provide them as part of their package. Prebuilt transformations expedite ETL development and implicitly capture transformation metadata. Common data transformations that exist in most ETL jobs include:

- **Source data extractions.** This could be as simple as an SQL SELECT statement or involve FTP or reading XML DTDs or mainframe Copy Books.

- **Surrogate key generators.** These can simply call a database sequence or involve complex routines that manage memory or involve third-party software. The last number inserted into the data warehouse is also metadata that needs to be maintained and presented as required.

- **Lookups.** Primarily used to get surrogate keys from the dimensions during a fact table load or referential integrity in the staging area. If you are using raw SQL, this involves all of your inner and outer joins and IN statements.

- **Filters.** This rule determines which rows are extracted and loaded. Metadata is the business rule or constraint used to apply the filter. Filters can be applied anywhere in the ETL process. It is a recommended practice to filter your data as early in the process as possible.

- **Routers.** Conditionally routes rows like a CASE statement

- **Union.** Merges two pipelines with compatible row sets

- **Aggregates.** When the fact table is not the same grain as the atomic-level transaction, you need to apply aggregates to source data. Metadata associated to the aggregate includes any calculations within the aggregate function, the function itself—count, sum, average, rank, and so on—and the columns on which the aggregate functions are grouped. The grouped columns declare the granularity of the aggregate.

- **Heterogeneous joins.** When your source's data comes from different systems, they are usually joined outside of any single database (unless you use a database *link*). The way you join heterogeneous systems outside of the DBMS environment needs to be defined and presented as metadata.

- **Update strategies.** The update strategy contains business rules that determine if a record should be added, updated, or deleted. It also contains the slowly changing dimension policy.

- **Target loader.** The target loader tells the ETL process which database, table, and column needs to be loaded. Additionally, this documents if any bulk-load utility is used to load data into the data warehouse.

Each transformation gets data, manipulates it to a certain degree, and passes it to the next transformation in the job stream. Metadata attributes that describe the transformation include:

- **Transformation name.** A single job can have a multitude of transformations, and identification of each is crucial for management and maintenance. Each transformation must have a unique name that is meaningful and complies with standard naming conventions. Transformation-naming conventions are outlined in this chapter.

- **Transformation purpose.** The purpose of the transformation must be easily identified. Many ETL tools color-code their predefined transformations. If you are hand-coding your ETL processes, make sure metadata is captured both within your code and your transformation matrix.

- **Input columns.** The data elements fed into the transformation

- **Physical calculations.** The actual code used to manipulate data

- **Logical calculations.** The textual equivalent of the physical calculations is required to make sense of the sometimes cryptic code required to physically manipulate data.

- **Output columns.** The result of the data transformation sent to the next transformation

Transformation Nomenclature

Transformations are the components of an ETL job. Each type of transformation requires a slightly different naming format. For maintainability, adhere to the following naming conventions while building your ETL transformations:

- **Source data extractions.** SRC_<table name>

- **Surrogate key generators.** SEQ_<name of surrogate key column being populated>

- **Lookups.** LKP_<name of table being looked up or referenced>

- **Filters.** FIL_<purpose of filter> (for example, FIL_SUPPRESS_BOTS to suppress hits on a Web site generated by bots)

- **Aggregates.** AGG_<purpose of aggregate> (for example, AGG_HITS_BY_MONTH to aggregate Web site hit counts to the monthly level)

- **Heterogeneous joins.** HJN_<name of first table>_<name of second table>

- **Update strategies.** UPD_<type of strategy (INS, UPD, DEL, UPS)>_<name of target table>

- **Target loader.** TRG_<name of target table>

Batch Metadata

Once all of the jobs are designed and built, they need to be scheduled for execution. The load schedule is a crucial piece of metadata for the team responsible for incrementally loading the data warehouse. Figure 9.3 illustrates what a typical load schedule might look like for a clickstream data mart.

In Figure 9.3, notice that the load schedule contains information for the following metadata attributes:

Load Schedule

- **Dependent batches.** Batches are nested to contain several levels of batched jobs to execute many jobs in parallel or to maintain integrity

```
B_Daily_DW_Load - Scheduled to kick off at 12:30 am each morning.
        S_DW_Prepare_logs – This session creates an excludes.txt file by querying the clickstream_excludes table
        in the staging area database. This list includes all image extentions and 'bots' that are
        excluded from the page_events_fact table.
                Pre-session process  –./Scripts/del_files.pl – Delete today's partial logs from /incoming/*
                Post-Session process -./Scripts/create_output_file.pl – create output.txt file containing
                all pages_views for the previous day. This command is dependent on the success of the creation of
                the excludes.txt files.
        S_DW_DB_Dim – All subsequent sessions are dependent on data from the operations database.
                B_DW_Content_Dim_Load
                        S_Content_Dim_Product – Load new Products since last data warehouse load.
                        S_Content_Dim_Category - Load new Categories since last data warehouse load.
                        S_Content_Dim_Ad - Load new Ads since last data warehouse load.
                        S_Content_Dim_Link - Load new Links since last data warehouse load.
                S_Last_Process_Date – Update the DW_LastProcess table in data staging database.
B_DW_DIMS_AND_FACTS
        S_DW_Stg_Web_Log – Load all Web Logs minus excludes into staging area
                        S_DW_Page_events_dims – Load all data warehouse clickstream dimension tables concurrently
                        B_DW_Load_Facts_tables – Load Clickstream Fact Tables in parellel
                        S_DW_Hits_Fact - Load Hits_Fact table
                        S_DW_Pages_Events_Fact - Load Page_Events_Fact table
        Post-Session process – ./Scripts/update_brio_repo.sql – this script triggers Brio Broadcasr
        Server to start producing reports.
                        S_DW_load_audit – Add activity to the Audit log table in the data warehouse
        Post-Session process – /Scripts/move_logs.bat – upon completion, move any logs in the /incoming/ directory
        to the /outgoing/ directory.
```

Figure 9.3 Clickstream data mart load schedule.

between jobs. For example, a batch that loads dimensions of a data mart must complete successfully before fact table jobs can be executed. Remember, the data warehouse database does not enforce referential integrity. Dependent batches are one of the ways to enforce integrity in the data warehouse.

- **Frequency.** Portions of the data warehouse are loaded monthly, weekly, daily, or are continuously fed data. This piece of metadata defines how often the batch is executed.

- **Schedule.** If a job is run daily, this metadata attribute captures the exact time the batch is executed. If it is run monthly, the exact day of the month is represented. Batches must have the ability to be scheduled on any give time of day, day of week, month, or year.

- **Recovery steps.** Actions required in the event of a midprocess failure. Recovery steps can be a lengthy process and are usually offered in a separate document. The steps to recover from a failed process must be walked through with the team that supports the operation of the execution of batched ETL jobs to ensure they understand the procedure.

Data Quality Error Event Metadata

Chapter 4 is an in-depth tutorial on capturing metadata describing data quality. The three main tables are depicted in detail in that chapter, but for uniformity, we list the data elements we captured in the cleaning and conforming steps.

First, the screen table includes:

- The **ETL Injection Stage** describes the stage in the overall ETL process in which the data-quality screen should be applied.

- The **Processing Order Number** is a primitive scheduling/ dependency device informing the overall ETL master process the order in which to run the screens. Data-quality screens with the same Processing Order Number in the same ETL Injection Stage can be run in parallel.

- The **Severity Score** is used to define the error severity score to be applied to each exception identified by the screen.

- The **Exception Action** attribute tells the overall ETL process whether it should pass the record, reject the record, or stop the overall ETL process upon discovery of an error of this type.

- The **Screen Category Name** is used to group data-quality screens related by theme—such as *Completeness*, *Validation*, or *Out-of-Bounds*.

- The **SQL Statement** captures the actual snippet of SQL or procedural SQL used to execute the data quality check. If applicable, this SQL should return the set of unique identifiers for the rows that violate the data-quality screen—so that this can be used to insert new records into the Data Quality Error Event fact.

Second, the main error event fact table includes:

- The **Staged Record Identifier**, which uniquely identifies the error record
- The **Error Severity Score**, which assigns a severity from 1 to 100 to the error condition

The error event fact table has foreign keys to calendar date, time of day, ETL batch, table, and source system dimensions. These dimensions provide the context for the measures in the error event fact table.

The audit dimension includes the following fields described in Chapter 4:

- Overall Data Quality Score
- Completeness Score
- Validation Score
- Out of Bounds Score
- Number of Screens Failed
- Maximum Error Event Severity
- Cleaning and Conforming Timestamps, including the begin times and end times of specific job runs
- Overall ETL Timestamps, including the begin times and end times of complete end-to-end ETL jobs
- The Overall ETL Release Version Numbers to identify the consistent suite of ETL software tools in use at a point in time
- Other Audit Version Numbers such as allocation version, currency conversion logic version, and conforming logic version, depending on the business-rules environment

Process Execution Metadata

Virtually all process metadata in the data warehouse is generated by the ETL. Each time a job or batch is executed, statistics or indicators of success need to be captured. Load statistics are a vital piece of metadata that captures information about the *execution* of the ETL process and contains information about the actual load-process results.

Run Results

Metadata elements that help you understand the activity in your jobs or batches and rate the success of their execution include:

- **Subject name.** This can be the data mart or a description of a *batch* of programs being run for a specific area.
- **Job name.** The name of the program executed
- **Processed rows.** The total number and percentage of rows read and processed from the source system
- **Success rows.** The total number and percentage of rows loaded to the data warehouse
- **Failed rows.** The total number and percentage of rows rejected by the data warehouse
- **Last error code.** The code of the last database or ETL exception raised during the load process
- **Last error.** The textual description of the last database or ETL exception raised during the load process
- **Read throughput.** Throughput is used to measure the performance of the ETL process. It is normally represented in rows per second. This is used to capture if the source system is causing a bottleneck.
- **Write throughput.** Throughput is used to measure the performance of the ETL process. It is normally represented in rows per second. This is used to capture if the target data warehouse database is causing a bottleneck.
- **Start time.** The date, time, and second that the job is initiated
- **End time.** The date, time, and second that the job ends, regardless of its success
- **Elapsed time.** The difference between the Start time and End time. This is an important element for analyzing performance. In most cases, rows per second are not enough, because it can vary depending on the number of rows being loaded.
- **Source file name.** The name of the table or file where the data in the process originates. This can include more than one table or file.
- **Target file name.** The name of the table or file where the data in the process is targeted. This can include more than one table or file.

Process-execution metadata should be retained in a data store so trend analysis can be performed. Metadata can reveal bottlenecks in the process, and trending can expose portions of the data warehouse that lack the required scalability. Measures of data quality should also be trended.

Exception Handling

This data records exceptional conditions that arose in the running of the ETL system and what action was taken:

- **Subject name.** This can be the data mart or a description of a *batch* of programs being run for a specific area
- **Job name.** The name of the program executed
- **Exception Condition.** One of a standard set of exception conditions
- **Severity.**
- **Action Taken.**
- **Operator.**
- **Outcome.**

Batches Scheduled

Batches are a collection of ETL jobs scheduled for execution. The name of the batch should reveal the subject area being loaded, the frequency that the jobs are run, and whether the jobs within the batch are executed sequentially or in parallel.

Metadata Standards and Practices

One aspect of metadata that is worth investigating is standards. Many organizations attempt to standardize metadata at various levels. If you are interested in standards on things such as naming conventions or domain standards, you may find the standards maintained by the Library of Congress to be helpful (www.loc.gov/standards/standard.html). Furthermore, links to additional standards organizations are offered. On their Web site, you'll find links to:

- **Metadata Encoding and Transmission Standard (METS).** A standard for encoding descriptive, administrative, and structural metadata regarding objects within a digital library
- **American National Standards Institute (ANSI).** The organization that coordinates the U.S. voluntary standardization and conformity-assessment systems
- **International Organization for Standardization (ISO).** The body that establishes, develops, and promotes standards for international exchange

Metadata relative to the ETL process includes not only standards in values and conventions but also in methodology on storing and sharing metadata. Organizations geared toward the organization and storage of metadata include:

- **Dublin Core.** The Dublin Core Metadata Initiative (DCMI) is an open forum created to develop metadata standards. DCMI hosts periodic working groups and conferences that promote metadata standards and practices worldwide. More information about Dublin Core can be found on their Web site at www.dublincore.org.

- **Meta Data Coalition.** The now defunct Meta Data Coalition (MDC) was created in 1995 as a consortium of approximately 50 vendors and end users whose efforts attempted to provide technical direction to exchange metadata between products in the data warehouse environment. During its existence, MDC helped to establish and encourage consistent means of sharing metadata. In 2000, MDC folded into the Object Management Group (OMG), who has a much larger agenda in the metadata space and combined MDC's objectives with their own broader plan.

- **Common Warehouse Metamodel.** The Common Warehouse Metamodel (CWM) was created as a result of the merger of MDC and OMG. You can find detailed information about CWM in books dedicated to the topic and the OMG Web site www.omg.org/cwm.

Establishing Rudimentary Standards

To maintain manageable jobs for all of your enterprise data warehouse ETL processes, your data warehouse team must establish standards and practices for the ETL team to follow. Whether you follow the recommendations of the organizations in this section or follow the practices outlined throughout this book, at the most rudimentary level, your organization should adhere to standards for the following:

- **Naming conventions.** Corporations usually have naming-convention standards in place for their existing software and database development teams. The data warehouse may be required to follow those standards. In practice, we tend to deviate from those standards when we can, especially while naming columns. But often, you must conform to corporate policies. Therefore, any corporate policies must be documented and provided to the data warehouse team.

- **Architecture.** Best-practice guidelines need to be captured as metadata for your ETL environment. In many cases, high-level architecture decisions are made before the ETL team is established or on the recommendation of your ETL vendor. Decisions such as whether you should run your ETL engine on your data warehouse server or on a dedicated box, whether you should have a persistent staging area (PSA), or whether your target data warehouse should be normalized or dimensional should be based on best practices that need to be established, documented, and followed.

- **Infrastructure.** Should your solution be on Windows or UNIX, mainframe or AS/400? Corporate standards influence the decision-making process for the products and hardware used for the ETL. Some ETL engines run only on UNIX or the mainframe, while others run on Windows. You must have established corporate infrastructure metadata before any purchasing decision is made for your ETL environment. Once your environment is established, the metadata of its infrastructure must be documented and reviewed with your internal infrastructure support team.

Naming Conventions

Naming conventions for the objects in the data warehouse environment should be established before the ETL team begins any coding. Conventions for tables, columns, constraints, indexes, checks, and so on should be offered by the existing DBA team within your organization or the data warehouse manager. The ETL team must adopt any conventions that exist in the rest of the data warehouse environment.

> If you decide that your existing corporate naming conventions are not applicable to your ETL environment, you must document your alternative naming conventions and seek approval from your corporate standards committee. Once approved, the corporate standards committee should incorporate the new ETL-specific conventions with their existing naming standards.

None of the organizations we recognize earlier in this section recommend naming standards specific to the ETL process. If your ETL processes consist only of raw SQL, follow your in-house programming practices and naming standards, with the exception of conventions explicitly defined in this chapter. In this section, we share conventions that prove to be effective in the ETL environment.

> The naming conventions recommended in this section include the common transformations found in most ETL tools. Use these conventions regardless of your tool, even if you are coding your ETL by hand. Tools can come and go—do not set

up new standards each time you change tools. Use the vendor-recommended naming conventions for transformations that are not mentioned in this book. It is acceptable to slightly modify these naming conventions for your purposes—the important thing is be consistent within your environment.

Impact Analysis

One of the key advantages of maintaining ETL metadata is to enable impact analysis. Impact analysis allows you to list all of the attributes in the data warehouse environment that would be affected by a proposed change. Ultimately, you should be able to analyze the impact of a change that would occur in any component of the data warehouse and list all of the attributes in all of the other components. An impact analysis solution must be able to answer the following questions:

- Which ETL jobs depend on this staging table?
- Is this table in the source system used by the data warehouse?
- Would the deletion of this source system column affect the ETL process?
- Which source systems populate this dimension?
- Which ETL jobs and data warehouse tables will need to be modified if we change this data type from VARCHAR(2000) to CLOB?

Tools designed specifically for ETL should be able to answer all of these questions. Without an ETL tool, you need to maintain spreadsheets to capture every table and column from the source systems and their mapping into the data warehouse. Each time an ETL job is altered, the spreadsheet needs to be manually modified to stay current.

Summary

In this chapter, we have brought order to the traditional chaos of metadata surrounding a data warehouse, first by focusing only on the metadata needed to manage the ETL system, and next by dividing the ETL metadata into three categories.

1. **Business metadata.** Describing the meaning of the data in a business sense and consisting of separate tables tracking business definitions, source system information, the data warehouse dictionary, and logical data mapping

2. **Technical metadata.** Representing the technical aspects of data, including attributes such as data types, lengths, and lineage, and consisting of separate tables tracking system inventory, data models, data definitions, business rules, ETL jobs definitions, specific data transformations, and batch job definitions

3. **Process execution metadata.** Presenting statistics on the results of running the ETL process itself, including measures such as rows loaded successfully, rows rejected, and amount of time to load. We proposed particularly important process metadata in the cleaning and conforming steps, including the screen dimension table, the error event fact table, and the audit dimension table. All of this metadata consists of separate tables tracking run results, exception handling, and the immediate operational schedule.

Responsibilities

In this chapter, we discuss managing the development and administration of a successful ETL system. We could have put this chapter at the beginning of the book, before the myriad responsibilities of the ETL system were discussed thoroughly, but we think by putting it at the end of the book, you will better be able to visualize how to manage a team effectively.

The first part of this chapter looks at planning and leadership issues, and the second part descends into more detail of managing the ETL system. Many of these perspectives were developed in *Data Warehouse Lifecycle Toolkit*.

PROCESS CHECK Planning & Design:
Requirements/Realities → Architecture → *Implementation* → Release to Ops

Data Flow: *Extract* → *Clean* → *Conform* → *Deliver*

Planning and Leadership

In some ways, the data warehouse and ETL process are just like any other software development project. When a data warehouse team is established, it usually requires three specialists. The following list contains common roles required to initiate a data warehouse project. The list includes the primary role and the secondary role (in parentheses) that the same individual can perform on small teams.

- **Data Modeler (Project Manager).** The data modeler must be specially trained in dimensional data modeling and educated in the principles of dimensional modeling.
- **ETL Architect/Programmer (DW Architect).** The ETL programmer is usually a SQL and database expert as well as an architect. This person establishes the technical infrastructure of the ETL system and data warehouse environment and designs the physical ETL processes.
- **Application Specialist (Business Analyst).** This person gathers and documents the business, analytical, and reporting requirements. This specialist writes the front-end interface and initial reports for the data warehouse. This position is often called the business intelligence (BI) specialist.

When a data warehouse is kicked off, the often compact team of highly specialized individuals builds the foundation for what evolves into the most visible, widely used database application in your enterprise. Like any other substantial structure, without a thoroughly planned and methodical construction of the foundation, anything built subsequently is certain to topple.

Having Dedicated Leadership

The data warehouse is a complex entity that requires specialized knowledge that most enterprise IT managers don't quite understand. Initially, the data warehouse must have a dedicated project manager who has experience implementing a data warehouse using the principles of dimensional modeling. As your data warehouse evolves, each component and subcomponent must have a dedicated project manager. A mature data warehouse must a have distinct ETL, data-modeling, and business-intelligence managers as well as a dedicated project manager who oversees all of the *departments* of the data warehouse team to ensure a cohesive solution is implemented across all areas.

It's been argued that a single person can manage the entire data warehouse, but we strongly recommend that specialists for each area be appointed. Each area requires specialized skills that become diluted if someone tries to encompass them all. Remember, a single mind, no matter how strong, is not as strong as a group.

 A group is always stronger than an individual, but that does not mean that design decisions are made by voting! Design decisions are best made autocratically, so that consistency is maintained.

Planning Large, Building Small

When you are building a data warehouse from scratch, it is often difficult to imagine that it is going to evolve from the single data mart you are working on into a major enterprise, mission-critical application that has more exposure than any other application within your company. The big picture is commonly lost because data warehouses are usually built in an iterative approach. They start and complete a single business process or *data mart*, such as human resources or campaign management, before development of the next data mart begins.

The data warehouse architect must utilize a methodology known as *data warehouse bus architecture*, which outlines the framework of the data warehouse so all of the resulting data marts work together in a cohesive fashion using conformed dimensions and conformed facts as we have described extensively in this book.

Part of the data warehouse bus architecture process includes devising a *data warehouse bus matrix*, a list of all the dimensions that need to be created and their associations to the various data marts in the data warehouse. The bus matrix helps the architect visualize which dimensions are shared or conformed across the various data marts in the data warehouse. Once the bus matrix is created, the physical data marts can be built one at a time. Figure 10.1 illustrates a sample data warehouse bus matrix.

Just as certain dimensions are reused throughout the data warehouse, certain ETL routines are reused over and over when you are building the ETL processes. For example, your first ETL process most likely includes generating a surrogate key for a dimension. The code that generates the surrogate key can be reused to generate all surrogate keys in the data warehouse—just by using different parameters. If you come from a software development background, you may have heard the saying, *Write once, use many*. That adage means to reuse as much code as possible. Not only does reusable code cut down development time of subsequent processes; it ensures consistency across them.

You need an effective code-reusability strategy. Establish an environment that encourages developers to share ideas and to trust each other's work. The following tips can help you build a team environment.

- **Agree as a group on strategies.** Have regular meetings that discuss technical and functional strategies and solve problems as a group.

- **Share ideas as well as code.** Reinforce that ETL development is not a competitive sport. Work together and share issues with others on your team. We've spent hours in isolation agonizing over situations. Then, by simply explaining the scenario to someone else, the solution

Data Mart / Dimension	DIM_AGREEMENT_TYPE	DIM_CURRENCY	DIM_DATE	DIM_DEPARTMENT	DIM_ABSENCE_REASON	DIM_OFFICE	DIM_EMPLOYEE	DIM_POSITION	DIM_ABSENCE_TYPE	DIM_EMPLOYEE_RATING	DIM_COMPENSATION_TYPE
Employee Monthly Snapshot		X	X	X		X	X	X			
Employee Transfer Transaction	X	X	X	X		X	X	X			
Attendence Transaction		X	X	X	X	X	X	X	X		
Compensation Monthly Summary		X	X	X		X	X	X		X	
Rating Monthly Summary			X	X		X	X	X		X	
Compensation Transaction		X	X	X		X	X	X			X
Rating Transaction			X	X		X	X	X		X	

Figure 10.1 Data warehouse bus matrix.

instantly came to mind. It's amazing how many ideas are born during simple conversation.

- **Use a repository.** Many ETL tools offer a repository for reusable code. Make sure your tool includes a repository that allows code to be reused and shared among various load routines and developers. If you have not yet invested in a dedicated ETL tool, at least use a source-code repository such as SourceSafe or PVCS. In mature installations, you need to develop multiple individual repositories which then must be managed as a single virtual repository.

Once your team is trained to work together and all of your core routines are in your repository, development efficiency is sure to increase. Also, working together helps developers understand the big picture of the project. Avoid isolating developers by subject area. Over time, each developer becomes an expert in the specific areas he or she develops. It is advantageous for the team to be exposed to other areas for which they are not directly responsible. Broadening the scope of ETL developers promotes cross-functional planning and builds morale within the team.

💡 **Your ETL team should be encouraged to share and reuse as much of their work as possible. Make sure appropriate metadata is associated to all of the sharable code in your repository. Metadata is crucial for identifying the purpose of the code and providing instructions for its use. But be realistic in your expectations for literally reusing code across separate operating systems and DBMS platforms.**

Hiring Qualified Developers

Skilled ETL developers are invaluable assets to your organization. However, skill alone does not qualify someone as an expert. We've interviewed many potential ETL developers over the years who knew various tools inside and out but could not grasp dimensional concepts such as hierarchy mapping tables. Developers must have the ability to comprehend new techniques quickly and implement them with minimal hand-holding. When we interview, we tend to spend less time talking about using tool features and more time on problem solving—technical and functional. We find that candidates with intelligence and character make much better ETL team members than those with only technical skill.

During candidate interviews, ask a specific question you know the interviewee does not know the answer to. Watch to see how he or she works it out. Remember, it's not whether the candidate gets the answer right, but the process he or she uses to solve it. The reality is that ETL and data warehousing can be quite complex and are quite specialized. Still, it's not splitting atoms. (If it were, a scientist would have to provide a specification!) So, when you are building your team, make sure that your developers are motivated to grow technically and professionally. They must be able to grow with you and your project and be able to accept and adapt new techniques and strategies.

Building Teams with Database Expertise

Part of the responsibility of the ETL manager is to inventory all of the source systems within your enterprise and align the appropriate skill sets in your development team according to the existing databases. If you use a dedicated ETL tool, staffing your team with specific database expertise might not be as critical. But even with the best toolsets, you never seem to get away from rolling up your sleeves and writing raw SQL at some point in the ETL development process.

Listing specific SQL coding tips and techniques is beyond the scope of this book—there are several SQL books on the market—but be advised that SQL is the foundation of any DBMS query. Tools alone cannot adequately fulfill all of your ETL requirements. When you interview potential candidates for your ETL team, be sure they are proficient in the specific *flavors* of SQL required both for your transaction DBMSs as well as the system you have chosen for your main ETL processing.

> 💡 Each source system DBMS that you encounter requires knowledge and implementation of specialized SQL syntax. Make sure your team has the specialized skills to navigate the various databases and that your ETL tool can seamlessly integrate native SQL code in the ETL process without leaving the application.

Don't Try to Save the World

The ETL system is just a portion of the data warehouse project, and some things that happen within it are beyond your control. Accept that the data warehouse is not, nor will be, perfect. You are going to encounter dirty data, and in many cases, you will not get the political backing to clean it. Our philosophy is that the best way to get data cleansed is to expose it. You've been asked to build the data warehouse because the existing data has been so difficult to analyze. Chances are that much of the data you are publishing with your ETL process has not been exposed before, especially to the extent that it is via the data warehouse. If your petition for ultimate data quality is ignored, be patient. As soon as blemished data is published, managers have to start explaining the anomalies, and you will witness a change in heart about the quality of the data and receive the support you need.

Enforcing Standardization

In large ETL projects, it is imperative that you establish standards early on. Without standards, developers write inconsistent ETL jobs and cause the maintenance of existing code to be horrendous. The ETL team must standardize their development techniques to provide a consistent and maintainable code environment. The following list contains areas of the ETL process that need standardization most:

- **Naming conventions.** Establish and enforce a standardized convention for naming objects and code elements in your ETL process. Begin by adopting existing naming standards in your organization. Add to your existing conventions with those recommended by your ETL tool vendor.

- **Best practices.** Document and follow best practices for building your ETL routines. Make standards for things such as the ordinal position of transformations in your routines or the best ways to recover from a failed process. This book is full of recommended strategies for your ETL processes. Standards to consider are:

- **Generating surrogate keys**. If you decide to use the database, ETL tool, or any other mechanism to generate surrogate keys, be consistent throughout your ETL jobs.

- **Looking up keys.** You may use mapping tables, look to the physical dimensions, or use other staging techniques to associate natural keys to their surrogates. Pick one and stick with it. If you mix techniques, maintaining these routines is a nightmare.

- **Applying default values.** Several approaches and values are acceptable means of defaulting missing values. Remember that missing values or NULL values have to be handled carefully in the data warehouse because those values can cause *blank* column or row headings on reports and because some databases do not include NULLs in their indexes. It's best to check incoming records for NULL values and to substitute them with actual values such as the single character ? during the ETL process.

Monitoring, Auditing, and Publishing Statistics

ETL statistics are invaluable to anyone who uses the data warehouse. If your data warehouse has a dedicated Web site—and it should—make sure it includes the daily statistics of your ETL processes. Users often want to know exactly when a table has been loaded or if any rows were rejected. Most ETL tools generate load statistics automatically. Make sure your tool has the ability to automatically publish the required statistical information upon completion of the daily data load.

CROSS-REFERENCE A list of the statistical elements that should be published as part of your metadata strategy can be found in Chapter 9.

Maintaining Documentation

Documentation of what your ETL processes do is an invaluable asset to the data warehouse team and has become mandatory in many phases of financial and regulatory-reporting data warehouses. Even with the most thorough logical data-map specification, only the developer knows *exactly* what is done to the data between the data warehouse and its source. It's the responsibility of the ETL team to maintain documentation for the lineage of each data element in the data warehouse with rigorous change control. Some documentation comes in the form of metadata, but not all forms of documentation are considered formal metadata. Metadata is a complicated entity that already has several books to explain its capacity. Regardless of how you categorize it, several pieces of documentation must exist and be maintained and published. Often, descriptions of processes cannot be captured in the allotted fields in the various tools designed to capture this information. Inevitably, you need to provide documentation that explains your ETL processes in Word documents, Excel spreadsheets, PowerPoint presentations, and so on. Use a version control system such as SourceSafe or PVCS to maintain the integrity of your documentation.

Providing and Utilizing Metadata

Metadata is crucial for sharing and reusing ETL processes. Virtually all ETL tools have the ability to capture and utilize metadata. Don't do your team an injustice by creating processes without metadata. Each time you create a new ETL process, keep this in mind: If it's not captured by metadata, it doesn't exist. This is true in established data warehouse environments. If you don't expose your work via metadata, someone else on your team may recreate from scratch something that you've already created and tested.

What's more, the ETL tool repository is often the home of the metadata repository. Some ETL tools have the ability to transmit existing metadata from other tools such as data-modeling or reporting tools and associate elements for impact analysis. Some business-intelligence tools can utilize the ETL repository to integrate metadata with the data warehouse user interface. If the metadata in the ETL environment is published, it must be maintained, or the toolset can publish out-of-date information to its users.

Keeping It Simple

If you think there has to be an easier way to so something, there usually is. When you are building your ETL processes, take a step back from time to time and look at your work from a design perspective. Is the design straightforward, or does it have complexities that could be avoided? The more complex your processes are, the more difficult they will be to maintain. Moreover, complex ETL designs are almost impossible to *evolve*. As business needs or source systems change, your ETL jobs must be adaptable enough to change with them. We were called on a project once where an ETL job was so complex it was untouchable. No one knew exactly what it did, so no one was able to modify it. It was so convoluted that we were hired to reverse-engineer, document, and redesign it into a more streamlined, manageable process.

Optimizing Throughput

No real limitation exists as to how elaborate your ETL processes can be to transform your source data into usable information for the data warehouse.

However, a restriction on how long your jobs can take to process does exist. One of the challenges to being an ETL developer is to have the ability to extract, clean, conform, and load data within the allotted load window. The load window is the time set aside each night to run the ETL processes. Usually, the data warehouse is not available to its users during the load window, so there is always pressure to keep the load window as small as possible.

Managing the Project

The ETL process is a critical piece of the data warehouse project. Until now, it has been thought of as the least glamorous aspect of the project and typically did not receive the attention it deserved. In the early days of data warehousing, the primary focus was on front-end tools; then as the size of data warehouses began to grow, the dimensional data model became the next focal point. As the data warehouse reaches its next level of maturity, ETL is finally getting appropriate time in the spotlight.

Most designers agree that at least 70 percent of the entire data warehouse project is dedicated to the ETL process. Managing the team that builds these tenacious processes responsible for transforming potentially billions of rows of unorganized data from disparate systems into a cohesive user-friendly information repository is an achievement that is highly regarded by technologists and executives alike. Managing the ETL team takes dedication and know-how.

The ETL manager position has been established to alleviate the over-whelming responsibility of the ETL process from the data warehouse project manager. Also, this position provides business sponsors with confidence that the ETL team can maintain a controlled, efficient environment to load the data warehouse with clean, consistent data. The tasks contained in this chapter should be read carefully by all members of the data warehouse team to make certain that they understand that the ETL process is not a trivial byproduct of the data warehouse project but rather the glue that holds the entire project together. To the ETL manager, this chapter offers the knowledge required to bring your ETL project to victory.

Responsibility of the ETL Team

At the most rudimentary level, the ETL team is responsible for extracting data from the source system, performing data transformations, and loading transformed data into the target data warehouse. More specifically, to achieve optimal ETL results, the following tasks are the responsibilities of the ETL team:

- Defining the scope of the ETL
- Performing source system data analysis
- Defining a data-quality strategy
- Working with business users to gather and document business rules
- Developing and implementing physical ETL code
- Creating and executing unit and QA test plans
- Implementing production
- Performing system maintenance

To effectively manage your team in the execution of the preceding tasks, we've outlined an actual project plan that incorporates these tasks and gives details of your functional responsibility for properly managing each.

Defining the Project

Although the ETL process is only one of the many components in the data warehouse lifecycle, it is the center of the data warehouse universe. Moreover, the ETL process is by far the most difficult component to manage. As users begin to see the resulting data in the beginning phases of the project, you will be faced with an onslaught of change requests. Without a properly executed project plan and change-management strategy, managing the ETL process will seem impossible, a never-ending task that could delay the project to the point of failure. As you go about defining your project, keep the following guidelines in mind:

- **For a seamless process, the management of the ETL must be closely coupled with the other components within the data warehouse lifecycle.** From the standpoint of those who work with it regularly, the data warehouse is never really finished. As new requirements are initiated, the modeling team, ETL team, and reporting team must work together to effectively accomplish these new goals and complete the tasks that lie ahead. Steps outlined in this chapter should be reused as each subject area is added to the ever-evolving data warehouse. Nailing down the methods outlined in this chapter is crucial to properly managing these iterative processes.

- **Be realistic when estimating completion dates and defining scope.** Do not let data modelers or business sponsors who do not have the knowledge to make an informed decision dictate the time frame of the ETL effort. Use the project plan in this chapter as a guide and make sure your business users and sponsors are aware of exactly what is involved in *loading* your data warehouse.

- **Make sure the ETL team is an active participant in the data warehouse project kick-off meeting.** Such a meeting can be a venue where you introduce the ETL team to key business users and discuss the ETL-specific goals, roles and responsibilities, and timeframes. Create an environment that fosters collaboration. This meeting helps participants understand project needs, and it gives you the opportunity to manage expectations.

Planning the Project

What is a plan? A plan is a method of action, procedure, or arrangement. It is a program to be done. It is a design to carry into effect, an idea, a thought, a project or a development. Therefore, a plan is a concrete means to help you fulfill your desires. — Earl Prevette

It is your ultimate goal as an ETL manager to successfully manage the ETL process and integrate the process into all other phases of the lifecycle. You might assume that managing the ETL process is identical to managing any other implementation, but it is quite different. In this section, we explain the methods that have helped us achieve successful implementations. Also, we expose many obstacles you may be faced with and provide suggestions to mitigate those risks to achieve your goals.

As a prerequisite to beginning the iterative portions of the project plan, you need to complete a few housekeeping responsibilities. These tasks include determining your ETL tool set and staffing your project team.

💡 The order in which these two tasks are executed is important. You want to select your ETL tool set prior to staffing your team. Doing so will enable you to recruit individuals who specialize in your selected tool set.

Determining the Tool Set

The ETL manager must determine whether it makes sense to build the ETL processes by hand or to purchase an ETL tool set, as discussed in Chapter 1. There are many arguments for either case. However, with the success of enterprise data warehousing and the expectations of executive sponsors, we feel there is no time for hand-coding, especially when you consider the iterative nature of data warehousing. Even the smallest projects benefit from the transformation reusability of dedicated ETL tools. The features available in these tools, right out of the box, would take months to design manually, not to mention coding the actual data-transformation processes. The reduced development time obtained via these tools makes them viable solutions for any data warehouse project.

Furthermore, ETL tools are specifically designed for the task at hand. The most popular case we hear for building over buying is that programmers already know SQL. Why waste time learning a tool that essentially has the same result: moving data? Two analogies immediately come to mind when we hear this. First, if the only tool you know is a hammer, everything around you is treated like a nail. Setting screws becomes very difficult, laborious, and sloppy. The second is the secretary that didn't have time to learn word processing because she was too busy typing. As silly as this may sound, it is synonymous to not training your SQL programmers in dedicated state-of-the-art ETL tools to perform their assignments.

To aid in the decision-making process, we recommend documenting your tool-selection criteria. Establish proof-of-concept decisive factors such as throughput performance, ease of modification, and vendor support and then perform a proof-of-concept for the tools (including a comparison with hand-coding) that you feel may meet your criteria. Upon evaluation of your proof-of-concept results, you will be able to make a firm decision on whether to build or buy an ETL tool set. If you are purchasing, you will have a firm idea of exactly which tool fits your needs.

Staffing Your Project

A crucial factor in managing the ETL process is establishing a superior team. Your team members must possess the necessary skills to perform the duties expected of them. A properly trained team is vital to your success. Ensuring that all team members fit into the company culture and work well together is equally important.

Before data warehousing reached its current point of maturity, all duties of the project were typically performed by just a few data warehouse experts. These all-encompassing experts interviewed business users, documented requirements, designed the data model, loaded the database, and so on. As the data warehouse project evolves, we are discovering that each of these specific tasks requires a unique set of specialized skills and that no individual can achieve expertise in all of them.

ETL Team Roles and Responsibilities

Staffing the roles of the ETL team is an undertaking that must be reckoned with. If you have appropriate knowledge internally, you may be able to recruit or train your internal staff. Otherwise, you need to work with recruiters to find the appropriate expertise required to construct your team.

The following bulleted list explains the roles and responsibilities we've found to be fundamental to building an optimal ETL team.

> Staffing one person per specific role would be ideal. However, as circumstances dictate, it is realistic to have people play multiple roles by overlapping some of their responsibilities, depending on the size of your project. Remember when you are staffing the project team, your main goal is to ensure that all duties will be performed. You do not necessarily have to fill each role with a dedicated person.

- **ETL Manager.** This individual is responsible for the day-to-day management of ETL team and the on-going data warehouse maintenance as it relates to the ETL process. The ETL manager is accountable for managing the development of the data-extract, transform, and load processes within the data warehouse and oversees its testing and quality assurance. The ETL manager also develops standards and procedures for the ETL environment, including naming conventions and best-development and design practices.

- **ETL Architect.** Primary responsibilities for this individual include designing the architecture and infrastructure of the ETL environment and designing the logical data mappings for the ETL development team. This architect must have a strong understanding of the business requirements and the source operational systems. The ETL architect is responsible for resolving complex technical issues for the team and migrating ETL routines to production.

- **ETL Developer.** This individual is accountable for building the physical ETL processes. The ETL developer works closely with the architect to resolve any ambiguity in specifications before actual coding begins. The developer is responsible for creating functional ETL routines and testing their reliability to ensure that they comply with business requirements. There are usually several ETL developers assigned to a data warehouse project.

- **Systems Analyst.** The systems analyst is accountable for business requirements definition activities and documenting those requirements throughout the data warehouse lifecycle. The systems analyst works closely with all members of the data warehouse team and the business users.

- **Data-Quality Specialist.** Data-warehouse quality includes the quality of the content and the information structure within the data warehouse. The data-quality specialist typically reports to the ETL manager but may also report directly to the data warehouse project manager. The data-quality specialist primarily works with the systems analyst and the ETL architect to ensure that business rules and data definitions are propagated throughout the ETL processes.

- **Database Administrator (DBA).** The DBA is primarily responsible for translating the logical database design into a physical structure and maintaining the physical database. Moreover, the DBA works very closely with the ETL team to ensure that new processes do not corrupt existing data. In some environments, the DBA actually owns the ETL process once it is migrated to production.

- **Dimension Manager.** The dimension manager is responsible for defining, building, and publishing one or more conformed dimensions to the extended data warehouse community that agrees to use the conformed dimensions. This is a truly centralized responsibility. Conformed dimensions must be version-stamped and replicated simultaneously to all fact table provider clients. There can be more than one dimension manager in an organization, since the data content of each dimension is largely independent. In any case, a given dimension is the responsibility of a single dimension manager.

- **Fact Table Provider.** The fact table provider owns a specific fact table. In a conformed dimension environment, the fact table provider receives periodic updates of dimensions from dimension managers, converts the natural keys in the fact tables to the dimension's surrogate keys, and exposes the fact table appropriately to the user community.

ETL Project Team Staffing Options

The old aphorism *you are only as good as your subordinates* holds special importance in a mission-critical environment like the ETL process of the data warehouse. An intelligent approach to preventing project failure is to build a superlative team to develop it. This section discusses various options available to you while building your ETL team.

Working with Recruiters

More often than not, you will need to look outside your organization while building your ETL team. Typically, organizations work with dedicated recruiters to seek the best candidates. But, just as a data warehouse needs to be fed complete, reliable information to be valuable to its users, you need to provide precise requirements to your recruiters for them to be effective. Be as detailed as possible when you supply job qualifications to ensure that you receive candidates that possess the skills and work habits you are looking for. Let the recruiter know the details of your environment, especially emphasizing your programming languages, vendor packages, and database systems. Also describe the dynamics of your team and exactly what type of person you are looking for. Provide the most detail possible to ensure that the candidates they send will meet your expectations.

Recruiting companies that specialize in data warehouse staffing will give you the benefit of working with recruiters who are knowledgeable in the data warehouse industry and the tools sets that support it. They are responsible for pre-screening candidates and weeding out under-qualified individuals before forwarding any resumes to you, limiting the number of lacking resumes and individuals you need to evaluate. You will be busy enough with many other tasks; the time saved using qualified recruiters is well worth their fees.

Hiring Internally versus Externally

There are advantages to building your team from either internal or external sources. The benefits of hiring internally include the following:

- The primary benefit of performing internal searches and hiring from within your organization is that internal individuals already have a strong understanding of your organizational structure and IT systems. They know who is responsible for what; who to go to for answers; and how to get things done politically. If you're lucky, they may already possess the skills needed to fill a specific role within the team. If an individual does not have the desired skill level but do have the potential and desire to be trained appropriately, this person may very well be a candidate worth considering.

- Providing internal employees who possess motivation with the opportunity to learn new things keeps them challenged and satisfies their needs.

- There is an economic benefit to hiring internally: It will most likely be more cost effective to hire from within than to go through a recruiter and incur placement fees, interview expense reimbursements, relocation costs, and so on.

If you hire externally, you hire an individual who possesses the skills you are looking for as well as experience using those skills in several different business cultures. This experience offers more than its face value. Experience saves you time and money while adding value to your team.

Selecting Team Members

Once you are armed with a handful of resumes, we recommend that you schedule a telephone interview to speak with potential candidates before bringing them in. Asking key questions over the phone instantly reveals their communication skills and level of understanding of the subject matter.

Candidates that pass phone screenings should be brought in for face-to-face interviews. Your candidates should be questioned not only by the ETL manager but also by technical developers, as well as by functional analysts. Having candidates meet both functional and technical individuals gives you the ability to gauge how broad their proficiency is. We've had many unpleasant experiences where team members were technically proficient but did not (and could not) grasp the functional picture. Their inability required extra work on the part of other team members to ensure their work actually met the business needs.

You need to be convinced, without a doubt, that all potential members of your team have sufficient knowledge in ETL process design, ample skill in required tool sets, and appropriate aptitude of business processes to comprehend functional requirements. The ability to work collaboratively with the rest of your team is crucial. Be sure to inquire about team dynamics on previous projects during your interviews.

During candidate screening and interviewing, it is essential that you and your recruiters are not only knowledgeable about the role they are seeking to fill but also know the appropriate questions to ask. Figure 10.2 includes an interview questionnaire that provides you with questions you need during the interview process. Using this questionnaire helps ensure your candidate's knowledge is sufficient for the specific role. Answers to the questionnaire are sprinkled throughout the book.

Building and Retaining a Winning ETL Team

Once you have staffed your team, your main responsibility as a manager begins. Retaining a first-rate team is among your biggest challenges. Superstar ETL personnel are in very high demand, and recruiters are not shy about poaching them from right under your nose. We find the best way to keep the majority of ETL developers and architects on our projects is to keep them challenged technically. In our experience, a bored technologist will be a departing one. It is your responsibility to assign projects that keep your team members interested and excited.

The tasks that the ETL developer accomplishes are not trivial. They step up to the plate acknowledging it is their responsibility to transform unorganized, disparate data into cohesive valuable information, an intense, sometimes grueling undertaking. Do not take them for granted. Be attentive of their needs; know what makes them tick and starts their fire. We've

Sample Interview Questionnaire

Analysis
1. What is a logical data mapping and what does it mean to the ETL team?
2. What are the primary goals of the data discovery phase of the data warehouse project?
3. How is the system-of-record determined?

Architecture
4. What are the four basic Data Flow steps of an ETL process?
5. What are the permissible data structures for the data staging area? Briefly describe the pros and cons of each.
6. When should data be set to disk for safekeeping during the ETL?

Extract
7. Describe techniques for extracting from heterogeneous data sources.
8. What is the best approach for handling ERP source data?
9. Explain the pros and cons of communicating with databases natively versus ODBC.
10. Describe three change data capture (CDC) practices and the pros and cons of each.

Data Quality
11. What are the four broad categories of data quality checks? Provide an implementation technique for each.
12. At which stage of the ETL should data be profiled?
13. What are the essential deliverables of the data quality portion of ETL?
14. How can data quality be quantified in the data warehouse?

Building mappings
15. What are surrogate keys? Explain how the surrogate key pipeline works.
16. Why do dates require special treatment during the ETL process?
17. Explain the three basic delivery steps for conformed dimensions.
18. Name the three fundamental fact grains and describe an ETL approach for each.
19. How are bridge tables delivered to classify groups of dimension records associated to a single fact?
20. How does late arriving data affect dimensions and facts? Share techniques for handling each.

Metadata
21. Describe the different types of ETL metadata and provide examples of each.
22. Share acceptable mechanisms for capturing operational metadata.
23. Offer techniques for sharing business and technical metadata.

Optimization/Operations
24. State the primary types of tables found in a data warehouse and the order which they must be loaded to enforce referential integrity.
25. What are the characteristics of the four levels of the ETL support model?
26. What steps do you take to determine the bottleneck of a slow running ETL process?
27. Describe how to estimate the load time of a large ETL job.

Real Time ETL
28. Describe the architecture options for implementing real-time ETL.
29. Explain the different real-time approaches and how they can be applied in different business scenarios.
30. Outline some challenges faced by real-time ETL and describe how to overcome them.

Figure 10.2 Sample interview questionnaire.

worked with some developers that just love to clean data. They find making consistent reliable data from garbage to be rewarding. Others cannot be bothered. They feel that if data is so important, it would be clean in the source; those developers would much rather be challenged with solving nearly impossible SQL puzzles like converting data from tremendously complex data models into simple dimensional ones. Other developers just love to race the clock. If an ETL process should take one week to develop, they work furiously to have it complete in just a few days. Part of your responsibility as manager is to know what kind of developers you have and keep them challenged.

If team members are eager and able to accept more responsibility, give it to them. It's your duty to navigate each individual's desires and try to fulfill them. Also, you need to provide team members with the training they need to ensure they are the best at what they do. If you let your staff stagnate, they will leave the project and move on to a more challenging environment.

An effective approach to keeping in tune with your subordinates needs is to hold weekly status meetings. The ETL environment is a volatile one, and letting more than a week elapse without receiving your team's feedback on progress could be detrimental to the project. These dual-purpose meetings make sure team members are meeting their goals and that you are meeting yours. Give them responsibility, empowering them to make decisions where doing so makes sense. Moreover, you should foster an environment where team members can voice concerns, convey development needs, and so on. They must be able to rely on their ETL manager to take action on rectifying their problems. A well-managed staff is a satisfied one.

Outsourcing the ETL Development

Outsourcing IT responsibilities is a hot topic as we write. Yet the overall numbers are smaller than the talk would suggest. In 2003, of the $119 billion spent in the United States on IT budgets, less than five percent was reportedly vulnerable to outsourcing. In recent reports, some of the hoopla surrounding outsourcing savings is being offset by realizing that over time, managing outsourcing projects involves extra communication, travel to foreign countries, and resetting of expectations and deliverables that did not appear in the original financial savings projections. We are not saying that outsourcing is a bad idea, but we are cautioning that outsourcing is a tricky topic as far as the data warehouse is concerned.

The data warehouse must always respond to the data sources *de jure*, as well as to the changing priorities of management and the end user community. As we have said many times, the data warehouse is not a *project* (with specifications and a final delivery) but is rather a *process* that is on-going. Data warehouse development tasks are iterative and changing. In fact, that is one of the reasons we like the dimensional approach; it is the most resilient architecture for adapting to new surprises and changes in scope.

For these reasons, we are generally negative about outsourcing many of the data warehouse development tasks to remote parties and do not engage in regular contact with the source data suppliers as well as the end users. Remember that the data warehouse is a decision support system judged solely on whether it effectively *supports decisions*.

ETL system development does provide selected opportunities to outsource development tasks, if you have a specific transformation that can be well specified.

Project Plan Guidelines

Now that you have decided on your tool set and staffed your ETL project team, you are ready to dive into the heart of the ETL project plan. In this section, we provide a detailed project plan that any ETL team can utilize.

> 💡 Given the cyclical nature of data warehouse phases, the project plan can, and should, be reused with each phase of your data warehouse project. Consistent use of these guidelines enforces standards and ensures that no steps are forgotten.

Details of each step are explained in the remaining portion of this chapter. High-level steps for managing the ETL process are shown as a project plan in Figure 10.3.

Building the Development Environment

To perform thorough data analysis and begin ETL development of any source system, it is good practice to have the DBA team build a development environment. Use of a separate development environment guarantees that data analysis and ETL development will not affect the production transaction system. Once the environment has been set up, the ETL architect and the DBA team work together to install the appropriate software and tool sets required to perform the analysis and development activities for your team.

Be sure to document the course of actions required and create the development environment during your first phase of the project. Documenting standards from lessons learned minimizes future errors and risk to the added systems during subsequent iterations.

Business Requirements Analysis

Although many of the business rules have been documented through analysis during data-modeling sessions, the ETL architect's is responsibility to take those rules to their completion. Typically, the ETL architect and

Task #	Task Description	Sub Task	Sub Task Description	Role
1	Build Development Environment	1	Set up Hardware Infrastructure	DBA
		2	Install Software / Tool Sets	DBA / ETL Architect
		3	Create Best Practices & Standards Document	ETL Manager / ETL Architect
2	Business Requirements Analysis	1	Review Existing Documentation with Data Modelers	ETL Architect/Systems Analyst
		2	Define & Document ETL Business Rules	ETL Architect/ Systems Analyst
		3	Analyze Source Systems	ETL Architect/Systems Analyst
		4	Define Scope for Phase of Project	ETL Manager
		5	Obtain User Sign-off	ETL Manager
3	Design Logical Data Mapping	1	Review Data Warehouse Data Model	ETL Architect
		2	Review Business Rules	ETL Architect
		3	Analyze Source Systems	ETL Architect
		4	Create Logical Data Mapping Document	ETL Architect
4	Data Quality Strategy	1	Define Data Quality Rules	ETL Manger / Data Quality Specialist
		2	Document Data Defects	ETL Manger / Data Quality Specialist
		3	Determine Data Defect Responsibility	ETL Manger / Data Quality Specialist
		4	Obtain Sign-off for ETL Correction Logic	ETL Manger / Data Quality Specialist
		5	Integrate rules with ETL Logical Data Mapping	ETL Manger / Data Quality Specialist
5	Build Physical ETL Process	1	Review Logical Data Mapping	ETL Developer
		2	Create Simple Dimension Load Processes	ETL Developer
		3	Develop Complex SCD-2 Dimension Processes (History)	ETL Developer
		4	Develop Complex SCD-2 Dimension Processes (Incremental)	ETL Developer
		5	Develop Fact Table Process (History)	ETL Developer
		6	Develop Fact Table Process (Incremental)	ETL Developer
		7	Automate Processes	ETL Developer

Figure 10.3   ETL Project Plan.

6	Test ETL Processes - Unit	1	Create Test Environment	DBA / ETL Architect
	- Quality Assurance (QA)	2	Create Test Plan and Scripts	Systems Analyst
	- User Acceptance (UAT)	3	Load Test Data (Historic & Incremental)	ETL Developer
		4	Execute Unit Test Scripts	Systems Analyst
		5	Validate Data Quality Controls	Systems Analyst
		6	Validate Loaded Data	Systems Analyst
		7	Validate Business Rules	Systems Analyst
		8	Obtain Sign-Off	ETL Manager
7	ETL Deployment	1	Create Production Support Documents	ETL Architect
		2	Create Failure Recover Procedures Document	ETL Architect
		3	Create Production Environment	DBA / ETL Architect
		4	Load Historic Data	ETL Architect
		5	Initiate ETL Scheduler for Incremental Processes	ETL Architect
8	Data Warehouse Maintenance	1	Develop Audit Reports for Known Issues	ETL Architect
		2	Review ETL Logs Regularly to Ensure Consistent/Efficient Loading	ETL Architect

Figure 10.3 Continued.

the systems analyst review all existing documentation and meet with data modelers to discuss questions that arise.

It is critical that the ETL architect and systems analyst have a solid understanding of the source systems and the data inside them. Be sure not to underestimate the time needed to complete this analysis, and keep in mind that the logical data mapping cannot be created until the source systems have been thoroughly analyzed. It is not uncommon for the ETL architect and systems analyst to meet with the data modelers, the source system DBAs, or system analysts for multiple sessions, depending on scope, to review details of the source systems. These sessions will facilitate the findings of business rules that will be used to build the logical data mappings and finally code the ETL process.

Figure 10.4 is a sample template for gathering and documenting business rules and data defects. The spreadsheet is broken out as such to allow the tracking of either data clean up or ETL details or both. We have combined the two into one template because the ETL architect typically has to tackle

Business Rules and Data Defects

No.	Business Rules or Data Defects	Resolution (Source Data Clean-up, ETL, or Both)	Data Clean-up Details	ETL Details	Audit Report/Detail, if Applicable	Report Sent to?
1	Employee Id's must be unique	ETL	N/A - no non-unique Employee Id's found in the source.	ETL process will check for non-unique Employee Id's and if any are found, they will be Employee Id's and if any are found, they will be generated.	Report will include the EMPL_ID, FULL_NAME, HIRE_DATE and DEPARTMENT for both duplicate Employee Id records.	Personnel Systems Team
2	Multiple cases found where do not use flag is set to 'Y' and status is Active	Source Data Clean-up	Source system team must determine if these products should be DNU or active and make the necessary adjustments in the source.	N/A - this can no longer occur, as a result of added business rules.	N/A	N/A
3	E-mail addresses must be unique. However, duplicate e-mail addresses exist in the source system.	ETL and Source Data Clean-up	Source system team must clean-up the duplicate e-mail address and put a business rule in place that will prevent duplicate e-mail addresses from being entered in the source. However, the source system team does not have the resources to implement the necessary business rule at this time.	Given the source system team does not have the resources to implement the business rule at this time, an ETL process must be built to identify duplicates, not load the data into the warehouse and generate a report that will be sent to the appropriate team.	Report will include the EMAIL_ADDRESS, EMPL_ID, FULL_NAME and DEPARTMENT of the duplicate e-mail address.	Systems Administration Team (responsible for assigning e-mail addresses)
4	Multiple cases were found where DEPARTMENT inactive flag is set to 'Y' but their end date is not populated	Source Data Clean-up	Source system team must determine if these departments are truly inactive and if so, enter an end date. A business rule will also be put into place which will require an end date to be populated when the inactive flag is set to 'Y'.	N/A - this can no longer occur, as a result of added business rules.	N/A	N/A
5	Users categorize Products differently then the source system does for reporting. They would like to include these categories in the data warehouse for ease of use when reporting.	ETL	A centralized picklist of products must be established and a business rule must be put in place in the source systems to prevent any non-unique Product ID's from being entered. Due to resource constraints, this enhancement will not be put in place until some time in the future.	Users will provide the the ETL team with a list of Products and their Product Categories. This information will be created in a staging table and loaded into the product dimension in the data warehouse. This will allow the users to easily group their Products into Categories when running reports from the warehouse.	N/A	N/A
6	Product ID's must be unique across departments.	ETL	A centralized picklist of products must be established and a business rule must be put in place in the source systems to prevent any non-unique Product ID's from being entered. Due to resource constraints, this enhancement will not be put in place until some time in the future.	Given the source system team does not have the resources to implement the business rule at this time, an ETL process must be built to identify any non unique Product ID's, prevent them from being loaded into the data warehouse and generate a report that will be sent to the appropriate team.	Report will include the PRODUCT_ID, PRODUCT_DESCRIPTION and DEPARTMENT_NAME	Personnel Systems Team
7						
8						
9						
10						

Figure 10.4 Business rules and data defect tracking spreadsheet.

the business rules and data clean-up transformations simultaneously for a cohesive, integrated solution. It is important that these rules and transformations are thoroughly documented in detail, not only for purposes of coding but also because this document is the foundation of the creation of unit, system, QA, and user acceptance testing test cases. This metadata is also used for end user training and procedures documents.

In theory, emphasis is always placed on documentation. Unfortunately, in reality it is common for project teams to start off with good intentions by creating the documentation, but they rarely go back and update the documents as things change. Do not fall into this trap. Keeping documentation up to date is crucial to the success of your project. Up-to-date documentation is mandatory to perform detailed impact analysis of future enhancements and subsequent phases of your project. Moreover, current documentation ensures that you have a handle on the data lineage of your warehouse. Maintaining your documentation may require time and effort, but consider the alternative: going back and trying to figure out what has changed within ETL processes, business rules, or data after the fact. It doesn't take a lot of imagination to visualize the wasted time, increased costs, and pure frustration that can be avoided by planning ahead and updating your documentation as modifications to your ETL processes are made.

Defining the Scope of the ETL project

Defining scope includes determining and documenting what will be included for each phase of the ETL process as it relates to subject areas, business rules, transformation, and data-cleansing strategies. It can also, and usually does, indicate what is not included in the phase. Documenting the scope of each phase and requiring business users to review and sign-off the scope documents aids in your management and prevents scope-creep.

Be realistic when defining each phase. Although your users expect you to fulfill your commitment, they will most likely make many changes and additions throughout the lifecycle of the phase. Changes to scope must be negotiated and prioritized, leaving low-priority changes for future phases. Keep potential scope-creep items on your radar when finalizing the scope documentation.

After business rules have been documented and scope has been defined, have a user-walkthrough of the documentation and obtain sign-off by the business users. Techniques for managing scope are discussed in the "Managing Scope" section of this chapter.

Designing the Logical Data Map

To help facilitate the design of the logical data map, the ETL architect must review the data warehouse data model and all business-rules documentation. Additional meetings may be needed to get answers for any remaining open questions and/or issues. If the existing business rules gathered during the business-requirements-analysis phase do not provide enough detail, the ETL architect needs to analyze the source systems manually. Once all questions and issues are resolved, the ETL architect creates the logical data-mapping document.

CROSS-REFERENCE Chapter 3 contains the exact details involved in creating the logical data map.

Defining a Data Quality Strategy

Other than being query friendly, the chief acceptance factor of any data warehouse is that the data is consistent and reliable. Therefore, conducting a data-quality assessment and defining a strategy is a vital part of the ETL process.

The ETL manager and the data-quality specialist are jointly responsible for defining data-quality rules. They are tasked with analyzing the quality of the source system data and documenting all identified data defects. This exercise not only ensures that the cleanest possible data is entering your data warehouse; it also benefits the source system from a data-quality perspective. This analysis exposes flaws in the source system applications and gives source system administrators the opportunity to make corrections to their application to prevent future data defects.

Options for cleaning data usually fall into two categories:

- Cleanse data at the source.
- Transform data in the ETL.

Cleansing data at the source is the most desirable and beneficial option. Unfortunately, it may be neither feasible, due to resource constraints, nor timely, due to the transaction application development lifecycle complexity and schedule. Additionally, data cleanup usually involves political navigation to settle on appropriate data defect correction activities.

After all details and deadlines are committed and agreed upon, document the details of each data-cleanup issue and associated cleanup resolution. Creating a project plan to track the issues to be cleansed in the source systems as well those to be cleansed by the ETL process will help you manage user expectations regarding data defects.

We recommend setting up weekly meetings with the administrators responsible for source system data cleanup. Use these meetings to review and update the project plan to accurately reflect progress and discuss any new findings. These meetings will determine the feasibility of cleanup and will provide a forum to agree on a strategy for cleaning up new findings. Be sure to stay on top of progress made to source-data cleansing, as your data warehouse is depending on source data being clean. It is a good idea to make the extra effort to query the source database to ensure the cleanup effort was successful.

> 💡 Although data is being cleansed in the source system, the source system owners may not have the ability to add business rules to prevent data from becoming dirty again. Therefore, it is a good idea for the systems analyst and ETL architect to meet to determine whether ETL code is necessary to prevent dirty data from entering the data warehouse. ETL code can either kick out or transform dirty data, depending on the business rules.

If ETL code is used as a preventative measure, whether through exclusion or transformation, it is a good idea to define audit reports for the ETL processes to capture and report dirty data. Such reports aid in the continual cleanup of the source data and provide a mechanism to tie the corrected data in the data warehouse back to its source. This metadata also serves as an audit trail that provides the ability to trace a data discrepancy to its place of origin, identifying the data owner responsible for its cleanup. Be sure to obtain user sign-off on the business rules and data cleanup logic being handled by the ETL.

Building the Physical ETL Process

Once the data analysis is complete and the business rules and logical data mappings are final, the ETL architect walks through the logical data mapping with the assigned ETL developer. This walkthrough ensures that the ETL developer understands the complete requirements before he or she begins coding. The ETL developer is responsible for forward engineering the logical data mapping into physical ETL routines. Whether SQL scripts are written or a dedicated ETL tool is used, the routines must be developed and tested and the resulting data must be validated by the developer before they are turned over to the ETL architect for migration.

When several routines are given to the developer at once, which is usually the case, an *ETL build sequence document* is usually prepared by the ETL architect for the developer to use as a guide. Shown in Figure 10.5, the document contains a listing of the expected tables to be loaded, the ordinal position to build the processes, and comments as to what challenges should be expected in the routine. This document is especially important during the first phase of the project or for developers new to your team.

Table Name	ETL JOB BUILD SEQUENCE	Comments
d_SHIP_TERM_FLAG	1	Straight load from flat file
d_DATE	1	Straight load from flat file
d_DEPARTMENT	2	Straight load From database table. Some constraints
d_PRODUCT_TYPE	3	Fairly straight load From database table. Need to select distinct
d_VENDOR	3	Fairly straight load From database table. Need to select distinct
d_CURRENCY	4	Some table joining, pretty straight forward.
d_ORDER_TERM_FLAG	4	Load Result of UNIONED selects.
d_REGION	4	Some table joining, pretty straight forward.
d_OFFICE	5	Some Validation Checking. Data comes from 2 different Sources
d_STORE	5	Fairly straight load From database table. Some Look-ups from Staging Table
d_SHIP_TYPE	5	Some constraints and substrings, pretty straight forward.
d_CLIENT	6	Very Complex Slowly Changing Dimension Logic
f_CLIENT_ORDER_TRANSACTION	7	Fact table load, Pretty straight forward but typically done after dims are complete
f_CLIENT_MONTHLY_SNAPSHOT	7	Fact table load. Pretty straight forward but typically done after dims are complete

Figure 10.5 ETL build sequence document.

Testing the ETL Processes

Most systems' lifecycle methodologies include three phases of testing. During your ETL, it is recommended that you follow the three-phase approach when going live with new source systems, subject areas, or any major release. Following are the three types of testing that should be conducted with each phase of your ETL project.

- **Unit Testing.** This testing occurs during and after development before going to QA testing. This testing is performed by the ETL developer and the systems analyst in the development environment.
- **Quality Assurance Testing (QA).** This is the testing that typically occurs by a separate group within your organization in a separate environment mirroring production. The environment is created and controlled by the DBA and QA team members. This environment will be used to ensure all ETL processes are performing as expected,

meeting all business rules and timeframe (load window) requirements. Given that it simulates the production environment, the QA group can validate that the ETL processes will work in production.

■ **User Acceptance Testing (UAT).** This phase typically occurs by your user group in a separate controlled environment created from the QA environment. This database is controlled by the DBA team members. In smaller organizations, after QA testing is complete, it is acceptable to open the environment to users for user-acceptance testing, reducing the cost of infrastructure maintenance and hardware. UAT is the testing phase that benefits the team by letting users have a hands-on look at the data to ensure processes are running as expected. At the end of UAT, obtain sign-off from your users. Once sign-off is received, you are ready to move to production.

We've been on projects where the user-acceptance testing phase is bypassed for small build releases and bug fixes, going directly from quality-assurance testing to production. In these cases, users inevitably detect issues after code has been pushed into production. Excluding the user-acceptance testing phase is a short cut that prevents you from discovering issues that only a user might find before it is too late: in production.

When testing new ETL processes, be sure to have users test for known data issues and source system anomalies. Not only will this validate your efforts; exposure to the clean data will excite your users and make them eager to use the new data warehouse. Clean data tends to have some positive effects. Users will enthusiastically spread the word of the success of the ETL and data warehouse project, causing other subject areas to flock to the data warehouse project manager begging to be next in line for their data to be transformed and loaded into the data warehouse.

Developing Test Cases

While ETL development is taking place, using the business rules and data defects document, the systems analyst and ETL architect are jointly responsible for developing detailed test plans for unit testing, QA testing, and UAT.

Test plans should include cases that test all business-rule scenarios. Validating test results against expected results ensures that the ETL code is correct and the transformations are working as designed. Your test cases should deliberately try to load poor data into the data warehouse. The ETL process should either prevent data from entering or transform data and load it. In either case, an audit report should be generated. Even when poor data is not intentionally loaded, be sure to include queries that test data quality in the data warehouse to ensure that data-cleansing transformations are working as expected.

Most likely, issues will be identified during the validation of the test cases. Some of these issues may be bugs discovered in your code, and some may be fresh ideas triggered by the users' exposure to their data in a format that is new to them. It's not uncommon to receive user requests for new requirements during this phase that may need to be added as enhancements. Be careful: Data is not the only thing being tested here. Managing the initial ETL processes is a task in itself; add on bug fixes, additional requests, and ever-changing business rules and the process can become completely unmanageable. In-depth change management techniques are detailed in the "Managing Scope" section of this chapter.

A sample test case template is illustrated in Figure 10.6. It is intended to capture the requirements you are testing; the detailed steps to perform the test; the expected results; and the status of the test: pass or fail. Sample test cases are given to display the level of detail you should capture. This template should be used for all three phases of the testing process.

ETL Deployment

Next comes the moment you have all been waiting for: ETL deployment. To make the migration to production as seamless as possible, be sure to create production support documents. These documents should include following information:

- The final lineage report
- Procedures for running (and restarting) the incremental load process
- Details about the automated load schedule

It is important to create and deliver documented failure recovery procedures. Should a load process fail, users could have access to bad data or data that is not up to date. A plan must be in place to avoid this before the production environment is unleashed to users. Document and test your failure recovery procedures, so that when failures occur, you can quickly recover data and make it available for your users in a timely manner.

Work with the DBA team to create a stable production environment. Load your historical data and kick off the ETL incremental load processes with your production scheduler. Be sure to run tests on data in production (historical and incremental) to ensure data was successfully loaded.

Test Case Template

No.	Test Subject	Step	Test Detail	Dependencies	Pass /Fail	Expected Results	Comments
1	Validate that new products entered in the transaction system are successfully being loaded into the warehouse via the incremental load.		A new product and detail will be entered and saved in the source system. The incremental load will run. The QA instance of the warehouse will be queried and results will be validated.	Test results are dependent on a successful incremental load.		Product ID 89076 and it's detail are displayed in the warehouse exactly as they were entered in the transaction system.	
		a	Log on to the QA instance of your source system.				
		b	Add a new product id of 89076 and detail of your choice to the transaction system (noting values you enter in the expected results field for test validation).				
		c	Save the new product record.				
		d	Contact the ETL Manger/DBA to request that the incremental load be run.				
		e	Log into the query tool to access the data in the warehouse.				
		f	Run the following query: Select * from d_Product where Product_Id = 89076			Product ID 89076 and it's detail are displayed in the warehouse exactly as they were entered in the transaction system.	
		g	Validate that the query results match exactly what was entered in the transaction system.			Query results match what was entered in the transaction system.	
2	Validate Duplicate Product Id's do not enter the warehouse via the incremental load and that a report is automatically generated by the incremental load.		A duplicate Product Id and detail will be entered and saved in the source system. The incremental load will run. The QA instance of the warehouse will be queried and results will be validated.	Test results are dependent on a successful incremental load.		Only one record exists for Product Id 89076 and a report is automatically generated, indicating the duplicate entry for clean up in the source transaction system.	Although duplicate Product Id's were cleansed in the source system, they did not have the resources to put the business rules in place to prevent duplicates from entering until a future release. Therefore, ETL code was written to prevent duplicate Product Id's from entering the warehouse and automatically generate a report indicating the duplicate records.
		a	Log on to the QA instance of your source system.				
		b	Add a new product id of 89076 and detail of your choice to the transaction system.				
		c	Save the new product record.				
		d	Contact the ETL Manger/DBA to request that the incremental load be run.				
		e	Log into the query tool to access the data in the warehouse.				
		f	Run the following query: Select * from d_Product where Product_Id = 89076			1 row is returned	
		g	Validate that only one Product Id of 89076 exists in the warehouse.				
		h	Validate a report indicating the duplicate Product Id is automatically generated.			Only one record exists for Product Id 89076 and a report is automatically generated, indicating the duplicate entry for clean up in the source transaction system.	

Figure 10.6 Test case template.

Maintaining the Data Warehouse (ETL)

Depending on how your organization is structured, the data warehouse project manager and DBA team are typically responsible for the ongoing maintenance of the data warehouse. However, you are the owner of the ETL process, and unless other arrangements have been made, its ongoing maintenance is your responsibility.

After you go *live* in production, it is important to continuously monitor your data warehouse for known content issues. Part of this maintenance includes the development of audit reports that will capture known issues. These audit reports should stem from the business rules and data defects document. The reports can automatically be sent to the appropriate contact personnel for action via e-mail.

Patches and upgrades are inevitable in any production IT environment. Such patches and upgrades are especially relevant in the data warehouse environment, where so many distinct tool sets are integrated for a single solution. Be diligent in applying patches and upgrades as necessary. It is recommended that you schedule regular system maintenance and perform these upgrades during this time. All patches and upgrades must go through the full development lifecycle, including unit testing in the development environment, QA testing, and user-acceptance testing. Passing the patches and upgrades through testing ensures that maintenance was performed correctly and that all processes are running as expected.

Keep your users abreast of new releases or enhancements as they are being rolled out to production. That communication helps users prepare for changes as they enter the data warehouse. Your users could be waiting for a specific release or enhancement. Giving them a heads up on the time frame of scheduled releases will boost their experience with the data warehouse.

Managing Scope

It won't be far into the project when you realize why defining scope and obtaining sign-off is so important. It's easy to lose control when you are trying to tackle the overwhelming bombardment of change requests.

Unmanaged ad-hoc changes to the ETL specifications can be detrimental to the success of the project. It is common to receive additional requirements during the development and testing phases. Issues will certainly be found and new ideas will most likely surface, all of which need to be implemented *immediately*. In our experience, when the data warehouse is unveiled, new wish lists and requirements excitedly begin to trickle in, picking up momentum exponentially as more subject areas are deployed. Before you know it, you will be bombarded with more work than you and your team can handle. Did someone say scope-creep? Creating a mechanism for tracking and managing these changes is crucial to your success. The next section provides the documents you need to track changes and recommends procedures that help you execute them.

Change Tracking

Implementing a process to track enhancement requests, bug fixes, or changes to the initially agreed scope is essential to your success as the ETL manager. Following is a list of elements that have proven to be significant while capturing and tracking change requests. You will want the ability to track and manage the following information even if it means creating a simple spreadsheet to do it. Capturing the following elements aids in the management of changes and helps minimize scope-creep.

> A system could easily be built in Microsoft Access or any small personal database application for this purpose. For larger groups, you can implement a small Visual Basic application or can leverage packaged systems that your organization has already invested in. And, of course, a good ETL tool may provide this capability.

- **Subject Area.** This is the name of the data mart (portion of the data warehouse) the request is being submitted for.
- **Request Date.** The date the request originates
- **Change Description.** This should capture a high-level description of the request.
- **Priority.** High, Medium, or Low. This is a negotiated rating of the importance of the request.
- **Change Type.** Indicates whether the request is for a new requirement or a change to an existing process
- **Status.** Status values can include anything that identifies the state of the request. Values we've used include New request, Developer investigating, Developer developing, More information needed, Cancelled, Passed unit testing, Passed QA, Passed UAT, Ready for production, and so on. The values in this field change throughout the life of the request.
- **Submitter.** The name of the person submitting the change request
- **Owner.** Indicates the person responsible for the request at a specific time. It usually begins with the data warehouse or ETL manager and then gets assigned to the appropriate developer, tester, or so on throughout the life of the request.
- **Version Found in.** This is the active version number at the time the bug is detected or the request is submitted.

- **Version Fixed in.** This is the number of the version that the request is packaged with when released to production.
- **State.** Open or Closed. Closed should be selected only when the Status is set to Released to production or Cancelled.
- **Date Closed.** This field should be populated at the time the state field is set to Closed.
- **Functional Description.** The information provided here should describe the user's experience prompting the request.
- **Technical Description.** The information provided here is usually filled in by power users or the ETL architect. It is used by the developer for coding the change or new requirement.

Having the ability to generate reports using the elements from this list is advantageous. If you have the resources to develop this as an IT system, consult with your team to get their input on the process, making sure the process meets the needs of everyone on your team.

However, minimizing changes to the production data warehouse environment is a good practice, if you can achieve it. Keep in mind, the more changes made, the greater the risk of affecting other processes. We recommend holding regularly scheduled meetings with appropriate team members to discuss the priority of each request. It is important that you make your users realize how critical it is to minimize changes to production. Make sure they understand the cost and effort it takes to fulfill each request. Have them ask themselves the following questions: What is their return on investment? Are the benefits of the changes worth making? Can they justify the change requests?

Once it is agreed that a change should be made, you must discuss the impact of the change. If the change affects another ETL process or another area, a detailed impact analysis must occur. Proposed changes can result in multiple new changes to existing ETL processes. Be sure to add these changes to your new tracking system.

A sample change/enhancement requisition form is shown in Figure 10.7. This form includes all of the necessary information you need to enter a new request and perform development to complete the request. This form, in conjunction with your change-request tracking system, supports effective management of the change-request process.

Scheduling Version Releases

Typically, a number of changes, enhancement requests, patches, and upgrades are bundled together as a single build or release. Each release must go through the full development lifecycle. Before going to production, be

---

Change/Enhancement Requisition

Subject Area: _____   Request Date: _____

Change Description: _____

_____

Priority: _____   Change Type: _____

(indicate if this is a new requirement or a
change to an existing requirement)

Submitter: _____   Owner: _____

Version found in: _____

Functional Description (attachments):

Technical Description (attachments):

All fields are required

Figure 10.7   Change/enhancement requisition form.

sure to unit, QA, and UAT test your changes. After the changes have passed the testing cycles, either the ETL architect migrates the routines or the DBA team pushes the code to production.

Tracking versions of your data warehouse is beneficial for troubleshooting problems discovered in production. Use the tracking mechanisms outlined earlier in this chapter to maintain control over your version releases. Normally, following standard-versioning techniques works well in the data warehouse/ETL environment. It is especially important for the ETL manager to adhere to this standard because much of the data warehouse code releases to production are created and deployed by the ETL team.

The version number consists of a series of three decimal delimited numbers (##.##.##). The first set of numbers signifies major releases; the second, minor releases; and the third, patches. For example, Version 1.2.1 means the data warehouse is in its first version and there have been two minor releases and one patch applied to it.

In the data warehouse environment, a *major version release* typically constitutes a new subject area or data mart that includes new facts, dimensions, and ETL processes. A *minor release* is defined as primarily ETL modifications, possibly including some minor structural database changes. *Patches* are usually a result of a *hot fix*, where a mission-critical error has been detected in the production environment and needs to be corrected immediately. If patches are bundled with minor changes or minor changes with a major, only the leftmost number in the series should be incremented and the right-hand numbers are reset. For example, if version 1.2.1 is in production and you have two patches, a minor change, and a major release scheduled for migration, bundling these changes would be considered a single major release. In this case, you would now be at release 2.0.0.

It is good practice to bundle and schedule major releases with enough time between to address hot fixes. With scheduled major releases, perhaps monthly, it is easier to bundle minor fixes into the controlled release environment to minimize code migrations.

Our recommended data warehouse versioning strategy is especially powerful when your project is using the data warehouse bus architecture. In such a case, each data mart in the bus matrix will be a major version release as it enters the physical data warehouse. If your data warehouse is at version 1.0.210, you are most likely not using this matrix and probably not sleeping at night, either.

Summary

In this chapter, we have finally stepped back a little from the myriad tasks of the ETL team to try to paint a picture of who the players are and what are they supposed to think about. We must keep in mind that this chapter and really the whole book are deliberately limited to the back-room concerns of the enterprise data warehouse.

We began by describing the planning and leadership challenges faced by the ETL team; then we descended into the specific tasks that these people face. In many cases, much more detail is provided in the main text of the book.

Real Time Streaming ETL Systems

CHAPTER 11

Real-Time ETL Systems

Building a real-time data warehouse ETL solution demands classifying some often slippery business objectives, understanding a diverse set of technologies, having an awareness of some pragmatic approaches that have been successfully employed by others, and developing engineering flexibility and creativity. This field remains young, with new technologies, emergent methodologies, and new vocabularies. Clearly, this situation can be a recipe for trouble, but real-time data warehousing also offers early adopters great potential to gain a competitive advantage—an intriguing risk versus reward trade-off. This chapter proposes a four-step process to guide the experienced data warehousing professional through the selection of an appropriate real-time ETL technical architecture and methodology:

1. This chapter examines the historical and business contexts of the state of the art real-time data warehouse—providing some *How did we get here*? and *Where are we going*? background.

2. Next, it describes a method for classifying your organization's real-time requirements in a manner that is most useful for selecting design solutions later.

3. The heart of the chapter is an appraisal of several mechanisms for delivering real-time reporting and integration services, the technologies most appropriate for each approach, and their strengths and weaknesses.

4. And finally, a decision matrix is presented; it uses the requirements classifications and approaches previously described, and it guides

the ETL team through the selection of a technical approach and methodology.

💡 It must be stated that this material falls short of a *recipe* for building a real-time ETL solution; as of this writing, such recipes do not exist. As this new technology becomes more popular, you are bound to come up against requirements for which solutions have not yet been perfected. Apply your creativity and the know-how you have gleaned from personal experience in fashioning a solution most appropriate for the specific challenges you face. By doing this, you are doing your part to help advance the progress of real-time data warehousing.

PROCESS CHECK

- Planning & Design: This chapter touches every aspect of the ETL system planning and design. We intend this chapter to be read as an *increment* to all the ideas developed in Chapters 1 through 10.

- Data Flow: Parts or all of the techniques in this chapter can be added to an existing ETL system framework. But as we emphasize, the conversion from batch-oriented ETL to streaming ETL is a profound end-to-end change.

Why Real-Time ETL?

Not very long ago, engineers vehemently defended the notion that the data warehouse needed to provide an unwavering set of data to business decision makers, providing a reliable information *floor* upon which to stand. For up-to-the-moment reporting against a *twinkling* database, business users were directed to the production applications that run the business. Therefore, users had to go to the data warehouse for a historical picture of what happened in the business as of yesterday and had to look across many OLTP systems for a picture of what was happening today. Business users never fully accepted this divide. Why could they not go to one place to get the business information that they needed?

Well, much has changed, and the data warehouse has now become a victim of its own success. Although the delay between a business transaction and its appearance in the data warehouse is typically less than 24 hours, for many organizations in fast-moving vertical industries, this delay is too much. The data warehouse has become mission critical, too, feeding enriched information back to operational systems that is then used to process transactions, personalize offers, and present up-sell promotions. The push for ever-fresher information is on.

Several other important factors have conspired to force data warehouse practitioners to rethink some earlier positions:

- **Customer relationship management (CRM).** Modern CRM demands a contemporary, consistent, and complete image of the customer available to all operational systems that directly or indirectly serve the customer—quite a tall order. Despite the marketing claims of leading packaged CRM vendors, this capability cannot be purchased off the shelf; unless all customer-facing systems are retired by the packaged CRM suite, businesses also need to integrate real-time customer information across all of their legacy transactional stovepipe applications. Data warehouses, of course, absolutely need constant customer information streams from operations, but increasingly, operational systems rely on data warehouse enrichment of customer information, too. Therefore, it is predictable that organizations have begun to explore architectural alternatives that can support more generalized integration scenarios—moving operational data between applications and simultaneously into and out of the warehouse—with ever-increasing urgency.

- **The zero-latency enterprise business ideal**. This ideal exhorts the benefits of speed and a single version of the truth. In a real-time, zero-latency enterprise, information is delivered to the right place at the right time for maximum business value. Some people call these *right-time* systems. Just-in-time inventory and supply chains and assemble-to-order/mass customization business models also amplify the need for absolutely current and pervasive information throughout the organization. At present, true zero latency is an unattainable ideal—it takes some time to synchronize information across several production systems and data marts—but the pressure on many modern data warehouses to provide a low-latency view of the health of the business is very real.

- **Globalization and the Web.** Finally, and perhaps most pragmatically, the combined effects of globalization and the Web, which demand round-the-clock operations and access to the data warehouse, in concert with requirements to warehouse ever-broader and deeper sets of data, have severely compressed the time window available to load the data warehouse. The amount of data needing to be warehoused continues to expand, while the window of *business downtime* continues to shrink, challenging the already overworked and under-loved data warehouse's ETL team. Wouldn't it be easier if you could somehow *trickle feed* your data warehouses throughout the day, rather than trying to shoehorn expanding data loads into shrinking windows of acceptable downtime?

These factors have conspired to drive the data warehouse to an increasingly real-time posture.

Defining Real-Time ETL

Real-time ETL is a misnomer for a category of data warehousing services that is neither true real-time nor, in many cases, ETL. Instead, the term refers to software that moves data asynchronously into a data warehouse with some urgency—within minutes of the execution of the business transaction. In many cases, delivering real-time data warehousing demands an approach quite different from the ETL methods used in batch-oriented data warehousing. Simply running conventional ETL batches on an ever-more frequent schedule throughout the day might not be practical, either to the OLTP systems or to the data warehouse. Conversely, including the data warehouse in the OLTP system's transaction commit logic cannot work either. The OLTP system does not have the luxury of waiting for the data warehouse loading transaction to *commit* before it proceeds with its next transaction, nor is any locking or two-phase commit logic practical across systems with different structures and different levels of granularity. Instead, you aspire simply to move the new transactions into a special *real-time partition* (defined later in this chapter) of the data warehouse within some timeframe acceptable to the business, providing analytic support for day-to-day operational decisions. For the time being, this procedure is our practical definition of real-time ETL.

💡 **This chapter explores some pragmatic approaches to achieving these objectives, using mainstream toolsets familiar to data warehousing engineers. However, real-time data warehousing is a young field, rife with all manner of software-vendor claims and higher risk. The approaches to real-time ETL explored in this chapter attempt to minimize risk through managed expectations and emphasis on mature approaches and execution strategies rather than groundbreaking tool selection. This chapter presents approaches that address the objective of achieving a few minutes latency between business transactions and their availability in the data warehouse.**

Challenges and Opportunities of Real-Time Data Warehousing

Real-time data warehousing presents a number of unique challenges and opportunities to the ETL engineer. From a technical architecture perspective, it has the potential to change the big-bang approach needed during the nightly batch ETL load windows to a continuous ETL-like flow throughout the day. System-availability requirements may escalate as the business comes to rely on low-latency availability of business transactions in the data warehouse. If the organization opts for the real-time dimension manager approaches described in this chapter, availability becomes a strategic advantage.

From a data architecture perspective, real-time data warehousing challenges the posture of the data warehouse as system of discrete periodic measurements—a provider of business *snapshots*—advocating instead a system of more comprehensive and continuous temporal information. This shift happens subtly if, for example, the frequency of fact loading increases from once per day to every 15 minutes, but more dramatically if the loading of facts and dimension records occurs continuously. The data warehouse might then capture a record of the business transactions and their dimensional context at all points in time. Slowly changing dimensions become rapidly changing dimensions, and the data warehouse's bearing becomes more operational in nature. In fact, should the real-time data warehouse also support real-time dimension conforming and synchronization, it then evolves into a logical extension of the operational systems themselves.

Real-Time Data Warehousing Review

The real-time approach to data warehousing can trace a clear lineage to what was originally called the ODS. The motivations of the original ODSs were similar to modern real-time data warehouses, but the implementation of real-time data warehouses reflects a new generation of hardware, software, and techniques. The following sections develop these ideas in more detail.

Generation 1—The Operational Data Store

The operational data store, or ODS, is a first-generation data warehousing construct intended to support lower-latency reporting through creation of a distinct architectural construct and application separate from the data warehouse. The ODS is half operational and half decision-support system, attempting to strike a balance between the need to simultaneously support frequent updates and frequent queries. Early ODS architectures depicted it as a place where data was integrated and fed to a downstream data warehouse, thus acting as a kind of extension to the data warehouse ETL layer. Later architectures depict it as a consumer of integrated data from the data warehouse ETL layer and categorize it as a Type 1 through 4 and *internal or external* ODS, depending on where within the overall architecture it resides and the urgency with which it must load data from the operational world.

In practice, the ODS has become a catch-all architectural component for data staging, data cleansing, and preparation, as well as operational reporting. By virtue of all these different roles, it is a compromise solution to each of these challenges. A simpler and less compromising alternative exists.

Generation 2—The Real-Time Partition

The use of the real-time logical and physical partition, as originally described by Ralph Kimball, is a pragmatic solution available for delivering real-time analytics from a data warehouse. Using this approach, a separate real-time fact table is created whose grain and dimensionality matches that of the corresponding fact table in the static (nightly loaded) data warehouse. This real-time fact table contains only the current day's facts (those not yet loaded into the static data warehouse table).

Figure 11.1 shows two star schemas associated with a real-time and static retail point-of-sale fact tables, sharing a common set of dimensions.

Each night, the contents of the real-time partition table are written to the static fact table, and the real-time partition is then purged, ready to receive the next day's transactions. Figure 11.2 gives an idea of how the process

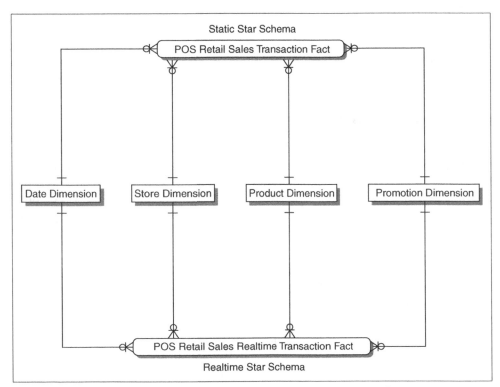

Figure 11.1 The relationship between the static and real-time star schemas.

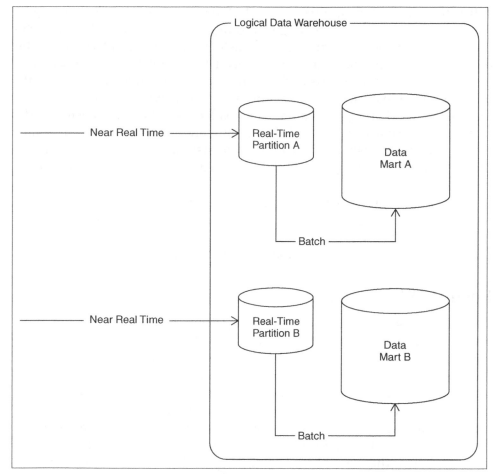

Figure 11.2   The logical relationship of the real-time partition to its data mart.

works. In essence, this approach brings the real-time reporting benefits of the ODS into the data warehouse itself, eliminating much ODS architectural overhead in the process.

Facts are *trickled in* to the real-time fact table(s) throughout the day, and user queries against the real-time table are neither halted nor interrupted by this loading process. Indexing on the real-time fact table is minimal, or nonexistent, to minimize the data-loading effort and its impact on query response times. Performance is achieved by restricting the amount of data in the table (one day only) and by caching the entire real-time fact table in memory. Optionally, a view can be created that combines (Unions) facts in both the real-time and static fact table, providing a virtual star schema to simplify queries that demand views of historical measures that extend to the moment.

If fact records alone are trickle-fed to the real-time partition, some policy is needed to deal with changes to dimensions that occur between the nightly bulk loads. For example, new customer records created during the day for which you have facts might need to be defaulted to a series of generic *new customer* records in the customer dimension to be updated into more descriptive customer records in the evening, when a complete batch load of new and changed customers is loaded into the static customer dimension. Alternatively, the real-time data warehouse can opt to maintain more frequent snapshots of changing dimensional images or to abandon the point-in-time concept altogether and instead capture all dimensional changes that occur.

Later, this chapter describes some of the issues associated with selecting an appropriate policy for dealing with dimensional changes, some pragmatic approaches to trickling data into real-time partition(s) throughout the business day, and the pros and cons of these approaches.

Recent CRM Trends

CRM demands a complete understanding of the organization's history with each customer across all customer *touch points* and insight into the challenges and priorities that the customer faces in their markets. In the past few years, packaged CRM systems have been widely adopted by businesses to support the first of these goals, unifying the simplest and most common customer touch points of the organization. However, while these systems represent an important advance for organizations that had fragmented customer support systems (or no systems support at all), they are not comprehensive. Often, there are older and more specialized systems that support customer interactions that fall outside of the packaged CRM system. These transactions never find their way back to the packaged CRM system. Also, packaged CRM systems typically fall short of equipping the organization with the customer knowledge it needs to be perceived as an intelligent collaborator and partner by its customers because they lack any mechanism for collecting, harvesting, and synchronizing customer and marketplace intelligence across the enterprise. The further splintering of the packaged CRM marketplace into Operational CRM versus Analytic CRM amplifies this divide. Businesses don't have *operational* or *analytic* customers; the same patron must be intelligently served by both operational and decision support systems, working together.

What is needed is a way to bring together with great urgency all of the data about the organization's past and present interactions with the customer, combined with external marketplace information, some mechanism to convert data into customer intelligence, and a means to share this with everyone in the organization. Bringing such things together represents a melding of data warehouse technologies and application integration technologies.

💡 **CRM vendors are keenly aware of the challenges facing organizations, so some are *bolting on* Business Intelligence capabilities to their operational CRM suites. Too often, the result is rudimentary, simplistic, and difficult to architecturally defend, ultimately failing to provide a differentiating competitive capability.**

Generation 2 CRM as we define it in this chapter is not an application that can be purchased and installed; rather, it demands a comprehensive data warehouse of all customer touch points, intelligently selected and utilized marketplace data, a continuous harvesting of customer intelligence from the data warehouse, and a mechanism for sharing and continuously synchronizing customer information across the enterprise. The task of providing such capabilities seems to be landing right in the backyard of the contemporary ETL architect.

The Strategic Role of the Dimension Manager

The glue that binds logically and/or physically separate subject areas (data marts) together in the dimensional data warehouse bus architecture is conformance of dimensions and facts, achieved through the use of dimension manager systems as described in this chapter. Traditionally, the dimension manager has been viewed as a role whose job is the definition, maintenance, and publication of a particular conformed dimension to all data marts that interoperate within the data warehouse bus architecture.

Ultimately, the real-time data warehouse plays a role in the larger objective of providing ready access to the most current and insightful data to all users throughout the enterprise. In addition, to quickly deliver fact records to the data warehouse, tremendous competitive advantage might be found in providing real-time synchronization of key dimensions such as customer or product across all operational systems in the organization. This information-synchronization function can be considered a logical extension of the dimension manager role and is an effective and consistent mechanism for closing the loop between the operational world and that of the data warehouse by providing a means of distribution of data warehouse-derived segmentations and other enrichment information to the operational world.

The customer dimension manager in a strategic real-time data warehouse might not only trickle-feed all data marts with new conformed customer information, but might also cooperate with some mechanism for synchronizing customer information across all interested (subscribing) operational systems. This real-time customer information should include customer intelligence generated by the data warehouse itself.

Clearly, these are ambitious objectives, and as of this writing, no packaged solutions or end-to-end toolsets dramatically simplify the process of building a bidirectional enterprise application integration (EAI)/real-time data warehouse solution. Nonetheless, such systems have been created; the basic building blocks for these systems exist and are getting more mature. The potential for business differentiation provided by such a system is striking, so it is likely that today's early adopters will enjoy marketplace advantages that drive more widespread adoption of such systems in the future. Consider building systems today that, at a minimum, do not impede the organization's ability to evolve to a real-time EAI/data warehousing solution in the future. Organizations under competitive pressures or seeking marketplace differentiation through customer intimacy might need to take the leap now.

Categorizing the Requirement

Clearly, this topic offers a lot to consider from an architectural perspective. Given the rather complex set of strengths and weaknesses associated with the mainstream alternatives for real-time data warehousing, it is important to nail down the scope of your real-time requirements.

Presented in the sections that follow are some litmus test questions that, once answered, help you categorize the set of real-time capabilities needed by your organization and select mainstream methodologies and toolsets appropriate for the task at hand. A matrix appears near the end of the chapter that summarizes this discussion and guides the ETL team in approach and architecture selection.

Data Freshness and Historical Needs

The developmental costs and complexity for reducing latency between OLTP and the data warehouse obey the law of diminishing returns, lowering latency increases complexity and cost in a nonlinear fashion. Therefore, you need to set realistic goals and expectations about the *freshness* of the data needed in the warehouse.

You also need a complete understanding of the set of hard business requirements that cannot be met either through conventional daily data warehouse publication or transactional reports from OLTP systems. Watch for the following red flags as you consider the needs of your would-be real-time data warehouse:

- **Less than five minutes of latency.** Reports with latency this low, as of this writing, cannot be reliably met through mainstream real-time data warehousing. This window of time shrinks continuously, but it always takes some nontrivial amount of processing and time to move, transform, and load information from the OLTP systems to the real-time partition. Organizations that absolutely must have information more than five-minutes fresh should consider running their reports directly against the operational system(s).

  > Enterprise Information Integration (EII) applications do not suffer this latency limitation and can deliver nearly up-to-the-second reports directly from the operational systems. However, they have other characteristics and limitations that must be considered. EII systems and these limitations are discussed later in this chapter.

- **Single data source requirements demanding little or no history**. These reports require none of the integrated and historical data features provided by the data warehouse and are best addressed through the operational system itself. Happily, they should present a very small reporting footprint on the OLTP systems and should not degrade transactional performance significantly. If Web-enabled, these reports can be presented through the business intelligence portal, and they then *feel* to the user community as if they are data-warehouse based.

- **Reports with an entirely different audience from that of the existing data warehouse.** These reports might demand new reporting vocabularies and mechanisms for dissemination, factors that can overly complicate an already complex real-time data warehousing development effort. While not an automatic project-killer, the real-time architect should be aware that business vocabularies and metrics employed by shipping versus marketing management, for example, are likely to be quite different and deeply rooted.

- **No real need for ad-hoc analysis.** If there is little demand for ad-hoc analysis of the low-latency part of data, you may be able to avoid a full-blown streaming ETL system redesign. Perhaps you can simply append a *flash report* of most-recent data from the transaction system to a conventional data warehouse report created with data up through yesterday.

- **Organizations that have not yet successfully implemented a data warehouse.** Attempting a real-time data warehouse as an initial business intelligence development effort, at least for now, is not recommended, simply because it demands mastery of too many simultaneous disciplines. Thankfully, dimensional data warehousing architectures and methods allow the organization to gracefully add real-time reporting capabilities later.

A symptom of one of these red flags should be a report that requires data fresher than last night but is tolerant of at least five minutes of latency. Such a report may also demand continuity in terms of data history, reporting vocabulary, and presentation with the existing non-real-time data warehouse. These red flag reports are appropriate candidates for the real-time data warehousing ETL approaches described.

The next sections discuss some basic requirements for real-time time reporting.

Reporting Only or Integration, Too?

Does the organization need a one-way solution for moving operational data into the data warehouse for reporting purposes only, or are there also requirements for *closing the loop* by moving conformed dimension data between operational applications themselves and/or the data warehouse? For example, is a mechanism needed for moving data warehouse-derived customer segmentations back into the operational systems? This question is perhaps the most influential in selecting a real-time data-warehousing approach.

Certainly, any strategic CRM initiative is likely to require a means of sharing the timeliest and most complete customer information available, which includes both operational customer data (information about recent sales or complaints, for example) and data-warehouse or data mining-derived customer marketing information such as customer segmentation, profiling, and lifetime value. Is the request for real-time reporting a first step in the journey of closing the loop between the operational and decision support systems of the organization (true CRM)?

Just the Facts or Dimension Changes, Too?

Business people and dimensional data warehouse architects describe the world in terms of facts and dimensions, but OLTP systems do not make such crisp distinctions. Nonetheless, as an engineer, you must understand and categorize the OLTP business transactions of interest to your end users and design appropriately.

Are the real-time report requirements focused exclusively on fresh facts, such as recent orders placed, recent telephone calls routed, recent stock trades executed, recent sales calls made, and so on, or are they also concerned with fresh dimension transactions, such as customer or product record updates? If real-time dimensional changes are needed for reporting, are they slowly or rapidly changing? In other words, does the user community need an accurate image of these dimensions as they were at the point in time of the transaction, or can all or some dimensional updates be destructively overwritten when new updates occur? Do reports need to be *repeatable*? Type 1 slowly changing dimensions, in which the changes to a dimension's attributes destructively overwrite the prior values, result in a data warehouse that continuously recasts history, reporting events not as they look at the time of the transaction but as they look in the context of today's dimensions. In this scenario, reports run against the same dimensional elements at different points in time might have slightly or dramatically different results. Type 1 changes are also dangerous because they can invalidate historical aggregates if the Type change is applied to a field used as the basis of an aggregate calculation.

Type 2 and 3 slowly changing dimensions maintain a more granular picture of the dimension images at certain points in time, perhaps daily, but they still do not capture the changes to dimensions that occur between extractions. Real-time dimensional refresh can drive this granularity up to every few minutes or can capture all dimension changes.

The architectural implications are not subtle. By adopting a policy of capturing increasingly frequent dimensional change images, the data warehouse moves away from its earlier posture as a system of periodic measurement (snapshots) and toward a zero-latency decision-support ideal. As data warehousing and application integration technologies begin to commingle, the data warehouse becomes, in effect, a true logical extension of the operational systems that run the enterprise. For the time being, as a practical matter, ETL systems probably need to be designed to provide as near zero latency for measured facts as possible, but allow some or all dimensional attributes to be updated in batches, or microbatches, as developed in this chapter.

Alerts, Continuous Polling, or Nonevents?

Although usually the ETL system has a very well-defined boundary where dimensionally prepared data is handed to the front room, in many cases a real time system cannot have this boundary. The architecture of front-end tools is affected at the same time. There are three data-delivery paradigms that require an end-to-end perspective reaching all the way from the original source to the end user's screen:

- *Alerts*. A data condition at the source forces an update to occur at the user's screen in real time.

- *Continuous polling*. The end user's application continuously probes the source data in order to update the screen in real-time.

- *Nonevent notification*. The end user is notified if a specific event does not occur within a certain time interval or as the result of a specific condition.

In each of these cases, the real-time ETL system is connected all the way to the end user's application, either by sending a notification or by receiving a direct request.

Data Integration or Application Integration?

Assuming that the real-time data warehouse requirement also entails some measure of integration across operational systems, you need to categorize your requirement as either data integration or application integration.

- In general, integration that can be satisfied by simply moving data between databases is called *data integration*. Often, these solutions are point-to-point, executed through (for heterogeneous databases) ASCII file extraction, triggers, database links, and gateways or for homogeneous databases replication services or table snapshots. In essence, data is shared across the back rooms of the participating applications, bypassing application logic entirely. Some higher-end data-integration tools provide centralized administration support for the scheduling and movement of data, supporting a bit more enterprise control and management for point-to-point data-integration chores.

- *Application integration* (sometimes also called functional integration) can be described as building new business solutions by gluing applications together through the use of some common middleware. Middleware is a class of software that is application independent, providing a means to capture, route, and execute transactional messages between applications. In general, connectors or adapters are used to connect the participating applications to the integration network, and brokers are used to route messages according to publication and subscription rules.

Point-to-Point versus Hub-and-Spoke

If your near real-time data warehouse is also supporting some degree of application (or functional) integration, an important factor in selecting an architecture is the number of publishing and subscribing systems that you anticipate supporting in the foreseeable (for example, 24 month) future. This

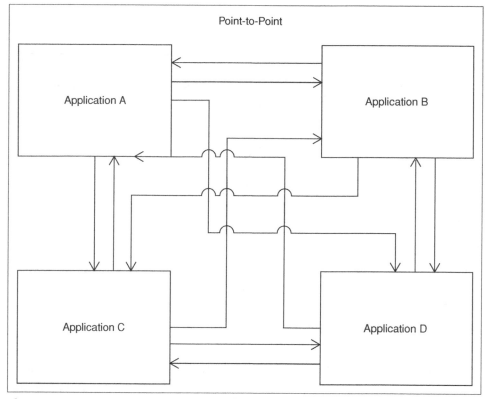

Figure 11.3 Point-to-point application integration.

number can help you decide if a relatively simple point-to-point solution will suffice or if a more robust hub-and-spoke architecture will be required.

Figure 11.3 shows that, even with a relatively small number of applications exchanging data, point-to-point solutions can demand a very large number of data-exchange interfaces, each of which requires maintenance whenever its source or target applications change.

Adding applications to the integration network also demands new data-exchange interfaces to all publishing and subscribing applications. Nonetheless, organizations that have a short, crisp list of applications demanding conformed dimension integration and that expect this list to remain stable for the foreseeable future might find a point-to-point integration approach quite attractive. It avoids the complexity of creating EAI middleware components and can be partially supported through the use of data-integration technologies such as Capture, Transform, and Flow (CTF) tools described later in the chapter.

In contrast to point-to-point architectures, the number of customer interfaces and cross-system dependencies can be minimized through the use of a hub-and-spoke integration approach (see Figure 11.4).

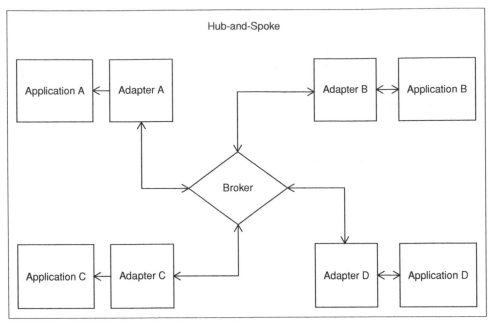

Figure 11.4   Hub and spoke application integration.

However, the additional burden of building EAI middleware adapters and broker components is not trivial. Each application that participates in the integration network needs an adapter capable of converting specified transactions into generic messages and of interpreting and executing generic messages on the local application. Adapter maintenance is required whenever an associated host application changes or if the set of generic messages changes.

Hard-and-fast rules on the decision boundary between point-to-point or hub-and-spoke architectures do not exist, but organizations anticipating integration across three or more applications or those that expect a growing number of integration-network participants in the foreseeable future can strongly consider hub-and-spoke EAI architectures. This admittedly elastic boundary can also be shaped by the organization's comfort with and commitment to EAI messaging technologies.

Customer Data Cleanup Considerations

If the organization needs real-time cleanup and synchronization of customer data, you need to consider some additional factors in selecting an approach. Does the organization have in place some centralized means of generating new customer keys, one that ensures that no redundant customer records are created? Such systems are quite rare, and it often falls upon the data warehouse customer dimension manager to provide this service for the enterprise.

Assuming that such a system is not in place, it may be appropriate for the real-time customer dimension manager to assume responsibility for matching (deduplicating) customer records. A number of deterministic and probabilistic matching tools available today can help support these requirements, but unfortunately, many of these tools currently run in batch mode only. Customer cleanup utilities that support postal address verification, propensity for fraud segmentation, credit worthiness, or householding might also demand batch processing. It is still possible to approximate real-time performance, however, by building an architecture for moving frequent microbatches, described later in the chapter, into and out of these utilities throughout the day.

Real-Time ETL Approaches

Through some creative recycling of established ETL technologies and tools, a mature and broad palette of technologies is available to address real-time data warehousing requirements. The sections that follow discuss these technologies.

Microbatch ETL

Conventional ETL, the file-based approach described throughout this book, is extremely effective in addressing daily, weekly, and monthly batch-reporting requirements. New or changed transactions (fact records) are moved en masse, and dimensions are captured as point-in-time snapshots for each load. Thus, changes to dimensions that occur between batch processes are not available in the warehouse. ETL, therefore, is not a suitable technique for data or application integration for organizations needing low-latency reporting or for organizations that need more detailed dimensional change capture. But conventional ETL is a simple, direct, and tried-and-true method for organizations that have more casual latency requirements and complex integration challenges. Figure 11.5 shows the conventional ETL process.

Microbatch ETL is very similar to conventional ETL, except that the frequency of batches is increased, perhaps to as frequently as hourly. These frequent microbatches are run through an otherwise conventional ETL process and directly feed the real-time partitions of the data marts. Once each day, the real-time partitions are copied to the static data marts and are emptied. Figure 11.6 shows a diagram of micro-batch ETL.

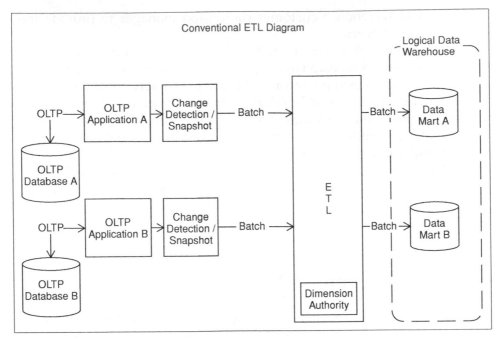

Figure 11.5 Conventional ETL diagram.

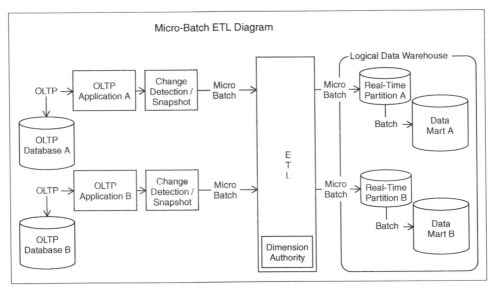

Figure 11.6 Microbatch ETL diagram.

The dimension manager systems generate new dimensional images in Type 2 or 3 slowly changing dimensions, but due to the increased run frequency, dimensions that change throughout the day may become rapidly changing and grow deep. An inelegant alternative is to ignore changes to dimensions that occur during the day and instead generate dimension records only for new instances, using default values in all columns. This compromise might suffice for organizations that generate few new records on a given day and are tolerant of dimensional context latency from the previous evening, but it clearly dilutes some of the benefits of real-time reporting. If unavoidable, the only practical solution for dealing with rapidly changing dimensions is the judicious use of a minidimension, where you create separate dimensions for the most frequently changing attributes of a large dimension and thereby reduce the number of new dimensional instances needing to be created by the ETL process.

An interesting hybrid alternative is to treat intra-day changes to a dimension as a kind of Type 1, where a special copy of the dimension is associated with the real-time partition exclusively. Changes during the day trigger simple overwrites. At the end of the day, any such changes can be treated as Type 2 as far as the copy of the dimension in the static portion of the data warehouse is concerned. That way, for instance, a credit-worthiness indicator could be set immediately for a customer in the real-time data warehouse.

Microbatch ETL demands a comprehensive job control, scheduling, dependency, and error-mitigation method, one robust enough to run unattended for most of the time and capable of executing data warehouse publication strategies in the face of most common data-loading issues. A number of job-control utilities support this functionality, but custom development work is likely to be needed to make the microbatch ETL data warehouse resemble a *lights out* automated operation.

Microbatch ETL also demands more frequent detection of new and updated transactional records on the OLTP systems, so the load imposed on the operational system must be considered and carefully managed.

Several methods exist for identifying changed record candidates for microbatch ETL load into the real-time data warehouse:

- **Timestamps.** Tried and true, timestamps maintained by the operational system for the creation and update of records can be used by real-time microbatch ETL to differentiate candidate data for extraction. While simple, this method does impose frequent writes of these timestamps on the operational systems for all changes and frequent reads whenever the ETL processes run. Indexing the timestamps improves read performance and reduces read overhead but increases the operational overhead on INSERTs and UPDATEs, sometimes prohibitively so. The ETL engineer must balance these concerns.

- **ETL log tables.** Another approach is to create triggers in the OLTP environment to insert the unique legacy identifiers of new and changed records into a series of special ETL log tables. These specialized tables exist solely to speed ETL processing and are used by the microbatch ETL process to determine which rows have changed since the previous microbatch. The ETL log tables contain the unique identifier of the new or changed dimensional record and perhaps a status value, a timestamp, and a run identifier of the microbatch ETL process that ultimately processes the changed record. The microbatch ETL process joins the ETL log tables to the operational tables where the ETL run identifier is null, extracts the resultant rows, and then deletes (or populates the run identifier of) the ETL Log records extracted. The overhead on the operational system is reduced using this method, because trigger-driven INSERTs do not unduly exercise the OLTP system.

- **Database management system (DBMS) log scrapers.** The DBMS audit log files, created as a byproduct of backup and recovery utilities, can sometimes be utilized to identify new and changed transactions by using specialized utilities called log scrapers. Some of these log-scraping utilities can selectively extract and recreate the SQL statements applied to the database tables of interest since some specified point in time, allowing the ETL to know not just which records have changed since the last extraction, but what elements have changed on these records as well, information that can be utilized by the ETL process in directly applying changes to the target tables in the staging area.

- **Network sniffers.** These utilities monitor some set of interesting traffic on a network and filter and record the traffic that they see. Network sniffers are often used for capturing Web Clickstream traffic because they eliminate the need to stitch together the Web logs from multiple servers in a Web farm, provide sessionizing of Web visits, and improve visibility into the actual Web content delivered from dynamic Web pages. Network sniffers are an ETL alternative wherever there is a stream of traffic requiring data-warehousing analysis, including telecommunication calls routing, manufacturing floor workflow, or EAI messaging traffic.

Microbatch ETL is an excellent choice for data warehouse requirements tolerant of hourly latency without intra-hour dimensional updates and that do not demand bi-directional synchronization of dimensional data between the data warehouse and the operational systems. It is by far the simplest approach for delivering near real-time data warehousing reporting.

Enterprise Application Integration

At the high end of the complexity spectrum lies enterprise application integration (EAI), sometimes called functional integration. EAI describes the set of technologies that support true application integration, allowing individual operational systems to interoperate in new and potentially different ways than they were originally designed.

EAI typically entails building a set of adapter and broker components that move business transactions, in the form of *messages*, across the various systems in the integration network, insulating all systems from knowledge or dependencies on other systems in the integration network. Application-specific adapters are responsible for dealing with all of the logic needed to create and execute messages, and brokers are responsible for routing the messages appropriately, based on publication and subscription rules.

Adapters and brokers communicate via application-independent messages, often rendered in XML. When a significant application event occurs such as the update of a customer record, a trigger is fired, and the application's adapter creates a new message. The adapter is also responsible for initiating transactions in its respective application when it receives a message containing information that it has chosen to receive, such as a newly conformed customer record from the customer dimension manager system. Brokers route messages between adapters, based on a set of publication and subscription rules. Messaging queues are often placed between applications and their adapters, and between adapters and brokers, to provide a staging area for asynchronous messaging and to support delivery guarantees and transaction consistency across the integration network.

In the Figure 11.7, applications A and B operate independently but are able to exchange data and interoperate through EAI messages.

For example, changes to a customer record on application A might fire a trigger detected by application A's adapter, which creates and sends an XML message of the change to a broker. If application B has subscribed to customer-change messages from application A, the broker forwards the message to application B's adapter, which can then apply all or a subset of the customer record change to application B.

Applications A and B do not need to know anything about one another; their respective adapters are responsible for capturing, interpreting, and applying messages for their application. This concept is a powerful one because it allows EAI networks to extend elegantly; introduction of new applications into the integration network requires only the creation of a

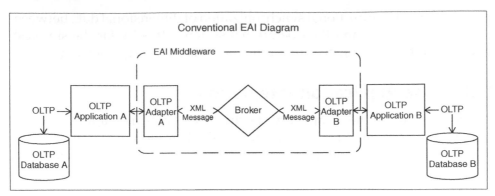

Figure 11.7 Conventional EAI diagram.

new adapter and new publication/subscription rules to the broker(s). When we say *only*, we do not imply that the creation of hardened industrial-strength adapters is trivial; quite the opposite is true. Each adapter must be capable of executing potentially complex transactions on its host system and gracefully handling the many concurrency issues that can appear whenever independent applications operate on common logical data. Regardless of the integration approach, certain issues must be dealt with somewhere in the architecture, and EAI adapters do so at the optimal position, as close to the application as is possible.

EAI technologies can be powerful enabling tools for the real-time data warehouse because they support the ability to synchronize important data like customer information across applications, and they provide an effective means for distributing data-warehouse-derived information assets, such as new customer segmentation values, across the enterprise.

The real-time EAI data warehouse architecture modularizes the monolithic ETL block by pulling the dimension manager system(s) out as separate architectural components, each with its own adapters, and placing responsibility for most of the transformation and loading chores of the data mart real-time partitions on the data mart adapters. Figure 11.8 is a diagram of a real-time EAI data warehouse.

A typical real scenario might involve implementing adapters for a set of OLTP systems such as enterprise resource planning, ERP, and sales-force automation, customer and product dimension manager systems (which perform real-time cleansing and deduplication), and data marts for orders and sales calls.

Any customer or product-change transaction would be captured from the OLTP application by an adapter, sent as a nonconformed dimension message to the broker, which then routes it to whichever systems subscribe to nonconformed dimension messages, typically only the appropriate dimension manager system. The dimension manager system conforms the

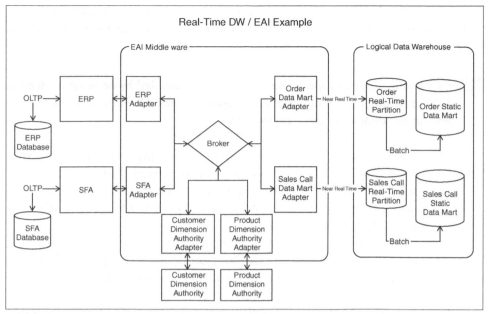

Figure 11.8 Real-time data warehouse EAI diagram.

dimensional record, and its adapter then sends it back as a conformed dimension message to the broker, which then forwards it to all systems that subscribe to conformed dimension data, typically the OLTP systems and data marts.

Consider this example. The ERP system updates a customer record; then the ERP adapter detects this change, generates an XML message labeled *Non-Conformed Customer Transaction from ERP*, and sends it to the broker. The broker forwards this message to the customer dimension manager, typically the only system that subscribes to nonconformed customer messages from system ERP. The customer dimension manager receives the message and places the nonconformed customer information in the work queue (or staging area, if micro-batch) of the customer dimension manager. The customer dimension manager works the transaction, and if it results in a change to one or more conformed customer records, the customer dimension manager adapter detects that these changes have occurred, packages these revised customer records into *Conformed Customer Transactions from the Customer Dimension Manager* messages, and sends them to the broker. Assuming that the orders data mart, sales-call data mart, ERP, and SFA systems have all subscribed to *Conformed Customer Transactions from the Customer Dimension Manager* messages, the broker copies and distributes the message to all four of these systems. Each of the four adapters is then responsible for applying the changes to the customer record to their respective applications.

The acceptance of the conformed customer record by the ERP and SFA systems might cause a change to their respective customer records, thereby triggering a new set of EAI transactions.

NOTE Endless loops, or *race conditions*, must be avoided by devising a selective publication strategy at the edges of the integration network, either at the OLTP systems or the dimension manager systems.

Fact transactions are also captured by the OLTP adapters, sent to the broker as an *Order or Sales Call* fact message, and then routed to all subscribers of these types of messages, typically data marts. The data mart adapter performs all transformations needed and inserts the new transaction directly into the data mart real-time partition.

EAI is a powerful means of synchronizing key business information, both for trickle-feeding data marts and for publishing and distributing data warehouse-derived segmentations to customer-facing OLTP systems. But it can be complex and expensive to implement.

EAI is an excellent approach for organizations whose requirements demand low-reporting latency, who are intolerant of loss of intra-day dimensional updates, or who require bidirectional synchronization of dimension data between the data warehouse and/or the operational systems.

Using EAI mechanisms for shoveling high-volume transaction data into the data warehouse may be inefficient if every transaction is separately packaged as an EAI message with significant communications overhead. Before commiting to this design approach, make sure you are anticipating the full volume of message traffic. Also, investigate whether your EAI broker interfaces allow for compact representations of transactional data.

Capture, Transform, and Flow

Capture, Transform, and Flow (CTF) is a relatively new category of data-integration tools designed to simplify the movement of real-time data across heterogeneous database technologies. The application layer of the transactional applications is bypassed. Instead, direct database-to-database exchanges are executed. Transactions, both new facts and dimension changes, can be moved directly from the operational systems to the data warehouse staging tables with low latency, typically a few seconds.

The transformation functionality of CTF tools is typically basic in comparison with today's mature ETL tools, so often real-time data warehouse CTF solutions involve moving data from the operational environment, lightly transforming it using the CTF tool, and then staging it. These light transformation tasks might include standardization of date formats, recasting data types, truncating or expanding field lengths, or applying application-specific code translations into descriptions. Once data is staged, additional transformations beyond the capabilities of the CTF tool are then applied as needed. This subsequent transformation can be invoked either by microbatch ETL or via triggers that fire on INSERT in the staging area. In either transformation scenario, records are then written directly into the real-time partition tables of the data mart. These subsequent transformations might include tasks like data validation, dimensions-record cleansing and matching, surrogate key lookups for dimensional records, and creation of new slowly changing dimensional records as needed. Figure 11.9 diagrams CTF.

Some CTF tools can also simplify the batch movement of information from the data warehouse back to the operational systems, such as periodic refreshment of customer data. Because they bypass the application-logic layer, utilizing these features places the burden on the CTF administrator to ensure that the resultant updates do not corrupt operational system transactions or cause transaction loss.

CTF is an excellent approach for organizations whose requirements demand near real-time reporting with some light data-integration needs and for organizations whose core applications enjoy common periods of low activity that can allow minimally disruptive data synchronization to occur. In situations like these, CTF can offer a compelling blend of the some of the benefits of EAI, while avoiding much its complexity.

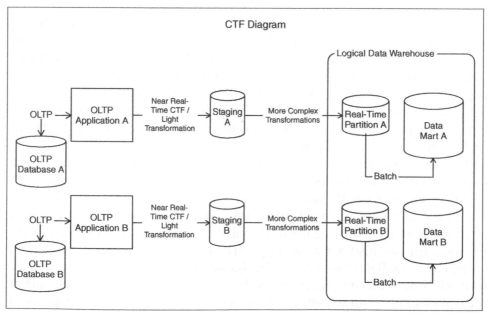

Figure 11.9 CTF diagram.

Enterprise Information Integration

Enterprise Information Integration (EII) is another relatively new category of software, built specifically to assist organizations in quickly adding real-time reporting capabilities to their business-intelligence systems. They are, in a sense, a virtual real-time data warehouse, a logical view of the current data in the OLTP systems, presented to the business user in a structure appropriate for analysis, and delivered on the fly via inline ETL transformation.

With conventional ETL, you identify a set of source structures in your OLTP world, a set of target structures in your data warehouse. Then on some schedule, perhaps nightly, a trigger is pulled, and the ETL tool extracts the data, transforms it, and loads it into data warehouse tables. EII operates in a somewhat similar vein, except that instead of a data warehouse, the target might be a report, spreadsheet, or OLE DB or XML object. The EII trigger is pulled by the business analyst whenever he or she needs up-to-the-second operational information. The EII system actually generates a series of queries, typically via SQL, at the moment requested, applies all specified transformations to the resultant data, and delivers the results to the business user.

The capabilities that emerge are quite interesting: a zero-latency reporting engine enhanced with the robust capabilities for data integration associated with mature ETL tools. No history beyond the data available in the OLTP environment is available in EII, so trending reports must still be met by the data warehouse. Of course, the data warehouse itself can be defined as a source of information to the EII system, so the integration of real-time data from the operational world with the historic data from the data warehouse is at least theoretically possible. EII transformational capabilities, while robust, are not without limits. Not all modern ETL and data-cleansing functionality can be supported inline (for example, probabilistic matching), so expectations must be reduced accordingly. Also, because extractions are directly against the OLTP systems, the frequency and complexity of these extractions must be managed in order to manage the size of the footprint on the OLTP technical architecture.

An important strength of EII is its ETL pedigree. EII can be used as an effective data warehouse prototyping device. Organizations that select ETL and EII toolsets from the same vendor might find that successful EII subject areas that need to *evolve* into data warehouse subject areas that can be jump-started by reusing the data-transformation rules developed in the EII tool. EII can also act as a supportive real-time reporting component within an overall data warehouse business intelligence system. Use of conformed dimensions and facts across the data warehouse and EII, as part of the dimensional data warehouse bus architecture, allows these systems to interoperate effectively. Conforming dimensions and facts on the fly, however, is easier said than done. In this scenario, at a minimum, you must place fact constraints on the EII queries to exclude facts that have already been loaded into the data warehouse to avoid double-counting and exercise care in presenting real-time facts associated with new dimension records that have not yet been loaded into the data warehouse.

EII may be a very compelling approach for organizations whose requirements demand near-zero latency real-time reporting of integrated information for a relatively small user base with little historical data. It may also be valuable to organizations that believe that they need to evolve into real-time data warehousing but are unsure of their strategic real-time business requirements or whose business requirements are rapidly changing. And finally, EII may be a compelling choice for organizations in the throes of reorganization or acquisition and need real-time integrated operational reporting as quickly as possible.

The Real-Time Dimension Manager

The real-time dimension manager system, as proposed in this book, used primarily on customer information, converts incoming customer records, which may be incomplete, inaccurate, or redundant, into conformed customer records. *Conformed* does not mean perfect, but it should mean that dimensional records are brought to the best condition that the organization is capable of achieving. In practice, this means that all reasonable measures have been taken to eliminate redundancy, remove untrustworthy data, compile as complete an image as is possible, and assign surrogate data warehouse keys. A general schematic of the real-time dimension manager is presented in Figure 11.10.

The EAI broker is the same EAI middleware component depicted in the other EAI diagrams, and it is responsible for routing messages between adapters, in accordance with its publication and subscription metadata. In the case of the real-time dimension manager, it routes messages associated with nonconformed dimension changes from operational systems to the dimension manager and routes the conformed dimension changes from the dimension manager back to any subscribing operational systems or data marts. The conformed customer messages that come from the real-time dimension manager must also include the set of all legacy keys from the OLTP systems that have been joined together by the conformance process. These keys are then used by the OLTP system adapters in figuring out how to apply the conformed customer message to their respective applications. The resultant changes to the OLTP system can result in the creation of a new record, the update of an existing record, or the *merging* of two or more records that have been deemed redundant by the dimension manager. The

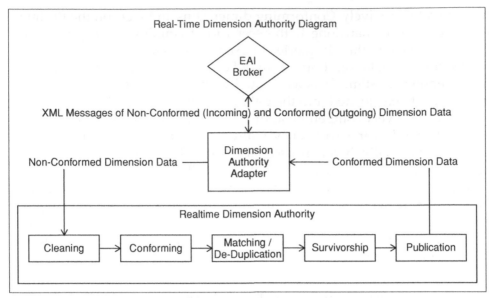

Figure 11.10 Real-time dimension manager diagram.

legacy keys are also used by the real-time data mart loading software to map the legacy keys that appear on incoming fact records to data warehouse surrogate keys.

This continuous exchange of dimensional images is the mechanism for synchronization across all systems that participate in the integration network. The net effect, though, transcends simple synchronization. From the CEO's perspective, the applications now appear to be working together.

Unless planned for, a kind of boomerang effect can develop between systems that participate in the integration network. After a nonconformed dimension record is processed by the dimension manager, the acceptance of the conformed dimensional record by subscribing applications generates messages of dimension change themselves. You must carefully manage this rebound (boomerang) effect and dampen any race conditions, including infinite loops of dimension conformance messaging. The importance of firm EAI architecture is critical to resolving these types of issues; you must establish sound policies governing message publications. Consider the following example policy: Integration network application participants, both OLTP and the dimension manager, might choose to publish messages *only* whenever they update an existing or create a new dimensional record. This policy implies that the dimension manager, for example, does *not* publish conformed messages for all incoming nonconformed messages, just those that result in a change to one or more conformed dimension records. Similarly, an OLTP system receiving a conformed dimension message publishes a new message only if the loading of this conformed image results in a change to its dimension table.

The dimension manager adapter is the EAI middleware component that interacts with the real-time dimension manager system by taking incoming messages of nonconformed data, placing them in a queue for the dimension manager, and listening for publication events triggered by the dimension manager, which it then converts to XML messages and sends on to the broker. The dimension manager adapter insulates the rest of the EAI architecture from any awareness or dependency on the real-time dimension manager system itself.

Referring to figure 11.10, the business of actually conforming dimensions in real-time is typically modularized into the following subcomponents:

- **Cleaning.** The cleaning component reads incoming nonconformed data and discards dimensional instances that are corrupt or invalid from the job stream. It ensures that required fields are present (which may vary across different sources) and that the data values contained in the attributes are valid—again, from the perspective of the originating system.

- **Conforming.** The conforming component accepts cleaned information from the job stream and performs field-by-field translations of the values from the set of valid values according to the originating system to a conformed domain, a set of enterprise-wide conformed values for each attribute of the dimension. In some cases, the conformed value is arrived at *deterministically*, through lookup tables that map all source system values to conformed values. In other cases, the conformed value is arrived at *probabilistically*, by deriving relationships using fuzzy statistical calculation. Specialized tools for probabilistic standardization are often used to clean up street addresses by putting them in a known format; correcting the spelling of street, city, and state names; and correcting postal zip codes. Some fuzzy tools also correct name misspellings and standardize common names.

- **Matching.** The Matching component accepts cleaned and conformed data from the job stream and attempts to identify and eliminate duplicate records. Again, specialized software tools are often employed to support matching, using deterministic and probabilistic matching techniques. Detailed descriptions of the workings of these tools are beyond the scope of this chapter, but suffice to say that these tools allow developers to define a number of matching scenarios and matching algorithms. The matching engines score the likelihood of a match for each pass and generate a combined score, which is a kind of balanced scorecard for overall likelihood of a match. This final score is then compared to high (certain match) and low (certain no match) thresholds that the dimension manager has defined, and matching group keys are defined. Records that fall between the high and low thresholds are marked for special treatment, typically manual review. The definition of the matching passes and setting of the matching thresholds is part science and part art and is shaped by the organization's tolerance for error, need for low latency, legal and regulatory considerations, and staff available for manual review. Undermatching (tending to err on the side of keeping similar but nonidentical customer records as separate dimensional instances) is generally regarded as more conservative and less intrusive than overmatching and is the norm. Undoing an incorrect match in a real-time EAI environment is not easily accomplished and often means that customer transactions that have been incorrectly consolidated by OLTP systems in response to a merge request from the dimension manager need to be manually split apart and retransmitted.

In a real-time environment, records requiring manual review are typically defaulted to a nonmatch state, and the manual review can then be performed later. For performance reasons, when dealing with large dimensions such as the customer dimension of a retailer, you must restrict the set of candidate records used for deduplication for match performance to meet a reasonable real-time performance obligation. Extracting candidates can speed these matching processes significantly, but it sometimes fails to deliver many candidate records that might have been found to match. Thus, real-time online matching is often a bit of a compromise, and periodic rematching of the entire dimension might be required. This monolithic rematching process can create a large number of conformed dimension messages and operational system updates, which you must managed carefully.

Specialized metadata is needed by the matching component to describe matching pass logic, matching thresholds, and matching override information for records that should never or always be matched. Often, you must develop a specialized user interface to support the manual matching processes and the maintenance of the matching metadata, including pass logic, match thresholds, and candidate extraction.

- **Survivorship.** Once a set of records has been identified as matches for one another, the best image of the dimension must be somehow distilled from the matched records to create a complete and accurate composite image. This distillation process is often referred to as *survivorship* because it ensures that only the best sources of dimensional attributes are survived in the overall dimension conformance process. The survivorship process utilizes business rules that identify, on an attribute-by-attribute basis, the source-system priorities to be applied in surviving the resultant conformed dimension image. Non-null source attribute values are survived into the final integrated dimension record based on a hierarchy of source-system rules captured ideally in metadata. The survivorship component should also support the ability to define groups of attributes that survive from the same source record as a block to avoid strange results when plucking, for example, address line 1 and address line 2 attributes from different source records. The survivorship module also typically handles the generation of distinct point-in-time surrogate keys for dimension records that are slowly changing, while simultaneously maintaining a single key value for all dimensional instances across time. So a customer whose profile has changed ten times must have ten distinct point-in-time surrogate key values, yet each of these should have the same overall customer surrogate key. These two key-handling perspectives are needed because the real-time dimension manager serves two constituencies: the data marts, which must have point-in-time surrogate keys, and the OLTP systems, which need only the most contemporary image of the dimension record.

- **Publication.** Once a dimension image has been fully integrated (cleaned, conformed, matched, and survived), you must determine if the resultant survived record is new or different enough from previous dimensional images to warrant publication to the integration network. The dimension manager typically needs to publish selectively to dampen infinite publication loops. If publication is warranted, the publication component's job is to awaken the dimension manager adapter, which is continuously listening for publication requests, so that it can gather all or a part of the dimensional record, convert it to a conformed dimension XML message, and push it to the EAI broker for distribution throughout the enterprise. Awakening the dimension manager adapter typically takes the form of applying an update to one or more records in a special repository of conformed data, an event which fires a trigger that the adapter is listening for.

Design publication policy to ensure that adequate dimension synchronization is possible throughout the enterprise, while avoiding any endless feedback or race conditions and without delving into application-specific publication and subscription rules, which are best handled by the EAI broker.

The ETL architect designing the real-time dimension manager's responsibilities must carefully dissect business requirements and tread bravely through sometimes difficult political territories. Many managers that seek one version of the truth assume that it will be their version, not the other guy's! Technically, the architect must also decide when and where complete or partial dimension records are passed between applications in the messages, which situations should cause conformed records to be published, how best to deal with possible contention and race conditions, how best to balance the need for application autonomy and conformance, and whether to use straight-through processing with very few disk touchdowns or microbatch processing, discussed in the next section.

Sound complex? Well, it is. But the real-time dimension manager is truly powerful medicine for the enterprise needing to synchronize enriched customer or other key dimensional information across the enterprise and can provide a competitive advantage to those organizations courageous enough to become early adopters.

Microbatch Processing

You will often face a common dilemma when designing real-time data mart partition or dimensional systems: Should the solution embrace straight-through processing or utilize more frequent microbatches? The current generation of toolsets that support low-latency data movement, such as CTF, often lack some of the transformation capabilities of well-established batch ETL tools. A number of ETL tool vendors have begun to offer real-time versions of their toolsets that process information in a more transactional manner but sometimes with restricted functionality. Designers of the real-time dimension manager systems often face a similar dilemma when selecting deterministic and probabilistic matching tools, some of which operate exclusively operate in batch mode. How can you best coax real-time performance out of tools that operate in batch mode?

One reasonable compromise to the conflicting demands of delivering near real-time performance within constraints imposed by batch-oriented toolsets is to design a solution that processes frequent microbatches, using state transition job control metadata structures.

Consider Figure 11.11. Each job in the job table represents either a fact or nonconformed dimension transaction record presented for processing to either the real-time data mart or dimension manager. These jobs must pass through several processes, each defined in the process table, such as cleaning and conforming, before they are ready for publication. In the data model in Figure 11.11, the microbatch table represents the invocation of a small batch of a given process, and each microbatch processes several jobs. The set of jobs processed by each microbatch are captured in the job

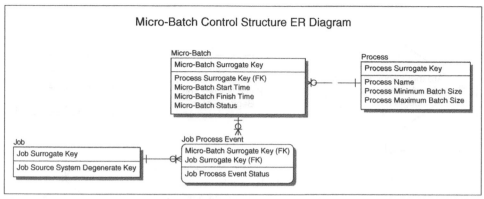

Figure 11.11 The microbatch table data model.

process event table shown in the figure, which also captures a job event process status attribute of the success or failure of the given job within the microbatch.

The processes run continuously, as daemons, looking for jobs that are at the appropriate state for processing. When they find some acceptable minimum number of jobs, they invoke a microbatch, process the jobs, and generate job process event records with appropriate status values; then they continue looking for more jobs to process.

The benefits of building modular process daemons, as opposed to using straight-through processing, is that they can be developed independently, have individually tunable batch-sizing specifications, and be replaced and/or upgraded independently as new toolsets with more features. Also, new processes such as specialized address verification or creditworthiness scoring can be more easily inserted into the job stream, and jobs that require selective processing are more easily accommodated.

But this flexibility comes at a cost. The microbatch process flow demands that each process have defined and persistent interfaces, typically database tables to pull data from and write to. The additional I/O and complexity imposed by this requirement can be significant. In practice, the complexity can be minimized by designing a single set of work tables used as common sources and targets by all processes, and the I/O can be minimized by caching these tables in the DBMS memory. Nevertheless, the microbatch approach does not perform as well as a straight-through processing approach. The control records associated with completed jobs should be purged or partitioned frequently to keep them as small as possible.

Each process flow of a typical process in the microbatch scenario is quite simple. As each batch process is invoked, a microbatch record is created, and some appropriate (between minimum and maximum specified batch size from the process table) number of job process event records are created

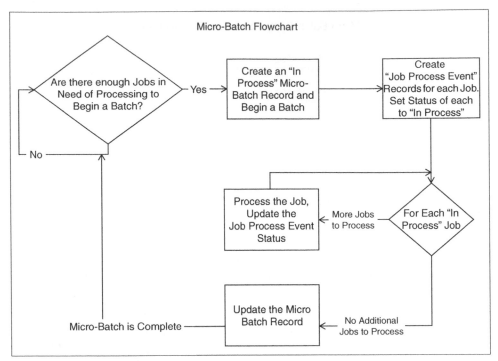

Figure 11.12 Microbatch flowchart.

too, one for each job to be processed in the microbatch. This basic technique provides enough information for managing many concurrent microbatches and keeping an adequate audit trail of all batch and job processing. Figure 11.12 shows how it works.

Figure 11.12 represents a single process. Each process runs continuously and simultaneously with other processes as daemons, working a mutually exclusive set of jobs to completion, setting the job process event and microbatch status values accordingly, and then continuing. So, a dimension manager system might have data cleaning, conforming, matching, survivorship, and publication process daemons sometimes working simultaneously on different sets of jobs. A data mart real-time CTF system might have transformation and surrogate key lookup process daemons, and so on. Each daemon is continuously looking for jobs to processes where jobs in this context are defined as job records that have previously been processed to a stage that makes them appropriate candidates for the given process.

As you can see in Figure 11.12, the status of the job process events is set to *In Process*, and a DBMS transaction begin set point is established. As each job is worked (cleaned, conformed, and so on), the job process event status is updated to either success or failure. Alternatively, to reduce processing overhead, this updating can occur at the end of the batch. Once all jobs have been processed, the batch completes, and the microbatch control table is updated. If it is successful with no fatal failures, and all job process event records have upgraded from *In Process*, a COMMIT is then executed, and the resultant changes are written to the database. If a failure occurs or if an unacceptably high number of job process events are of status Failure, a ROLLBACK is executed and the database returns to the state it was in before the microbatch began.

> **ROLLBACK events must not rollback error messages or status values on CONTROL tables. Many DBMSs offer autonomous transaction control options that support this restriction.**

Microbatch ETL applied to a real-time dimension manager is shown in Figure 11.13 as a series of process daemons that read from and update control, staging, and conformed libraries of tables.

Each process updates the status values of the job process event table and modifies and creates data in the staging or conformed dimension libraries.

- Cleaning reads nonvalidated records from the staging library and writes status values only to the control library.

- Conforming reads from cleaned and nonconformed records from staging and writes conformed values back to reserved conformed attributes in staging.

- Matching reads conformed and unmatched records from staging and writes match key values back to staging.

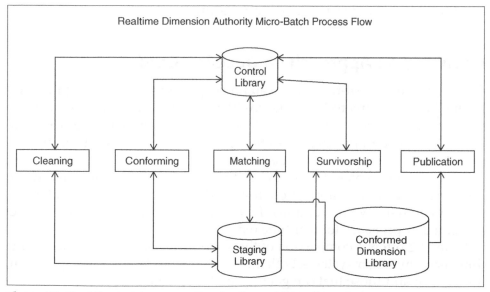

Figure 11.13 Microbatch process flow for the real-time dimension manager.

- Survivorship reads matched and nonsurvived records from staging and inserts or updates records in the conformed dimension library.
- Publication reads conformed records from the conformed dimension library and awakens the dimension manager adapter, which then publishes the record to the integration network.

A microbatch ETL system can also be used in concert with CTF for real-time data warehouses that demand more complex data transformations than those supported by CTF tool alone. CTF can be used for near real-time extraction of data from operational systems and light transformation services, dropping data into a staging area. From the staging area, microbatch ETL can be run to handle complex transformations and trickle feed data into the real-time data mart partition tables. From there, real-time reporting is supported, and the normal nightly batch process moves the data to the static data mart tables, emptying the real-time partition tables in the processes, ready for the next day's transactions.

A properly designed microbatch system exhibits good performance, reduced latency, and good scalability due to its high degree of parallel processing. It also supports the ability to logically *insert* jobs at various stages in the job stream by allowing administrators or other processes to create new control records with status values set as needed. This capability can be extremely helpful for dealing with special-case processing that might be needed by the real-time dimension manager: such as injecting manually matched records into the job stream for normal survivorship and publication services. It is a good trick to have in your arsenal for coaxing near real-time-like behavior from batch-processing toolsets.

Choosing an Approach—A Decision Guide

The entire area of real-time data warehousing, at present, can be quite confusing. With so many technologies to choose from, surrounded by so much vendor and analyst hype, and with so few successful case studies from which to draw best practices, selecting an appropriate architecture and approach can be a very daunting task.

The following tables attempt to cut through some of this uncertainty by distilling some of the information discussed in this chapter into guidelines to help you narrow your options. Table 11.1 is a comparison matrix of the presented approaches for real-time reporting.

Table 11.2 offers a comparison of the approaches presented for real-time dimension manager systems, both those that demand real-time application integration and those that can get by with batch-data integration.

Table 11-1 Real-Time Reporting Decision Guide Matrix

		EII ONLY	EII + STATIC DW	ETL	CTF	CTF-MB-ETL	MB-ETL	EAI
		ENTERPRISE INFORMATION INTEGRATION IN PLACE OF REAL-TIME DATA WAREHOUSE	ENTERPRISE INFORMATION INTEGRATION IN CONCERT WITH CONVENTIONAL NON-REAL-TIME DATA WAREHOUSE	STANDARD ETL PROCESSING	CAPTURE, TRANSFORM, FLOW FEEDING REAL-TIME DATA WAREHOUSE	CAPTURE, TRANSFORM, FLOW WITH MICRO-BATCH ETL FEEDING REAL-TIME DATA WAREHOUSE	MICRO-BATCH ETL FEEDING REAL-TIME DATA WAREHOUSE	ENTERPRISE APPLICATION FEEDING INTEGRATION REAL-TIME DATA WAREHOUSE
Historical Data Supported		✓	✓	✓	✓	✓	✓	✓
Reporting Data Integration Complexity	Low	✓	✓	✓	✓	✓	✓	✓
	Moderate	✓	✓	✓	✓	✓	✓	✓
	High		✓	✓		✓	✓	✓
Data Freshness/ Maximum Latency	1 Minute	✓	✓		✓			✓
	15 Minutes	✓	✓		✓	✓	✓	✓
	1 Hour	✓	✓		✓	✓	✓	✓
	1 Day	✓	✓	✓	✓	✓	✓	✓

This matrix suggests a couple of natural decision boundaries for selecting an approach for real-time reporting, based on reporting latency and integration complexity:

Organizations facing (or expecting to soon face) significant data-integration challenges should look toward ETL, microbatch ETL, and EAI solutions. These organizations include those with data-integration challenges that demand specialized tools for matching, name and address standardization, postal address verification, householding, and so on. Selecting between an ETL-based approach and an EAI-hybrid approach, in this scenario, should be driven primarily by any anticipated needs for a low-latency real-time dimension manager; EAI technologies are uniquely appropriate for these situations.

Organizations with, or expecting, low-latency reporting requirements should look toward EII, CTF, and EAI solutions. Again, the jump to the EAI arena is driven primarily by any requirements for the low-latency real-time dimension synchronization features of the real-time dimension manager.

Table 11-2 Dimension Authority Decision Guide Matrix

		ETL STANDARD ETL PROCESSING	CTF CAPTURE, TRANSFORM, FLOW FEEDING DIMENSION AUTHORITY	CTF-MB ETL CAPTURE, TRANSFORM, FLOW WITH MICRO-BATCH ETL FEEDING DIMENSION AUTHORITY	MB ETL MICRO-BATCH ETL FEEDING DIMENSION AUTHORITY	EAI ENTERPRISE APPLICATION INTEGRATION FEEDING DIMENSION AUTHORITY	EAI–MB–ETL ENTERPRISE APPLICATION INTEGRATION AND MICRO-BATCH ETL FEEDING DIMENSION AUTHORITY
Dimension Data Integration Complexity	Low	✓	✓	✓	✓	✓	✓
	Moderate	✓	✓	✓	✓	✓	✓
	High	✓	✓	✓	✓	✓	✓
Data Freshness / Maximum Latency	1 Minute		✓			✓	
	15 Minutes		✓	✓	✓	✓	✓
	1 Hour		✓	✓	✓	✓	✓
	1 Day	✓	✓	✓	✓	✓	✓
Enterprise Integration	Data Mart Feeds Only	✓	✓	✓	✓	✓	✓
	Light Data Integration		✓	✓		✓	✓
	Substantial Data Integration					✓	✓
	Application Integration					✓	✓

Pure ETL techniques are appropriate for dimension-manager scenarios tolerant of high-latency data integration services to a set of data marts (say, one dimension publication per day). CTF is appropriate for dimension-manager situations that demand low-latency data integration with simpler integration challenges and a small universe of applications to serve. EAI-based approaches are appropriate for dimension manager situations demanding application integration services, such as synchronizing a customer dimension across the enterprise and feeding fresh dimension information to real-time data marts.

Summary

Real-time ETL is much more than a fad or a new feature. Moving to real-time delivery of data challenges every aspect of the ETL pipeline, both physically and logically. Perhaps the best sound bite for real-time systems is that they replace batch-oriented ETL with streaming ETL. In this chapter, we have presented the state-of-the-art of practical approaches to real-time ETL, and we have pointed out as many of the challenges as we can.

Conclusions

Designing and building an ETL system for a data warehouse is an exercise in keeping perspective. This is a typical complex undertaking that demands a comprehensive plan up front. It's easy to start transferring data from a specific source and immediately populate tables that can be queried. Hopefully, end users don't see the results of this prototype because such an effort doesn't scale and can't be managed.

Deepening the Definition of ETL

We go to considerable lengths in Chapter 1 to describe the requirements you must *surround*. These include business needs; compliance requirements; data-profiling results; requirements for such things as security, data integration, data latency, archiving and lineage tracking; and end-user tool delivery. You also must fold in your available skills and your existing legacy licenses. Yes, this is an overconstrained problem.

If you simultaneously keep all these requirements in mind, you must make the *BIG* decision: Should you buy a comprehensive ETL tool or roll your own with scripts and programs? We've made a serious effort to not bias this book too heavily in either direction, but the bigger the scope and the longer the duration of your project, the more we think a vendor-supplied ETL tool makes sense. Your job is to prepare data, not be a software development manager.

The real value of this book, in our opinion, is the structure we have put on the classic three steps of extract, transform, and load. This book describes a specific set of interwoven techniques that build on each other. This is not a book surveying all possible approaches to building an ETL system! We have expanded the classic three ETL steps into four steps: extract, clean, conform, and deliver. The deliverables of these four steps that uniquely differentiate this book include:

- **Extract:** Methods for choosing the specific original data sources and then combining the logical data map and the data-profiling efforts into a plan for the ETL system. It all begins with the sources. We also suggest specific transformations that take place here rather than in the more traditional cleaning step that follows.

- **Clean:** Schema designs for an error event fact table, an audit dimension, and a series of data-quality screens. We show how these deliverables are usefully integrated into your ETL system.

- **Conform:** Precise definitions for conformed dimensions and conformed facts (with a full discussion of the dimension manager's responsibilities and the replication and publication strategy for dimensions and facts). Conforming is the basis for what is now being called *master data management* in the industry.

- **Deliver:** Detailed structural specifications for the full range of dimensional models, including slowly changing dimensions, the major fact table types, and bridge tables for multivalued dimensions and hierarchical structures. We show how to build all the dimensional schema variations, and we provide specific detail for managing surrogate keys in each of these situations.

The deliverables in each of these steps provide the foundation for the ETL metadata. Much of the mystery and difficulty of dealing with ETL metadata can be reduced by promoting metadata to the status of real data. The audit dimension described in the cleaning step captures this perspective directly. Since dimensions always describe the context of measurements, we see that the state of the ETL system at the time of delivering a table is just another kind of context. With this in mind, we gracefully attach variations of the audit dimension to all of the data seen by end users through their familiar tools.

In Chapter 7, which covers development, we take you on a tour of many of the specific transformation steps and utilities you need to build an ETL system. If you chose to roll your own, the code snippets we provided are directly relevant. If you have purchased a vendor's ETL tool suite, most of these steps and utilities show up as tangible *transformers* in the graphical depiction of your ETL data flow. In the second half of Chapter 7, we give you some guidance on DBMS specific techniques for performing high-speed bulk loads, enforcing referential integrity, taking advantage of parallelization, calculating dimensional aggregates, and troubleshooting performance problems.

In Chapter 8, which covers operations, we start with a comprehensive discussion of scheduling the jobs in your ETL environment, keeping in mind that each environment has its own unique bottlenecks. We then make suggestions for certain control documents to help you manage the ETL system on a day-to-day basis. These include a datamart release document, an ETL performance-tracking document, and a list of usage metrics. We conclude Chapter 8 with recommendations for security and archiving architectures.

In Chapter 11, we open the door to the design of real-time data warehouse systems. Real-time is *anything too fast for your current ETL*. But more to the point, the migration to a real-time perspective almost always requires a jump from batch-oriented ETL to streaming ETL. When making this jump, it is likely that every step of your ETL system and your end-user tools will need to be redesigned. Obviously, this is a step not to be taken lightly. However, nearly all the important steps of batch-oriented ETL must be addressed in a streaming ETL design. You still need to extract, clean, conform, and deliver. For these reasons, we can use the lessons developed in the first ten chapters as the basis for the real-time design.

The Future of Data Warehousing and ETL in Particular

IT really has only two complementary missions: Get data in, and get data out. Getting the data in, of course, is transaction processing. Over the last 30 years, organizations have spent more than a trillion dollars building progressively more powerful transaction-processing systems whose job is to capture data for operational purposes. But data cannot be a one-way flow: At some point, we must consume data and derive value from it. There is a profound cultural assumption in the business world that *if only we could see all of our data, we could manage our businesses more effectively*. This cultural assumption is so deeply rooted that we take it for granted. Yet this is the mission of the data warehouse, and this is why the data warehouse is a permanent entity in all of our organizations, even as it morphs and changes its shape. Viewed in this way, it seems reasonable that in the long run, the overall investment in getting data out will rival that of getting data in.

In the last five years, a number of important themes have become the drivers for data warehousing:

- The honeymoon phase for the data warehouse is over. Businesses have lost their patience for technology, and they are insisting that the data warehouse deliver useful business results. The name, at least for now, of this theme is *business intelligence* (BI). BI is driven by end users, and BI vendors all control the final screens that the users see.

- The data warehouse has become distinctly operational. The old classic distinction between the data warehouse and operational reporting has disappeared. This operational focus gives rise to two huge requirements for the data warehouse. First, the data warehouse must have access to the atomic transactions of the business. If you want to see if a particular order was shipped, you can't look at aggregated data. Every subject area in the data warehouse must have smooth access to the most atomic data at the individual transaction level. Second, many of the operational views of the business need to be available in real-time. Of course, we've developed the definition and the technical responses to this real-time challenge in depth in this book.

- Businesses expect a 360 degree view of their operations. The lightning rod for the 360 degree view is the customer. Every customer-facing process in the business is expected to be available in the data warehouse, and end users want a single view of the customer list across all these processes. This places an enormous burden on the cleaning and conforming steps of the data warehouse, especially if little thought has been given to rationalizing all the views of customer in the operational systems. Although the customer is the most important dimension driving the 360 degree requirement, products, citizens, and vendors present the same challenges in other environments.

- Finally, the explosion of data continues unabated. Technical advances in data capture (especially RFIDs) and data storage are swamping many of our data warehouses, creating the expectation that every data mote be available for analysis.

So, how will these themes change the nature of the ETL task?

In our view, the most important reality is the stunning complexity of developing and running an ETL system. As we've stated, this is an over-constrained problem. Read the list of requirements in Chapter 1 one more time. As the sheer size of data and the number of software and hardware processes mushrooms, it will become less and less feasible to roll your own system. The future will belong to systems that allow you to assemble high-level building blocks of logic.

Ongoing Evolution of ETL Systems

Other technology areas have gone through similar phases where thresholds of complexity have simply forced the level of tool integration to be much more comprehensive. Integrated circuit designs with millions of components on each chip and software development with millions of lines of code are examples of this evolution. The development of ETL processing pipelines must inevitably respond in the same way if we are to keep up with the increasing volumes of data flowing in.

This means that the ETL designer must be increasingly oriented toward system integration, system monitoring, and system building block assembly, rather than coding. There simply isn't enough time to program very much at a low level.

The theme of analyzing atomic data ever-more precisely will only accelerate. Micromarketing is already descending to the individual customer level, and marketing analysts will want to perform queries that isolate custom subsets of customers based on very complex combinations of attributes and sequential behavior. We see a hint of the challenges of analyzing sequential behavior in Chapter 6 when we place text facts in a positional time series in the customer dimension. Again, we repeat our fundamental belief that the ETL system must be aware of, and participate in, the nature of key analysis modes such as sequential behavior analysis in order to make end-user applications possible. The ETL system is very much like the kitchen of a fine restaurant: The ETL system must arrange the plate before it is brought out of the kitchen.

Sequential behavior analysis will also create much more pressure to query distributed systems. RFID tags *go on journeys through doorways*. Each doorway is a data-collection device that records the passage of RFID tags. Sequential behavior analysis is possible only when the separate databases at each doorway can be merged into a single data view. Then the journey of an individual RFID tag and whole groups of tags can be analyzed. This is clearly an integration and conforming challenge. The recent *mad cow* scare was a great example of these issues. The implanted RFID tags in each cow were already in place. But no one could analyze where the specific cow in question had come from or been because the separate RFID generated databases were not accessible or integrated.

Finally, it is appropriate to return to a theme that underlies the whole approach of this book and, indeed, the authors' careers. The *gold coin* for the data warehouse is being able to respond to the true business needs of the organization. In the final analysis, the most important characteristics of ETL system designers are business-oriented, higher-level system skills that keep the data warehouse aimed in the right direction and succeed most effectively in delivering the data warehouse mission: getting data out.

Index

Printed and bound by CPI Group (UK) Ltd, Croydon, CR0 4YY

08/10/2024

14570371-0001